Education and Training in Europe

Previous reports for the Fondazione Rodolfo Debenedetti published by OUP

Structural Reforms Without Prejudices, edited by Tito Boeri, Micael Castanheira, Riccardo Faini, and Vicenzo Galasso

Women at Work: An Economic Perspective, edited by Tito Boeri, Daniela Del Boca, and Christopher Pissarides

The ICT Revolution: Productivity Differences and the Digital Divide, edited by Daniel Cohen, Pietro Garibaldi, Stefano Scarpetta

Immigration Policy and the Welfare System, edited by Tito Boeri, Gordon H. Hanson, and Barry McCormick

The Role of Unions in the Twenty-First Century, edited by Tito Boeri, Agar Brugiavini, Lars Calmfors

Education and Training in Europe

Edited by
Giorgio Brunello, Pietro Garibaldi,
and Etienne Wasmer

With

Andrea Bassanini, Alison Booth, Maria De Paola,
Peter Fredriksson, Ana Lamo, Edwin Leuven,
Julián Messina, and Giovanni Peri

OXFORD
UNIVERSITY PRESS

This book has been printed digitally and produced in a standard specification
in order to ensure its continuing availability

OXFORD
UNIVERSITY PRESS

Great Clarendon Street, Oxford OX2 6DP

Oxford University Press is a department of the University of Oxford.
It furthers the University's objective of excellence in research, scholarship,
and education by publishing worldwide in

Oxford New York

Auckland   Cape Town Dar es Salaam   Hong Kong   Karachi
Kuala Lumpur Madrid Melbourne Mexico City   Nairobi
New Delhi Shanghai Taipei Toronto
With offices in
Argentina Austria Brazil Chile Czech Republic France Greece
Guatemala Hungary Italy Japan South Korea Poland Portugal
Singapore Switzerland Thailand Turkey Ukraine Vietnam

Oxford is a registered trade mark of Oxford University Press
in the UK and in certain other countries

Published in the United States
by Oxford University Press Inc., New York

ISBN 978-0-19-921097-8

Table of Contents

List of Figures   xi
List of Tables   xiii
List of Contributors   xvii
Preface   xix

Part I. The Macroeconomics of Education
Etienne Wasmer, Peter Fredriksson, Ana Lamo, Julián
Messina, and Giovanni Peri   1

Introduction   3
  Background   3
  Organization and summary of the report—Part 1   4
    Theory and facts   4
    Part A: The growth vs. cohesion trade-off   4
    Part B: Improving the trade-off: a study of mismatch,
    mobility and skill specialization   6
    Policy Implications   8

1. Theory and Facts   9
  1.1 A brief theoretical perspective on human capital
      investment with a focus on institutions   9
    1.1.1 Introduction   9
    1.1.2 Theory   9
      1.1.2.1 Perfect financial markets   9
      1.2.2.2 Financial imperfections   10
      1.2.2.3 Life-cycle and on-the-job investments   13
      1.2.2.4 Labour market frictions   13
      1.2.2.5 Conclusions of the theory part   14
  1.2 Classification of education   15
  1.3 The supply of education and its trends   18

1.4 Financing and quality   22
1.5 Returns to education: unemployment, wages, mobility   25
    1.5.1 Wage returns to education   25
    1.5.2 Employment and unemployment   28
    1.5.3 Geographical mobility   31
1.6 Conclusion   35

PART A—EDUCATION PRIORITIES: GROWTH VS. COHESION
2. Cohesion and the Supply of General Skills in Europe   36
    2.1 Introduction   36
    2.2 Schooling and skills by cohort: a long-run perspective   36
      2.2.1 Data description   37
      2.2.2 Schooling and skills by cohort   39
    2.3 The skills among those still in school   47
      2.3.1 Mean student performance   47
      2.3.2 Student/teacher ratios   49
      2.3.3 Equality   51
    2.4 Implications for wage inequality   52
    2.5 Concluding remarks   54

3. Higher Education, Innovation and Growth   56
    3.1 Introduction   56
    3.2 A survey of the effects of education on growth   57
    3.3 International migration, the brain drain and 'talents'   59
      3.3.1 Immigration to the EU and the USA:
         size and composition   59
      3.3.2 'Talents': analysing their mobility and contribution   63
    3.4 Highly educated, productivity and innovation   66
      3.4.1 Quality of highly skilled foreign-born in the US   66
      3.4.2 Effect on innovation   68
    3.5 Conclusions   70

PART B—THE MARGINS OF IMPROVEMENT OF EDUCATION
INSTITUTIONS: SKILL MISMATCH, SKILL PORTABILITY AND MOBILITY
4. Internal Mobility, Skills and Education   71
    4.1 Introduction   71
    4.2 Internal mobility: EU versus USA   72
    4.3 Mobility and education in Europe   73
      4.3.1 Introduction   73
      4.3.2 Data: ECHP and geographical mobility   75
      4.3.3 More descriptive statistics on mobility   76

4.3.4 Theory 78
4.3.5 First strategy: comparing job-related
mobility and mobility for other reasons 80
4.3.6 Second strategy: estimating the income gain
from migration 85
4.3.7 Further comments on mobility and education 88
4.4 Determinants of mobility of highly skilled workers
across US state data 88
4.5 Conclusions 90

5. Skill Mismatch and Over-qualification in the Enlarged Europe 91
5.1 Introduction 91
5.2 A brief survey of the literature 92
5.3 Skill mismatch and over-qualification in the EU-15 93
5.3.1 Who is over-qualified or mismatched? 97
5.3.2 Over-qualification, skills mismatch and wages 101
5.4 Education mismatch in a transition economy:
the case of Poland 104
5.4.1 Returns to over-under-education 106
5.4.2 Nature of education mismatch in Poland 108
5.5 Overall conclusions 110

6. Specificity of Skills and Reallocation 111
6.1 Introduction 111
6.2 Skill specialization in Europe 111
6.3 Measurement of specific skills 114
6.4 An application to two accession countries,
Poland and Estonia 115

7. Policy implications 118

References 122
Appendices 131
Comments 134
Juan J. Dolado 134
Daniel Gros 140

Part II. Workplace Training in Europe
*Andrea Bassanini, Alison Booth, Giorgio Brunello, Maria De
Paola, and Edwin Leuven*

143

8. Introduction 145

9. An Overview of the Theoretical Framework   158
  9.1 The received wisdom   158
  9.2 Challenges to this orthodoxy   159
  9.3 An overview of the various approaches and their
     empirical predictions   161
    9.3.1 General training in a perfectly competitive
       labour market   161
    9.3.2 Imperfect capital markets and general training   161
    9.3.3 Pure specific training   162
    9.3.4 Mixture of training types   162
    9.3.5 Oligopsonistic wage setting   163
    9.3.6 Asymmetric information   164
  9.4 Comparisons of predictions of these models   165
  9.5 A clarification of wage compression   165
  9.6 Is there under-provision of training?   167
  9.7 Is there an equity issue?   169
  9.8 Institutions   170
    9.8.1 Trade unions   170
      9.8.1.1 Otherwise competitive labour markets   171
      9.8.1.2 Imperfectly competitive labour markets   171
      9.8.1.3 Union concern over the wage-employment
         package   173
      9.8.1.4 Labour turnover   173
      9.8.1.5 Unions' use of training to control labour
         supply   174
      9.8.1.6 Selectivity and other issues   174
    9.8.2 Minimum wages   175
    9.8.3 Taxes and social security systems   176
    9.8.4 Product market competition and deregulation   176
    9.8.5 Schooling institutions   177
  9.9 Summary   177

Appendix 1   179
Appendix 2   182
Appendix 3   184
  A3.1 Unions   184
  A3.2 Product market regulation   185

10. Stylized Facts about Workplace Training   187
  10.1 Measurement issues   188
  10.2 The distribution of training across countries and regions   193

10.3 Who pays for training?   197
10.4 The distribution of training investments across firms   201
10.5 Training differences across employees   205
10.6 Summary   214

Appendix 4: Description of the Datasets and Supplementary
            Tables   216

11. Training and Labour Market Institutions   232
11.1 Previous empirical literature   233
      11.1.1 Unions and training   233
      11.1.2 Minimum wages and training   234
      11.1.3 Flexible labour contracts and training   235
      11.1.4 Product market competition, employment
              protection and training   235
      11.1.5 Schooling and training   236
      11.1.6 Training and pensions   236
11.2 The data   237
11.3 The empirical set-up   243
11.4 The empirical results   244
11.5 Summary   251

12. The Costs and Benefits of Workplace Training   253
12.1 Estimating the private returns to training   254
      12.1.1 Identification   254
      12.1.2 Rates of return   256
12.2 Returns to employees   257
      12.2.1 The US evidence   258
      12.2.2 The European evidence   261
      12.2.3 Evidence from the ECHP   263
      12.2.4 Are the wage returns to training really high?   265
      12.2.5 Summary   267
12.3 Returns to employers   267
12.4 Training and growth   270
12.5 Summary   270

13. Is There Scope for Policy?   272
13.1 Policy responses to market failures in training provision   273
13.2 Under-provision: what is the evidence?   273
      13.2.1 Training and turnover   276
      13.2.2 Credit constraints   278
13.3 Is there an equity issue?   278

Contents

13.4 What do we learn from the empirical evidence?   282
13.5 A political economy approach   282
13.6 Policies offering financial support to workplace training   283
13.7 Labour market policies and training   287
13.8 Summary   289

Appendix 5: A Simple Political Economy Model of Training
           Subsidies   290

Appendix 6: Training Policies in Europe   293
   A6.1 Regulation: pay-back clauses, time working
       accounts and apprenticeship contracts   293
   A6.2 Co-financed schemes directed at firms   301
   A6.3 Co-financed schemes directed to individuals   306

References   310
Comments   324
   Giuseppe Bertola   324
   Jörn-Steffen Pischke   330

Final Remarks   343
   John P. Martin

Index   349

List of Figures

1.1 Determination of the level of schooling   11
1.2 Comparison between two individuals   11
1.3 Links between inequality of human capital
and redistribution   12
1.4 ISCED-1997 Transition pattern   17
1.5 Long-run public expenditure patterns,
percentage of GDP, 1970–2000   26
2.1 Schooling by cohort in the EU, the UK,
Ireland, and the US   39
2.2 Skills by cohort in the EU, the UK, Ireland and the US   40
2.3 Schooling by cohort in Belgium, Germany,
the Netherlands, and Switzerland   41
2.4 Skills by cohort in Belgium, Germany, the
Netherlands, and Switzerland   42
2.5 Schooling by cohort in Denmark, Finland,
Norway, and Sweden   42
2.6 Skills by cohort in Denmark, Finland,
Norway, and Sweden   43
2.7 Schooling by cohort in the Czech Republic,
Hungary, Italy, and Poland   44
2.8 Skills by cohort in the Czech Republic,
Hungary, Italy, and Poland   44
3.1 Percentage of foreign-born by skill group in the USA, 2000   64
3.2 Percentage of foreign-born by skill group
in the EU-12, 1999   65
4.1 Mobility rate in the last three years, job-related
reason and outside the area/city, by education
(EU-15 less Luxembourg and Sweden, 1995–2001)   78
5.1 The incidence of skill mismatch in EU-15, time series   95
5.2 The incidence of skill mismatch in EU-15, cross-country   96

5.3 Skill mismatch and employment protection
legislation in Europe: Rank correlations   97
6.1 Macroeconomic context during the transition
to a market economy, Poland   113
6.2 Macroeconomic context during the adhesion
to the European Union, Poland   114
8.1 Training participation and training intensity   147
8.2 R&D investment and training, by country   150
8.3 Product market regulation and training, by country   150
8.4 Temporary workers and training, by country   151
8.5 Training incidence and schooling   154
8.6 Training participation and returns in Italy and Finland   156
9.1 Wage structure and training   163
10.1 Comparison of training participation
rates across datasets   192
10.2 Training participation and training hours
per participant in OECD countries   193
10.3 Dispersion of training participation rates
in EU countries, by region   196
10.4 Share of employer-sponsored training   198
10.5 Employers' investment in training: by firm size   203
10.6 Training participation in innovative and
non-innovative firms   205
10.7. Training age gaps and employment
rate of older workers   213
11.1 Training incidence and tracking in secondary schools   239
11.2 Training in 1997 and the employment
protection of regulars in 1995   241
11.3 Training in 1997 and the employment protection
for temporary workers in 1995   241
11.4 Training of older workers and the implicit
tax on continuing work   242
12.1 Returns to training and training incidence, by country   265
13.1 Training and PISA scores   287
C1 Mortgage loan-to-value (1980s)   327
C2 EPL, residuals from regression on LTV and constant   328

List of Tables

1.1	Educational attainment: adult population (2002)	19
1.2	Population that has attained tertiary education (2002)	20
1.3	Trends in the educational attainment of the population aged 25–64, 1960–2002	21
1.4	Total education expenditure as a fraction of GDP and expenditure per student as a fraction of GDP per capita, percent, 1991 and 2001	23
1.5	Expenditure and enrolment shares by level of education, percent, 1991 and 2001	24
1.6	Share of private expenditure in total expenditure, percent, 2001	25
1.7	Relative earnings across countries	27
1.8	Private rates of return associated with tertiary education	28
1.9	Employment rates and educational attainment (2002)	29
1.10	Unemployment ratio and educational attainment (2002)	30
1.11	Geographical mobility in the last three years, 15–64 population, by reason and country	32
1.12	Geographical mobility in the last three years, by education	32
1.13	Summary of internal mobility and immigration, USA and EU 1990–2000	33
2.1	Test scores in the adult population	38
2.2	Changes in the 'quality of education' (change in residual skills)	46
2.3	Literacy test scores	48
2.4.	Student/teacher ratios in lower secondary schools, 2002 and 1992	49
2.5	Variations in maths skills across students and the share of the variance attributable to schools	50
2.6	Earnings regressions, pooled country/cohort data	54

3.1 Foreign-born residents of the EU, 1992–99   60
3.2 Foreign-born residents of the USA, 1990, 2000   60
3.3 Skill distribution of immigrants, 1990–2000   62
3.4 Wage differentials of foreign high-skilled
      workers relative to US-born, 2000   67
3.5 Impact of high skills on innovation   69
4.1 Internal geographical mobility in the EU   72
4.2 Internal geographical mobility in the USA   73
4.3 Geographical mobility rate in the last year
      and in the last three years, any reason, active
      15–64 population, head of households, by
      unemployment status   76
4.4 Geographical mobility rate in the last year, any
      reason, occupied 15–64 population, head of
      households, by occupation   77
4.5 Geographical mobility rate outside the area in the
      last three years, active 15–64 population, head of
      household, by country   78
4.6 Geographical mobility rate outside the area,
      active 15–64 population, head of household,
      by education level   79
4.7 Mobility in the last three years, by reason and
      distance, heads of households   81
4.8 Multinomial models of mobility, 3-level-mlogit   82
4.9 Multinomial models of mobility, 6-level-mlogit   83
4.10 Probit model of household job-related mobility
      and income model   87
4.11 Determinants of mobility for highly educated workers   89
5.1 A taxonomy of mismatch in Europe   95
5.2 The determinants of over-qualification: marginal
      effects from probit analysis   99
5.3 The determinants of skill mismatch. Multinomial
      logit analysis. Pooled country sample   100
5.4 Over-qualification and wages   102
5.5 Skill mismatch and wages   103
5.6 Percentage of under/over-educated workers by year   106
5.7 Coefficient on the over/under-education variables
      of an augmented standard Mincer equation   107
5.8 Coefficient on the over/under-education variables
      of equation [5.1]   108

5.9 Occupational/career mobility and education
      mismatch. Extract of education coefficients   109
6.1 Sectoral composition of employment, OECD
      and Eastern Europe   112
6.2 Human capital specificity and mobility in
      Poland and Estonia   117
A5.1 Definition of variables: EU-15   133
9.1 Some predictions of human capital theory   161
9.2 Predictions about unions and training   172
10.1 Cross-country distribution of training
       expenditures by firms, European countries   201
10.2 Individual characteristics and training
       incidence. ECHP 1995–2001. Average partial effects 207
A4.1 Training participation rates by source of
       financing in the ECHP   219
A4.2 Percentage of employers-sponsored training
       courses that are entirely paid by employers,
       selected OECD countries (IALS sample)   219
A4.3 Hours of training per participant and source of
       financing, selected OECD countries (IALS sample)   220
A4.4 Ratio of employer-sponsored training to
       total training in the ECHP, by course duration   220
A4.5 Share of total wage and salary employees who
       receive employer-sponsored training in
       innovative and non-innovative firms, by
       firm size. European countries   221
A4.6 List of industries used in the regressions   222
A4.7 Individual characteristics and training. Alternative
       models for sponsored and non-sponsored training   222
A4.8 Individual characteristics and training duration.
       ECHP 1995–2001. Interval regression models   225
A4.9 Individual characteristics and training incidence.
       ECHP 1995–2001. Average partial effects, by
       gender, skill group and age   227
A4.10 Individual characteristics and training incidence.
       ECHP 1995–2001. Average partial effects, by country 229
11.1 Changes of institutional and other indicators
       between 1995 and 2001, by country   243
11.2 Summary statistics   246

11.3 Employer provided training and time varying
institutions. ECHP 1995–2001. Dependent variable:
logistic transformation of the proportion of trained
individuals. Weighted least squares.   247

12.1 Wage returns studies   259

12.2 Private returns to training. ECHP 1995/97/99/2001   264

13.1 Different types of market failures and policy
interventions aimed at restoring efficiency   274

13.2 Estimates of the probability of separation in year
t+1 as a function of employer provided training in
years t−2 to t. Linear probability model. Fixed
effects. 1996–2000   277

13.3 Enrolment in education. 1996–2001. Average partial
effects. Weighted estimates. Dependent variable:
workplace training   280

13.4 Enrolment in education, 1996–2001. Average partial
effects. Weighted estimates. Dependent variable:
employer provided training   281

13.5 Private returns to training by education   286

A6.1 Regulation: pay-back clauses, time working
accounts and apprenticeship contracts   294

A6.2 Apprenticeship contacts in selected OECD countries   297

A6.3 Co-financed schemes directed at firms   302

A6.4 Co-financing schemes directed to individuals   308

C1 Sources of job-relevant skills in Germany (in percent)   332

C2 Sources of job-relevant skills and firm size (in percent)   333

Contributors

Andrea Bassanini, OECD and CEPN-University of Paris XIII

Giuseppe Bertola, University of Turin

Alison Booth, Australian National University and University of Essex

Giorgio Brunello, University of Padua

Maria De Paola, Calabria University

Juan J. Dolado, Universidad Carlos III, Madrid

Peter Fredriksson, Uppsala University

Pietro Garibaldi, Fondazione RODOLFO DEBENEDETTI and University of Turin

Daniel Gros, Centre for European Policy Studies

Ana Lamo, European Central Bank

Edwin Leuven, University of Amsterdam and CREST

John Martin, OECD

Julián Messina, European Central Bank, Universitat de Girona and IZA

Giovanni Peri, University of California, Davis

Steve Pischke, London School of Economics

Etienne Wasmer, Sciences-Po Paris

Preface

While Europe is certainly one of the richest and most educated areas of the world, some of the challenges faced by the 'old' continent are staggering: low economic growth, structural difficulties in the labour market, and stiffer international competition. Discussions about a European decline are now taken seriously by politicians and policymakers. Academic scholars, international organizations and media analysts constantly underline the urgency for reform in Europe. Some stress the need for Europe to fully embrace competition and market discipline in labour, goods, and financial markets. Others argue that Europe needs to shrink and redesign its social model and its welfare state. Despite these subtle differences, everyone agrees that to overcome the risk of decline, Europe needs foremost to strengthen human capital, its ultimate comparative advantage in the world economy.

The accumulation of human capital takes place either before entering the labour market—through formal education, or during market participation—through professional training. The returns on the investment, conversely, always take place inside the labour market and critically depend on the functioning of such markets. In light of the structural difficulties in European labour markets, there are important and complex interactions between formal education, professional training, high unemployment, low market mobility, inefficient wage setting and poorly designed institutions. These interactions are key to this book. Specifically, the aim of the book is threefold. First, it takes stock of the core facts and characteristics of education and training in Europe, extending much beyond the conventional and simple analytical description of a statistical report. Secondly, and most importantly, it asks crucial questions about the fundamental problems of education in Europe. Thirdly, it discusses which policies are necessary to make the existing educational systems more efficient, and high skills more accessible to a wider range of people.

The key questions addressed in the book are easily identifiable. In the new globalized world, should Europe drastically shift resources from secondary toward tertiary education? What drives over-education, or the fact that European workers are often employed in jobs inadequate to their skill? What is the interplay between labour market institutions, educational mismatch, and low labour market mobility? Why does training differ markedly across European countries? In light of the structural difficulties in the labour market, should European governments subsidize professional training? Are there spillovers between labour market reforms and training participation?

Europe, like the United States, has invested massively in human capital over the last three decades. Total spending for formal education is around 5 per cent of GDP in most advanced OECD economies. The main difference between the US and Europe is not so much in the total amount spent in education, but rather in the difference in composition between second and tertiary education, with a much larger proportion of money being spent on tertiary education in the US. The disproportionate European investment in secondary education over the last twenty years certainly contributed to preventing a widespread increase in income and wage inequality. But the under-funding of tertiary education did not come without costs. This book makes the case that the recent low innovation and low growth in Europe is partly the result of this allocation of funds.

With limited public finances, the increase in tertiary education necessary to stimulate invention, research and growth is likely to require, as a by-product, a reduction in spending in secondary education. Does that mean that European workers need to accept larger income and wage inequality in response? This is not necessarily the case. On the one hand, despite low overall mobility, the new European graduates are much more mobile than their parents were, thus providing an endogenous channel to the reduction of persistent inequality in employment rates across regions. On the other hand, structural reforms aimed at increasing mobility are likely to play a role. Full real portability of pension rights across Europe, just to name an example, is likely to support workers' mobility and reduce labour market inequalities, even if total spending on secondary education were to fall. There are thus important spillovers from structural reforms in Europe to the returns to education. Policymakers should be aware of this.

A tough European problem is a large 'mismatch' that exists between workers' supply of skills, and labour demand. The book presents substantial empirical evidence of this mismatch, a phenomenon often described as over-education. Arguably, an education system that is not able to supply the right skills needs serious reform. Here it is not simply a matter of resources. In this, as well as in various other contexts, the book argues that a more efficient human capital investment requires serious reforms in the incentive mechanisms of the educational sector in general, and the university system in particular. European universities should be rewarded on the basis of their research output and their ability to supply the right type of skill. The former implication is standard, while the latter is novel. The long term frustration of European graduates, who far too often land up in jobs that are an inadequate match to their skills, should be taken into account not only when discussing labour market reforms but also when discussing reforms of education. Only an overhaul reform of the upper education system, with strong emphasis on the incentive mechanism, can succeed simultaneously in spurring growth and innovation and alleviating mismatch in the market place.

Professional training is the second key dimension of human capital investment. Both participation rates and training intensity differ significantly among European countries. Whereas the UK, France and Scandinavian countries invest more in training than does the US, countries in the 'olive belt' (Greece, Italy, Spain and Portugal) invest substantially less. The low training incidence of the 'olive belt' countries is only partly linked to their larger proportion of smaller firms—empirically considered low training intensity. Conversely, it seems that statistically similar firms do provide less training around the Mediterranean.

As in the US, Europe's training incidence also grows with education and decreases with age. While women feature larger training incidence, younger women absorb less training than younger men. Temporary workers, a key feature of the ongoing labour market deregulation in Europe, also feature lower training intensity. The large difference between countries in the North and South of Europe is further linked to difference in propensity to R&D and ICT spending, with much more spending in the North. Training appears to be lower also in countries with product market regulation that is largely anti-competitive. Along the latter dimension there is evidence that reduced regulation in Europe over the last decade has led to larger training rates. Labour market regulation, conversely, seems to have ambiguous effects on training: on the one hand, increase in temporary workers reduces training incidence; on the other hand, reduction in employment protection legislation among regular workers has the opposite effect.

One needs to be very cautious before advocating policies aimed at fostering training. This is true for vocational training, regulatory changes (such as recovery clauses), apprenticeships, training certification policies, and co-financing policy towards firms and workers that invest in training.

In this book there is very little evidence that training provided in the market is inferior to the socially desirable training.

There are also indirect ways to making training more effective. Most scholars and policymakers agree with the need for Europe to invest more in R&D and increase labour market participation. The book shows that these types of policies have a positive side effect on training. For example, policies aimed at increasing female participation in the labour market—including childcare assistance and extended maternity leave—lead to larger training rates. Similar mechanisms work for deregulation in the product market and reduction in early retirement.

Pietro Garibaldi
February 2007

PART I

THE MACROECONOMICS OF EDUCATION

*Etienne Wasmer, Peter Fredriksson, Ana Lamo,
Julián Messina, and Giovanni Peri**

*Affiliations in order: Sciences-Po Paris, OFCE, IZA and CEPR; Uppsala University, IZA, CESifo and IFAU; European Central Bank, DG-Research; European Central Bank, DG-Research, Universitat de Girona and IZA; UC Davis, UCLA and NBER. The views expressed here are those of the authors and not of the European Central Bank. We thank Anna Sanz de Galdeano for help with the ECHP, and Adriana Kugler, Joshua Angrist and Sascha Becker for providing help with the European Labour Force Survey data and with their authorization to use them. We also thank Juan Dolado, Pietro Garibaldi, Arianna Degan and Pierre Lefebvre for discussions and comments, as well as CIRPÉE for hosting a meeting.

Introduction

Background

One year after the major enlargement to 10 new member states, the European Union is facing several challenges. The EU has experienced a relatively long period of slow growth, with growth rates that were one or two percentage points lower than in the US during the last decade. As a consequence of the enlargement, the EU is facing a huge redistribution of political and economic powers, both internally and vis-à-vis its partners. Furthermore, Europe has to cope with an ever-growing integration of international markets. Most notably the emergence of the two low-wage giants, China and India—sometimes characterized as the 'world suppliers' of labour intensive goods and services—will increase competition in the world market.

The success with respect to these challenges is mixed. Although Europe remains one of the wealthiest areas in the world and its new members grow at a fast rate, it still faces several structural problems. Most big countries in Europe—including France, Germany, Italy, Spain and Poland—have relatively inefficient labour markets and are plagued with high unemployment rates and low participation rates particularly among the less educated workers. In a rapidly evolving macroeconomic context, more adaptability of individuals and institutions is needed to preserve living standards and the welfare state.

In particular, Europe should invest more than ever in the factor that provides its comparative advantage, *human capital*, which is in the long-term the only source of growth and of better living standards and of cohesion at the same time. We will discuss these links throughout our report and will show that, in some dimensions, European education is under-funded as compared to the US. The answer, however, cannot be simply quantitative: more money injected in the system may not be a solution in the absence of a serious reflection on the nature of education, on its macroeconomic and labour market impact and on the various imperfections. The report does not intend to provide an exhaustive analysis of these issues. Instead, it aims at taking stock of the large economic literature on the subject, and at providing some useful policy guidelines, organized as follows.

Organization and summary of the report—Part I

Theory and facts

In Chapter 1, we develop a few theoretical insights and present a large set of facts to be discussed in subsequent sections. The theory deals with the interaction between labour market institutions and the incentives to accumulate various skills. It starts with a brief theoretical survey on human capital, in relation to the efficiency of credit markets and labour markets. We then show how various institutions play different roles in human capital accumulation. Notably, the nature of skill investments is itself shaped by the nature of institutions. Employment protection may well increase the duration of employment and raise the returns to job specific skills, and may raise the duration of unemployment. This in turn reduces the returns to general skills, augmenting the cost of labour reallocation.

We then examine various types of education as classified by UNESCO with ISCED-1997 (International Standard Classification of Education) and their supply in several OECD countries. We look at the relation between wages and education, unemployment and education and mobility and education. We also survey the financing of education (as a fraction of GDP, per pupil/student and by origin i.e., public or private). Finally we note that Europe drastically differs from the US in that the higher priority given to secondary education is accompanied with under-funding of tertiary education and notably advanced tertiary education.

Part A: The growth vs. cohesion trade-off

After this first preliminary exploration of the vast subject of the macroeconomics of education, we can organize thinking around a first policy guideline: the well-known trade-off between efficiency and equality, as represented in Figure 1 (see p. 7), where here, we reinterpreted this trade-off in terms of cohesion vs. growth. Priorities set by policy affects the position in this trade-off, and a reallocation of funding from higher education to lower levels of education may favour one objective (i.e. cohesion) over another (i.e. growth). Along the curve, representing a *short-run arbitrage*, one can either raise efficiency, say by reducing progressive taxation at the cost of deteriorating equality, or instead, by improving equality at some efficiency cost.

Part A is thus devoted to the growth–cohesion trade-off. We shall investigate how education policies can affect the position on this curve: a policy targeting the most elitist tertiary education institutions will generate more research, innovations and growth, while a policy targeting secondary education will raise educational attainment of the population, qualitatively as well as quantitatively, thus generating more cohesion.

In Chapter 2 we emphasize that Europe has invested massively in secondary education during the past decades. These investments appear to have paid off, as the supply of skills has grown at a faster rate in Europe than in the US. Further, they have prevented large increases in wage and income inequality, at least to some extent. In the most recent cohorts, the overwhelming majority of individuals spend as much as 12 years in initial education; they start at the age of 6 in primary education and fully complete secondary education at the age of 18. In 1999, 78 per cent of the 25–34 year old population in the entire OECD had at least upper secondary education.[1] The corresponding fraction for the 55–64 year old population was only 45 per cent. This indicates that the education sector expanded dramatically during the last three decades. Since the 1960s, the average number of years of education of the working age population has grown by 3.5 years, and half of the gap with the US has been bridged.

Overall, this educational effort in Europe as in other advanced countries represents a sizeable fraction of GDP: according to the OECD Education at a Glance, the OECD countries spent on average 5.23 per cent of GDP in 1998. This aggregate number may be decomposed into: 3.64 per cent of GDP in primary and secondary education (3.28% public and 0.37% private) and 1.59 per cent in tertiary education (.93 public and .67 private).

There are, however, some differences across countries in both the allocation of funds and their origin. Interestingly, in two very different countries—the US and France—public expenditure in tertiary education as a fraction of GDP is exactly the same, 1 per cent of GDP. But in total, the US spent 2.29 per cent of its GDP in tertiary education while France spent only 1.13 per cent; the entire difference between the two countries actually came from private money. Spain, Italy and Germany are very close to

---

[1] The average is calculated including Turkey and Mexico, where this share was only 25 and 26 per cent respectively.

France in the sense that private money is marginal, resulting in an under-funding of tertiary education. In other words, tertiary education is under-funded in Continental Europe, where public money is primarily concentrated on secondary education.

What are the consequences of these facts? Could this be a cause of lower growth and technology adoption in Europe during the last decades? This is explored in Chapter 3. Indeed, it has for long been recognised that education, particularly tertiary education, is an important vehicle for growth and aggregate economic performance. In spite of this, the gap vis-à-vis the US in terms of scientific and technological advancement appears to have widened during the 1990s (Daveri, 2002). Certainly, many EU countries are late in adopting the recent information technologies and biotechnologies; and in the field of applied sciences, the US lead is at best not narrowing (see Gordon, 2004). Further, we will present evidence that Europe faces difficulties in attracting the most skilled and talented workers, with potentially large adverse consequences on long-run growth.

Part B: Improving the trade-off: a study of mismatch, mobility and skill specialization

Part B investigates the role of education on mismatch, mobility and adaptability of the labour force. The reason for raising these issues is that a more efficient allocation of labour will reduce the trade-off between equality and growth, thus pushing out the growth–equality frontier in Figure 1. We are interested in the question: How can we increase growth for given egalitarian ambitions and educational funding? In other words, can we shift the short-run constraint of Figure 1 from the solid line to the dashed line?

Beyond the quantitative aspects of education, this part develops an analysis of its skill content. Indeed, for investments in education to pay-off, the skills provided by education must match with the actual demand of skills. We will point out several mechanisms through which an inefficient allocation of labour and skills may occur in Europe, and provide evidence of mismatch between demand and supply of skills and workers.

As pointed out in Chapter 4, geographical mobility of labour is very low in Europe—even among the most educated—especially compared to the US. This section also shows that the gradual increase in the number of years of education has led the recent cohorts of young graduates in Europe to be more mobile than low-skilled workers. This partly mitigates the claim that there is a general problem of over-education in Continental Europe. Over-education is more directly addressed in Chapter 5. For

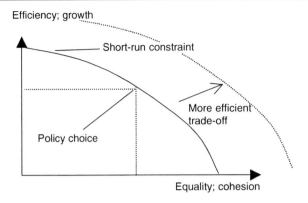

Fig. 1. Efficiency–equality trade-offs

several countries, we show that over-education appears to be a misnomer for a different phenomenon that we believe to be one of Europe's main problems: there is a very large share of European workers reporting they do not have the right skills for the job: the problem is not so much the level of education, but rather its quality and the mismatch between demand and supply.

Analysing these issues in the European context is complex because of the existing labour market institutions such as employment protection and social insurance policies. These institutions have potential pros and cons. On the one hand, they promote the stability of employment relationships and accordingly raise incentives to acquire sector or job specific skills. On the other hand, in rapidly changing environments, labour market institutions may affect mobility incentives by raising costs and reducing returns.[2] Related to these findings, Chapter 6 illustrates that when labour market institutions promote longevity of jobs, they favour specific skills while the increasingly volatile demand for labour would require general skills instead. This is discussed in the context of the European Enlargement, which precisely requires increased adaptability from workers given the likely patterns of country specialization predicted by trade theory. Further, the European population is ageing: the median age in Western and Eastern Europe is now around 40 years, 10 years more than twenty years ago. The ability of societies to deal with aggregate and distributional changes is thus likely to be lower than in the past, making it even more important to

---

[2] See Bertola and Ichino (1995), Bertola and Rogerson (1997) and Blanchard and Wolfers (2000) on the interaction between shocks and institutions.

design relevant institutions and particularly educational institutions to cope with these transformations.

Policy implications

Part A suggests raising investments in tertiary education, without sacrificing too much of cohesion. Indeed, inequality per se may lead to lower growth over a very long run. As pointed out in Benabou (2000), poorer families may not be able to invest in education, which may result in a loss of growth potential. As a matter of fact, improving individuals' access to financing educational investments can promote the dual objective of reducing inequality and increasing efficiency (Okun, 1975). Thus, well-designed educational policies create a win-win situation where the usual trade-off between equality and efficiency is absent.

Part B suggests that, if more investments in education are required, they must come with well-thought out provisions of incentives: first, incentives to do well must be imposed on the supplier of skills (secondary schools and tertiary establishments); and second, incentives to follow the right curriculum must be brought to the consumers of education (students and trainees).

It is only if these conditions are fulfilled that Europe can simultaneously reach the dual objective of promoting equality and generating growth. Investing in secondary education is probably a good way to promote equality. On the other hand public–private competition and merit-based incentives are necessary if Europe wants to produce universities with the same worldwide prestige and attractiveness as Harvard, Princeton, or MIT, and ultimately develop a knowledge-based economy.

1

Theory and facts

1.1 A brief theoretical perspective on human capital investment with a focus on institutions

1.1.1 *Introduction*

Various labour market institutions (minimum wages, collective wage bargaining, employment protection, passive and active labour market policies) are known to have a big impact on unemployment. Layard and Nickell (1999) argue that unions and unemployment compensation have the most adverse effects, while the impact of the other components of institutions is not that evident, and can even be ambiguous. Labour market institutions also have a large impact on workers' incentives and effort (Ichino and Riphahn, 2004) and on the flexibility of labour markets, notably regional mobility and labour reallocation (see Bertola and Ichino, 1995 and Bertola and Rogerson, 1997). In this chapter, we focus on the direct or indirect effects of institutions as well as market imperfections on workers' supply of skills. We focus, in particular, on the way labour market institutions affect the nature of education and the type of skills acquired.

1.1.2 *Theory*

1.1.2.1 PERFECT FINANCIAL MARKETS

In this part, we develop the common theoretical framework, which we use to analyse the nature of investments in skills and to draw implications in the next part. The concept of human capital has been widely used in the last 40–50 years, since the pioneering work by Theodore W. Schultz, Gary Becker and Jacob Mincer. Human capital typically refers to a set of knowledge, skills, and know-how characterized by the following three features. First, they are costly to acquire, both because of direct financial cost and because of time and effort. Secondly, they increase potential earnings through the life-cycle: like a financial investment, their return is deferred to the future. Finally, they are embedded in an individual: skills cannot be sold or transferred from one individual to another—only their services can be rented.

Note that human capital is similar to physical capital in the first two characteristics, but differs in the third one. Despite this difference, Becker (1964) established in the context of perfect markets, that the internal rate of return on education (defined as the discount rate equalizing costs and returns on investments) had to be equal to the interest rate. A key condition for this result is that financial markets are perfect. This means that individuals should invest in education and possibly borrow to finance their investment, up to the point where the rate of return to education is equal to the interest rate.

All individuals stop studying at one point or another, suggesting decreasing returns to schooling. In this case, a first implication of human capital theory is that the amount of schooling falls with the rate of interest. Alternatively, years of education increase with the return to schooling, for a given interest rate. Figure 1.1, where i denotes the interest rate, s the number of years of schooling and s^* the chosen level of schooling, illustrates the optimal schooling choice.

A second implication of this analysis is that decentralization of education choices to the market is efficient: individuals choose optimal investments when they pay for education. Of course, the real world features several market imperfections leading to drastically different policy conclusions. The general consensus among economists is indeed that education should not be entirely financed by households or individuals. But, this by no means implies that education should be freely provided, as many free goods tend to be over-consumed. Where to draw the line between public and private funding is actually difficult to know. This question is beyond the scope of this report and in any case, cannot be addressed at a European level: these are primarily the responsibility of national policies. Among other things, the answer depends on the magnitude of the market imperfections, which we now describe.

1.2.2.2 FINANCIAL IMPERFECTIONS

First, what happens in the presence of financial imperfections, such as borrowing constraints? One can easily reinterpret Becker's analysis as follows. The internal rate of return on education has to be equal to the interest rate faced by borrowing individuals—a number typically larger than the riskless interest rate. If an individual has no access at all to financial markets, the interest rate can be replaced by the (risk-neutral) individual's rate of pure time preference—typically a very high rate.

Still under the assumption of decreasing marginal returns to education, differences in the level of education across individuals can be due to differences in the access to financial markets: the higher the interest rate faced by an individual, the lower the investment in education he/she will afford. Figure 1.2 illustrates the schooling choices made by two individuals: individual 1 has poor access to capital markets and chooses a low level of schooling, while individual 2 has good access to capital markets and chooses a higher level of schooling. Note that, in the total absence of capital markets, individual 1 would be interpreted as an impatient individual, while individual 2 would be interpreted as more patient.

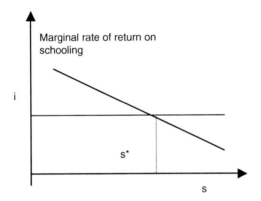

Fig. 1.1 Determination of the level of schooling

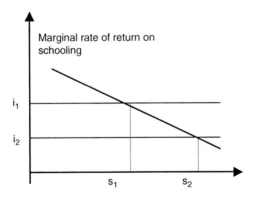

Fig. 1.2 Comparison between two individuals

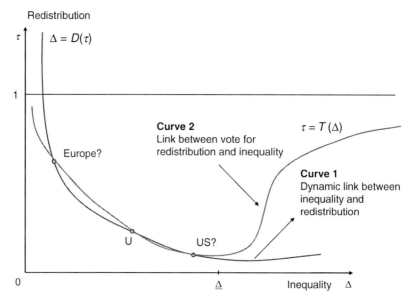

Fig. 1.3 Links between inequality of human capital and redistribution
Notes: Inequality: Δ^2 = inequality in human captial (variance of log-normal).
Redistribution: $\tau \leq 1$ = degree of progressivity/equalization in fiscal (taxes + transfers) or education (school finance), or labour market (minimum wage, unions) policy.
Benabou (2000 and 2005).

Analyses of this kind are mostly static; Benabou (2000, 2005) is an exception, however. An eloquent summary of the dynamic trade-off between inequality and redistribution in a world of imperfect information is illustrated in Figure 1.3. On the one hand, less redistribution leads, dynamically, to a less efficient transmission of human capital across generations, and thus to more inequality as poorer families remain un-skilled. This is the downward sloping curve 1 (in blue), which depends heavily on the failure of financial markets. On the other hand, median voters would normally tend to choose more redistribution as inequality increases which is the upward sloping part in curve 2 (in red). Unfortu-nately, there is also a downward sloping part to that curve: more inequality distorts democratic decisions through lobbying or influence, resulting in less redistribution when there is more inequality. The outcome is a multi-plicity of equilibria, where the European case (more redistribution, less inequality) may be represented by the first intersection to the left between the two curves, and the US case can be represented by the third intersection with the opposite characteristics (more inequality, less redistribution).

1.2.2.3 LIFE-CYCLE AND ON-THE-JOB INVESTMENTS

Ben-Porath (1967) has analysed human capital decisions in a dynamic context and shown that the optimal time allocated to learning should decrease monotonically with age: full-time education is optimal in the beginning of an individual's life; part-time learning, meaning being trained part time and working the rest of the time, is optimal afterwards; and no learning at all should be optimal as the retirement age is getting closer and closer as returns to learning eventually drop to zero. Blinder and Weiss (1976) show that this result survives an extension of the model, where labour supply decisions and notably retirement decisions are incorporated.

It is implicit in the analysis described above that the nature of initial education and, say, on-the-job learning is similar: they apply to any job held, without any distinction. However, as noted earlier on by Becker (1964), on-the-job skills should be usefully separated in two broad categories: skills that are useful in any job—called 'general human capital'—and skills that are specific to a job—'specific human capital'. One can then easily extend the distinction to 'sector-specific' skills or 'occupation specific skills'.

A drastic difference between general and specific skills is that purely general skills are theoretically paid by employees: they accept a lower wage today in order to be more productive and hence better paid tomorrow. The reason is that general skills raise productivity in all possible jobs. It is therefore possible for a worker in a perfect labour market to obtain a wage increase as soon as he/she becomes more productive. In contrast, specific skills cannot be transferred to other jobs. They simply generate a surplus or quasi-rent that can be shared between the employer and the employee. In other words, depending on the relative bargaining power of workers vis-à-vis employers, the cost of specific skills is shared between the bargaining partners.

1.2.2.4 LABOUR MARKET FRICTIONS

With labour market frictions, it is useful to distinguish between the wages return to education and the return to employability (Charlot, 2003). Frictions affect the return to education in two opposite ways. Factors leading to wage compression may reduce the propensity to invest in all types of skills. But private incentives are increased by the existence of longer spells of unemployment and lower job durations for the less skilled workers.

In terms of on-the-job skills, Acemoglu and Pischke (1999a and b) have shown that to a large extent, employers pay for general human capital. Their interpretation is that one must relax the assumption of frictionless labour market, since this assumption implies that employers are unable to appropriate the returns to general skills. In fact, in the presence of market frictions such as search frictions, workers incur a loss when they leave their employer, even if they were able to find a job elsewhere, in the same occupation with the same general skills. Search frictions imply that it will take some time and some resources to the worker before becoming employed again. Frictions thus create a specificity of the employer–employee relationship, in the sense developed by Caballero and Hammour (1998). Interestingly, specific skills and search frictions have similar features. They create some specificity as well as a surplus of the relationship and thus lead naturally to sharing the surplus, via bargaining for instance.

Wasmer (2002, 2006) has investigated the relation between another market imperfection: employment protection and the type of skills chosen by individuals. When employees are protected by lay-off costs, they anticipate a longer duration in the current job. In response to a small shock, it is simply too costly for employers to fire; they thus prefer to retain workers even if they are temporarily unproductive. In partial equilibrium, this raises the return to specific skills relative to general skills, as workers obtain a reward to their skills over a longer time horizon. This mix of highly specific skills and long-duration jobs has several implications: it is conducive to low turnover in the labour market (as workers with specific skills have no incentive to quit and lose their skills); it makes the cost of displacement extremely high (as workers having over-invested in specific skills and under-invested in general skills require huge retraining). Interestingly, *ceteris paribus*, employers tend to prefer workers with specific skills and low mobility, as long as they remain productive, because such workers are attached to the firm and have low outside options. On the other hand, workers with too specific skills are more likely to demand more employment protection (precisely because their outside options are typically low) and are more likely to unionize (as their only option to improve wages is through bargaining over the surplus, not by raising outside options).

1.2.2.5 CONCLUSIONS OF THE THEORY PART

This brief review of the theoretical literature brings together a few points that are worth emphasizing and which are useful for the following sections, and for the policy conclusion, namely:

1 Human capital is costly to acquire but it improves individual labour market opportunities (wages, employability, careers etc.).

2 Individual incentives to learn decrease over time.

3 Financial market imperfections lead to under-investment in human capital.

4 In the absence of labour market imperfections, employed workers pay for general skills and the costs of specific skills are shared.

5 With labour market imperfections, employers are partly willing to finance on-the-job general skills.

6 Employment protection raises the return to specific skills.

7 Investing in specific skills rather than in general skills raises the individual cost of displacement.

We have not made any statement on whether education and more generally on-the-job training should be publicly or privately financed. Pure gratuity is probably conducive to waste, while fully private funding is probably conducive to inequality and inefficiency in the presence of market imperfections and externalities.

After this theoretical review, we will describe the main facts. All OECD countries have drastically increased their effort to improve educational attainments. We now review the trends in the supply of education, the financing issues and exhibit some simple statistics on employment, unemployment, wages and mobility rates by education levels. We start with a short description of the ISCED-classification, the methodology used by the United Nations Educational, Scientific and Cultural Organization (UNESCO) to compare educational outputs across countries.

1.2 Classification of education

To describe the educational attainments and their evolution, we will use the well-known ISCED-97 classification designed by UNESCO. As stated in the operational manual (UNESCO, 1999)

> The world's education systems differ considerably not only in respect to their structures but also in respect to their educational contents. In consequence, it is often difficult for national educational policy-makers to compare their own education systems with those of other countries and to draw useful lessons from the educational experiences of other countries. For this reason, UNESCO has been concerned since the Organization's earliest days with the design of a standard classification system for education that would facilitate

15

comparisons of education statistics and indicators of different countries on the basis of uniform and internationally agreed definitions for the different levels and fields of education.

The number of years of schooling is well captured by the six following levels of education:

Level 0 — Pre-primary education

Level 1 — Primary education or First stage of basic education

Level 2 — Lower secondary or Second stage of basic education

Level 3 — Upper secondary education

Level 4 — Post-secondary non-tertiary education

Level 5 — First stage of tertiary education (not leading directly to an advanced research qualification)

Level 6 — Second stage of tertiary education (leading to an advanced research qualification).

Roughly speaking, this would correspond respectively to: level 0, less than 5 years; level 1, 5–7 years; level 2, 8–10 years; level 3, 10–12 years; level 4, 12–14 years; level 5, 14+ years, and level 6, 16+ years of education, with some overlap across levels and large cross-country differences (up to $+/-2$ years).

In addition, ISCED-97 characterizes the type of education with three letters (A, B and C), corresponding to the destination of pupils/students: C usually means that the completion of the degree is associated with the entry to the labour market and typically refers to entirely vocational types of skills; B means access to the next educational level with likely termination and/or short duration (i.e. a type C programme in the next level) and typically refers to a programme with a mix of general and pre-vocational skills; A means access to any of the next levels and typically refers to predominantly general education, although it also includes some purely vocational skills leading to longer duration programmes in the next stage (e.g. engineering). See Figure 1.4 for the transition pattern.

For economists, the adequacy between the thin subdivisions of this classification and the theoretical concepts derived from human capital theory they may want to use is good, but not perfect. On the positive side, the number of years of schooling can be imputed reasonably well, even though there is an obvious measurement problem due to the diversity of schooling systems across countries. On the negative side, the letters A, B and C imperfectly match the degree of specificity of the training. As just explained, A, although dominantly general in that it gives an access to all superior levels, is also consistent with vocational skills. C typically

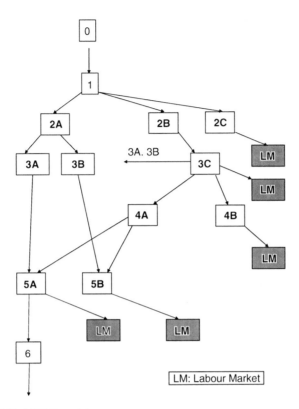

Fig. 1.4 ISCED-1997 Transition pattern
Source: UNESCO (1999).

refers to vocational skills but is actually meant to capture a curriculum leading straight away to the labour market. More generally, these letters are a measure of the expected duration of education in the next stage rather than of the nature of skills provided in the curriculum. Economists interested in knowing the degree of sectoral or occupational specialization of workers, and hereby, their adaptability in a world of labour reallocation across sectors, cannot use these classifications with certainty. Given the importance of skill mismatch and the needs of adaptability of the labour force in modern economies which we consistently point out in this report, it would certainly be interesting to develop a new classification harmonizing the degree of specialization of educational attainments instead of limiting the classification to the main destination after the completion of the diploma.

1.3 The supply of education and its trends

The basic education figures in year 2002 are shown in Table 1.1 for 14 European countries (EU-15 except Luxembourg), as well as for the US and Canada. The average years of education for the population aged 25–64 is around 11.6 in Europe. The differences across countries, however, are quite large: Southern European countries have a less educated population (8.0 years in Portugal, 9.4 years in Italy, 10.3 in Spain) while individuals in the Nordic countries are more educated (13.3 in Denmark, 12.4 in Sweden and Finland). The average individual in the US and in Canada has completed one more year of education than the average European (12.7 and 12.9 years respectively). On average, in our sample of Western European countries (hereafter denoted by EU-14), workers have completed 1.3 fewer years than their US counterparts.

It is interesting to understand the nature of the gap, and notably which educational categories are responsible for the difference between Europe and North America. Inspection of Table 1.1 suggests that it can be attributed in equal parts to a lack of tertiary education in Europe and to lower general upper-secondary education (ISCED 3A). Furthermore, the difference in tertiary education can mostly be attributed to differences in the population with degrees from general and advanced research programmes: only 14.2 per cent of the EU population earned such degrees, while 29 per cent of the US population did.

Where does the gap between Europe and US in type-A tertiary education come from? Additional unreported statistics allow for a gender decomposition of educational attainments. It appears that only 15 per cent of European males had type-A tertiary education versus 30 per cent of the US male population, suggesting that a part only of the gap is due to insufficient access of females to tertiary education. One may also think that the main part of the gap between Europe—or more precisely, Southern Europe—and North America is due to a catching-up effect, as the US may have invested earlier into higher education. Table 1.2 shows that the answer is partly in the negative. In this table, we present the attainment in tertiary education of various age categories. Notice that for the cohort aged 25–34, the Europe–US gap is 14.1 percentage points (between 16.9% type-A tertiary educated in Europe vis-à-vis 31% in the US) while for the cohort aged 55–64 the gap is only marginally larger and equal to 16.6 percentage points (between 9.4% in Europe and 26% in the US). This means that in the last 40 years, Europe has not been able to catch up more than 2.5 of the 16.6 percentage points difference.

Table 1.1 Educational attainment: adult population (2002)
(Distribution of the 25 to 64-year-old population, by highest level of education attained)

| | Pre-primary and primary education | Lower secondary education | Upper secondary education | | | Post-secondary non-tertiary education | Tertiary education | | All levels of education | Average years of schooling |
| | | | ISCED 3C Short | ISCED 3C Long/3B | ISCED 3A | | Type B | Type A and advanced research programmes | | |
	(1)	(2)	(3)	(4)	(5)	(6)	(7)	(8)	(9)	
Austria	x(2)	22	na	49	7	7	7	7	100	11.3
Belgium	19	21	na	8	24	1	15	13	100	11.2
Denmark	na	20	x(2)	46	5	1	8	20	100	13.3
Finland	x(2)	25	na	na	42	n	17	16	100	12.4
France	17	18	27	3	10	n	12	12	100	10.9
Germany	2	15	na	52	3	5	12	13	100	13.4
Greece	37	10	2	2	25	5	6	13	100	10.5
Ireland	21	18	na	na	23	12	10	16	100	12.7
Italy	20	33	2	6	26	2	x(8)	10	100	9.4
Netherlands	12	22	x(4)	24	13	5	3	22	100	13.5
Portugal	67	13	x(5)	x(5)	11	x(5)	2	7	100	8.0
Spain	32	26	na	6	11	na	7	17	100	10.3
Sweden	8	10	na	x(5)	49	x(7)	15	18	100	12.4
United Kingdom	na	16	19	22	15	x(9)	8	19	100	12.7
EU-14	**na**	**20.1**	**na**	**na**	**14.1**	**na**	**na**	**14.2**	**100.0**	**11.6**
United States	5	8	x(5)	x(5)	49	x(5)	9	29	100	12.7
Canada	6	12	a	x(5)	28	12	22	21	100	12.9

Notes: x indicates that data are included in another column. The column reference is shown in brackets after x *e.g.* x(2) means that data are included in column 2. EU-14 refers to EU-15 except Luxembourg.

Source: OECD Education at a Glance 2004, Table A1.1 and authors' calculations.

Table 1.2 Population that has attained tertiary education (2002)
(Percentage of the population which has attained tertiary-type B education or
tertiary-type A and advanced research programmes, by age group)

	Tertiary-type B education					Tertiary-type A and advanced research programmes				
	25–64	25–34	35–44	45–54	55–64	25–64	25–34	35–44	45–54	55–64
	(1)	(2)	(3)	(4)	(5)	(6)	(7)	(8)	(9)	(10)
Austria	7	7	8	8	6	7	7	8	7	5
Belgium	15	20	16	13	10	13	18	13	11	8
Denmark	5	6	6	5	4	23	23	24	25	18
Finland	17	19	21	16	12	16	21	17	14	11
France	12	17	12	9	6	12	19	11	10	9
Germany	10	8	11	11	10	13	13	15	14	11
Greece	6	7	8	4	3	13	17	14	12	7
Ireland	10	14	10	7	5	16	23	15	12	9
Italy	5	6	6	5	4	5	6	6	5	4
Netherlands	3	2	3	2	2	22	25	23	21	17
Portugal	2	3	2	2	2	7	12	7	5	3
Spain	7	12	7	4	2	17	25	18	13	8
Sweden	15	17	18	14	10	18	22	16	17	16
United Kingdom	8	8	9	8	7	19	23	18	18	13
EU-14	8.5	10.0	9.3	7.7	6.1	13.5	16.9	13.8	12.6	9.4
United States	9	9	10	10	7	29	31	29	30	26
Canada	22	25	23	21	16	21	26	20	20	16

Notes: For Italy, data in columns 2–5 are missing. One has assumed that the profile of columns 2–5 is the same as the profile of columns 7–10 and that half of students are in each broad category (type A and B). Assuming 0 in B and 10 per cent in A does not change much EU averages. EU-14 refers to EU-15 except Luxembourg.
Source: OECD Education at a Glance 2004, and authors' calculation.

We then investigate the trends, going back to the 1960s. In Table 1.3 we provide indicators of educational attainment for the population aged 25–64 in some countries. The sample includes some of the new EU member states.[1] Three facts emerge from the table. First, between 1960 and 2002, the difference between Europe and the US in the share of less skilled workers in total population was significantly reduced. In 1960, 76 per cent of European workers had less than secondary education, versus 48 per cent of Americans, that is 28 percentage points less in the US. In 1980 and 1990 (unreported numbers), the gap was still a 30-percentage points difference. In 2002, that fraction was 34 per cent in Europe and 13 per cent in the US,

---

[1] The educational attainment data for 2002 come from OECD (2004a). To obtain estimates for 1960 and 1980 we combine OECD data with estimates of the changes in educational attainment in the data compiled by De La Fuente and Domenech (2001). It is well known that human capital measures in changes are plagued by measurement errors to a great extent. However, Serrano (2003) shows that the reliability of the De La Fuente and Domenech (2001) data, in changes, is much better than in the data derived by Barro and Lee (2001) that are most commonly used.

Table 1.3 Trends in the educational attainment of the population aged 25–64, 1960–2002

Country	Less than upper secondary (%)			Upper secondary and post-secondary non-tertiary (%)			University (%)			Years of schooling		
	1960	1980	2002	1960	1980	2002	1960	1980	2002	1960	1980	2002
Austria	58	45	22	39	50	63	3	6	14	9.7	10.9	12.5
Belgium	84	60	39	8	25	33	8	15	28	7.9	9.7	11.3
Czech Republic	na	na	12	na	na	76	na	na	12	na	na	12.4
Denmark	40	27	20	51	53	53	9	20	27	11.5	12.2	12.7
Finland	84	56	25	8	26	42	9	19	33	7.9	10.3	12.3
France	83	58	35	11	30	41	6	11	24	7.2	9.2	11.0
Germany	62	31	17	33	54	60	5	15	23	9.4	12.0	13.1
Greece	83	73	47	11	17	34	6	10	18	7.4	8.2	10.3
Hungary	na	na	29	na	na	57	na	na	14	na	na	11.5
Ireland	86	73	40	10	21	35	3	6	25	7.3	8.4	11.2
Italy	90	76	54	7	17	36	3	6	10	6.3	8.0	10.2
Netherlands	87	64	34	7	23	42	6	14	24	8.3	10.2	12.1
Norway	61	35	13	28	44	55	11	21	31	10.6	11.7	12.8
Poland	na	na	18	na	na	70	na	na	12	na	na	11.9
Portugal	94	90	80	4	5	11	2	5	9	6.5	6.8	7.8
Spain	96	89	58	1	3	17	3	8	24	5.5	6.3	9.6
Sweden	68	48	18	26	37	49	6	15	33	8.4	9.9	12.2
Switzerland	44	28	15	48	57	59	8	15	25	10.8	12.1	13.2
United Kingdom	54	40	16	38	47	57	8	14	27	10.0	10.9	12.4
United States	48	24	13	44	57	49	8	19	38	10.2	11.7	12.8
EU-14	**76**	**56**	**34**	**19**	**32**	**44**	**5**	**11**	**22**	**8.0**	**9.6**	**11.5**

Notes: EU-14 refers to EU-15 except Luxembourg. Values for 1960 and 1980 have been imputed using OECD (2004a), OECD labour force statistics 1995–2000, and De La Fuente and Domenech (2001). To link the different data sources we have used the 1995 values reported in De La Fuente and Domenech (2001) and OECD labour force statistics on the educational attainment in the population for the year closest to 1995. Then we used the growth rates during 1960–80 and 1980–95 reported in De La Fuente and Domenech (2001) to impute values for 1980 and 1960. Years of schooling have been calculated from the attainment data generated by this procedure. In general, we have used the mapping between years of schooling and attainment provided by De La Fuente and Domenech (2001). Years of schooling for the Czech Republic, Hungary and Poland come directly from OECD (2004a).

Sources: OECD (2004a); OECD labour force statistics 1995–2000; and De La Fuente and Domenech (2001).

that is, a difference of 21 percentage points. In other words, about one-third of the gap has been filled in a decade. A related observation is that Europe had a much lower share of individuals with upper-secondary schooling in 1960 than the US did, but by 2002 that gap had been more or less closed.

Secondly, interestingly, there was not such a big difference at the tertiary level in 1960, the difference being only of 3 percentage points (8% in the US, 5% in Europe). However, in 2002, the difference had reached 16 percentage points (38 vs. 22). Thus, over the 40 years spanned by these data, the EU–US gap in attainment has moved from the upper secondary level to the tertiary level. The gap has actually stabilized in the last decade: in 1991 (unreported), the difference was of 15 percentage points (30% vs. 15%).

Thirdly, combining the two trends, there appears to be a general catch-up in terms of the average number of years of education. To see this, Table 1.3 also provides estimates of the number of years of schooling.[2] In 1960, the average European had completed 8 years of schooling, while the average American had 10.2 years of education. By 2002, this gap had been reduced by almost a year. The reduction of the gap comes mostly from the educational improvements in Southern European and some continental European countries. The overall picture shows a fair amount of convergence in average educational attainments across European countries, and between Europe and the US.

1.4 Financing and quality

We now turn to the issue of the financing of different types of education. The figures we present provide useful information, particularly about changes over time. Cross-country comparisons may be more difficult to interpret due to imperfect comparability of source data, but we can still discuss with a fair amount of confidence whether individual countries target education at the primary, secondary, or tertiary level.

Table 1.4 presents total expenditure as a fraction of GDP along with expenditure per student as a fraction of GDP per capita for the EU-14. These numbers are reported at two points in time, in 1991 and 2001. While expenditures increased in the US over the considered period, in Europe they actually decreased. By normalizing the total expenditure data with respect to the relative size of the student population we obtain the last two columns reported in Table 1.4. In the US, expenditure per student, relative to GDP per capita, did not change between 1991 and 2001 while in Europe it experienced a small decline. For some individual countries the decline was large, however. In particular, in the Nordic countries and in the UK expenditure per student declined substantially. The largest decline was experienced in Sweden, a country that was the most ambitious in 1991 but had dropped to the European average by 2001.

---

[2] The average years of schooling is imputed using the attainment data and information on the typical length of schooling corresponding to each attainment level. In general, we use the 'mapping' between educational attainment and years of schooling provided by De La Fuente and Domenech (2001). There are two exceptions and those pertain to years of schooling at the primary level in Switzerland and the US. This is most likely an upward biased estimate of the actual number of years of schooling in the population. Notice also that we have used a finer division into different attainment levels when predicting years of schooling; furthermore, we use the same mapping for all years.

Table 1.4 Total education expenditure as a fraction of GDP and expenditure per student as a fraction of GDP per capita, percent, 1991 and 2001

Country	Total expenditure		Expenditure/student	
	1991	2001	1991	2001
Austria	5.4*	5.8 (5.6*)	27*	27*
Belgium	5.4*	6.4 (6.0*)	23	26
Denmark	6.1	7.1	31	28
Finland	6.6	5.8	32	24
France	6.0	6.0	24	25
Germany	5.4	5.3	29	25
Greece	na	4.1	na	22
Ireland	5.9	4.5	21	18
Italy[a]	5.1*	5.3 (4.9*)	26*	30*
Netherlands	5.8	4.9	26	22
Portugal	5.5*	5.9 (5.8*)	28*	28*
Spain	5.6	4.9	22	24
Sweden	6.8	6.5	38	26
United Kingdom	5.3*	5.5 (4.7*)	28*	19*
EU-13	**5.5**	**5.3**	**27**	**25**
United States	7.0	7.3	30	30

Notes: [a] Data refer to 1992 rather than 1991.
* Expenditure data are from public sources only. Total expenditure includes all levels from pre-primary to tertiary education. EU-13 average is the population-weighted average for the 13 EU countries where data are available 1991 and 2001; the sizes of the populations in 2001 are used as weights; if only public expenditure is reported in one year we use public expenditure for the other year as well.
Source: OECD (1993, 1995, 2004).

In Table 1.5 we look at the allocation of the overall education budget at various levels. The first number in each country/year cell reports the allocation of expenditure; the second number (in italics) is the enrolment share; and the third number (in bold face) is the ratio of expenditure and enrolment shares. In all countries investment per student is increasing with the educational level, but the allocation across levels differ markedly between the US and Europe: the European countries allocate more resources per student (for given level of overall expenditures) to the secondary level while the US favours the tertiary level (see the bold face numbers). With respect to the changes over time in the allocation of expenditures per student, there are no major changes in Europe. In the US, however, there appears to have been a redirection of investment per student from the primary and secondary levels towards the pre-primary level.

Table 1.6 reports the share of total educational expenditure that comes from private sources. The main message of the table is well known and was already discussed in our general introduction: the private share of total expenditure is far greater in the US than in Europe. The EU average is

Table 1.5 Expenditure and enrolment shares by level of education, percent, 1991 and 2001

(Expenditure (resp. enrolment) shares are reported in normal fonts (resp. italics), while bold face numbers are ratios of expenditures to enrolment)

Country	Pre-primary		Primary		Secondary		Tertiary	
	1991	2001	1991	2001	1991	2001	1991	2001
Austria	7	9	19	21	51	48	23	22
	13	*14*	*24*	*25*	*48*	*46*	*16*	*15*
	0.54	**0.64**	**0.79**	**0.84**	**1.06**	**1.04**	**1.44**	**1.47**
Belgium	10	9	20	23	51	45	19	22
	17	*16*	*34*	*31*	*25*	*40*	*11*	*13*
	0.59	**0.56**	**0.59**	**0.74**	**2.04**	**1.12**	**1.73**	**1.69**
Denmark	4	11	28	28	46	36	21	27
	5	*21*	*34*	*29*	*46*	*34*	*15*	*15*
	0.80	**0.52**	**0.82**	**0.97**	**1.00**	**1.06**	**1.4**	**1.8**
Finland	2	6	31	23	43	41	24	30
	4	*11*	*38*	*31*	*42*	*40*	*16*	*17*
	0.50	**0.55**	**0.82**	**0.74**	**1.02**	**1.02**	**1.5**	**1.76**
France	10	11	20	19	52	51	18	18
	18	*17*	*29*	*27*	*41*	*42*	*12*	*14*
	0.56	**0.65**	**0.69**	**0.70**	**1.27**	**1.21**	**1.5**	**1.29**
Germany	4	11	11	13	66	55	19	21
	15	*14*	*21*	*21*	*50*	*52*	*15*	*13*
	0.27	**0.79**	**0.52**	**0.62**	**1.32**	**1.06**	**1.27**	**1.62**
Greece	na	na	na	29	na	40	na	31
				37		*37*		*26*
				0.78		**1.08**		**1.19**
Ireland	8	0.15	28	32	40	35	24	31
	13	*0.21*	*42*	*46*	*36*	*37*	*8*	*17*
	0.62	**0.72**	**0.67**	**0.70**	**1.11**	**0.95**	**3.00**	**1.82**
Italy[a]	8	9*	24	24*	50	48*	18	19*
	11	*12*	*27*	*27*	*48*	*44*	*14*	*17*
	0.73	**0.64**	**0.89**	**0.89**	**1.04**	**1.10**	**1.29**	**1.12**
Netherlands	6	7	23	28	41	39	30	26
	11	*11*	*34*	*37*	*42*	*39*	*13*	*13*
	0.55	**0.56**	**0.89**	**0.76**	**0.98**	**1.00**	**2.31**	**2.00**
Portugal	2	na	42	na	38	na	17	na
	4		*50*		*40*		*7*	
	0.50		**0.84**		**0.95**		**2.43**	
Spain	8	10	22	25	52	40	18	25
	10	*14*	*29*	*31*	*48*	*38*	*13*	*17*
	0.80	**0.71**	**0.76**	**0.81**	**1.08**	**1.05**	**1.38**	**1.47**
Sweden	3	7	35	31	44	35	18	26
	6	*15*	*40*	*34*	*41*	*39*	*13*	*12*
	0.50	**0.47**	**0.88**	**0.91**	**1.07**	**0.90**	**1.38**	**2.17**
United Kingdom	4*	8	28*	24	47*	48	21*	20
	7	*7*	*40*	*33*	*44*	*49*	*9*	*11*
	0.57	**1.14**	**0.70**	**0.73**	**1.07**	**0.98**	**2.33**	**1.82**
EU-12	6	9	21	21	53	48	20	21
	12	*13*	*30*	*28*	*45*	*45*	*13*	*14*
	0.50	**0.69**	**0.70**	**0.75**	**1.18**	**1.07**	**1.54**	**1.50**
United States	6	7	28	27	31	29	34	37
	12	*8*	*38*	*39*	*33*	*35*	*17*	*18*
	0.50	**0.88**	**0.74**	**0.69**	**0.94**	**0.83**	**2.00**	**2.06**

Notes: [a] 1992 data are used in place of 1991 data.

* Expenditure data are from public sources only. EU-12 average is the population-weighted average for the 12 EU countries where data are available 1991 and 2001; the size of the populations in 2001 are used as weights. Enrolment data for 2001 are based on full-time equivalents. In 2001, expenditures not allocated by level have been distributed to the remaining educational levels in proportion to their expenditure shares. In 2001, expenditure (enrolment) at the post-secondary, non-tertiary level, have been allocated to the secondary and tertiary level in proportion to the expenditure (enrolment) shares.

Source: OECD (1993, 1995, 2004).

Table 1.6 Share of private expenditure in total expenditure, percent, 2001

Austria	3.4
Belgium	6.3
Denmark	4.2
Finland	1.7
France	6.7
Germany	18.9
Greece	4.9
Ireland	6.7
Italy	7.5
Netherlands	8.2
Portugal	1.7
Spain	12.2
Sweden	3.1
United Kingdom	14.5
EU-14	10.8
United States	31.5

Notes: EU average is the population-weighted average for the 14 EU-15 countries where data are available; the sizes of the populations in 2001 are used as weights.

Source: OECD (2004).

some 20-percentage points lower than in the US and the private share of expenditure for no single European country surpasses that of the US.

Figure 1.5 presents long-run expenditure patterns. The reported numbers pertain to public expenditure on education as a percentage of GDP. The solid line shows public expenditure for the US. The dashed line labelled 'EU-6' reports the population weighted average for six EU countries (Austria, Germany, Ireland, the Netherlands, Sweden, and the UK) where such data are available starting in 1970, while the line labelled 'EU total' pertains to the EU-15 countries (excluding Luxembourg). As shown by the figure, public expenditure has been fairly similar in the US and Europe over the past thirty years. The US, however, had a much higher share of private expenditure in overall expenditure, resulting in larger total expenditure.

1.5 Returns to education: unemployment, wages, mobility

1.5.1 *Wage returns to education*

How does Europe compare to the US in the returns to education? Table 1.7 provides some information on this question by reporting relative earnings by educational attainment, gender and country. The earnings of upper-secondary graduates are normalized to 100. For most countries, earnings are gross of individual income taxes and reported on an annual

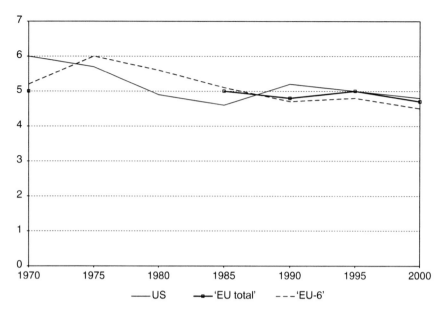

Fig. 1.5 Long-run public expenditure patterns, percentage of GDP, 1970–2000
Notes: EU-6 is the population weighted average for Austria, Germany, Ireland, the Netherlands, Sweden, and the UK. EU total is, generally, the population weighted average for the EU-15 countries, excluding Luxembourg; no data are available for Greece in 1990, however. Notice also that there are some time series breaks in these data; see OECD (1996) for further details.
Source: OECD (1996, 2003).

or monthly basis. Thus, relative earnings will capture hours as well as wage variation across educational categories.

The main message conveyed by Table 1.7 is well known: the earnings distributions of the European countries are in general much more compressed than in the US. The main exception from this rule is Portugal where earnings inequality appears to be on par with the US. We also see from the table that vocational tertiary education (type B) has a lower pay-off than general tertiary education (type A). Interestingly, the relative earnings of type B graduates are very similar in the US and in the EU. The relative earnings for those with less than university education are not too different in the EU and the US. It is primarily at the top end of the earnings distribution where Europe and the US differ. In relative terms, individuals with the highest educational level are paid much more in the US than in Europe.

Of course, gross earnings are not the sole determinants of the return to higher education. Taxes, employment probabilities, as well as study grants and subsidized student loans are also of some importance.

Table 1.7 Relative earnings across countries
(By level of educational attainment and gender for 30 to 44-year-olds (upper secondary education = 100))

	Year	Gender	Below upper secondary education	Tertiary-type B education	Tertiary-type A and advanced research programs	All tertiary education
Belgium	2002	Males	97	120	149	136
		Females	83	124	185	146
Denmark	2001	Males	83	109	135	128
		Females	89	112	122	121
Finland	2001	Males	89	125	180	155
		Females	94	124	167	141
France	2002	Males	86	132	173	157
		Females	80	135	159	148
Germany	2002	Males	87	113	152	137
		Females	72	112	153	138
Ireland	2000	Males	77	123	140	133
		Females	61	126	155	144
Italy	2000	Males	72	m	140	140
		Females	80	m	132	132
Netherlands	1997	Males	86	130	133	132
		Females	73	136	154	152
Portugal	1999	Males	57	155	194	185
		Females	58	139	206	185
Spain	2001	Males	82	97	135	122
		Females	65	88	138	126
Sweden	2001	Males	86	114	162	149
		Females	85	109	137	126
United Kingdom	2001	Males	67	126	162	151
		Females	74	133	216	183
United States	2002	Males	70	122	205	195
		Females	67	122	191	182
Canada	2001	Males	78	115	183	147
		Females	65	120	179	145
EU-12		**Males**	**80**	**120**	**154**	**143**
		Females	**75**	**120**	**161**	**146**

Notes: The numbers generally pertain to earnings before tax. The earnings concept for Belgium is, however, tax-adjusted. The reference period is: a week for Ireland and the UK; a month for France, Germany, and Portugal; a year for the remaining countries. The EU-12 average is a population-weighted average of EU-15 countries reported here.
Source: OECD (2004).

The OECD (2004) has calculated returns that take taxes and employment probabilities into account for a small sub-set of countries listed in Table 1.7.[3] In Table 1.8 we reproduce some of these estimates. The numbers in the table refer to the private rate of return from upper-secondary to tertiary education. They are presented for tertiary education as a whole (there is thus no distinction between type A and B programmes). The calculations

---

[3] It is not clear whether the rate of return's calculation takes the availability of subsidized study grants and loans into account.

Table 1.8 Private rates of return associated with tertiary education

Country	Males	Females
Denmark	6.7	6.1
Finland	14.2	15.2
Spain	9.2	8.5
Sweden	8.8	7.3
United Kingdom	11.2	13.7
United States	11.0	7.9
EU-5	10.3	11.2

Notes: Rates of return take taxes and employment probabilities into account. EU-5 is the population-weighted average of the five EU-15 countries in the table.
Source: OECD (2004).

are based on the assumption that an individual proceeds to tertiary education immediately upon completion of upper-secondary education.

The returns reported in Table 1.8 are fairly similar across countries. The EU average return is slightly lower than the US counterpart for males; for females, however, the EU average return exceeds that of the US.[4] Presumably, it is the adjustment for differences in employment probabilities that makes the male returns in the EU countries more similar to the US counterparts. Adjusting for taxes should have increased the spread between Europe and the US, since European tax systems tend to be more progressive than the American one. The low return for American females is quite surprising, but it may reflect the fact that they proceed to tertiary type-B education to a greater extent than American males.

1.5.2 Employment and unemployment

Education has a strong impact on the relative economic performance of individuals in the labour market. We review some well-known facts here. First, Table 1.9 describes the employment rate by education group in 14 European countries, the United States and Canada in 2002. The employment rate is the fraction of the population in working age actually contributing to production. It is therefore a useful index of the ability of an economy to mobilize its human resources in production. The comparison of the EU average with the US and Canada shows that differences in employment rates (by education and in the aggregate) are not very

---

[4] One should probably be slightly careful here since the UK has a higher relative weight in the EU average in Table 1.8 than in Table 1.7. But this cannot be the entire story; compare, for instance, the estimated returns in Sweden and Finland with that of the US.

Table 1.9 Employment rates and educational attainment (2002)
(Number of 25 to 64-year-olds in employment as a percentage of the population aged 25 to 64, by level of education attained and gender)

		Pre-primary and primary education	Lower secondary education	Upper Secondary	Tertiary education		All levels of education
						ISCED 5A and advanced research programmes	
		ISCED 0/1	ISCED 2	ISCED 3A	ISCED 5B	(ISCED 6)	
		(1)	(2)	(3)	(4)	(5)	(6)
Austria	Males	x(2)	65	77	86	91	80
	Females	x(2)	48	66	81	85	64
Belgium	Males	49	74	83	87	88	77
	Females	25	45	65	79	82	57
Denmark	Males	na	73	84	88	92	83
	Females	na	52	71	86	84	74
Finland	Males	x(2)	61	77	84	89	76
	Females	x(2)	54	72	83	85	72
France	Males	57	77	83	88	86	79
	Females	43	56	71	80	80	64
Germany	Males	54	65	63	84	88	77
	Females	33	45	54	78	80	62
Greece	Males	75	84	83	81	88	81
	Females	36	42	45	73	76	47
Ireland	Males	64	86	89	91	91	84
	Females	30	47	63	80	84	60
Italy	Males	52	79	82	x(5)	88	77
	Females	18	39	61	x(5)	77	46
Netherlands	Males	63	82	91	91	91	84
	Females	35	50	74	80	82	64
Portugal	Males	82	88	85	84	93	84
	Females	60	77	80	78	90	67
Spain	Males	69	86	83	88	87	81
	Females	28	44	58	68	76	48
Sweden	Males	67	80	83	85	89	83
	Females	51	69	80	83	88	79
United Kingdom	Males	na	59	88	88	90	82
	Females	na	48	77	84	86	72
EU-14	Males	na	75	82	na	91	82
	Females	na	49	66	na	83	62
United States	Males	67	69	80	86	89	82
	Females	39	49	68	77	79	69
Canada	Males	55	72	82	86	86	81
	Females	31	51	68	78	79	69

Notes: x indicates that data are included in another column. x(2) means that data are included in column 2, etc.

Source: OECD Education at a Glance 2004, Table A1.1 and authors' calculations; na: not applicable.

Table 1.10 Unemployment ratio and educational attainment (2002)
(Number of 25 to 64-year-olds who are unemployed as a percentage of the population aged 25 to 64, by level of education attained and gender)

		Pre-primary and primary education	Lower secondary education	Upper Secondary ISCED 3A	Post-secondary non-tertiary education	Tertiary Type B	Type A and advanced research programmes	All levels of education
		(1)	(2)	(3)	(4)	(5)	(6)	(7)
Austria	Males	x(2)	5.9	1.5	2.6	1.0	2.2	3.2
	Females	x(2)	2.9	2.7	1.5	1.0	2.4	2.5
Belgium	Males	6.7	5.3	3.6	5.9	2.6	3.1	4.5
	Females	4.5	6.0	4.8	4.6	2.8	3.9	4.6
Denmark	Males	na	3.5	1.4	7.2	3.5	3.2	3.1
	Females	na	4.6	2.9	4.7	2.5	4.8	3.2
Finland	Males	x(2)	8.0	7.4	na	4.8	3.1	6.5
	Females	x(2)	8.1	7.0	na	4.8	3.1	6.2
France	Males	6.0	9.8	6.0	na	5.0	4.8	5.8
	Females	5.4	9.4	6.0	na	3.9	4.8	6.4
Germany	Males	17.7	12.8	5.4	5.2	3.9	3.6	7.4
	Females	7.7	6.4	3.7	3.9	4.7	3.8	5.9
Greece	Males	3.4	5.6	4.4	5.9	4.6	3.6	4.3
	Females	3.9	8.8	7.8	12.6	8.4	7.0	6.6
Ireland	Males	5.6	4.0	2.8	1.7	2.3	1.9	3.3
	Females	1.7	2.5	2.0	2.3	1.4	1.1	1.9
Italy	Males	4.8	5.2	4.1	6.6	x(6)	3.3	4.5
	Females	3.2	6.1	5.6	10.5	x(6)	5.9	5.4
Netherlands	Males	2.8	2.4	1.6	1.7	1.1	1.9	1.9
	Females	2.1	2.2	2.1	2.7	1.7	2.0	2.1
Portugal	Males	3.0	3.6	3.5	x(3)	4.5	1.8	3.1
	Females	3.4	5.0	4.0	x(3)	2.8	4.8	3.8
Spain	Males	6.5	6.5	5.0	na	4.7	4.7	5.8
	Females	5.8	10.1	8.6	na	10.4	8.4	8.3
Sweden	Males	3.8	4.5	4.5	x(5)	3.3	3.2	4.0
	Females	4.4	3.9	3.3	x(5)	2.4	2.1	3.1
United Kingdom	Males	na	6.8	3.1	x(7)	2.6	2.5	3.8
	Females	na	3.2	2.4	x(7)	1.5	1.8	2.7
EU-14	**Males**	**na**	**8**	**5**	**na**	**na**	**4**	**5**
	Females	**na**	**7**	**5**	**na**	**na**	**5**	**5**
United States	**Males**	6.9	7.9	5.3	x(3)	3.8	2.8	4.7
	Females	5.1	5.5	3.7	x(3)	2.5	2.1	3.3
Canada	Males	7.8	8.6	5.8	5.9	5.4	4.5	5.9
	Females	4.5	5.7	5.0	5.1	3.9	3.9	4.6

Notes: x(2) means that data are included in column 2. etc.

Source: OECD Education at a Glance 2004, Table A1.1 and authors' calculations; na: not applicable.

large among males, while they are much larger among females. Over all educational levels, the female employment rate is 7 percentage points lower in the EU compared with the US (as well as with Canada).

Two regularities characterize the relationship between employment rates and schooling. First, in each country, higher education is associated with higher employment rates for both men and women. In some cases the differences are very pronounced (see, for instance, the differences pertaining to females in Italy or Belgium). Second, the gap between women and men's employment rates decreases as educational attainments grow. In the group with lower secondary education, the average female employment rate in Europe was 49 per cent, 26 per cent lower than the corresponding number for males (75%). For the group with tertiary education, the difference was only 8 per cent (83% for women relative to 91% for men). The higher participation of women and the higher levels of education in the North American countries explain most of the overall differences in employment rates with the EU.

As usual, the average across the EU countries masks large differences between 'southern' European countries (such as Spain and Italy) exhibiting very low employment rates for women (44–46%) and 'northern' European countries (such as Finland or Denmark) having very high employment rates (72–9%); in fact, in 2002, female employment rates in the Nordic countries were higher than in US and Canada. Notice that these differences across the EU countries are much more pronounced when we look at the groups with low schooling than when we consider those with high schooling (especially tertiary education).

Table 1.10 presents a similar picture, using unemployment ratios (unemployment as a percentage of the population in working age) across educational groups and countries. Again, the aggregate unemployment ratio for Europe as a whole is significantly larger than for the US or Canada only for females. In each country, the unemployment ratio is negatively related to the level of education of a group. Increased education is likely to make the skills of a worker more valuable in production (increasing their employment rate) and may also increase the efficiency of the matching process (highly educated workers are more mobile and have a broader range of search) decreasing the unemployment rate.

1.5.3 Geographical mobility

Geographical mobility has two dimensions. The first one is the mobility between residential areas or between regions within countries. The second

Table 1.11 Geographical mobility in the last three years, 15–64 population, by reason and country

# obs. 152902		Primary reason for move			
Country	Mobility rate	Job related	House related	Personal reason	Total
DK	0.237	0.1234	0.6219	0.2547	1
NL	0.201	0.1217	0.4457	0.4325	1
B	0.167	0.0659	0.6503	0.2838	1
F	0.214	0.1625	0.5704	0.2671	1
IRL	0.0647	0.056	0.6001	0.3438	1
I	0.0871	0.0869	0.3815	0.5316	1
EL	0.0752	0.0955	0.6744	0.2301	1
E	0.105	0.0877	0.5521	0.3603	1
P	0.101	0.0611	0.5953	0.3436	1
A	0.010	0.0978	0.5622	0.34	1
FIN	0.270	0.1534	0.5607	0.2859	1
L	0.282	na	na	na	1
D	0.206	0.0974	0.722	0.1806	1
UK	0.2054	0.1631	0.5855	0.2514	1
S	0.252	na	na	na	1
Total	0.162	0.1153	0.5723	0.3125	1

Notes: Sample 1995–2001, survey weights. Columns 2–4: division based on the main reason for move, sum is 100 per cent. 'Total' is the EU-15 average excluding Luxembourg and Sweden.

one is the mobility between countries. Both are relevant for our analysis because education affects mobility and notably human capital is an increasingly mobile factor. We first investigate residential mobility within countries and present summary statistics in Tables 1.11 and 1.12. These descriptive statistics are based on computations using the European

Table 1.12 Geographical mobility in the last three years, by education

	Mobility rate, Any reason	# obs.
All	0.145	750168
Primary	0.113	730422
Secondary	0.154	730422
Tertiary	0.205	730422
	Mobility rate, Job-related reason	# obs.
All	0.083	58337
Primary	0.055	57093
Secondary	0.080	57093
Tertiary	0.110	57093

Notes: Samples. Any reason: all individuals 15–65, 1995–2001; job-related reason: active population, head of households 15–65, 1995–2001. Numbers pertain to EU-15 excluding Luxembourg and Sweden. Survey weights are used in the computation.

Table 1.13 Summary of internal mobility and immigration, USA and EU 1990–2000

Year		Early 90's			2000	
Variable	Total labour force	% Labour force born outside Union	% Labour force living in a state (country) different from that of birth	Total labour force	% Labour force born outside Union	% Labour force living in a state (country) different from that of birth
USA	124,772,500	9.3%	35.3%	138,733,660	12.4%	35.6%
EU-12	154,007,000	4.1%	2.5%	160,780,000	4.9%	2.5%
EU-15	167,000,000	4.6%	2.2%	171,668,000	5.0%	2.6%

Community Household Panel (ECHP) in 15 European countries between 1995 and 2001.[5]

Table 1.11 reports substantial heterogeneity between European countries: high mobility countries are Denmark, the Netherlands, France, the UK, Finland, Germany, Sweden and Luxembourg, with 20 per cent or more of individuals having moved from one dwelling to another. Ireland, Italy, Spain, Portugal, Austria and Greece all report a mobility rate below 12 per cent. Table 1.11 also reports the frequency of reasons for moving, conditional on mobility, by country. Job-related reasons for a move are most common in Denmark, the UK, Finland and France, while they are substantially less frequent in Ireland, Belgium, Portugal, Spain and Italy. This ranking is similar to the overall mobility ranking; the only exception is Germany, which has a relatively low job-mobility rate in this table.

Table 1.12 restricts the sample to heads of households (to identify the level of education) in the labour force, and reports that on average, 14.5 per cent of individuals have moved from one place to another in the last three years, whatever the reason for the move. It also indicates a substantial heterogeneity across education levels. Among individuals with primary education, the mobility rate is 11.2 per cent, while it reaches 15.4 per cent for those with secondary education and 20.5 per cent for those with tertiary education. The fraction of heads of households reporting geographical mobility in the last three years with the main reason being related to job is, on average, 8.3 per cent, but it is merely 5.5 per cent for workers with primary education, 8.0 for workers with secondary education and 11.4 per cent for workers with tertiary education.

---

[5] See Ch. 4 for a definition of mobility in ECHP.

These figures raise a few interesting points. First, overall mobility, particularly job-related mobility, is pretty low in Europe. Secondly, mobility outside the residential area is even lower. Thirdly, there are significant cross-country differences: the UK, Finland, Denmark and France having relatively high job mobility rates while countries in Southern Europe and Germany are lagging behind. Finally, less educated individuals are less mobile, even though they are most exposed to unemployment. We will come back on the links between education and mobility in Chapter 4.

We now investigate the second facet, mobility between states or countries. Table 1.13 summarizes some statistics on long-run mobility of labour into the European Union (immigration from outside) and within it (here, by 'within', we shall mean between countries). By way of comparison, the Table also reports the measures pertaining to immigration into the US and to mobility of US workers across states within the country. We capture long-run immigration into the EU (US) as the percentage of the labour force born outside the EU (US). Similarly we capture the extent of internal mobility as the percentage of people in the labour force working in a country of the EU (state of the US) and born in a different EU country (US state).

The data, based on US Census and European Labour Force Data compare the very early nineties (1990 in the US and 1992 in the EU) with the year 2000. Two facts emerge clearly at a first glance to Table 1.13. First, the US had a much larger share of foreign-born immigrant workers than the EU already at the beginning of the considered period (1990) and increased the lead by attracting more foreign-born workers during the nineties. Hence, by 2000, one worker in eight was foreign born in the US while only one in 20 in the EU was born outside the Union. Second the degree of internal mobility of US citizens is more than ten times higher than the mobility of EU citizens between different countries of the Union. Hence, less than 3 per cent of the labour force in Europe works in a country different from the country of birth, while, in the US, more than 35 per cent of the labour force moved out of the state of birth to work in a different one. We recognize that the comparison is somewhat forced since US states are more homogenous than EU countries, but the difference is still strikingly large. As a matter of fact, the degree of cross-country mobility has not changed at all between 1992 (Maastricht Treaty) and 2000, after nearly a decade of potential (*de jure*) freedom of movement of workers in the Union. This fact may be a source of concern.

These statistics illustrate a substantially smaller capacity of the EU to attract and absorb foreign workers, as well as to promote mobility within its boundaries, when compared to the US. We will develop the analysis in Chapter 3, which, *inter alia*, addresses the issue of immigration and skills.

1.6 Conclusion

1 In the European macroeconomic context of the Enlargement and more generally volatility of demand, one can expect large workers' reallocation flows.
2 Education must provide skills to ease transition between sectors.
3 In an ageing Europe, such transitions may be costly, since labour market institutions—particularly employment protection—do not encourage the acquisition of general skills.

2

Cohesion and the Supply of General Skills in Europe

2.1 Introduction

In this chapter we examine the evolution of the skills provided by the schooling systems across Europe. We primarily focus on primary and secondary schooling and thus the analysis presumably has more implications for inequality than growth. Important questions asked in this chapter are: What do the European countries get for their resource investments, that is, what skills are provided by these schooling systems? How have these general skills evolved over time? What is the implication of the evolution of skills for wage inequality? Throughout this chapter, we use the US as a benchmark and present data for a selection of European countries. The actual selection of European countries is mostly determined by the availability of data.

We analyse skills first in the oldest cohort and then proceed to successively younger cohorts. Section 2.2 examines basic skills brought to the labour market by successive cohorts born from 1935 until 1970. In section 2.3, we look at skills for those still in schools. Section 2.4 examines the relationship between skills and wage inequality across countries. Section 2.5 offers concluding remarks.

2.2 Schooling and skills by cohort: a long-run perspective

We begin by describing the evolution of years of schooling and skills across cohorts within countries. To provide details on the evolution of general skills, we utilize data from the International Adult Literacy Survey (IALS), described in OECD and Statistics Canada (1995). The great virtue of the IALS data is that it provides an internationally comparable measure of skills in the adult population. Although IALS data impose a restriction on the number of European countries included.[1]

2.2.1 Data description

The IALS data were collected in 1994, 1996, and 1998.[2] The IALS test consisted of three domains: prose, document, and quantitative literacy. It is mainly a test of basic skills. It is thus primarily designed to detect variations in skills at the lower end of the skill distribution; it is presumably less apt to fully detect variations in skills at the top end of the distribution.

Table 2.1 reports a basic set of statistics obtained using these data with different samples. The measure of skills used is the IALS score obtained by averaging over the three domains. The first two columns show the mean and the standard deviation (SD) for the target populations (aged 16–65). The country obtaining the highest score on this literacy test is Sweden, while Poland has the lowest score. The US is slightly above average and has the highest variance in skills. The average score in the US target population is almost identical to the EU average reported in the table. That average skills are so similar in the US compared to the EU is perhaps surprising given the large attainment differences we reported in the last chapter in Table 1.3. To some extent this lack of a difference is driven by the fact that EU countries that did not participate in the IALS tend to be those with low levels of human capital (e.g., Greece, Spain, and Portugal). But this is not the entire story: consider indeed the EU countries that have an educational attainment similar to the one of the US: European countries do better on a comparison of basic literacy skills than they do when examining formal attainment.

We decided to exclude immigrants from the analyses that follow, as it is not clear whether they went to school in the host country. The columns headed 'Natives' report the mean and standard deviation in skills when

---

[1] For instance, Spain did not participate in the survey and France elected to opt out of the survey.

[2] The data for Germany, Ireland, the Netherlands, Poland, Sweden, Switzerland (French and German-speaking regions), and the United States were collected in 1994. Data for the Flemish community in Belgium and Great Britain were collected in 1996, and data for the Czech Republic, Denmark, Finland, Hungary, Italy, and Norway in 1998. The target populations were individuals aged 16–65 and the sample sizes were around 3,000 per country. A potential drawback of these data is thus that the samples are small. Small sample error is therefore likely to be an issue, in particular at the cohort level.

Table 2.1 Test scores in the adult population

Country	Target population (ages 16–65)		Natives (ages 16–65)			Natives & ages 25–64		
	Mean	SD	Mean	SD	Sample (% of target)	Mean	SD	Sample (% of target)
Belgium	277	55	279	53	96	275	55	65
Czech Republic	283	46	284	46	99	282	47	83
Denmark	289	40	289	40	98	289	41	80
Finland	288	48	289	47	98	285	47	78
Germany	285	42	287	41	92	286	42	79
Hungary	254	48	254	48	99	250	47	77
Ireland	263	57	262	57	94	258	59	73
Italy	244	60	244	61	97	238	62	81
Netherlands	286	44	288	42	94	286	42	82
Norway	294	45	296	42	93	295	42	73
Poland	229	64	230	64	98	225	65	77
Sweden	304	49	308	44	91	308	44	71
Switzerland	271	57	285	39	75	283	40	65
United Kingdom	267	62	270	58	95	270	59	80
United States	272	65	284	55	78	287	55	63
All Europe	266	54	268	52	95	266	52	79
EU-9	271	52	273	51	95	271	51	80

Notes: Row headed All Europe reports the population-weighted average of all European (Western and Eastern) countries included in the table. Row headed EU-9 reports the population-weighted average of the nine countries in the Western EU-15. Columns headed 'Sample' report the percent of the target population that remains after making the indicated sample exclusions.

immigrants are excluded.[3] The final three columns report summary measures of skills for the sample that comes closest to our sample of analysis. The sample is restricted to those aged 25–64 to eliminate those who have not yet finished their educational careers from the data. As can be seen, this sample restriction has a minor effect on measured mean skills, although it is slightly surprising to see that mean skills increases in the US. In the final analysis sample, the variation in skills is comparable for the US and Europe and the average native-born American perform slightly better on the test than the average native-born European.

---

[3] Natives are defined as those who responded 'yes' to the question of whether they were born in the country of the interview. This sample restriction has a big effect on the reported mean and variance in the US—the mean increases, and the standard deviation falls, substantially. The European numbers are only affected to a minor extent. This mainly has to do with the immigrant population being much greater in the US, but a greater fraction of sample non-response to the question on nativity is probably also an issue. With only those reporting that they were born in the country in question included in the sample, the sample size is reduced by 22 per cent in the US, but only by 5 per cent in Europe.

2.2.2 Schooling and skills by cohort

The IALS also report educational attainment as measured by years of schooling. In this chapter, we thus use both measures; still we shall focus on test scores as they provide a better measurement of the quality of the education than years of schooling.

Figure 2.1 shows years of schooling by cohort for the Anglo-Saxon countries along with the EU average.[4] It conveys a similar message to Table 1.3. The educational expansion in the US preceded that of the EU. For the cohorts observed in the data there is in fact little increase in the US; the increase amounts .5 years from the cohort born in 1935 to the cohort born in 1970. For Europe, on the other hand, there is a substantial rise in attainment for successive cohorts. For the time period spanned by these cohorts the increase is 2.9 years. Note that the deceleration in growth rates of human capital in the US has been observed by others, for example, DeLong et al. (2003).[5]

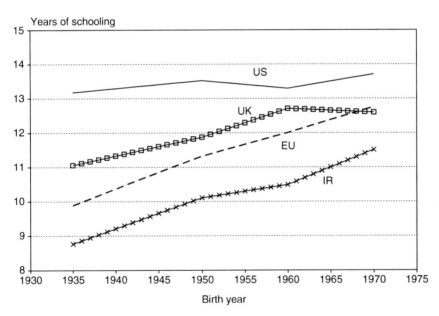

Fig. 2.1 Schooling by cohort in the EU, the UK, Ireland, and the US
Notes: The figure shows smoothing splines with knots in 1950 and 1960 fitted to raw cohort data. EU is the population-weighted average across the EU countries. UK = United Kingdom; IR = Ireland; US = United States.

[4] To avoid the variability due to small samples we have fitted a smoothing linear spline with knots in 1950 and 1960 to the raw cohort data.
[5] The evolution of years of schooling for the US, according to the IALS is not quite consistent with the figures reported in DeLong et al. (2003). For the cohorts born before 1950, years of schooling is higher in the IALS than in the census data used by DeLong et al.

How is the increase in attainment translated into skills? Figure 2.2 examines this question by showing the evolution of skills (as measured by the sum of the scores in all three domains of the IALS) by cohort.[6] In looking at these estimates one should bear in mind that skill depreciation will affect the slope of these relationships. However, we do not expect the rate of skill depreciation to vary substantially across countries, so this problem should not bias the cross-country comparison.[7]

There are a couple of interesting patterns in Figure 2.2. First, starting out from a much lower level in the 1935 cohort, the skills in the average European country have actually surpassed the skills in the US for the 1970 cohort. Second, skills are actually declining for those born during the 1960s in the US (this decline is statistically significant). Similarly, in the UK there is no increase in skills for those born after 1950. For those born in the 1960s, the rate of increase in skills thus appears to be much lower in the Anglo-Saxon countries than in the average European country. This is particularly interesting given that it is in Anglo-Saxon countries

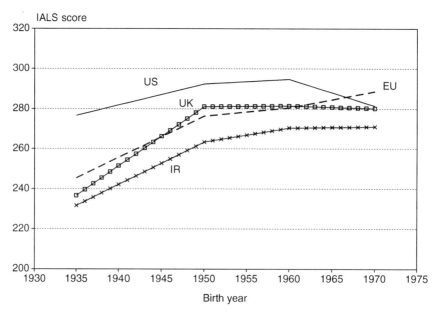

Fig. 2.2 Skills by cohort in the EU, the UK, Ireland and the US
Notes: The figure shows smoothing splines with knots in 1950 and 1960 fitted to raw cohort data. See notes to Fig. 2.1 for a description of the legends.

[6] Again, we have smoothed the data by fitting a spline to the cohort data.
[7] Moreover, Nathanelsson (2003) shows that skill depreciation is a minor issue using IALS panel data for Sweden collected in 1994 and 1998.

where we have observed the greatest surge in wage inequality during the 1980s; we return to this issue in section 2.4.

Figures 2.3 and 2.4 report years of schooling and skills by cohort for four continental European countries. Looking at Figure 2.3 we see that educational attainments are initially almost identical in the Netherlands and Switzerland, but then grow at a faster rate in the Netherlands. The comparison between Belgium and Germany exhibits a similar feature. The average educational attainment is very similar through the cohort born in 1950. Afterwards, the schooling attainment of new cohorts continued to grow in Belgium, but not in Germany. Again, we look at how the attainment differences are translated into skill differences in Figure 2.4. Comparing Figures 2.3 and 2.4 it seems that the increase in schooling was translated into skill increases to a greater extent in Belgium than in the Netherlands.

Next we turn to the Nordic countries. Figures 2.5 and 2.6 report the evolution of years of schooling and skills for Denmark, Finland, Norway, and Sweden. These countries start out at fairly similar educational attainments in the 1935 cohort but then they seem to diverge. The country showing the most exceptional growth in attainment is Finland. It starts off

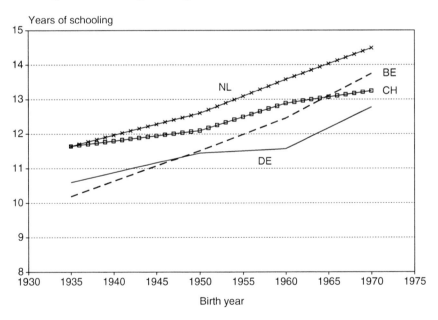

Fig. 2.3 Schooling by cohort in Belgium, Germany, the Netherlands, and Switzerland
Notes: The figure shows smoothing splines with knots in 1950 and 1960 fitted to raw cohort data. BE = Belgium; DE = Germany; NL = the Netherlands; CH = Switzerland.

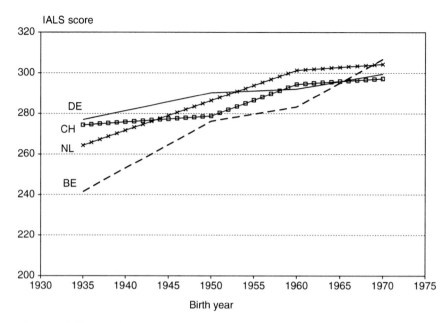

Fig. 2.4 Skills by cohort in Belgium, Germany, the Netherlands, and Switzerland
Notes: The figure shows smoothing splines with knots in 1950 and 1960 fitted to raw cohort data. See Fig. 2.3 for a description of the legends.

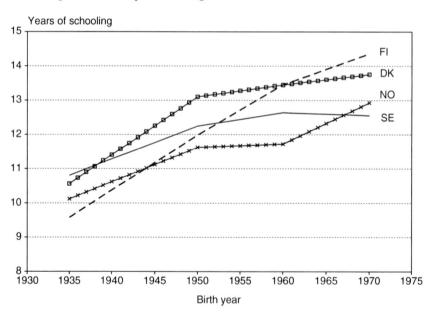

Fig. 2.5 Schooling by cohort in Denmark, Finland, Norway, and Sweden
Notes: The figure shows smoothing splines with knots in 1950 and 1960 fitted to raw cohort data. DK = Denmark; FI = Finland; NO = Norway; SE = Sweden.

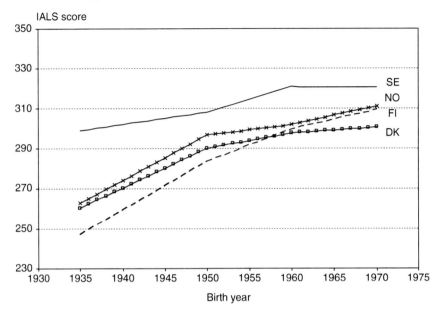

Fig. 2.6 Skills by cohort in Denmark, Finland, Norway, and Sweden
Notes: The figure shows smoothing splines with knots in 1950 and 1960 fitted to raw cohort data. See Fig. 2.5 for a description of the legends.

having the lowest attainment level and, over the next 35 years it surpasses the other three countries. Conversely, if we look at the evolution of literacy skills, there seems to be convergence rather than divergence among the Nordic countries. The country ranking is fairly different when it comes to skills rather than attainment. In the skills dimension, Sweden manages to keep its early advantage throughout the period despite slipping down the ranking when it comes to investment in formal schooling. Skills are growing at the fastest rate in Finland, which largely mirrors the increase in educational attainment.

Finally, we consider four countries from Southern and Eastern Europe. Figure 2.7 shows years of schooling by cohort for the Czech Republic, Hungary, Italy, and Poland, while Figure 2.8 shows cohort skills for these countries. The development of formal schooling is similar in the three Eastern European countries. Educational attainment falls for the cohorts born during the 1960s, perhaps as a result of poor incentives to invest in schooling. In Italy, on the other hand, educational attainment increases precipitously starting from a very low level for the cohort born in the mid-1930s.

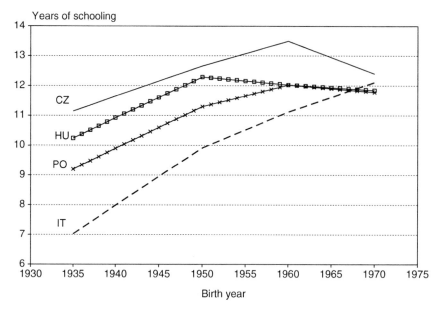

Fig. 2.7 Schooling by cohort in the Czech Republic, Hungary, Italy, and Poland
Notes: The figure shows smoothing splines with knots in 1950 and 1960 fitted to raw cohort data. CZ = the Czech Republic; HU = Hungary; IT = Italy; PO = Poland.

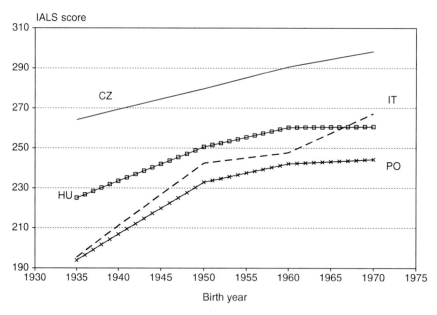

Fig. 2.8 Skills by cohort in the Czech Republic, Hungary, Italy, and Poland
Notes: The figure shows smoothing splines with knots in 1950 and 1960 fitted to raw cohort data. See Fig. 2.7 for a description of the legends.

The evolution of cohort skills to some extent mirrors the development in educational attainment. The skill increase levels off in Hungary and Poland for those born in the 1960s. This does not appear to happen in the Czech Republic, however, where the test score increases throughout the period. Indeed, the skill evolution in the Czech Republic is roughly comparable to the development in the Netherlands, despite the fact that attainment evolves rather differently in these two countries.

If we look at Figures 2.1 through 2.8 it is clear that there is a fairly close match between educational attainment and skills as measured by the test in the IALS. Nevertheless, for some countries during some time periods they deviate from one another. To give a more systematic account of these differences, we estimate the relationship between skills and educational attainment using the cohort data for all countries.

$$s_{ic} = \alpha_i + \alpha_{50s} + \alpha_{60s} + \beta e_{ic} + \gamma d_{e \geq 8}(e_{ic} - 8) + \delta d_{e \geq 10}(e_{ic} - 10)$$
$$+ \lambda d_{e \geq 12}(e_{ic} - 12) + \eta_{ic} \tag{2.1}$$

where s_{ic} denotes skills in country i and cohort c and e_{ic} years of education. We include country fixed effects (α_i), time-period fixed effects (e.g., α_{50s} equals unity for the cohorts born during the 1950s), and allow the 'effect' of schooling on skills to vary by years of schooling.[8] The break points where the skills/schooling gradient may change slope are somewhat arbitrarily set at 8, 10, and 12 years of education (thus, e.g., $d_{e \geq 8} = I(e_{ic} \geq 8)$). We think of the time variation in the deviation between actual skills and the prediction obtained from the regression equation as a measure of the time variation in the quality of the education provided by the schooling system of individual countries.

Table 2.2 reports the annual changes in residual skills relative to the standard deviation within the country. Let us take a concrete example to illustrate what the table shows. According to Figures 2.1 and 2.2, skills are improving substantially in the UK between the cohorts born 1935 and 1950. At the same time, the average years of schooling rises. However, the increase in years of schooling is not sufficient to 'justify' the substantial increase in skills. Hence, we have a positive coefficient during 1935–50 for the UK. The opposite happens during the 1950s. Then there are no improvements in measured skills, despite the fact that there is

---

[8] There are several arguments for estimating a non-linear relationship between formal attainment and skills. For one thing the IALS was not primarily designed to pick up skill variations at the top end of the skills distribution. Thus one should expect the 'effect' of an additional year of schooling on measured skills to be lower for higher levels of formal attainment.

Table 2.2 Changes in the 'quality of education' (change in residual skills)
(Each cell reports the annual change in residual skills relative to the standard deviation
within country)

Country	Birth cohorts		
	1935–50	1950–60	1960–70
Belgium	**0.4**	−0.2	**0.3**
	(2.9)	(1.7)	(2.3)
Czech Republic	−0.3	−0.1	**1.6**
	(1.5)	(0.5)	(6.1)
Denmark	0.0	0.0	−0.1
	(0.1)	(0.1)	(0.1)
Finland	0.6	−0.3	0.3
	(1.8)	(0.9)	(0.9)
Germany	0.0	−0.3	−0.2
	(0.3)	(1.8)	(1.3)
Hungary	−0.4	**1.1**	0.3
	(1.7)	(4.7)	(1.1)
Ireland	**1.1**	−0.3	**−0.8**
	(6.5)	(1.5)	(4.8)
Italy	0.3	**−0.9**	**0.4**
	(1.7)	(4.7)	(2.2)
Netherlands	**0.6**	0.1	−0.3
	(3.1)	(0.6)	(1.4)
Norway	**1.1**	−0.2	−0.1
	(4.9)	(1.0)	(0.6)
Poland	**0.9**	**−0.5**	0.3
	(4.2)	(2.3)	(1.6)
Sweden	**−0.8**	0.3	0.0
	(4.0)	(1.6)	(0.0)
Switzerland	−0.3	0.2	0.0
	(1.2)	(1.0)	(0.0)
United Kingdom	**1.2**	**−0.5**	0.0
	(10.0)	(4.5)	(0.2)
United States	**0.4**	−0.1	**−0.7**
	(2.7)	(0.4)	(4.5)
EU-9	**0.8**	**−0.8**	0.0
	(5.3)	(4.9)	(0.1)
All Europe	**0.9**	**−0.8**	0.1
	(5.4)	(4.6)	(0.6)

Notes: Bold face numbers are significant at conventional levels (t-values in parentheses). 'Residual skills' is estimated
from a regression relating the cohort IALS score to a country fixed effect, a spline (with knots at 8, 10, and 12 years
of education) in the cohort years of schooling, and two time period indicators equaling unity for cohorts born
during the 1950s and 1960s respectively. EU-9 and All Europe: see Table 2.1.

similar growth in educational attainment as during the earlier time period.
Thus there is a negative coefficient during 1950–60.

According to Table 2.2, almost half of the countries saw an increase in
residual skills for the cohorts born during the 1940s (and earlier). This may
reflect an increase in the ambition of educational authorities, such
that they expanded the resources invested per student at each level of

attainment. The table also shows that the EU as a whole did worse than expected for the cohorts born during the 1950s. The negative coefficient for the US during the 1960s may also indicate that the quality of the education provided to children born during this decade has deteriorated. In passing, note that this also implies that skills deteriorated within educational groups in the US. Indeed, for the US, the measured skills for those born in the 1960s are lower for the university-educated as well as for those with less than upper-secondary education than in the previous cohorts; see Björklund et al. (2005).

2.3 The skills among those still in school

We now focus on the most recent cohorts and investigate the skills of children who are still in school. We look at mean student performance (sub-section 2.3.1), the variation in student/teacher ratios (sub-section 2.3.2) as well as the variance in student achievement (sub-section 2.3.3).

2.3.1 *Mean student performance*

The first column of Table 2.3 gives a snapshot picture of mean performance by reporting a subset of the latest PISA (Programme for International Student Assessment) tests results. The tests in PISA are taken at age 15 in mathematics, science, and reading literacy. We report the scores in reading literacy and maths according to PISA 2003 along with estimated changes in reading literacy and maths since 1991 and 1995 respectively. The data for the earlier time points are taken from the Reading Literacy Study and the TIMSS (these two studies tested students at age 14).[9] The top performers in the PISA study are the students in Finland. This is true for all three domains tested by PISA; indeed, country rankings are rather similar across the three domains. The EU as a whole does as well as US students in reading but better in mathematics.

The last two columns attempt to examine the changes in performance during the 1990s. Rather than presenting the changes in the actual scores we present the changes of the rank order of countries.[10] It seems

---

[9] TIMSS is short for Third International Math and Science Study. Beaton et al. (1996) report results for TIMSS while the results for the Reading Literacy study are contained in Elley (1992).

[10] The reason for focusing on the rank order is that the scores are relative in nature; the scores are set such that the average student among all participating countries gets a score of 500. Therefore, the scoring depends on which countries participated in the study.

Table 2.3 Literacy test scores

Country	PISA 2003		Change in rank order*	
	Reading	Maths	Reading 1991→2003	Maths 1995→2003
Austria	491	506	na	−4
Belgium	507	529	na	−2
Czech Republic	489	516	na	−3
Denmark	492	514	−2	7
Finland	543	544	0	na
France	496	511	−5	−1
Germany	491	503	−2	0
Greece	472	445	−1	−1
Hungary	482	490	−6	−6
Ireland	515	503	11	−3
Italy	476	466	−3	na
Netherlands	513	538	8	3
Norway	500	495	5	0
Poland	497	490	na	na
Portugal	478	466	−4	1
Spain	485	485	3	1
Sweden	514	509	0	1
Switzerland	499	527	−3	−1
United Kingdom[a]	517	532	na	9
United States	495	483	−2	−1
EU-14	**494**	**501**	**−1**	**2**
All Europe	**494**	**501**	**−1**	**1**

Notes: [a] Score refers to England. The 2003 score has been predicted using the PISA 2000 results on all three domains.
* In calculating the change in rank order we have first ordered the countries from best to worst among the tabulated countries participating at both time points and then calculated the change from the base year to the last year. Positive numbers thus reflect improvements in the rank order. EU-14 and All Europe: see Table 2.1.
Sources: Elley (1992), OECD (2004b), and Beaton et al. (1996).

that students in Ireland and the Netherlands improved substantially in reading, while students in France and Hungary moved down the rank order. In mathematics the big improvers are the UK and Denmark while losses are recorded in Austria and Hungary.

An obvious observation is that it is difficult to make strong inference about within-country changes in performance, because PISA and TIMSS are different studies. Further, differences in the cross-country variation in the age of testing may have a substantial impact on estimated changes in the rank-order. In the TIMSS, however, there are attempts to look at the trends in achievement for a small sub-set of countries. According to these estimates, there were significant losses in maths achievement in Belgium, Sweden, and Norway while students in the US improved significantly. For reading literacy, there are also some trends estimates pertaining to 10-year-olds. According to the International Reading

Literacy study, there is a significant reduction of the reading performance of Swedish students.[11]

2.3.2 Student/teacher ratios

The next question we raise is what accounts for the variation in student performance over time. The most natural place to start looking for an answer to this question is by examining the variation in resources, in general, and the variation in class size in particular. Table 2.4 shows the number of students per teacher—the student/teacher ratio—in 1992 and 2002. The most useful information in Table 2.5 pertains to the changes over the 1990s.[12] Since the early 1990s, the number of students per teacher has been reduced in the US while it appears to have been constant in

Table 2.4. Student/teacher ratios in lower secondary schools, 2002 and 1992

Country	2002	1992	Relative change (%)
Austria	9.8	7.7	27.3
Belgium*	13.1	13.7	−4.4
Czech Republic	14.4	17.0	−15.3
Denmark*	10.9	10.9	0.0
Finland*	15.8	19.0	−16.8
France*	19.4	20.4	−4.9
Germany	15.7	14.6	7.5
Greece	9.3	na	na
Hungary	10.7	11.6	−7.8
Ireland*	19.5	25.6	−23.8
Italy	9.9	9.0	10.0
Netherlands*	17.0	23.6	−28.0
Norway	10.3	8.5	21.2
Poland	14.1	na	na
Portugal	9.3	na	na
Spain	13.7	17.6	−22.2
Sweden	12.2	10.6	15.1
Switzerland	na	na	na
United Kingdom	17.6	15.9	10.7
United States	15.5	16.8	−7.7
EU-9	**14.9**	**15.5**	**0.8**
All Europe	**15.3**	**14.6**	**0.4**

Notes: * Numbers refer to the primary level. EU-9 and All Europe: see Table 2.1.
Source: OECD (2004a) and OECD (1995).

[11] There is also a significant gain for Hungarian students. But it is difficult to place much emphasis on this gain given that the average age at testing increased by almost half a year.
[12] This is one of the cases where the cross-sectional variation is probably not informative. Differing reporting principles presumably drive the difference between e.g. Portugal (9.3) and the UK (17.6) to a large extent.

Table 2.5 Variations in maths skills across students and the share of the variance attributable to schools

Country	Variation across students (Coefficient of variation, percent)		Share of variance attributable to schools, percent	
	PISA 2003	Change (PISA 2003– TIMSS 1995)	PISA 2003	Change (PISA 2003– TIMSS 1995)
Austria	18.4	1.3	55.5	22.5
Belgium*	20.8	4.5	56.9	20.9
Czech Republic	18.6	1.9	50.5	28.5
Denmark	17.8	1.0	13.1	7.1
Finland	15.4	na	3.9	na
France	18.0	3.9	na	na
Germany	20.4	2.7	56.4	9.4
Greece	21.1	2.9	68.1	54.1
Hungary	19.1	1.8	66.0	49.0
Ireland	17.0	−0.7	13.4	−31.6
Italy	20.5	na	56.8	na
Netherlands	17.2	0.8	54.5	3.5
Norway	18.6	1.9	6.5	0.5
Poland	18.4	na	12.0	na
Portugal	18.9	4.8	30.3	14.3
Spain	18.1	3.2	17.2	1.2
Sweden	18.6	2.2	10.9	−0.1
Switzerland	18.7	2.5	36.4	−2.6
United States	19.7	1.5	27.1	−3.9
EU-13	**19.2**	**2.9**	**45.5**	**7.6**
All Europe	**19.7**	**2.5**	**41.7**	**9.4**

Notes: * The measures of the variation in TIMSS pertain to the Flemish community in Belgium. EU-13 and All Europe: see Table 2.1. Population-weighted averages.

Sources: OECD (2004b) and Beaton et al. (1996).

Europe. There is a good deal of variation behind this constant average. Some countries have expanded a lot (i.e. reduced student/teacher ratios): the reduction of the number of students per teacher is roughly 25 per cent in Ireland and the Netherlands. Other countries have moved in the opposite direction: for instance, in Austria and Norway the student–teacher ratio increased by 27 and 21 per cent respectively.

The interesting question is, of course, whether, and how much, students gain by being in a smaller class. This is one of the most controversial issues in the economics of education. The disagreement is so profound that not even the quantitative reviews of the literature are in agreement. Some reviews (e.g. Hedges et al. 1994 and Krueger, 2003) find positive impacts of smaller classes on student outcomes, while others (most prominently, Hanushek, 1997) find no beneficial effects of smaller classes.

Our reading of the voluminous literature on class size is that the students gain by reductions in class size; the gains are particularly apparent for disadvantaged students. We come to this conclusion by placing more weight on studies that are based on an experimental or quasi-experimental design (e.g. Angrist and Lavy, 1999, and Krueger, 1999), that is, studies that have a credible source of variation to identify the causal effects. On this reading of the literature, US students should have gained from the resource development during the 1990s.

Is there any support for the conclusion that students benefit from reductions in class size in the data presented in Tables 2.3 and 2.4? There is some support when it comes to reading literacy. A regression of the change in the rank order across countries on the change in the log student/teacher ratio produces a coefficient with the expected (negative) sign with a t-ratio of 1.64.[13] Of course, one should not place too much emphasis on this estimate, given that there are only 12 observations. Moreover, we find no systematic relationship between performance and the student/teacher ratio when it comes to maths and science.

2.3.3 *Equality*

A potentially important policy concern is the variation in skills across students and schools. The individual variation in skills during adolescence will eventually contribute to the observed variation in market outcomes. The between-school variation in student performance is related to issues concerning segregation and equality of opportunity. With a high share of the overall variance being explicable by the schools that students attend, this may signal variations in the quality of schooling that the students get.

Table 2.5 reports various dimensions of cross-sectional inequality among students and how these have evolved over time. The variance measures are derived from the maths test in PISA since this is the only test where the between-school variance is reported in OECD (2004b). The development of cross-sectional inequality is obtained by comparing the PISA results to those obtained in TIMSS 1995. The total variation across students appears to be similar across all countries. In all countries, apart from Ireland, the variation has risen but the increases seem to be rather minor (apart from possibly Belgium, France, and Portugal). The variation across students has increased more in Europe than in the US.

---

[13] If we use the actual change in performance (with an adjustment of the means such that the scores are comparable), the coefficient has a t-ratio of 1.97.

There is considerably more variation between schools. The between-school variance is particularly low in the Nordic countries. It is considerably higher in continental Europe and the Eastern European countries. The US is in between these two extremes. Interestingly, the between school variance seems to move in opposite directions when the US is compared to Europe. In the US, the share of the variance that can be attributed to schools has declined since 1995, while in Europe it has increased on average. The opposite changes in the between-school variance begs the question of why this has occurred. According to OECD (2004a), decision-making in most European countries became more decentralized between 1998 and 2003. Thus, decentralization of authority to the school level is one potential explanation; however, there is not sufficient data to back up this statement, so this is a somewhat speculative conjecture at this point.

2.4 Implications for wage inequality

At this stage, it is of course tempting to try to relate the changes in skills (described in section 2.2) to the changes in the wage distribution. Can the supply of skills account for the variation in wage inequality observed across countries? By now, there is a fairly substantial literature revolving around this issue.[14] It is well known that the greatest increases in wage inequality during the 1980s were observed in the US and the UK (e.g. Katz and Autor, 1999). In the 1980s, cohorts born during the 1960s entered the labour market. It is interesting to note that the US and the UK are among the countries with the weakest increases in skills. Indeed, the US stands out as the country with the most marked *decrease* in the inflow of skills.

Skill dispersion will affect wage dispersion for two reasons. First, there is the obvious direct effect: for given price of skills, countries with high skill dispersion will have more wage dispersion. Second, there is an indirect effect working through the price of skills: increases in the net supply of

---

[14] See, e.g. Gottschalk and Joyce (1998), Blau and Kahn (2001), Devroye and Freeman (2002), Acemoglu (2003), and Leuven et al. (2004). One strand of the literature (Blau and Kahn, 2001; Devroye and Freeman, 2002; and Leuven et al., 2004) uses the spread in the IALS test score to examine if the (cross-sectional) variance of skills can account for the (cross-sectional) variation in wage inequality. Another strand of the literature (e.g. Gottschalk and Joyce, 1998, and Acemoglu, 2003) examines whether changes in the relative supply of, e.g. educated labour can account for the changes in wage inequality across countries. In Gottschalk and Joyce (1998) the answer is affirmative: they conclude that changes in relative supplies can explain much of the changes in returns to skills (education and age).

skills will lower the price of skills. The papers by Blau and Kahn (2001) and Devroye and Freeman (2002) look only at the direct effect. The evidence suggests that the direct effect of skill dispersion on wage dispersion may be fairly small. Devroye and Freeman (2002) present a simple variance decomposition exercise that suggests that only a small part of the cross-country differences in wage inequality is driven by differences in skill dispersion (given the US price of skills). They therefore conclude that the differences in wage inequality between the US and European countries are mainly driven by different wage setting institutions. Similar evidence is reported by Blau and Kahn (2001). In contrast to Devroye and Freeman (2002), however, Blau and Kahn allow for different effects of skills at different parts of the wage distribution. An interesting aspect of their results is that the contribution of measured characteristics (including skills) to wages is higher at the lower end of the wage distribution. Comparing two extreme countries when it comes to wage inequality—the US and Sweden—they find that differences in age, schooling, and skills account for 26 per cent of the 50–10 log wage differential between the US and Sweden. A recent paper by Leuven et al. (2004) attempts to include the indirect effect as well—the effect of the net supply of skills on the price of skills. Applying the methodology of Katz and Murphy (1992), Leuven et al. find much stronger effects of cross-country differences in skills; about one-third of the variation across countries in the relative wages of skill groups can be attributed to the net supply of skill groups. Their analysis does an even better job in explaining differences in relative wages in the lower parts of the wage distribution, where differences in skills account for about 60 percent of the variation. Taken at face value, their estimates then suggest that the relative supply of skills has a rather big impact on relative wages, in particular at the lower end of the wage distribution.

To come back to the initial question, what should we expect about the evolution of wages, given the evolutions of the supply of skills shown in Figures 2.1–2.8? In the remaining part of the section we examine this question. In particular we show that the variation in skills and the quality of education has some importance to the labour market. We do that by running earnings regression at the cohort level. In particular, we estimate versions of the following simple regression using IALS data

$$y_{ic}^q = \alpha_i + \alpha_c + \beta s_{ic} + \gamma e_{ic} + \delta(pop_{ic}/pop_i) + \eta_{ic} \qquad (2.3)$$

where y_{ic}^q is the average male earnings quintile rank for cohort c in country i, α_i (α_c) is a country (cohort) fixed effect, s denotes skills, e years of education, and (pop_{ic}/pop_i) is the relative size of the cohort population.

Table 2.6 Earnings regressions, pooled country/cohort data

	All countries				EU	
	(1)	(2)	(3)	(4)	(5)	(6)
Years of education	.089	−.020	.101	−.090	.086	−.074
	(.022)	(.028)	(.017)	(.022)	(.024)	(.032)
IALS score	−	.013	−	.020	−	.017
		(.002)		(.002)		(.002)
Relative cohort size	−9.25	−9.46	.261	−6.11	2.02	−6.25
	(2.85)	(2.75)	(2.54)	(2.30)	(3.77)	(3.68)
Weighted by country size	No	No	Yes	Yes	Yes	Yes
# observations	540	540	540	540	324	324
R-squared	.835	.846	.879	.907	.823	.850

Notes: Standard errors in parentheses. All regressions include country and cohort fixed effects. Columns headed EU report population-weighted estimates for the nine EU-15 countries included in the data.

Notice that the quintile rank ranges from 1 to 5 and that the inclusion of the cohort fixed effects captures the age/earnings profile flexibly. We include relative cohort size in order to capture labour supply effects on earnings.

Table 2.6 presents the results. We begin with specifications that exclude skills; see columns 1, 3 and 5. The estimates suggest a 'healthy' return to schooling. An increase of years of schooling by one year moves the cohort up in the earnings distribution by two percentile ranks. However, controlling for skills, schooling has no impact (and in some specifications the impact is even negative and significant). A standard deviation increase in the IALS score (cf. Table 2.2) yields an increase of roughly 20 percentile ranks. Controlling for skills, we also find evidence suggesting that the relative size of the cohort has a negative effect on the earnings rank. The bottom line of these estimates is that what matters for relative wages is the quality of schooling that the education system produces. Increases in attainment without corresponding increases in skills have little value on the labour market.

2.5 Concluding remarks

1 US educational expansion long preceded the European one: there was a substantial gap in attainment some 40 years ago.
2 Some of this gap has now been closed, but there still exists a marked difference in attainment, particularly at the tertiary level; see section 1.2.

3 Despite the gap in attainment, Europe appears to have closed the gap in terms of basic skills. The basic skills that individuals bring to the labour market have grown at a faster rate in Europe. In the latest cohort in our data (born in 1970) skills in the average EU country have surpassed those of the US.

4 According to the latest PISA results, European (lower secondary) students do as well (reading) or slightly better (maths) than their American counterparts. It is difficult to get an idea about how student performance has changed during the 1990s, but the available data suggest that there have been no major changes in the position of Europe relative to the US.

5 Looking at the resource data it seems that the US invested more heavily in education during the 1990s. For instance, student/teacher ratios at the lower secondary level were reduced in the US but stayed largely constant in Europe.

6 Moreover, there is evidence suggesting an increase in heterogeneity of outcomes in Europe. In particular, the between-school variance in outcomes appears to have increased in Europe while it has been reduced in the US.

7 Finally, we documented that the basic skills that individuals bring to the market are important determinants of their labour earnings. Moreover, the variation in skills across countries can account for a substantial fraction of the variation in wage inequality across countries, in particular inequality at the lower end of the wage distribution. Thus the quality of the skills provided by the education systems has important repercussions on the labour market.

3

Higher Education, Innovation and Growth

3.1 Introduction

The recent growth performance of Europe since the mid-1990s has been disappointing when compared with that of the US. Growth of total GDP, of GDP per capita and of productivity have been much more anaemic in Europe than in the US (see e.g. Gordon, 2004). In addition, growth in employment, in labour market participation (particularly for young and women) in hours worked and even wage growth has fallen behind (see e.g. Phelps, 2003). Several causes have been identified as potentially responsible for the poor growth performance of Europe post-1995. Some have blamed excessive regulation and rigidities of goods and labour markets, excessive taxes (Prescott, 2005), limited integration of cross-county markets and lags in the adoption of information technologies. In this chapter we explore a complementary explanation: the role of education.

As documented in Chapter 1, while large variation exists across European countries, the educational attainments at the tertiary (College) level were on average, for Europe, well below those for the US as late as year 2002. Further, they have not been growing at a comparable pace for the previous two decades. Highly educated professionals and workers are functional to the creation and adoption of highly productive technologies that are, in turn, a fundamental engine of growth (Benhabib and Spiegel, 1994; Klenow and Rodriguez Clare, 2006).

In this chapter we present an overview and some suggestive evidence about the role of highly educated workers on promoting technological and scientific progress and ultimately economic growth. We first review the evidence on education and growth. We then review international migrations with an emphasis on highly-skilled scientists and engineers. Migration of human capital could be a viable and effective way of increasing supply of skills in Europe. Unluckily the migration channel in most cases has not worked to improve the skills of the European labour force. Finally, we present suggestive estimates of such 'dynamic effect' of highly-educated and talented workers on the rate of scientific and technological innovation.

3.2 A survey of the effects of education on growth

Since the early work on the determinants of economic growth across countries (Barro, 1991) and on the determinants of income per capita across countries (Mankiw et al., 1992) average schooling attainments and their improvements over time have been identified as crucial determinants of levels and growth rates of income per capita. Human capital, most often captured by schooling, has been associated with two distinct contributions to the growth of income per worker. Human capital as a factor of production, accumulated by individuals through education, increases their productivity by providing them with valuable skills that increase their private returns. Hence, increases in the schooling levels of a country result in more human capital and higher production per worker for that country. Such a channel (analysed by so called 'growth accounting' or 'development accounting' literature) has been found responsible for up to one-third of the increased income per worker in the US during the twentieth century (Jones, 2002), as well as for a similar fraction of growth in the fast growing economies of East Asia (Singapore, Hong Kong, South Korea and Taiwan, as documented in Young, 1995).

A second and, for our purposes, even more important channel through which education affects growth is via the positive impact of high education on research, technological adoption and total factor productivity growth. In this case, higher shares of tertiary education could increase growth rates of income per worker (Barro and Lee, 2001) by promoting invention and technological adoption and development. The original idea of 'human capital driven' productivity growth is due to Nelson and Phelps (1966). After that, several models of 'endogenous' growth (particularly Lucas, 1988) have emphasized the growth-effect of human capital, due to creation of ideas and technological innovation. It is important to emphasize that this 'growth-promoting' role of higher education is crucial both for economies at the technological frontier, as well as for less developed or emerging economies. In the first group of countries, scientists and engineers are needed to produce and develop technological innovations; in the second group, scientists, engineers and skilled professionals are needed to adapt and adopt those technologies 'imported' from the leaders. Europe can be seen as playing the role of leader in some technological sectors, while it is trailing behind the US in others; in either case an essential part of its technological growth is related to its ability of producing, attracting and retaining highly educated professionals.

Interestingly, empirical studies of the growth effect of schooling have emphasized that the quality of schooling, as captured by international mathematic and science test scores (e.g. Hanushek and Kimko, 2000; De La Fuente and Domenech, 2001) matters as much as (if not more than) the quantity of schooling (years of schooling, share of college educated). This notably echoes with the findings of Chapter 5. The quality measures have often been identified as more relevant than simple attainment measure (Hanushek and Kimko, 2000), although, using data on schooling that improve on the Barro and Lee (1996) measures, there seems to be consistent and robust evidence of a positive and significant effect of schooling attainments on growth (De La Fuente and Domenech, 2001).

All in all, combining the two effects (the private returns to education and the effect on productivity via technological adoption) tertiary education is a very effective investment for a country in generating economic growth. College graduates and post-graduate degree holders' contribution to human capital, are the main input in R&D and innovation and are the main agents in adopting new technologies.

Another recent line of research (Acemoglu, 1998, 2002; Acemoglu and Zilibotti, 2001; Caselli, 2006) has found that the educational attainment of workers drives the direction as well as the intensity of technological change. The presence of a large share of college educated workers in the labour force promotes the invention and the adoption of technologies that complement skills of highly-educated workers and this, in turn, increases their demand (this phenomenon is called skill-biased technological progress). The reinforcing dynamics between high education and technological innovation/adoption, while potentially causing increased wage inequality when left unmitigated are nevertheless a potent stimulus to promote education. 'Skill-biased' technologies induce higher returns to high education and this produces, in turn, higher supply as people respond to returns by increasing their schooling. Recent sweeping innovations in the information and communication technologies represented general purpose, skill-biased technological changes. They increased the returns to highly-educated as well as the demand for them. The delay in their introduction into Europe (as argued by work of R. Gordon, 2004, and F. Daveri, 2002) may be both a consequence of the smaller supply of college-educated in these countries as well as the cause of slower growth of their returns and of overall productivity.

Finally, as recognized by economists since Solow (1956) and re-emphasized by the literature on endogenous growth that has followed Romer (1990), Grossman and Helpman (1991) and Aghion and Howitt (1992), 'talent', that is, creative minds in the fields of science, engineering and technology have an incomparable role in advancing economic development and well-being.[1] Anecdotal evidence shows that many of the great inventions of the twentieth century (such as the first controlled nuclear reaction achieved by Enrico Fermi, the first form of plastic produced by Leo Baekeland, the first microprocessor built by Federico Faggin) were the products of foreign-born (European in the cases mentioned above) talent working in the US. This emphasizes the fact that even attracting very few extraordinary talents may have a relevant scientific (and later economic) impact.

3.3 International migration, the brain drain and 'talents'

Beyond domestic investments into higher education, attracting international migrants is another way to raise the supply of highly educated workers. At the same time, the ability of European countries to attract, retain and employ highly-educated individuals is a relevant indicator of its growth potentials.

3.3.1 *Immigration to the EU and the USA: size and composition*

In recent decades (notably during the eighties and the nineties), the US has regained its role as the primary destination for a large number of migrants,[2] mainly from Asia and Latin America. During the same period

---

[1] We provide in section 3.4, suggestive evidence to help quantify the impact of talents on innovation.

[2] The percentage of foreign-born residents in the US at the peak of the era of mass-migrations from Europe, in 1910, was equal to 14 per cent of the population. As of year 2004, such percentage was still unmatched as the percentage of migrants was only slightly above 13 per cent of the population.

the European Union has emerged as the destination of choice for those seeking better economic alternatives from Eastern Europe and North Africa. Tables 3.1 and 3.2 contain some summary statistics that capture the presence of foreign-born people in the population and labour force of the US and EU at the beginning and end of the nineties. Due to limited availability of comparable data we consider 1992 as the earliest year for

Table 3.1 Foreign-born residents of the EU, 1992–99

Year	1992			1996			1999		
Variable	Total labour force[a]	% Workers born outside EU-15	% Population born outside EU-15	Total labour force[a]	% Workers born outside EU-15	% Population born outside EU-15	Total labour force[a]	% Workers born outside EU-15	% Population born outside EU-15
EU-12	154,007	4.1%	3.9%	156,338	4.7%	4.4%	160,780	4.9%	4.7%
EU-15	na	na	na	167,000	4.8%	4.6%	171,668	5.0%	4.8%
France	24,525	7.1%	7.2%	25,335	8.2%	8.2%	25,875	8.2%	8.3%
Spain	15,141	1.1%	1.0%	15,872	1.4%	1.1%	16,339	1.8%	1.4%
UK	28,556	5.4%	5.5%	28,514	5.3%	5.4%	29,127	5.7%	6.1%
Germany[b]	38,994	5.1%	4.7%	39,082	6.1%	5.8%	39,595	6.1%	5.8%
Italy[b]	22,769	0.6%	0.6%	22,787	0.3%	0.2%	23,346	0.8%	0.6%

Notes:
[a] In thousands
[b] Data on place of birth are not available, therefore statistics are based on nationality of residents.

Source: Author's calculation using the Extract of the European Labour Force Survey, (1992–99) produced by Eurostat for Angrist and Kugler (2003).

Table 3.2 Foreign-born residents of the USA, 1990, 2000

Year	1990			2000		
Variable	Total labour force	% Labour force born outside USA	% Population born outside USA	Total labour force	% Labour force born outside USA	% Population born outside USA
USA[a]	124,772,500	9.3%	7.9%	138,733,660	12.4%	11.0%
California	15,237,296	25.4%	21.7%	15,984,433	28.0%	26%
New York	8,969,551	18.2%	15.9%	9,037,552	23.1%	19.9%
Texas	8,270,447	10.5%	8.9%	9,929,292	15.7%	13.9%
Florida	6,269,753	15.1%	12.8%	7,469,356	19.2%	16.5%
Illinois	5,720,396	10.5%	8.4%	6,189,302	14.2%	12.4%

Notes:
[a] In thousands.

Source: Author's calculation on US Census 1990 and 2000 data, available at Minnesota Population Center, http://www.ipums.org.

European data and 1999 as the latest year. This choice allows us to use accurate and detailed statistics from the European Labour Force Survey.[3] Table 3.1 reports the aggregate values of foreign-born residents for the EU-12, EU-15 and for the five largest economies within the EU (Germany, France, UK, Italy and Spain). Our analysis considers the totality of EU countries as one large economy to be compared to the US. We define, therefore, 'foreign-born' as those workers who were born in a country outside EU-15[4] and work in one of its countries.[5] Table 3.2 reports aggregate values for the US economy and for each of its five largest states (which happens to be those that also attract the largest percentage of immigrants). These data are obtained from the US Census of Population held in 1990 and 2000.[6] For the EU-12 as a whole, the presence of immigrant workers (born outside EU-15) increased from 4.1 per cent of the labour force in 1992 to 4.9 per cent in 1999. The corresponding percentages for the US were 9.3 per cent in 1990 and 12.4 per cent in 2000. If we calculate the rate of growth of the foreign-born population during the nineties, that turns out to be faster in the US (+ 0.45% a year) than in Europe (+ 0.14% a year), thereby increasing the gap between the presence of foreign-born workers in the two economies.

In Table 3.1, we also show data for the five largest economies in the EU and compare them with the five largest US states (whose data, for 1990 and 2000, are reported in Table 3.2). Two facts emerge. First, not only the US economy attracts more foreign-born on average, but its largest state economies are the main attractors of foreigners. California and New York, the largest poles of attraction for immigrants, have a percentage of foreign-born in the year 2000—two to three times the US average. To the contrary, some large European economies (such as Italy and Spain) are still hardly affected by immigration, while even France, the major attractor

---

[3] We are very grateful to Adriana Kugler and Joshua Angrist for providing their dataset covering information on nationality, country of birth, sex, working status, education and country of residence for a representative sample of the EU-15 labour force (from the European Labour Force Survey). The data used here are the same used in Angrist and Kugler (2003) and are described in detail in that article.

[4] For Italy and Germany data on nationality, rather than country of birth, have to be used to compute immigrants. See Munz (2004) for details.

[5] Both the US census and EU survey attempt to reach all people present on the territory, including illegal aliens. It is likely, however, that illegal immigrants are somewhat underestimated. Hanson and Spilimbergo (1999) try to assess the extent of under-estimation for US immigrants.

[6] The statistics are based on our calculations using data from the Integrated Public Use Micro data Samples (Minnesota Population Center, IPUMS, http://www.ipums.org).

of immigrants among large economies, had a percentage of non-EU foreign-born in 1999 only 3 percentage points higher than the EU-15 average. Moreover, no large country in Europe experienced an increase in the share of foreign-born larger than 1.1 per cent of the total labour force during the period 1992–99. To the contrary no large US state experienced an increase in the foreign labour force smaller than 4 per cent in the period 1990–2000.

Table 3.3 reports the composition of foreign-born residents across education groups. Considering the first two rows, we can see that, both in the early nineties and at the end of the nineties, the 'central' skill group of high school graduates is under-represented among immigrants, while the two extreme groups (high school dropouts and college graduates) are over-represented both in the US and Europe. Considering the US in the year 2000, the average share of foreign-born residents was 12.4 per cent of the labour force overall, but as many as 26 per cent of high school dropouts and 12.5 per cent of college graduates were foreign-born, while only 8.6 per cent of high-school graduates were foreign born.[7] The corresponding numbers for Europe (EU-12) in 1999 were 5.1 per cent of

Table 3.3 Skill distribution of immigrants, 1990–2000

	Beginning of Nineties[a] (1990–92)				End of Nineties[b] (1999–2000)			
	Overall	HSD	HSG	COG	Overall	HSD	HSG	COG
USA	9.3%	18.6%	6.1%	9.4%	12.4%	26%	8.6%	12.5%
EU-12	4.1%	4.1%	3.1%	4.9%	4.9%	5.1%	3.5%	5.3%
California	25.4%	55%	17.2%	19%	28%	57%	21%	25%
New York	18.2%	32%	14.7%	15.4%	23.1%	42%	18.5%	19%
Texas	10.5%	25.5%	5.8%	7.7%	15.7%	38%	9%	12.5%
France	7.1%	6.9%	6.5%	9.3%	8.2%	9.7%	5.9%	9.1%
Germany	5.1%	8.9%	2.8%	2.7%	6.1%	11%	3.5%	3.5%
UK	5.4%	6.8%	3.8%	8.2%	5.7%	7.2%	3.3%	7.3%

Notes:
[a] The data are relative to year 1992 for the EU countries and to 1990 for the USA.
[b] The data are relative to year 1999 for the EU countries and to year 2000 for the US.
HSD: High School Dropouts, for EU data these are worker with only a primary school degree, HSG: High School Graduates, for EU data these are workers with a secondary school degree, COG: College Graduates, for EU data, these are workers with a tertiary school degree.

Sources: For US, our calculations using the 1990 and 2000 US Census data from the US bureau of Census. For Europe our calculations using ELFS data.

---

[7] Interestingly, most of the literature on the impact of foreign-born in the US has concentrated on the effect of unskilled foreign born, e.g. Borjas (1987, 1999, 2003), Borjas et al. (1997), Card (1990, 2001), Card and DiNardo (2000). The effect of highly-educated foreign-born on the US economy has rarely been central.

foreigners in the group of high school dropouts, 3.5 per cent in the group of high school graduates and 5.3 per cent in the group of college graduates. Europe was drawing relatively more immigrants in the same two skill groups as the US (low and high schooling, with a lower percentage of intermediate schooling levels). However, at the top of the skill distribution, migration differs in three respects. First, between 1990 and 2000 the growth of high skilled (college-educated) migrants was faster in the US than in Europe. The share of college-educated foreigners grew 3.1 percentage points in the US (in line with the 3.1 per cent increase of the overall foreign born share in the labour force), while in Europe it only grew by .4 per cent (against a .8 per cent growth of the share of foreign born overall). Second, while the foreign labour force of all the large US states reproduce the 'V'-shaped skill distribution (low in the middle skills and higher at the extremes), Germany, the largest EU economy, clearly attracts mostly low skilled workers with a significant under-representation of both medium and high skilled workers. Third, while highly educated foreign-born workers in the US come from all over the world including developed countries (Europe) and fast growing countries such as China and India (more on this later) highly educated foreign-born in Europe are mainly from Africa.

3.3.2 'Talents': analysing their mobility and contribution

We now focus our attention on the top of the skill distribution: those highly educated scientists and engineers who are an essential part of research, innovation and growth. We may call this group the 'Talents'. Recent studies (Saint Paul, 2004; EEAG, 2003; Becker et al., 2004) have argued that the EU is losing some of its best talent to the US. In Figure 3.1, we report the percentage of foreign-born individuals in each of six 'skill' groups in the US in the year 2000 (solid black line). While the first three groups are those reported in Table 3.4 (high school dropouts, high school graduates and college graduates), the last three groups try to identify workers with progressively higher 'skills' and talent. The fourth group identifies workers with a Masters or a Ph.D. degree, the fifth group identifies those with a Masters or Ph.D. working in science, management or engineering, and the last group are the US-based Nobel laureates in natural sciences during the preceding decade. Strikingly, both in 1990 (not reported) and 2000, the foreign-born are increasingly represented the higher the quality of the skill group. While 12.5 per cent of college graduates were foreign-born, 15.3 per cent of the Masters–Ph.D.s and 20.1 per cent of the Masters–Ph.D.s working in science–management–engineering were of foreign origin. Finally, a stunning 26 per cent (one out of four) of the Nobel laureates in the sciences that worked in the US (in the decade 1990–2000) were foreign-born.[8] The dashed line in Figure 3.1 represents the percentage of foreign-born in each group for the year 2000, were they distributed homogeneously across skills. While clearly the size of groups decreases as we move to the right, their relevance to economic productivity and growth (and even more to technological and scientific growth) increases dramatically. The US has attracted, and continues to attract, a disproportionate fraction of the very highly educated, and among them, the very best brains seem to be even more over-represented.[9]

Figure 3.2 shows the same graph for Europe. While we could not find the overall share of those with a Masters or a Ph.D. born outside the EU-12, we could construct, from national data reported in European Commission (2003), the share of foreign-born among the individuals with doctoral

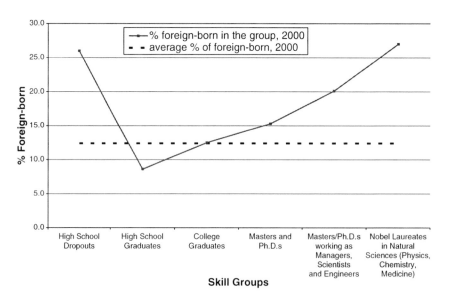

Fig. 3.1 Percentage of foreign-born by skill group in the USA, 2000

Sources: US census IPUMS data, 2000 plus website of the Nobel Foundation: http://nobel prize.org/nobel/.

[8] The data for Nobel laureates, their place of birth and their affiliation were found at the official website of the Nobel Foundation: http://nobelprize.org/nobel/.
[9] We calculated the distribution of foreign-born by skills also for the year 1990 and the shape is the same (at lower overall percentage levels).

degrees operating in the fields of science or engineering. We then calculated the percentage of EU-based, foreign-born Nobel laureates in the sciences. Figure 3.2 summarizes these percentages, including those of the first three groups (high school dropouts, high school graduates and college graduates). It is clear from the graph that the 'V'-shape of the distribution disappears: among the college-educated foreign-born workers, the European Union does not attract the 'highest quality' ones. The percentage of foreign-born Ph.D. holders in science and technology is a paltry 4.1 per cent, and no Nobel laureate (1990–2000) among those operating in the EU was of foreign origin.

One of the next indicators is the origin of migrations flows. First, consider China and India, which are roughly equidistant to Europe and the US. Further, these countries have a growing college-educated population, part of which emigrated (see Bound et al., 2006). Given that the EU-12 and the US are of comparable size in terms of labour force, a simple measure of the number of college graduates from China and India who moved to each economy during the nineties is a good measure of the relative ability to attract brains. In 1992, 6126 Chinese college graduates worked in the EU, this number grew to 30,675 in 2000. For Indian college graduates the corresponding figures were 84,733 and 77,371. The overwhelming majority of these college graduates from either country

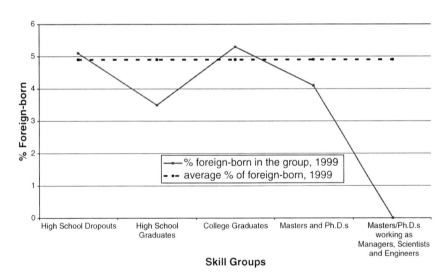

Fig. 3.2 Percentage of foreign-born by skill group in the EU-12, 1999

Sources: European LFS data, 1999, plus website of the Nobel Foundation: http://nobelprize.org/nobel/.

worked in the UK. We observe, therefore, an inflow of Chinese college graduates of 24,569 units and an outflow of Indian graduates of 7,362 units during the period 1992–99. These numbers seem very small, and they hardly represent a sizeable brain drain. In 1999, Indian and Chinese contributed less than .3 per cent of the college graduates working in Europe. A very different picture emerges for the US. During the nineties, the Chinese college graduates working in the US grew by 222,903 units (from 247,242 in 1990 to 470,145 in 2000), and Indian graduates grew by an even more starling 329,032 units (from 255,916 in 1990 to 584,948 in 2000). These inflows are an order of magnitude larger than those towards Europe. In the year 2000, Chinese and Indian college graduates constituted almost 3 per cent of the overall population of US College graduates.

Finally, in 1992, the number of US-born college graduates working in Europe (EU-12) was 72,330 units, while in 1999 it was 94,700. Conversely, college graduates born in the EU-12 and working in the US were 460,000 in 1990 and 643,700 in 2000. These are values five to six times larger than their American counterparts. During the nineties Europe had a net outflow of 176,300 graduates flocking to the US, while only 22,470 US college graduates left the US to work in Europe. In the year 2000, almost 2 per cent of all college graduates working in the US were born in a country of the EU-12. In Europe, less than .02 per cent of college graduates in the year 1999 were from the US. Overall, Europe had a very substantial outflow of its own 'brains' to the US.

This discussion is of course preliminary and mostly aims at generating a debate. It is however uncontroversial that Europe, in spite of attracting a respectable share of college-educated immigrants, is not able to select the most talented ones among them.

3.4 Highly educated, productivity and innovation

Measuring the contribution of talent to the economic well-being and development of a country is a difficult task. One reason, as suggested in section 3.2, is that a very small number of extremely talented individuals may have a very large impact, because the externalities of major scientific innovations are huge. Here, however, we attempt to do so in two steps.

3.4.1 Quality of highly skilled foreign-born in the US

First, we use wage (productivity) data and personal characteristics of the highly educated, to capture the unobserved quality of highly educated foreign-born workers in the US. Under the assumption that wages reflect productivity, we select groups of progressively more educated workers in the US labour force and, after controlling for observable characteristics of individuals (age, sex, race, marital status), we estimate the productivity (wage) premium for people born in selected foreign countries using a 'Mincerian' regression. We consider some specific locations as potential places of origin of 'talented' professionals, namely the EU-15 countries and Canada, as well as China and India, two large countries, as we saw, that experienced a significant siphoning of talent to the US. The reference group is always US-born workers with the same observable characteristics. The natural interpretation of the wage premium for (say) a European-born professional is that it measures the average (unobserved) quality of a European relative to the average (unobserved) quality of a US-born person in the considered group. This difference is measured as productivity differential.

Table 3.4 reports the estimated coefficients for four different definitions of highly skilled workers and for four groups of foreign-born individuals. The groups considered are increasingly selective as we move to the right of Table 3.4. First we consider college-graduates, then holders of a post-graduate degree, then the interesting sub-group of *young* holders of a post-graduate degree (less than 45 years of age), and finally, people with a graduate degree working in science, engineering or management. The coefficients are obtained from an individual Mincerian regression using

Table 3.4 Wage differentials of foreign high-skilled workers relative to US-born, 2000

Origin	College graduates		Post-graduate degrees		Young post-graduates degrees		Post-graduate degree working in engineering, science, management	
	Weekly wage	Yearly wage	Weekly wage	Yearly wage	Weekly wage	Yearly wage	Weekly wage	Yearly wage
EU-15 Born	0.17	0.19	0.17	0.18	0.16	0.17	0.18	0.19
	(0.01)	(0.01)	(0.02)	(0.02)	(0.02)	(0.02)	(0.02)	(0.02)
Canada-Born	0.19	0.20	0.20	0.21	0.20	0.22	0.18	0.17
	(0.02)	(0.02)	(0.03)	(0.03)	(0.04)	(0.04)	(0.04)	(0.04)
India-Born	0.08	0.074	0.12	0.15	0.13	0.16	0.12	0.11
	(0.01)	(0.02)	(0.02)	(0.02)	(0.03)	(0.02)	(0.03)	(0.03)
China-Born	0.07	0.05	0.05	0.06	0.04	0.06	−0.01	0.01
	(0.01)	(0.02)	(0.02)	(0.02)	(0.02)	(0.02)	(0.03)	(0.03)
Observations	307,103	307,103	108,933	108,933	55,632	55,632	36,825	36,825

Notes: The estimates are from individual regressions using public use microdata sample data, Census 2000 data. The dependent variable is ln(wage) (using weekly or yearly wages). Each column is a separate regression. Each regression includes 5-years' experience dummies, gender dummy, race dummy and marital status dummies. The reported value is the coefficient on a dummy that identifies the country of birth. Standard errors are reported in parenthesis.

individual data from the 1 per cent sample of the US Census (Public Use Microdata), year 2000. The reported numbers measure the wage premium for an individual born in a foreign economy relative to a US-born worker with the same observable characteristics, in the specific skill group. For instance, if we consider the first column, we see that a EU-born college graduate earns a 17 per cent higher weekly wage (19% higher yearly wage) than a US-born college graduate with the same experience, race, sex and marital status. Our interpretation is that the productivity (quality) of the EU-born college-educated working in the US in 2000 was 17–19 per cent higher than that of the average US-born college graduate. Consistent with our previous evidence, we interpret this as yet another indication that the US draws Europeans from the high end of the quality distribution, so that they end up being among the most skilled workers in the US.

Moving down the column we observe that Canadian-born college graduates are also 19–22 per cent more productive than US College graduates. The college graduates attracted from India and China are respectively 8 and 5 per cent more productive than US-born ones (and the difference is significant).[10] Moving to the other columns we can observe that the wage premium for EU-born is also between 16 and 19 per cent for holders of a graduate degree (column 3 and 4) or for young holders of a graduate degree (column 5 and 6) or for holders of a graduate degree working in science, engineering or management. Similarly, for Canadian-born, the wage premium fluctuates between 17 and 22 per cent depending on the skill group, and for Indians it seems to increase from 7 per cent to 12–16 per cent as we move to more highly skilled groups (columns 3–4 and then 7–8) and as we consider younger workers (columns 5 and 6). Finally, Chinese-born workers seem to be of slightly better quality than US-born in the groups of college-graduate and post-graduate degree holders. The conclusion here is that individuals attracted to the US appear to be more talented and productive than the average US-born skilled worker.

3.4.2 Effect on innovation

In this section, we try to quantify the impact of highly educated (talents) on innovation. Following previous work in this field (Branstetter, 2001;

---

[10] Notice that the sign and magnitude of the coefficients on the country of birth vary depending on the country. In general, Latin American and African countries have slightly negative coefficients while other Asian countries have close to zero. Our main interest is to show that the US attracts high quality talent from Europe as well as from some large and important countries experiencing emigration (such as China and India).

Pakes and Griliches, 1980; Peri, 2005) we use patent count as a measure of innovative output of a US state.[11] Patents are awarded to the innovations that show originality, non-trivial characteristics and potentially profitable applications. In spite of all the caveats (see Griliches, 1994) this is the best measure of innovative output we have. Moreover, empirical work (see Peri, 2004 for a review) indicates that innovation measured as patents is highly correlated with total factor productivity at the country level. We use innovation across US states to measure the importance of 'talents' in producing new ideas. In order to better capture the 'quality' of innovation, we weight patents by the average yearly citations received during the first three years after their publication. The number of citations is an indicator of the relevance of a patent, so the weights adjust for the importance of patents. We control for state and decade fixed effect and we include the stock of R&D at the beginning of the decade and the number of Ph.D. in science and engineering working in the state as main determinants of the innovation output.

The results of the regressions, reported in Table 3.5 and run on 50 US states for the 1970–2000 decennial data, measure the importance of highly

Table 3.5 Impact of high skills on innovation

Dependent variable	1 Patent count	2 Patent count adjusted for quality	3 Patent count	4 Patent count adjusted for quality
Log of R&D stock	0.16*	0.17*	0.17*	0.14*
	(0.07)	(0.08)	(0.07)	(0.07)
Log of Ph.D.	0.16*	0.14*		
	(0.06)	(0.06)		
Log of US-born Ph.D.			0.06	0.04
			(0.06)	(0.05)
Log of foreign-born Ph.D.			0.08	0.08*
			(0.05)	(0.04)
State fixed effects	Yes	Yes	Yes	Yes
Time fixed effects	Yes	Yes	Yes	Yes
R^2	0.98	0.98	0.98	0.98
Observations	150	150	150	150

Notes: Period 1970–2000 Panel, 3 decades 51 US states. Columns 1 and 3: dependent variable is average yearly count of patent granted during each decade. Columns 2 and 4: dependent variable is average yearly count of patent weighting each of them by 1 plus the average citation number received per year in the first 3 years. Explanatory variables are all measured at the beginning of the decade.
* = Significant at 5 per cent level. Huber-White robust standard errors.

Sources: Data on number of US-born and foreign-born Ph.D.s are from the 2000 US Census public use microdata. Data on the number of patents are from the NBER dataset described in Jaffe and Trajtenberg (2002). Patents have been assigned to a state according to the address of the first inventor. Data on R&D by state are from the National Science Foundation/Division of Science Resources Studies, Survey of Industrial Research and Development: 1998.

[11] See among others Griliches (1994) and Jaffe and Trajtenberg (2002).

educated workers in innovation, once we control for institutional effects (state fixed effects) secular trends (time fixed effects) and R&D inputs. Specifications 1 and 2 estimate the overall effect of Ph.D.s on innovation and show that even controlling for R&D spending increasing the Ph.D.s working in the state by 1 per cent increases its innovation rate by .14–.16 per cent. As innovation rates are likely to translate in similar growth rates of total factor productivity, the above estimates imply that increasing the share of Ph.D.s by 3 per cent in a country would increase innovation rates and TFP growth by a full 1 per cent per year. This is a very large effect and provides a sense of the importance of talents for innovation and growth. We then try to decompose this contribution between the contribution of US and foreign-born Ph.D.s. As the two 'inputs' to innovation are highly correlated the precision of the estimate deteriorates, however consistently foreign-born Ph.D.s have a larger and more precisely estimated impact than US-born Ph.D.s. This is remarkable in particular as they are, on average, only 20 per cent of total Ph.D.s. Either because they are disproportionately employed in R&D or because they are highly talented, the contribution of foreign-born Ph.D.s to US innovation seems very important. Ultimately and in the long run this may very well be the most important effect of foreign-born on the US economy.

3.5 Conclusions

1 Empirical evidence points out that both quantity and the quality of highly educated workers in a country provide a significant contribution to income per capita growth.
2 Higher education has both large private returns and social (external) returns, the latter through invention or adoption of better and more productive technologies that increase total factor productivity.
3 The EU is lagging behind in generating a large supply of highly-educated and is losing many of them to the US. Further, Europe does not compete effectively with the US in attracting brains from the rest of the world.
4 While it is hard to quantify exactly, there seems to be evidence that the contribution of highly skilled Europeans and foreign-born in general, to the US economy in static terms (wages) and in dynamic terms (innovation and growth) is important and beneficial to that country.

PART B—THE MARGINS OF IMPROVEMENT OF EDUCATION INSTITUTIONS: SKILL MISMATCH, SKILL PORTABILITY AND MOBILITY

4

Internal Mobility, Skills and Education

4.1 Introduction

This chapter first documents the differences in internal mobility in Europe and the US, then investigates the determinants of internal migration with a focus on the determinants of the migration of the most skilled workers. By internal mobility, we mean, first within EU (resp. US), that is, across countries (resp. across states). The fact that Americans or Europeans are potentially fully mobile within the boundaries of the US or the EU has important consequences on the efficiency of their skill allocation as well as on the impact of foreign skills on these economies. If the native labour force is very mobile (as turns out to be the case for Americans), this is a sign that people move in search of their best opportunity (best match between skill and job). Moreover, high internal mobility allows the diffusion (over time) of the positive (or negative) effects of local shocks such as immigration from outside. Mobility of labour, as pointed out by Mundell (1961) in his analysis of optimal currency areas, can be a way to arbitrage away asymmetric shocks.

Within the EU, mobility of highly skilled workers across its countries has been very small. While in the US highly educated and talented people move to the states and cities where their reward (and productivity) is higher, in the EU they are still, to a very large extent, confined to their country of birth.[1]

---

[1] It may seem unfair to compare cross-state mobility in the US and cross-country mobility within Europe, but this will illustrate the segmentation of the European labour markets. Section 4.3 will be devoted to within-country mobility in Europe instead.

This chapter is organized as follows. First we focus on internal mobility (section 4.2) of native workers, for Europe and the US, focusing on their skill composition. Section 4.3 attempts to measure the impact of education on internal mobility in Europe and shows that education reduces costs of migration, thus raising mobility and the efficiency of the allocation of labour. Finally, in section 4.4, we carry out an empirical analysis of the determinants of migrations between US states between 1970 and 2000. We find that higher median wage, higher wage dispersion and higher R&D spending attract more highly educated workers, especially foreign-born.

4.2 Internal mobility: EU versus USA

The present section measures the extent of internal mobility of the population and labour force within the US and the EU. Table 4.1 shows two measures of long-run mobility across countries in Europe and then details it for the five largest countries. The values presented in columns 1, 3 and 5 of Table 4.1 are the percentages of individuals in the labour force who reside in one of the EU-12 countries that is different from their EU-12 country of birth. Columns 2, 4 and 6 report the percentage of individuals in the population of the EU-12 states born in a different EU-12 state. The percentages are similar for population and labour force and they increase by a modest .3 per cent in seven years, from 2.2 per cent in 1992 to 2.5 per cent in 1999. France, which attracted the largest share of

Table 4.1 Internal geographical mobility in the EU

Year	1992		1996		1999	
	Labour force	Population	Labour force	Population	Labour force	Population
EU-12	2.2%	2.1%	2.2%	2.1%	2.5%	2.4%
EU-15	na	na	2.2%	2.0%	2.6%	2.4%
France	3.8%	3.9%	3.7%	3.7%	3.5%	3.6%
Spain	0.8%	0.7%	0.9%	0.8%	1.0%	0.9%
UK	2.2%	2.4%	2.1%	2.3%	2.2%	2.5%
Germany[a]	2.8%	2.4%	2.8%	2.3%	2.7%	2.2%
Italy[a]	0.2%	0.2%	0.1%	0.1%	0.2%	0.1%

Notes:
[a] The data on place of birth are not available, therefore statistics are based on nationality of residents.
The number in each cell represents the percentage of EU-born labour force/population born in a EU country different from the country of residence. The first two rows reports the average for the whole Union (EU-12 or EU-15) and each of the following lines reports the percentage of residents (labour force) of the specific country who were born in a different country of the EU.

EU citizens born in a different country, had a mere 3.5 per cent of non-French Europeans in 1999. Italy and Spain confirm their small power of attraction even for EU citizens, counting less then 1 per cent of foreign Europeans among their residents. The contrast between the EU and the US economies is stunning. Table 4.2 shows that in the average US state, one-third (30–33%) of the labour force and population in the year 2000 was made up of individuals born in a different state. This percentage decreased somewhat from 35 per cent in 1990, although the decreased 'out of state' presence was probably offset by the increased share of immigrants. Some US states are 'open' labour markets to an extent positively alien to EU countries. For instance, more than half of Florida's population in the year 2000 was born outside the state. As reference, we also consider geographical units larger than states in the US, namely the nine census regions,[2] and measure mobility as the percentage of people residing in a region and born in a different one. This percentage was 26 per cent in the year 2000 (25% in year 1990), somewhat lower than for states (as regions are much larger units) but still ten times larger than for EU countries.

4.3 Mobility and education in Europe

4.3.1 Introduction

The previous sub-section provides evidence of highly segmented labour markets for the EU. Let us investigate this further and consider now

Table 4.2 Internal geographical mobility in the USA

Year	1990		2000	
	Labour force	Population	Labour force	Population
USA	35.3%	32.1%	33.6%	29.2%
California	36.2%	30.6%	28%	23.7%
New York	17.8%	16.6%	16.1%	14.5%
Texas	32.4%	26.1%	30.4%	24.1%
Florida	61.1%	56.6%	55.6%	50.6%
Illinois	25.7%	22.5%	23%	20.7%

Notes: The number in each cell represents the percentage of US-born labour force/population born in a US state different from the state of residence. The first row reports the average for the whole US and each of the following lines reports the percentage of residents (labour force) of the specific state who were born in a different state.

[2] Each census region is a group of states, the nine regions are: New England, Middle Atlantic, East North Central, West North Central, East Atlantic, East South Central, West South Central, Mountain, and Pacific.

within-country mobility in the European Union, and notably the role of education. In section 1.5 (pp. 31–4), we already explored preliminary links between education and mobility and showed that more educated workers are more mobile. If unemployment in Europe is partly due to a lack of mobility of workers as suggested by many (e.g. Bertola and Ichino, 1995), the natural questions to ask here are: 'what is the role of human capital in determining mobility?' and more precisely: 'why is the impact of education on mobility so large and common in all countries?'

Here, we will show evidence that in Europe within-country mobility of more educated workers is greater than of less educated workers. The same is true in the US. In 2000, 43 per cent of college graduates worked in a state different from their state of birth, versus 32 per cent of high school graduates and 20 per cent of high school dropouts.

In theory, education may affect the migration decision for two reasons: it may raise gross returns to mobility; and it may reduce the costs to mobility. The first effect is rather obvious: education has an effect on earnings. Suppose workers receive job offers in a log-normal wage distribution. Workers with a higher level of education have access to proportionally better paid jobs than uneducated workers. Some of these job offers imply a geographical move. If mobility costs are independent of education, educated workers will therefore be more likely to move.

The second mechanism is usually disregarded, but is not necessarily less important. Higher education is associated with general skills, adaptability of individuals and, in the case of higher education, some experience of studying in another city or region. Many studies report that, conditional on many observable characteristics, the migration probability increases with previous mobility experience (e.g. Axelsson and Westerlund, 1998). Individuals with higher education are more likely to have studied elsewhere, having been confronted with classmates from other sub-regions or areas, thus raising the ability to exchange and communicate. Overall, higher education may reduce psychological costs to mobility.

The effect of education on both costs and returns produce the same observable effects as the ones displayed in Tables 1.11 and 1.12 (see p. 32): education and mobility are positively associated. This chapter will first provide multivariate analysis of the links between mobility and education with no strong claims on causality. We then make a rough attempt to disentangle the two effects (costs vs. returns). If we find that education seems to reduce mobility costs, the general increase in educational attainment in Europe may be beneficial to geographical mobility.

One could argue that it is difficult, both empirically and theoretically to dissociate costs from returns.[3] This is true, and we try to make modest claims about how to disentangle the two aspects. Nevertheless, the effect of education on returns and costs is important in normative terms. If education affects mobility positively because of higher wages, education should be privately financed, or at least not more publicly financed. If however education reduces mobility costs and is not internalized by students, or it acts through an external effect (e.g., if my mate is mobile, I am mobile too), then there is an additional rationale for the large recent increase in general education that is not always present in labour market analysis.

4.3.2 Data: ECHP and geographical mobility

The European Community Household Panel (ECHP) is a household survey collected from all EU-15 countries that includes detailed information about individual and household characteristics. We will use this survey here and in Chapter 5 on over-education and mismatch. The longitudinal nature of ECHP allows following individuals over time throughout the seven years covered in the survey (1994–2001). Moreover, the data also includes supplementary information at the country level such as PPP exchange rates, CPI national deflators and aggregate population information. Throughout this chapter we use the cross-sectional weights provided by ECHP. Education is defined as a categorical variable (primary, secondary or tertiary) in descriptive tables, and in years of schooling in regression analysis. (See the Appendix to Chapters 4 and 5 for details.)

Defining mobility in ECHP is relatively straightforward. The household files contain information of the year of the move into the current dwelling (left-truncated in 1979). For recent moves, the month of the move is also declared in most cases. Knowing the year and month of the interview, one can easily estimate the number of months elapsed since the last move for all household members and thus define a 'recent mobility variable'. For all 15 countries in ECHP and for all years but 1994 (due to lack of reliability), we construct two variables defining a recent episode of mobility if the household has moved within 12 and 36 months preceding the interview. We also know the main reason for the move for 13 of the 15

---

[3] For instance, in a compensating wage differential approach, wages may reflect moving costs. Here, we have in mind a take-it-or-leave-it model of wage offers where firms face an elastic supply of labour and thus have *ex-post* the monopoly power.

countries of ECHP (Luxembourg and Sweden being the exceptions). The reasons fall into three categories: mainly job-related, mainly house-related, or personal reasons. The last possibility corresponds to marriage or divorce or death of a relative, while the second one corresponds to a situation in which the current dwelling is inappropriate. Drawing the line between these two possibilities is not necessarily easy, but house-related mobility is typically associated with either the dwelling being too small or too expensive. We finally know whether the move was within the city/area, from outside the city/area or from another country. (See Appendix A4 for the definition of related variables.[4])

4.3.3 More descriptive statistics on mobility

Here we present additional descriptive statistics on mobility for the sample of heads of households (reference person) in the active population. Tables 4.3 to 4.4 report summary statistics on the relation between mobility rates and various variables related to the skill level and employment status of the head of household. Here we focus on mobility for any reason and refine the analysis later on. Table 4.3 indicates that mobility rates for the unemployed are substantially greater than for employed workers: the mobility rate of the unemployment in the last 36 months is 3.5 percentage points above the rate for the employed workers (21.3% compared with 17.8%). Table 4.4 reports mobility rates by occupation. The relatively

Table 4.3 Geographical mobility rate in the last year and in the last three years, any reason, active 15–64 population, head of households, by unemployment status

	Mobility rate	# obs.
Last year		
Employed	0.065	218,765
Unemployed	0.086	15,369
Last three years		
Employed	0.178	218,765
Unemployed	0.213	15,369

Notes: EU-15 less Luxembourg and Sweden, 1995–2001, survey weights.

---

[4] There are now many studies on mobility based on ECHP. Two recent works, Barcelo (2002), and Tatsiramos (2004), use a definition of geographical mobility similar to the one used here, in that it is not based on the change in the macro-region of residence to define mobility. The main reason is that, in several countries, macro-regions (which are a group of regions, corresponding to the geographical level NUTS1) are so large that geographical mobility would be strongly underestimated.

Table 4.4 Geographical mobility rate in the last year, any reason, occupied 15–64 population, head of households, by occupation

Grouped occupation	Mobility rate
Legislators, senior officials and managers	0.058
Professionals	0.079
Technicians and associate professionals	0.078
Clerks	0.065
Service workers, shop and market sale workers	0.071
Skilled agricultural and fishery workers	0.022
Craft and related trades workers	0.053
Plant and machine operators, assemblers	0.060
Elementary occupations	0.060
Total	0.063

Notes: EU-15 less Luxembourg and Sweden, 1995–2001, survey weights.

more skilled occupations (professionals, technicians) and service workers tend to have higher mobility rates than less skilled occupations and occupations specific to industry or agriculture.[5]

Figure 4.1 reports the measured mobility rate of heads of households for a job-related reason, outside the area/city in which they lived. For all countries, this mobility rate is higher, the higher the level of education. On average in Europe, this rate is 2.1 per cent for workers with tertiary education, .8 per cent for workers with secondary education, and .4 per cent for workers with primary education. Tables 4.5 and 4.6 examine mobility outside the residential area/city. Table 4.5 shows that the UK, Denmark and Finland exhibit the highest mobility rates outside the (previous) area of residence. Other countries, notably Belgium and Southern European countries, have low or very low mobility outside the current residential area. France and Germany are in intermediate positions in this table. The last column in Table 4.5 restricts mobility to job-related moves. This roughly corresponds to the observations to the right side in Figure 4.1, except that in this table, international mobility is excluded while it was included in Figure 4.1. Finally, Table 4.6 shows that the mobility rate outside the area is more than 3 times higher for workers with higher education (4.5% of households have experienced a move

---

[5] Other unreported statistics indicate that self-employed and workers in family enterprises are much less mobile than the regular employees, themselves less mobile than workers in training and apprenticeship. There is clearly an age effect here, as younger workers are at the same time more likely to be geographically mobile and more likely to be in a training or apprenticeship status. We did not find any clear trend in the data: mobility rates simply show a peak in 1997 and 1998 and subsequently decline.

Table 4.5 Geographical mobility rate outside the area in the last three years, active 15–64 population, head of household, by country

Country	Any reason	Job-related reason
DK	0.054	0.020
NL	0.029	0.010
B	0.013	0.003
F	0.042	0.025
IRL	0.01	0.003
I	0.011	0.005
EL	0.008	0.006
E	0.009	0.005
P	0.007	0.001
A	0.015	0.006
FIN	0.058	0.024
D	0.021	0.008
UK	0.072	0.027
Total	0.025	0.011

Notes: EU-15 less Luxembourg and Sweden, 1995–2001, survey weights.

outside the area in the last 3 years) than for workers with primary education (merely 1.4%).

4.3.4 Theory

We now present a simple model of migration. For simplicity we abstract from complex intra-household decisions and treat households and

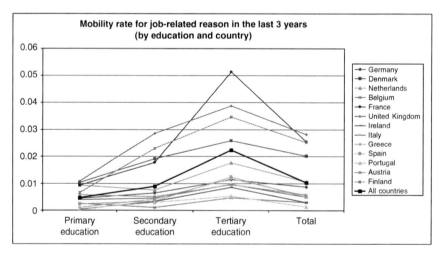

Fig. 4.1 Mobility rate in the last three years, job-related reason and outside the area/city, by education (EU-15 less Luxembourg and Sweden, 1995–2001)

Table 4.6 Geographical mobility rate outside the area, active 15–64 population, head of household, by education level

Education	Mobility rate
Primary	0.014
Secondary	0.023
Tertiary	0.045
Total	0.024

Notes: EU-15 less Luxembourg and Sweden, 1995–2001, survey weights.

individuals interchangeably. The presentation draws on Axelsson and Westerlund (1998) with some adaptations. Typical migration models go as follows: each household i has access to J possible places indexed by j. Households derive random utility U_{ij} from being located in j and chose the optimal location j^* as: $j^* = \text{Armax}\ (U_{ij})$

Now introduce time variability. Denote by $l = j^*(t-1)$ the optimal location last period. At time t, if $j^*(t)$ differs from l, the household moves. One can thus estimate a migration model such as:

$$M = 1\ (\text{or } 0)\quad \text{if } M^* = W\gamma + \omega > 0\ (\text{or } \leq 0) \qquad [4.1]$$

where W is a vector of households characteristics, γ a vector of coefficients, and ω a random error term, assumed to be normally distributed with zero mean and variance $(\sigma_\omega)^2$. This approach implicitly focuses on returns to migration and ignores costs.

To disentangle returns and costs to education, one can adapt the model as follows:

$$j^*(t) = \text{Armax}\ (U_{ij} - C_{ilj}) \qquad [4.2]$$

where now, the optimal location depends on the current location and C_{ilj} is the cost for household i to move from place l to place j, with $C_{ill} = 0$. Estimation of equation [4.1] is however not going to help, as the determinants of the returns to moving W are now the determinants of *net* gains from migration, thus still mixing up costs and gross returns. We need to adapt the existing empirical strategies to attempt to decompose the effects of education on costs and returns to mobility. Here, we will propose two alternative strategies. A first one can be thought of as a reduced-form empirical strategy. The second one represents a more structural approach.

4.3.5 *First strategy: comparing job-related mobility and mobility for other reasons*

Here we exploit an interesting feature of ECHP: individuals report the main reason for having moved to the current dwelling. As already discussed, the reason can be either primarily job-related, house-related or for personal reasons. The main idea in our empirical strategy is as follows. The effect of human capital on returns to mobility is presumably stronger for job-related moves than for moves induced by other reasons. Denote again by $W\gamma$ the determinants of mobility with $W\gamma = R\gamma_r - X\gamma_c$, where R is a set of variables affecting returns to mobility, and X a set of variables affecting costs to mobility. By estimating a multinomial logit model of migration, where the categorical variable takes values 0 if no recent move, 1 if job-related move, 2 if house-related move and 3 for personal reasons, one has an estimate of γ per type of mobility. We use the mobility rate in the last three years instead of the last year to obtain more mobility events, and thus have a better identification of parameters of interest.

A possible identifying assumption, denoted by (H_o), is that the coefficient of the variable education on returns to mobility (one coefficient of the array γ_r) is zero for house-related moves or personal reasons. In this case, we would obtain an estimate of the cost-effect of education (which is the corresponding coefficient of the γ_c). Nevertheless, this is a rather strong assumption. A refinement of the method is to run a higher-level multinomial logit model, making use of the distance of the move; individuals indeed declare whether the previous location was in the same area/city or outside. One can then create a categorical variable taking the following values (0 if no recent move, 11 if job-related move in the same area, 12 if job-related move to another area, 21 if house-related move to the same area, 22 if house-related move to another area, 31 if personal reason move to the same area and 32 if personal reason move to another area; see Table 4.7). One would expect the effect of education to be more important for house-related moves if the move is to another area, the same for moves motivated by a personal reason.

Table 4.8 reports the results of the three-level multinomial logit where individual clustering is taken into account in the computation of the variance-covariance matrix.[6] We present the relative risk ratios. As is

---

[6] We restrict the analysis to a sample of active individuals who are the reference person in the household. A missing variable is attributed to the categorical variables when the reason for move or its origin is missing. We use data covering the time period 1995 to 2001 for 13 countries (Sweden and Luxembourg excluded because of data availability) and obtain a

Table 4.7 Mobility in the last three years, by reason and distance, heads of households

	# obs.	Percent	Cum.
0 No move	434,247	79.44	79.44
11 Job-related move, same area	3,650	0.67	80.10
12 Job-related move, other area	4,517	0.83	80.93
21 House-related move, same area	32,072	5.87	86.80
22 House-related move, other area	3,271	0.60	87.40
31 Personal reason move, same area	19,547	3.58	90.97
32 Personal reason move, other area	3,401	0.62	91.59
0 Missing	45,955	8.41	100.00
Total	546,66	100.00	

Notes: EU-15 less Luxembourg and Sweden, 1995–2001, survey weights.

clear, whatever the specification retained (with or without industry and occupation effects, with or without control for household total net real income or unemployment status), the effect of education is positive and significant for all types of moves. Unsurprisingly, the coefficient on education is larger for job-related mobility (8% in the first specification), but it remains positive and significant for house-related and for moves due to personal reasons (3.5% and 2.0% respectively). Under the assumption (H_o), significantly, this would mean that mobility costs depend negatively on the level of education.

Table 4.9 decomposes the multinomial analysis further, using the information on the distance of the move. In the top table, we present the estimated coefficients both in level and in their exponential form. In the benchmark specification, one can observe that the coefficient of education in columns 'Outside the area' is between two and three times larger than in columns 'Same area'. The ratio almost reaches 4 if the move is for a personal reason. A similar finding emerges from alternative specifications in the bottom of the table. This means that, whatever the reason for the move, a higher level of education implies that individuals are two to three times more mobile outside the area than within the area, with everything else controlled for. Hence, since psychological mobility costs are presumably larger when distance of the residential change is larger, we take these results as an additional indication that mobility costs are significantly reduced by education.

partition of the sample as described in Table 4.7. Missing observations represent 9 per cent, no mobility 79 per cent. The remainder is mobility mostly due to house-related moves, mostly in the same area. In contrast, job-related moves tend to be marginally more outside the area (.83%) than within the area (.67%).

Table 4.8 Multinomial models of mobility, 3-level-mlogit

(With and without control for unemployment status, with and without control for total net (PPP adjusted) household income and with occupation and industry dummies. Columns 1–3: first model; columns 4–6: second model; columns 7–9: third model; columns 10–12: fourth model. Relative Risk Ratios.)

	(1)	(2)	(3)	(4)	(5)	(6)	(7)	(8)	(9)	(10)	(11)	(12)
	1	2	3	1	2	3	1	2	3	1	2	3
Reason	Job	House	Perso	Job	House	Perso	Job	House	Perso	Job	House	Perso
Sex	0.730	0.900	0.863	0.738	0.904	0.862	0.740	0.913	0.861	0.763	0.865	0.868
	(0.042)**	(0.026)**	(0.032)**	(0.043)**	(0.026)**	(0.032)**	(0.043)**	(0.026)**	(0.032)**	(0.051)**	(0.029)**	(0.037)**
AgeD1	2.796	1.629	2.304	2.843	1.643	2.302	2.927	1.700	2.278	3.390	1.768	2.466
	(0.228)**	(0.092)**	(0.130)**	(0.232)**	(0.093)**	(0.130)**	(0.243)**	(0.097)**	(0.130)**	(0.309)**	(0.111)**	(0.155)**
AgeD3	0.301	0.296	0.238	0.301	0.296	0.238	0.297	0.292	0.238	0.293	0.297	0.230
	(0.016)**	(0.008)**	(0.008)**	(0.016)**	(0.008)**	(0.008)**	(0.016)**	(0.008)**	(0.008)**	(0.017)**	(0.008)**	(0.008)**
AgeD4	0.103	0.119	0.112	0.105	0.120	0.111	0.102	0.117	0.112	0.092	0.123	0.106
	(0.012)**	(0.006)**	(0.007)**	(0.013)**	(0.006)**	(0.007)**	(0.012)**	(0.006)**	(0.007)**	(0.012)**	(0.007)**	(0.008)**
Educ	1.080	1.035	1.020	1.078	1.035	1.020	1.076	1.031	1.020	1.044	1.028	1.021
	(0.005)**	(0.003)**	(0.003)**	(0.005)**	(0.003)**	(0.003)**	(0.005)**	(0.003)**	(0.003)**	(0.006)**	(0.003)**	(0.004)**
Burden	0.886	0.754	0.786	0.871	0.750	0.788	0.873	0.742	0.787	0.826	0.731	0.777
	(0.027)**	(0.011)**	(0.016)**	(0.027)**	(0.011)**	(0.016)**	(0.027)**	(0.011)**	(0.016)**	(0.028)**	(0.012)**	(0.017)**
Unemp.				0.618	0.870	1.046						
				(0.060)**	(0.037)**	(0.052)						
Log. Inc.							1.146	1.166	0.974			
							(0.056)**	(0.026)**	(0.022)			
HSize D.	Yes	Yes	Yes	Yes	Yes	Yes	Yes	Yes	Yes	Yes	Yes	Yes
Year D.	Yes	Yes	Yes	Yes	Yes	Yes	Yes	Yes	Yes	Yes	Yes	Yes
Ctry D.	Yes	Yes	Yes	Yes	Yes	Yes	Yes	Yes	Yes	Yes	Yes	Yes
Ind. D.	No	No	No	No	No	No	No	No	No	Yes	Yes	Yes
Occ. D.	No	No	No	No	No	No	No	No	No	Yes	Yes	Yes
Obs.	200,091	200,091	200,091	200,091	200,091	200,091	199,426	199,426	199,426	171,646	171,646	171,646
PseudRsq:	13.70			13.69			13.69			14.51		

Notes: EU-15 less Luxembourg and Sweden, 1995–2001; dependent variable: 0 if no recent move, 1 if job-related move, 2 if house-related move, 3 if personal reason move Robust to clustering standard errors in parentheses.

* significant at 5 per cent level;

** significant at 1 per cent level; AgeD1 = 16–24 y.o.; AgeD2 (ref.) = 25–34 y.o.; AgeD3 = 35–54 y.o.; AgeD4 = 54–65 y.o.; Burden = 1 (Shelter costs represent a heavy burden); 2 (some burden) or 3 (not a burden); Unemp= 1 if unemployed, 0 otherwise Outcome (No mobility) is the comparison group. HSizeD: dummy variable for household size (1, 2 …, 5 & 6+).

Table 4.9 Multinomial models of mobility, 6-level-mlogit

(Benchmark specification. Columns 1–6: Coefficients; columns 7–12: Relative Risk Ratios)

| Reason | Job | Job | House | House | Perso | Perso | Job | Job | House | House | Perso | Perso |
Place	Same area	Outside	Same area	Outside	Same area	Outside	Same area	Outside	Same area	Outside	Same area	Outside
Sex	−0.196	−0.403	−0.110	−0.172	−0.168	0.085	0.822	0.668	0.896	0.842	0.845	1.089
	(0.090)*	(0.079)**	(0.032)**	(0.091)	(0.043)**	(0.082)	(0.074)*	(0.053)**	(0.028)**	(0.077)	(0.036)**	(0.090)
AgeD1	0.953	1.053	0.436	0.506	0.713	0.790	2.594	2.865	1.547	1.658	2.041	2.204
AgeD3	−1.120	−1.297	−1.183	−1.678	−1.431	−1.434	0.326	0.273	0.306	0.187	0.239	0.238
	(0.132)**	(0.113)**	(0.062)**	(0.153)**	(0.065)**	(0.128)**	(0.342)**	(0.324)**	(0.096)**	(0.254)**	(0.133)**	(0.282)**
AgeD4	−2.073	−2.393	−2.108	−2.583	−2.196	−1.813	0.126	0.091	0.121	0.076	0.111	0.163
	(0.178)**	(0.176)**	(0.060)**	(0.178)**	(0.073)**	(0.154)**	(0.022)**	(0.016)**	(0.007)**	(0.013)**	(0.008)**	(0.025)**
Educ	**0.048**	**0.134**	**0.036**	**0.072**	**0.011**	**0.041**	**1.049**	**1.144**	**1.037**	**1.075**	**1.011**	**1.042**
	(0.010)	**(0.008)**	**(0.003)**	**(0.011)**	**(0.005)***	**(0.010)**	**(0.010)**	**(0.009)**	**(0.004)**	**(0.011)**	**(0.005)***	**(0.011)**
Burden	−0.114	−0.119	−0.280	−0.285	−0.260	−0.131	0.892	0.888	0.755	0.752	0.771	0.877
	(0.047)*	(0.042)**	(0.016)**	(0.051)**	(0.022)**	(0.049)**	(0.042)*	(0.037)**	(0.012)**	(0.038)**	(0.017)**	(0.043)**
HSize D.	Yes	Yes	Yes	Yes	Yes	Yes	Yes	Yes	Yes	Yes	Yes	Yes
Year D.	Yes	Yes	Yes	Yes	Yes	Yes	Yes	Yes	Yes	Yes	Yes	Yes
Ctry D.	Yes	Yes	Yes	Yes	Yes	Yes	Yes	Yes	Yes	Yes	Yes	Yes
Ind. D.	No	No	No	No	No	No	No	No	No	No	No	No
Occ. D.	No	No	No	No	No	No	No	No	No	No	No	No
Obs.	196,158	196,158	196,158	196,158	196,158	196,158	196,158	196,158	196,158	196,158	196,158	196,158

(Additional specifications: with and without control for total net (PPP adjusted) household income and with and without occupation and industry dummies. Columns 1–6: first model (Relative Risk Ratios); columns 7–12: second model (Relative Risk Ratios)

| Reason | Job | Job | House | House | Perso | Perso | Job | Job | House | House | Perso | Perso |
Place	Same area	Outside	Same area	Outside	Same area	Outside	Same area	Outside	Same area	Outside	Same area	Outside
Sex	0.831	0.686	0.911	0.891	0.843	1.101	0.895	0.662	0.851	0.804	0.833	1.171
	(0.076)*	(0.054)**	(0.029)**	(0.081)	(0.036)**	(0.091)	(0.093)	(0.060)**	(0.032)**	(0.090)	(0.041)**	(0.114)
AgeD1	2.617	3.143	1.614	1.932	2.031	2.224	2.746	3.726	1.657	2.073	2.173	2.438
	(0.352)**	(0.359)**	(0.100)**	(0.297)**	(0.134)**	(0.288)**	(0.401)**	(0.487)**	(0.114)**	(0.338)**	(0.158)**	(0.350)**

(contd.)

Table 4.9 (*Contd.*)

(Additional specifications: with and without control for total net (PPP adjusted) household income and with and without occupation and industry dummies. Columns 1–6: first model (Relative Risk Ratios); columns 7–12: second model (Relative Risk Ratios)

Reason Place	Job Same area	Job Outside	House Same area	House Outside	Perso Same area	Perso Outside	Job Same area	Job Outside	House Same area	House Outside	Perso Same area	Perso Outside
AgeD3	0.325	0.266	0.301	0.179	0.240	0.238	0.306	0.276	0.308	0.179	0.233	0.217
	(0.026)**	(0.019)**	(0.008)**	(0.015)**	(0.009)**	(0.020)**	(0.026)**	(0.022)**	(0.009)**	(0.016)**	(0.009)**	(0.019)**
AgeD4	0.126	0.089	0.119	0.073	0.112	0.163	0.111	0.080	0.127	0.075	0.105	0.158
	(0.022)**	(0.016)**	(0.007)**	(0.013)**	(0.008)**	(0.025)**	(0.022)**	(0.016)**	(0.008)**	(0.015)**	(0.009)**	(0.026)**
Educ	**1.047**	**1.133**	**1.030**	**1.059**	**1.011**	**1.039**	**1.026**	**1.077**	**1.026**	**1.031**	**1.011**	**1.023**
	(0.010)**	**(0.009)****	**(0.004)****	**(0.012)****	**(0.005)***	**(0.011)****	**(0.012)***	**(0.011)****	**(0.004)****	**(0.013)***	**(0.006)***	**(0.013)**
Burden	0.888	0.861	0.741	0.712	0.770	0.874	0.844	0.812	0.730	0.727	0.765	0.842
	(0.042)*	(0.037)**	(0.012)**	(0.037)**	(0.017)**	(0.043)**	(0.043)**	(0.038)**	(0.013)**	(0.043)**	(0.019)**	(0.047)**
log. Inc.	1.055	1.326	1.188	1.668	0.988	1.054						
	(0.078)	(0.093)**	(0.028)**	(0.146)**	(0.025)	(0.073)						
HSize D.	Yes	Yes	Yes	Yes	Yes	Yes	Yes	Yes	Yes	Yes	Yes	Yes
Year D.	Yes	Yes	Yes	Yes	Yes	Yes	Yes	Yes	Yes	Yes	Yes	Yes
Ctry D.	Yes	Yes	Yes	Yes	Yes	Yes	Yes	Yes	Yes	Yes	Yes	Yes
Ind. D.	No	No	No	No	No	No	Yes	Yes	Yes	Yes	Yes	Yes
Occ. D.	No	No	No	No	No	No	Yes	Yes	Yes	Yes	Yes	Yes
Obs.	195,498	195,498	195,498	195,498	195,498	195,498	168,416	168,416	168,416	168,416	168,416	168,416

Notes: EU-15 less Luxembourg and Sweden, 1995–2001; dependent variable: 0 if no recent move, 11 if job-related move in the same area, 12 if job-related move in another area, 21 if house-related move in the same area, 22 if house-related move in another area, 31 if personal reason move in the same area, and 32 if personal reason move in another area; robust to clustering standard errors in parentheses.

* significant at 5 per cent level;

** significant at 1 per cent level; AgeD1 = 16–24 y.o.; AgeD2 (ref.) = 25–34 y.o.; AgeD3 = 35–54 y.o.; AgeD4 = 54–65 y.o.; Burden = 1 (Shelter costs represent a heavy burden); 2 (some burden) or 3 (not a burden). HSizeD: dummy variable for household size (1, 2 …, 5 & 6+). Outcome (No mobility) is the comparison group.

We also explored the determinants of mobility for Germany, France, the UK and Italy. We do not report the results, but for job-related moves the results are consistent with those in Table 4.9: the marginal impact of an additional year of education on the probability of moving outside the current residential area is larger than for moves within the current residential area. On the other hand, the coefficient on education is not larger for 'big' moves in Germany and the UK when it comes to moves that are not job-related. It is much larger in France and Italy, however.

4.3.6 Second strategy: estimating the income gain from migration

Equation [4.1] is a reduced-form approach to model the migration decision, where the explanatory variables are personal characteristics. A more structural approach would incorporate the income change due to migration. In our case, this would be very useful, because the effect of education net of income change would be a good measure of the cost-reducing effect of education. Of course, the income change from migration is only observed for those having moved, a typical selection problem analogous to the problem of estimating wage equations when the wage of non-participants is not observed.

To deal with the problem, a second equation—an income change equation—is typically estimated. Suppose income is determined by

$$Y = X\beta + \alpha M + Z\delta + \varepsilon \qquad [4.3]$$

where X are observable characteristics affecting income, while Z is a set of time-independent variables such as education, and β and δ are vectors of coefficients. The stochastic component ε is assumed to be normally distributed variable with zero mean and variance $(\sigma_\varepsilon)^2$. The correlation between the two error term ε from equation (4.3), and the error term ω from equation (4.1) is given by ρ.

The method is the following: in a first step, equation (4.1) is estimated. In a second stage, equation (4.2) is estimated. In this second step, the correlation between ε and ω is taken into account by adding the variable $Inv.Mills = \phi(W\gamma)/\Phi(W\gamma)$ if $M = 1$ and $\phi(W\gamma)/(1 - \Phi(W\gamma))$ if $M = 0$. The estimated coefficient on this variable delivers the product $\rho\sigma_\varepsilon$.[7]

---

[7] Identification will come from housing tenure and 'rent is a financial burden' variables in the mobility equation, and different functional forms (potential exp. vs. age dummies) in the income and mobility equations.

One thus obtains $E(Y|M = 1)$, $E(Y|M = 0)$ and their difference is thus the expected gain from migration, imputed notably to households for which no migration was observed. See the Appendix for the computation of these variables. Denote by

$$\Delta Y_{E,imp} = E(Y|M = 1) - E(Y|M = 0) \qquad [4.4]$$

the imputed, expected gain from migration. One can thus in a third stage re-estimate a migration equation similar to [4.1], but with this variable as an additional explanatory variable. The effect of education, given the inclusion of this variable, is thus the effect of education net of the effect of the potential gain from migration. It is thus the effect on the cost.

In order to see why it is important to estimate the income equation for stayers and movers separately in this two-stage analysis, one can simply report gross statistics on the yearly income growth of household real income (PPP adjusted). It is on average 2.4 per cent a year over the sample of 13 EU countries. Movers for job-related reasons have on average a 6.7 per cent income growth. Movers for a job-related reason who moved outside the area further experience on average a 8.3 per cent income growth.

We report in Table 4.10 the first stage (a probit equation for mobility) in the first column and the semi-structural mobility equation in the second column where the imputed income growth is added as a regressor. We also report the income model, corrected for selection, for stayers and movers, respectively, in columns 3 and 4.[8] Some interesting results emerge. First, in the income growth equations, the product $\rho\sigma_\varepsilon$ is positive and significant, contrary to Axelsson and Westerlund (1998) who find it to be statistically insignificant. The main reason is that we estimated the income model in levels, while they estimate an income growth model. The impact of education on income is large, and, though marginally, larger for movers. Other variables playing the dominant role in this equation are family status and family size. Second, the imputed income growth variable has a large and significant coefficient in the mobility equation. Finally, the coefficient of education is about .033 in the reduced-form probit, and is not much smaller in the semi-structural approach: it falls to .030. We also

---

[8] We also tried four different specifications, including additional variables: unemployment status and occupation and industry dummies but do not report these results, as they are very similar.

Table 4.10 Probit model of household job-related mobility and income model

	(1) Model of mobility reduced form	(2) Model of mobility semi-struct.	(3) Model of income, stayers only	(4) Model of income, movers only
Imputed income growth		0.108 (0.034)**	–	–
Inv. mills Ratio	–	–	2.956 (0.100)**	0.552 (0.075)**
Sex	−0.081 (0.026)**	−0.049 (0.036)	−0.082 (0.006)**	−0.108 (0.045)*
AgeD1	0.392 (0.041)**	0.267 (0.079)**		
AgeD3	−0.341 (0.024)**	−0.310 (0.033)**		
AgeD4	−0.695 (0.052)**	−0.702 (0.069)**		
Educ	**0.033 (0.003)****	**0.030 (0.004)****	**0.053 (0.001)****	**0.057 (0.005)****
Burden	−0.014 (0.016)	−0.035 (0.021)	–	
hhszD2	−0.002 (0.032)	−0.074 (0.045)	0.465 (0.010)**	0.621 (0.055)**
hhszD3	−0.131 (0.035)**	−0.167 (0.047)**	0.563 (0.010)**	0.610 (0.062)**
hhszD4	−0.199 (0.037)**	−0.204 (0.048)**	0.609 (0.010)**	0.517 (0.074)**
hhszD5	−0.121 (0.048)*	−0.116 (0.061)	0.666 (0.011)**	0.560 (0.076)**
hhszD6	−0.181 (0.075)*	−0.160 (0.092)	0.767 (0.014)**	0.687 (0.086)**
htenD2	0.505 (0.025)**	0.450 (0.033)**	–	–
marD2	–	–	−0.209 (0.020)**	0.029 (0.130)
marD3	–	–	−0.142 (0.010)**	−0.293 (0.078)**
marD4	–	–	−0.061 (0.016)**	−0.443 (0.167)**
marD5	–	–	−0.008 (0.007)	−0.108 (0.047)*
potexp	–	–	0.014 (0.001)**	0.048 (0.009)**
potexpsq	–	–	−0.000 (0.000)**	−0.001 (0.000)**
Year D.	Yes	Yes	Yes	Yes
Ctry D.	Yes	Yes	Yes	Yes
Observations	201,397	148,787	199,022	1,597
R-squared			0.9	0.9

Notes: EU-15 less Luxembourg and Sweden, 1995–2001; robust (to clustering) standard errors in parentheses.
* significant at 5 per cent level;
** significant at 1 per cent level; NB, there is no correction of s.e. for the two-stage procedure; AgeD1 = 16–24 y.o.; AgeD2 (ref.) = 25–34 y.o.; AgeD3 = 35–54 y.o.; AgeD4 = 54–65 y.o.; Burden = 1 (Shelter costs represent a heavy burden); 2 (some burden) or 3 (not a burden); Outcome (No mobility or mobility for non-job reason) is the comparison group of probit analysis. hhSizeDn takes value 1 if household size is n if n<6; hhSizeD6 takes value 1 if household size is >=6; marital status variables: reference = married. Rent = 1 if dwelling rented in the private sector. Reference is owner.

undertook the same analysis by country for Germany, France, the UK and Italy, in retaining the same benchmark specification.

4.3.7 *Further comments on mobility and education*

Interestingly, what is true within EU-countries is no longer true if we consider mobility across these EU-countries. It happens that college educated workers are less mobile across countries than the average worker, while low skilled (high school dropouts) turn out to be the most mobile of all workers across countries, with 2.7 per cent of them living in a country different from the country of birth. This percentage is only 2.2 per cent for college graduates and 1.7 per cent for high school graduates. We will come back on this important point in Chapter 7 and provide some tentative interpretations.

4.4 Determinants of mobility of highly skilled workers across US state data

We complement the previous analysis by investigating the determinants of high-skill location across US states. Can we quantify the respective role of wages, wage dispersion and the research and technological environment? The question is highly relevant in a European perspective: if wages (at the top of the distribution) are the main attractors of 'talents', then labour market reforms should be considered. On the other hand, if research spending has a relevant role, policies should target the development of research poles and research institutions instead. In order to test whether these two factors affect the mobility of the highly-educated and in particular attract the highly-educated from abroad, we use data on US states.

We use decennial census data on 50 US states over three decades (1970–2000). Controlling for a fixed state effect, a time effect and the initial endowment of highly educated workers in a state, we analyse whether the immigration during each decade depended on the initial value of median wage, initial wage dispersion and initial stock of R&D in that state. The idea is that, other things equal, a state with higher median wage, larger wage dispersion (measure as the percentage wage difference between median and top 90th percentile) and larger real spending in R&D would be more attractive to highly educated workers. The regression

Table 4.11 Determinants of mobility for highly educated workers

Dependent variable:	1 Foreign-born Ph.D.	2 US-born Ph.D.	3 Foreign-born college graduates	4 US-born college graduates
Initial log of R&D stock	0.04*	0.22*	0.01*	0.21*
	(0.01)	(0.05)	(0.005)	(0.05)
Initial log of skill level	−0.06*	−0.79*	−0.02*	−0.54*
	(0.01)	(0.10)	(0.01)	(0.07)
Log of median yearly	0.12*	0.44	0.18*	0.14
wage	(0.05)	(0.52)	(0.04)	(0.30)
Yearly wage dispersion	0.20	1.20	0.27*	0.58
	(0.11)	(1.10)	(0.11)	(0.80)
State fixed effect	Yes	Yes	Yes	Yes
Time fixed effect	Yes	Yes	Yes	Yes
R^2	0.20	0.33	0.13	0.34
Observations	150	150	150	150

Notes: Period 1970–2000. Panel, 3 decades, 50 US states. Dependent variable is the change in skilled workers during the decade as percentage of the initial size of employment in that skill group. The explanatory variables are all measured at the beginning of the period.
* = Significant at 5 per cent level.
Huber-White robust standard errors.

Sources: Data on wages and education are from the US census public use microdata 1970–2000, data on R&D for each decade and in each state are from the National Science Foundation/Division of Science Resources Studies, Survey of Industrial Research and Development: 1998. Foreign-born are defined as those workers who were born outside the US and without US citizenship at birth.

results for the group of college-educated and Masters–Ph.D.-educated, US-born and foreign-born, are reported in Table 4.11. Interestingly for both groups of highly skilled foreign-born the stock of R&D, median wage and wage dispersion are all (at least marginally) significant and economically important. R&D is also very important to attract the US-born while wage dispersion has a very imprecisely estimated effect. Doubling R&D, a state would attract 22 per cent more Ph.D.s born in the US plus 4 per cent of foreign-born Ph.D.s. Increasing the wage dispersion between median and the top 90th percentile by 20 per cent would also attract extra foreign-born Ph.D.s in an amount equal to 4 per cent of initial Ph.D.s.

We performed few robustness checks of this regression (excluding some decades such as the nineties, and some important states such as California) and the results are robust and do not seem driven by a particular decade or state. Even within the US, for given institutions and policies, states which, due to their industry composition, technological choices and local incentives, have more dispersed wage distribution and higher R&D investments, attract a larger flow of highly educated workers from inside and outside the country.

4.5 Conclusions

1 The EU as a whole is not promoting an adequate degree of internal mobility of highly educated workers.

2 Geographical mobility is positively associated with the level of education unconditionally as well as conditionally on other characteristics.

3 The effect of education is larger for job-related moves and for long-distance moves (outside the area of residence).

4 The results suggest that mobility costs, and notably psychological costs, are reduced by higher levels of education.

5 We find mild evidence of a role of wage dispersion and strong evidence of the role of R&D spending as a determinant of mobility. This suggests that the EU should emphasize R&D and high technology and reward merit rather than insider status in the competition to attract talented foreigners, and by doing so could succeed even without dramatically altering its overall wage distribution.

5
Skill Mismatch and Over-qualification in the Enlarged Europe

5.1 Introduction

Every year, the European economy generates a large number of high school and college graduates who begin their search for a first job. The transition from school to work is often slow and associated with long spells of unemployment.[1] Paradoxically, companies also claim that their posted vacancies cannot be filled in by the numerous jobseekers, due to a lack of sufficiently qualified or available labour force.

This chapter attempts to measure the magnitude of such mismatch, and provide some suggestions to correct it. The chapter is divided into two. First, we study the causes and consequences of skill mismatch in the EU-15 using data from the European Community Household Panel (ECHP) for the period 1994–2001. The data allow us to characterize the phenomenon of skill mismatch and over-qualification on a consistent basis across countries and time, based on workers' self-assessments on the relationship between their skills and those required by their jobs. After presenting a short overview of the phenomenon of skill mismatch in the EU-15 economies, the analysis concentrates on the five largest EU-15 countries.

Secondly, we complement the analysis by focusing on Poland, a country that similarly to nine others of the new enlarged Europe has recently gone through a process of structural change and transition to a market economy while its educational system was tailored to the needs of a regulated economy. The data source used for the analysis is the Polish Labour Force Survey (PLFS) for the period 1997–2003, which allows us to look at formal education mismatches (both under- and over-education), but does

---

[1] For a survey of the issue and recent international comparisons see OECD (1999).

not allow us to directly characterize the broader phenomenon of skill mismatch. This partially prevents us from comparing measures and trends of education mismatch in Poland and the other large countries of the European Union. Therefore, the second part of this chapter offers new empirical evidence of the labour market consequences of under- and over-education in Poland, and when possible, draws some tentative lines of comparison with the other EU countries.

5.2 A brief survey of the literature

Following Freeman's (1976) seminal book, a recent empirical literature has focused on the determinants and causes of the mismatches between the formal education of individuals and the educational requirements of their jobs in European countries. One limitation in this literature, which mostly develops cross-country comparisons, is the lack of comparability of methods and data. Groot and van den Brink (2000) present a meta-analysis of previous studies on the effects of over-education on wages, but their focus is on laying out cross-country regularities rather than identifying idiosyncratic features. Moreover, while looking at educational mismatches is interesting in itself and from a policy perspective, these mismatches might not necessarily imply an inefficient allocation of resources. Workers identified as over-educated might well be properly matched if their productivity is lower than average due to unobserved characteristics. Similarly, under-educated workers might compensate this lack of education with other forms of human capital such as firm-specific training.

There are two main perspectives in the interpretation of skill and educational mismatch. According to some views, skill mismatch is a temporary phenomenon at the individual level. This phenomenon might be related to inefficiencies in the functioning of the labour market due to lack of perfect information and mobility (Jovanovic, 1979), or might instead reflect a desire from the part of workers to acquire skills that complement their qualifications at earlier stages of their career (Sicherman and Galor, 1990). Over time, workers are expected to improve the matches by mobility either within or outside the firm. Instead, if formal education is used as a screening device by employers (Spence, 1973) skill mismatch can become a permanent phenomenon. Recently, Albrecht and Vroman (2002) and Dolado et al. (2004) have shown that mismatch can be a long-lasting phenomenon in matching models with jobs and worker heterogeneity, where high skilled workers can compete with low skilled workers for low skilled jobs. These structural mismatches can be attributed to supply forces such as rapid educational upgrading of the labour force, or demand forces such as skilled bias technological change. In both cases, they imply a rapid change in the demand or supply of skills that cannot be easily matched by the other side of the market.

5.3 Skill mismatch and over-qualification in the EU-15

In this section, we exploit the information of the European Community Household Panel (ECHP) to study the determinants and consequences of skill mismatch and over-qualification in Europe. The analysis concentrates on the five largest countries of the EU-15; namely, France, Germany, Italy, Spain and the UK, but presents summary statistics for all EU-15 countries in an attempt to provide a full picture of the skill mismatch phenomenon.[2]

Over-qualified individuals can be identified in the ECHP as those individuals answering affirmatively the following question: 'Do you feel that you have skills or qualifications to do a more demanding job than the one you have now?' Some aspects are worth noting regarding the formulation of this question. First note that the question refers to skills or qualifications rather than educational levels. In this respect, the information provided is broader than in previous studies that focused on over-education. For instance, an experienced individual with the right educational level for a given job might feel over-qualified when she compares herself with a younger worker employed for the same job with the same educational attainment. One drawback of this measure is that it does not allow us to distinguish by how much the phenomenon of over-qualification occurs. As an illustration, think about two individuals working as waiters; one holds a high school degree and the other a college-graduate certificate. It is very likely that in this case both individuals feel over-qualified for the job, but we will not be able to distinguish by how much each of them exceeds the required educational level of a waiter.

A second question in the ECHP questionnaire allows us to go further in the classification of skill and educational mismatch: 'Have you had formal training or education that has given you skills needed for your present type of work?' Crossing the information contained in both

---

[2] Sweden and the Netherlands are excluded from the sample since questions on skill mismatch are not available in the ECHP questionnaire.

questions we can construct four types of individual classes according to their type of match:

- NOWM. 'Non-over-qualified and well matched' if non-over-qualified and education and training is suited for their job.
- NOBM. 'Non-over-qualified and mismatched' if non-over-qualified but education and training is not suited for their job.
- OWM. 'Over-qualified but correctly matched' if over-qualified but education and training are suited for their job.
- OBM. 'Over-qualified and mismatched' if over-qualified and education and training are not suited for their job.

An example can help to illustrate the differences between the four types of individuals. An individual with a Ph.D. in mathematics working as a university professor will be classified as NOWM. Instead, if this individual is employed as a research assistant s/he will probably classify her/himself as OWM, since s/he has the right training to do the job but would be suitable for a more qualified set of tasks. Imagine instead that s/he is appointed as the CEO of a multinational firm. In this case, her/his formal qualification would not be well suited for the job although s/he is certainly not over-qualified (NOBM). Finally, if s/he worked as an electrician s/he would certainly feel over-qualified and with an education not suited for the job (OBM). It is important to note that strictly speaking, only NOWM workers are properly matched. OWM, although having the training demanded by the job could be assigned to more demanding tasks according to their qualifications. Thus, we label them as 'correctly matched' in the sense that their formal training is directly related to their job, although their actual (either formal or acquired on the job) qualifications would allow them to do a more demanding job.

Table 5.1 presents the results from the cross-tabulations of type of match, pooling all countries and years where information is available.[3] We restrict the sample throughout the chapter to full time employees in the working age (15–64) population, resulting in 279,655 observations. According to these tabulations, about 54 per cent of the population is considered to have skills for a more demanding job than the one they hold at the moment of the interview. Among the four categories described above, OWM workers are the most common, accounting for 33 per cent of

---

[3] These questions are only formulated in the common independent questionnaire of ECHP. This limits data availability in the cases of Germany and the UK to the first three waves (1994–97).

Table 5.1 A taxonomy of mismatch in Europe

	Formal training or education that has given you skills needed for your present type of work?		Total
	Yes	No	
Non over-qualified (%)	69,097.32	59,404.03	128,501.30
	(21.2)	(24.7)	(45.9)
Over-qualified (%)	92,269.88	58,883.78	151,153.70
	(33.0)	(21.1)	(54.1)
TOTAL (%)	161,367.20	118,287.80	279,655
	(57.7)	(42.3)	(100)

the total number of employees. Instead, the number of workers correctly matched (NOWM) is the lowest among the four categories (21.2 per cent).

Figure 5.1 shows the evolution of the different categories of skill match during the period of analysis for the European average. During the 7 years of study, the incidence of skill mismatch has remained relatively stable with a mild decline of OWM coupled with a raise of properly matched individuals (NOWM).

There are important cross-country differences in the incidence of the different categories of skill mismatch. Figure 5.2 shows the share of the

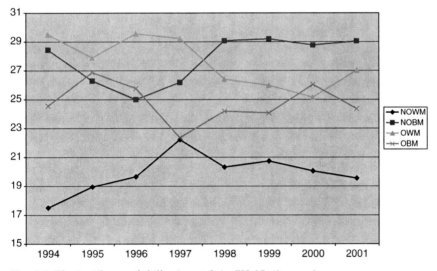

Fig. 5.1 The incidence of skill mismatch in EU-15, time series

Notes: Weighted averages (using population shares in 2001) of 10 European countries (Austria, Belgium, Denmark, Finland, France, Greece, Ireland, Italy, Portugal and Spain). Germany and the UK are excluded from the averages since data is only available for the period 1994–96.

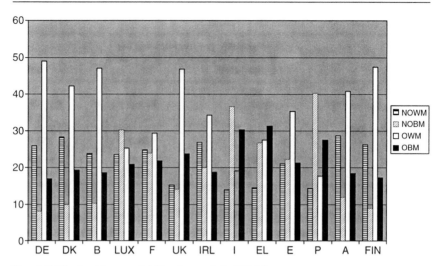

Fig. 5.2 The incidence of skill mismatch in EU-15, cross-country

four types of match in the 13 European countries for which information is available. In all countries, with the exception of Portugal, Italy and Greece, the modal category is OWM, involving almost 50 per cent of the employees in Germany, Belgium, Finland and the UK. In southern Europe, there is instead a relatively higher incidence of mismatch, either coupled with over-qualification in the cases of Italy and Greece or in the form of pure mismatch in the cases of Portugal and France.

These differences across countries can be attributed to a large number of factors. They could be caused by the design and efficiency of the different educational systems in providing the skills demanded by the market. Alternatively, they might be related to the interplay of institutions, educational choices and the functioning of the labour market in matching the supply and demand of skills. Regarding the latter, firing costs are expected to reduce labour flows with ambiguous effects on average employment, but unambiguous effects regarding efficiency, since they prevent workers being employed where more are needed at each point in time.[4] Moreover, they are expected to play a significant role in segmenting the labour market, by insulating insiders from employment fluctuations at the cost of lower (higher) employment (unemployment) of outsiders (typically younger and female workers). It might be argued then that in countries where reallocation of labour is costly, and finding a first job is difficult due to the presence of employment protection, the incidence of

---

[4] See Bertola (1999) and the references therein for a detailed analysis.

skills mismatched might be larger. At the same time, mismatched individuals would stay longer spells on the job due to stringent firing restrictions. Figure 5.3 shows the rank correlations between the different categories of skill match and a ranking of EPL.[5] In line with the previous arguments, we find that there is a positive association between skill mismatch and the stringency of EPL. However, there are not significant differences between the different categories of skill mismatch regardless of whether individuals are over-qualified for their jobs or not (NOBM and OBM).

5.3.1 *Who is over-qualified or mismatched?*

In this section we examine the individual and job characteristics most typically associated with the different categories of skill mismatch outlined in the previous section for the largest countries in the EU-15.

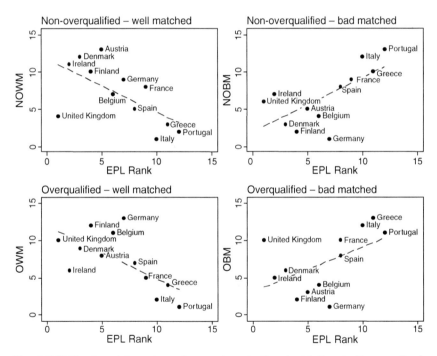

Fig. 5.3 Skill mismatch and employment protection legislation in Europe: Rank correlations

[5] The EPL ranking is constructed by averaging the OECD 2004(b) index of employment protection for the period 1994–2001.

The analysis is divided into two. First, we study the individual characteristics associated with over-qualification regardless of the matching status
of the individual. A probit model is estimated, where the dependent
variable takes value 1 if the individual declares to be over-qualified. Control
variables include personal- (gender, marital status, size of household, years
of education, potential experience and a set of previous unemployment
experience dummies) and job- (tenure, 10 industry and 10 occupational
dummies) related characteristics. Secondly, we differentiate between the
four categories of matching outlined above and estimate multinomial
logit models of the different categories of skill mismatch. Appendix A.5
provides a description of the construction of some of the variables, and
Table A.5.1 provides a full list of variables included in the analysis.

Table 5.2 presents marginal effects of the expected changes in the predicted probability of over-qualification evaluated at the mean of the covariates as a function of personal and job characteristics. Standard errors are
robust to clustering at the individual level.[6] Columns 1 to 5 present the
results for each individual country while column 6 pools the information
for all countries and years. Some common features across countries stand
out. Regarding personal characteristics, male workers tend to consider
themselves over-qualified in greater proportion than female workers and
over-qualification increases with years of schooling (except in Germany).
According to the average across countries, 10 additional years of education
increase the probability of being over-qualified by .21 percentage points.
Conversely, with labour market experience, the probability of being over-
qualified declines in all countries. This result goes in line with a transitory
interpretation of the incidence of over-qualification.

There are also some important differences across countries. In Italy and
Spain workers with more than 10 years of tenure on the job have a
significantly lower probability of being over-qualified, but this is not the
case in the other countries. In Germany and the UK, we find a positive
association between over-qualification and having experienced a spell of
unemployment during the previous last five years, suggesting that some
workers are willing to accept a job for which they are over-qualified to
avoid unemployment. Lastly, note that the country dummies are all
highly significant at standard confidence levels in column 6, suggesting
that cross-country differences remain after controlling for a wide set of
personal and job characteristics. According to this set of dummies, the

---

[6] Assuming that the individual heterogeneity is random and estimating the probit model
by random effects yielded qualitatively similar results, which are therefore not reported.

Table 5.2 The determinants of over-qualification: marginal effects from probit analysis

	(1)	(2)	(3)	(4)	(5)	(6)
	Germany	UK	France	Italy	Spain	All
marry	−0.006	0.004	0.018	0.020	0.021	0.012
	(0.32)	(0.20)	(1.14)	(1.38)	(1.76)	(1.67)
sex	−0.116	−0.090	−0.136	−0.074	−0.033	−0.081
	(5.75)**	(4.84)**	(8.58)**	(5.42)**	(2.70)**	(11.51)**
hhsize	−0.004	−0.001	−0.009	−0.001	−0.000	−0.002
	(0.59)	(0.18)	(1.75)	(0.21)	(0.05)	(1.01)
yeduc	0.003	0.017	0.021	0.024	0.025	0.021
	(1.37)	(5.65)**	(7.70)**	(10.80)**	(13.74)**	(20.26)**
exper	−0.004	−0.002	−0.004	−0.003	−0.005	−0.004
	(4.69)**	(2.96)**	(4.10)**	(4.37)**	(9.41)**	(12.36)**
tend2	0.006	−0.016	0.020	−0.039	−0.010	−0.017
	(0.30)	(0.81)	(1.29)	(2.68)**	(0.81)	(2.33)*
tend3	0.046	−0.009	−0.004	−0.010	0.002	−0.006
	(1.85)	(0.39)	(0.20)	(0.52)	(0.13)	(0.73)
tend4	0.004	−0.029	−0.020	−0.059	−0.037	−0.037
	(0.17)	(1.17)	(1.07)	(3.43)**	(2.45)*	(4.21)**
unem	0.062	0.072	−0.004	−0.031	0.022	0.012
	(2.29)*	(2.81)**	(0.15)	(1.18)	(1.34)	(1.15)
nunem	−0.034	−0.007	0.044	−0.001	0.007	0.003
	(0.76)	(0.18)	(1.33)	(0.03)	(0.41)	(0.21)
lunem	0.063	−0.041	0.006	0.036	0.025	0.020
	(1.28)	(0.90)	(0.16)	(1.30)	(1.53)	(1.63)
Dummy France						−0.073
						(6.24)**
Dummy UK						0.074
						(5.61)**
Dummy Italy						−0.114
						(9.92)**
Dummy Spain						−0.053
						(4.67)**
Sectoral dummy	Yes	Yes	Yes	Yes	Yes	Yes
Occupation dummy	Yes	Yes	Yes	Yes	Yes	Yes
Year dummy	Yes	Yes	Yes	Yes	Yes	Yes
Observations	10,474	7,960	20,343	31,424	31,556	101,757

Notes: Robust (to individual clustering) z-statistics (in absolute value) in parentheses.
* significant at 5 per cent level;
** significant at 1 per cent level.

likelihood of being over-educated is lower in Southern Europe, being highest in the UK and lowest in Italy.

Next we study the determinants of the four categories of skills match outlined in the previous section. Table 5.3 presents results for multinomial logit regressions, where the reference group are those individuals not over-qualified and well-matched (NOWM). The first three columns present the

Table 5.3 The determinants of skill mismatch. Multinomial logit analysis. Pooled country sample

	Coefficients			Relative Risk Ratios		
	(1)	(2)	(3)	(4)	(5)	(6)
	NOBM	OWM	OBM	NOBM	OWM	OBM
marry	−0.124	−0.009	−0.034	0.883	0.991	0.967
	(2.94)**	(0.23)	(0.76)	(2.94)**	(0.23)	(0.76)
sex	0.006	−0.381	−0.260	1.006	0.683	0.771
	(0.14)	(10.36)**	(6.09)**	(0.14)	(10.36)**	(6.09)**
hhsize	0.056	0.003	0.042	1.057	1.003	1.042
	(4.00)**	(0.20)	(2.49)*	(4.00)**	(0.20)	(2.49)*
yeduc	−0.186	0.048	−0.048	0.830	1.049	0.953
	(26.56)**	(9.47)**	(7.48)**	(26.56)**	(9.47)**	(7.48)**
exper	0.006	−0.017	−0.009	1.006	0.983	0.991
	(3.06)**	(8.54)**	(4.21)**	(3.06)**	(8.54)**	(4.21)**
tend2	−0.009	−0.024	−0.128	0.991	0.976	0.880
	(0.19)	(0.56)	(2.71)**	(0.19)	(0.56)	(2.71)**
tend3	0.014	0.085	−0.131	1.015	1.088	0.877
	(0.26)	(1.69)	(2.38)*	(0.26)	(1.69)	(2.38)*
tend4	−0.202	−0.080	−0.471	0.817	0.923	0.625
	(3.85)**	(1.64)	(8.69)**	(3.85)**	(1.64)	(8.69)**
unem	0.157	0.066	0.182	1.170	1.068	1.199
	(2.43)*	(1.11)	(2.76)**	(2.43)*	(1.11)	(2.76)**
nunem	0.077	0.049	0.091	1.080	1.050	1.095
	(1.02)	(0.66)	(1.17)	(1.02)	(0.66)	(1.17)
lunem	0.117	0.087	0.210	1.124	1.091	1.234
	(1.52)	(1.15)	(2.63)**	(1.52)	(1.15)	(2.63)**
Dummy France	0.974	−0.209	0.411	2.649	0.811	1.509
	(12.91)**	(3.67)**	(6.16)**	(12.91)**	(3.67)**	(6.16)**
Dummy UK	0.865	0.508	0.687	2.375	1.661	1.988
	(9.62)**	(7.45)**	(8.74)**	(9.62)**	(7.45)**	(8.74)**
Dummy Italy	1.986	−0.206	1.235	7.288	0.814	3.438
	(26.29)**	(3.43)**	(18.34)**	(26.29)**	(3.43)**	(18.34)**
Dummy Spain	0.584	−0.074	0.019	1.794	0.929	1.019
	(7.79)**	(1.31)	(0.29)	(7.79)**	(1.31)	(0.29)
Constant	1.366	0.346	0.326			
	(6.39)**	(1.74)	(1.50)			
Sectoral dummy	Yes	Yes	Yes	Yes	Yes	Yes
Occupation dummy	Yes	Yes	Yes	Yes	Yes	Yes
Time dummy	Yes	Yes	Yes	Yes	Yes	Yes
Observations	99,535	99,535	99,535	99,535	99,535	99,535

Notes: Robust (to individual clustering) z-statistics (in absolute value) in parentheses.
* significant at 5 per cent level;
** significant at 1 per cent level.

coefficients, and should guide us regarding the sign of the effects, while the last three columns present the relative risk ratios, which help interpreting the effects of the covariates in the odds of being in each category with respect to the reference group. To simplify the presentation of the results, we include only the specifications polling all countries and years and including country and year dummies.[7]

The multinomial logit regressions confirm the higher incidence of over-qualification among male workers. However, gender differences are not significant between NOWM and NOBM. An interesting difference between the two classes of over-qualified workers emerges. While the incidence of OWM workers increases with respect to comparison group (NOWM) with years of education, OBM are more concentrated than NOWM among individuals with a lower educational background. This is consistent with a higher concentration of OBM in elementary occupations (not shown in the table) such as clerks, service and trade workers and plant and machine operators, and a lower representation in more demanding occupations such as professionals and associate technicians.

The weaker association between over-qualification and experience is maintained in the multinomial framework, and no substantial differences are observed between both types of over-qualified individuals. Surprisingly, experience increases the probability of being NOBM. More than 10 years of tenure reduces the probability of being mismatched regardless of the over-qualification status (for NOBM and OBM), but it is only for the latter group that we observe a clear pattern of declining incidence of mismatch with increasing tenure. Having an unemployment spell, or experiencing long term unemployment in the recent past increases the likelihood of being OBM, although these effects are not always statistically significant at the country level. Finally, country differences remain important after controlling for compositional effects.

The multinomial logit analysis uncovered important differences among the four classes of workers. We have tested whether we can pool the different categories using standard Wald tests, and for all pairs of combinations of outcome categories the null of equal coefficients was rejected.[8] This evidence thus suggests that the determinants of each type of over-qualified workers differ significantly, depending on whether they are properly matched or not.

5.3.2 Over-qualification, skills mismatch and wages

Having established the main characteristics of the different classes of mismatched workers, we move next to the analysis of the consequences

---

[7] Separate specifications for the 5 largest EU-15 countries are available upon request.

[8] The independence of irrelevant alternatives (IIA) was also tested. The Hausman test did not reject the null of IIA.

of skill mismatch and over-qualification. In this section, we investigate the link between over-qualification, skill mismatch and wages. Although the previous analysis suggested that the rationales behind different types of mismatch are diverse, we start this section by estimating standard Mincer regressions augmented to include a dummy variable for over-qualification only. This first set of regressions has the virtue of being to some extent comparable to the analysis of Poland carried out in the next section. During a second stage we differentiate between the different types of mismatched workers and try to disentangle the different impact of each category on the determination of wages.

Table 5.4 presents the results of augmented OLS Mincer regressions including an over-qualification dummy.[9] The first 5 columns present the results for each of the countries separately and column 6 presents the results pooling all countries. The other covariates included in the regression (not shown in the table) presented the expected signs: wages increasing with education, tenure and experience (albeit at a decreasing rate), and falling for singles and female workers as well as for those individuals who experienced an unemployment spell in the recent past. In line with the rest of the literature, over-qualified workers have a wage penalty with respect to properly matched employees according to column 6. However,

Table 5.4 Over-qualification and wages

	(1) Germany	(2) UK	(3) France	(4) Italy	(5) Spain	(6) All
	OLS regressions					
Over-qualified	−0.015	0.017	0.002	−0.008	−0.032	−0.010
	(1.35)	(1.36)	(0.23)	(1.44)	(4.56)**	(2.75)**
Observations	10,614	8,160	20,781	32,123	31,164	102,842
R-squared	0.31	0.32	0.36	0.42	0.45	0.41

Notes: Robust (to individual clustering) z-statistics (in absolute value) in parentheses in the OLS regressions.
* significant at 5 per cent level;
** significant at 1 per cent level.
The regressions include a full set of time and country dummies (column 6), male, married and household size dummies, experience and its square, and three dummies of unemployment experience during the last 5 years: ever unemployed, unemployed more than once and unemployed for more than 1 year.

[9] To eliminate the possible impact of wage outliers we drop the 1st and 99th percentiles from the hourly wage distribution in all the wage regressions. A possible drawback of OLS estimates is the failure to control for individual heterogeneity. Messina (2006) accounts for individual effects in similar regressions and finds that the wage penalties discussed in the text retain their sign and statistical significance, but are significantly reduced in magnitude once individual heterogeneity has been accounted for.

the magnitude of the effect is relatively small (1% lower wages). Moreover, the pooled results hide important differences across countries, as it is only in Spain where the wage penalty of over-qualified workers is negative and statistically significant.

Our second set of regressions extends the approach in the over-education literature by allowing to distinguish between the three different types of skill mismatch already defined. Are these differences translated in wage differentials among these three groups of workers and between mismatched and correctly matched individuals? Table 5.5 presents OLS standard Mincer regressions augmented to include three dummy variables that capture each of our mismatch categories of workers, leaving those workers properly matched (NOWM) as the reference group.

Both categories of mismatched workers present a negative return in all countries. The effect is large, suggesting that on average NOBM and OBM workers earn about 11 per cent less than properly matched individuals. Interestingly, with the exception of the Spanish case where being over-qualified and mismatched carries an extra negative premium with respect to being NOBM, there are not substantial differences between the negative returns of NOBM and OBM. Hence, we can conclude that once the individual is mismatched there is no additional wage penalty from being over-qualified. If instead, the individual has the skills required for the job

Table 5.5 Skill mismatch and wages

	(1) Germany	(2) UK	(3) France	(4) Italy	(5) Spain	(6) All
			OLS regressions			
NOBM	−0.097	−0.165	−0.087	−0.101	−0.118	−0.112
	(4.54)**	(8.07)**	(8.61)**	(11.34)**	(11.93)**	(21.36)**
OWM	−0.012	−0.011	−0.001	−0.029	−0.045	−0.022
	(0.97)	(0.63)	(0.11)	(2.83)**	(4.75)**	(4.24)**
OBM	−0.110	−0.149	−0.089	−0.106	−0.149	−0.121
R-squared	0.32	0.35	0.37	0.44	0.46	0.42

Notes: Robust (to individual clustering) z-statistics (in absolute value) in parentheses in the OLS regressions.
* significant at 5 per cent level;
** significant at 1 per cent level.
The regressions include a full set of time and country dummies (column 6), male, married and household size dummies, experience and its square, and three dummies of unemployment experience during the last 5 years: ever unemployed, unemployed more than once and unemployed for more than 1 year.

(well-matched) but is over-qualified (OWM), a wage penalty is found in the cases of Spain and Italy. This fact together with the highest negative wage penalty for OBM workers in Spain is consistent with the view that the current expansion of tertiary education here has not been sufficiently accommodated by an increase in the demand for skilled jobs (Dolado, Jansen and Jimeno, 2004). However, it should be noted that the magnitude of the wage penalty from being OWM is about one-third of the wage penalty suffered by OBM workers. Thus, we can conclude that in the five EU countries studied, it is to a large extent skill mismatch that drives the wage penalty on wages and not over-qualification.

5.4 Education mismatch in a transition economy: the case of Poland

In this section we measure education mismatch in Poland using data from the Polish Labour Force Survey (PLFS) over the period 1997–2003. Next, we analyse its consequences in the determination of wages. And finally, we study the nature of this mismatch, focusing on whether it is a transitory phenomenon at the individual level, related to inefficiencies of the labour market, or a more structural or long lasting one.

Imposed by the nature of our data, we follow the strand of the literature that uses the so-called data-based indexes of over/under-education. This strand looks at the actual distribution of workers' educational attainments by type of occupation, to define the (estimated) adequate level of education per occupation. Indexes of over/under-education are based on measures of the deviations between actual and adequate education levels. We use two alternative indices. First, a *mean-based index* that takes as adequate education per occupation one standard deviation mean-centred interval. It classifies as under/over-educated those workers whose schooling is under/over the limits of this interval (Verdugo and Verdugo, 1989). Secondly, a *mode-based index*, according to which the adequate education for each occupation is represented by the mode of the distribution; any deviation from above/below the mode will be taken as over/under-education (Mendes de Oliveira et al., 2000). In this case, occupations for which less than 60 per cent of the individuals had an education level at the mode were dropped from our sample.

The main arguments in favour of data-based indexes, put forward by their supporters, are that (1) they do not suffer from subjectivity, when compared with measures based on the worker's own evaluation, and (2) they are much simpler (and often more accurate) than indexes based on exogenously designed criteria, which define the adequate educational level for each occupation relying on occupational classifications of job analysts (e.g. information on general educational development (GED) from the US Dictionary of Occupational Titles). The problem with this sort of information is that its transformation into equivalent schooling can be very complicated and arbitrary. Additionally, these job classifications are costly and not frequently updated.

The main drawbacks of the data-based indices are that different data-based indexes usually deliver different results and their accuracy heavily relies on how disaggregate is the available data on occupations. We think that these two problems are minor in the case of our study, because, first, the PLFS data provides data on a three-digits classification of occupations, adding to 122 occupations. And secondly, we use two alternative data-based indexes of over/under-education and the results turn out to be quite robust to the choice of the index. Additionally, it should be kept in mind that data-based measures are based on realized matches that involve labour demand and supply, being therefore inadequate as measures of the demand side.

We restrict the sample to full-time employees in the working age (15–65) population, including all activities but agriculture.[10] Additionally, we exclude observations with wage values in the 1st and 99th percentiles of the wage distribution.[11]

Table 5.6 displays the percentage of the sample that is over- and under-educated over time according to the two indexes. Over-education shows in both cases a clear trend upward while under-education has decreased during the sample period.

Estimations on the probability of being over/under-educated showed that it is more likely that a worker is over-educated if he is male and has high levels of education. While tenure, potential experience out of the job, having attended some training recently, and working in the public sector

---

[10] We re-did all the analysis in this chapter with a sample including agriculture: results did not change substantially. Nevertheless, it should be noted that, in the full sample, agriculture is under-represented because the PLFS sample under-represents rural areas, and because we have dropped self-employed workers.

[11] For more details on the data see Appendix A.5.

Table 5.6 Percentage of under/over-educated workers by year

Year	Mean-based		Mode-based	
	Under	Over	Under	Over
1997	0.158	0.116	0.147	0.130
1998	0.148	0.119	0.140	0.134
1999	0.136	0.121	0.130	0.139
2000	0.126	0.125	0.116	0.139
2001	0.118	0.137	0.110	0.141
2002	0.113	0.149	0.108	0.153
2003	0.104	0.158	0.095	0.153
Total	0.130	0.131	0.122	0.140

all have negative effects on the probability of being over-educated, and vice versa on the probability of being under-educated.[12]

5.4.1 Returns to over/under-education

To examine the returns to over/under-education we estimate two specifications for wage equations that have been frequently used in this literature. First, a standard augmented Mincer equation where a dummy on over/under-education is included among the covariates. This allows us to directly compare which workers suffer education mismatch, with others who have similar features but are adequately matched (i.e. have a job that requires their level of education). Table 5.7 shows that, according to the two indexes of education mismatch, on average, the wage of over-educated workers is around 8.5 per cent lower than the one of similar workers adequately matched; while in the case of under-education wages are between 10–14 per cent higher. This result contrasts with the evidence presented in Table 5.4, where wage penalties in the largest EU-15 countries for over-qualified individuals were found to be negative but small and not always different from zero, except in the case of Spain. Although measures of over-education and over-qualification refer to slightly different concepts, the comparison of both sets of results suggests a greater penalty of educational mismatch in Poland than in the EU-15 countries.

Secondly, we estimate the following equation:

$$\ln(W_{it}) = \alpha X_{it} + \beta YAE_{it} + \gamma YOE_{it} + \delta YUE_{it} + \varepsilon_{it} \qquad [5.1]$$

---

[12] Probit analysis results available upon request.

Table 5.7 Coefficient on the over/under-education variables of an augmented standard Mincer equation

	Mean-based	Mode-based
Years of education θ	0.071	0.072
	(86.76)**	(57.25)**
Over-educated τ	−0.083	−0.087
	(19.09)**	(16.85)**
Under-educated ρ	0.107	0.147
	(19.41)**	(17.26)**

Notes: Robust (to individual clustering) z-statistics (in absolute value) in parentheses in the OLS regressions.
* significant at 5 per cent level;
** significant at 1 per cent level.
The regressions also include a full set of regions, sectors and firm size dummies, male, married, disable, head of household, on the job training, vocational education and public firm dummies, tenure and its square, age and its square.

where $\ln(W_{it})$ is the logarithm of monthly real wages net of taxes. X is a vector of personal and job characteristics, YAE are the number of years of education that are adequate for the performed job, and YOE and YUE are measures of years of over- and under-education respectively. Thus, in this specification, years of education are decomposed as: YAE + YOE − YUE.

Then, γ and δ measure the return to an additional year of over/under-education with respect to the co-workers who are adequately educated for the job. $\gamma - \beta$ measures the return to an additional year of over education with respect to workers with the same level of education who are not mismatched, and $\beta + \delta$ is the wage differential due to a year of under-education with respect to workers with the same education, but who are well matched. A relatively large number of papers has followed this approach for several countries and periods. Hartog (2000) surveys this literature and concludes that the returns to required schooling are higher than the returns to actual schooling. Typically, returns to over-education are positive but lower than returns to required education while returns to under-education are negative but again lower than the returns to actual education, such that under-educated workers earn more than workers performing similar jobs with lower educational attainment but less than workers with their educational level, who are allocated to a more demanding task.

Table 5.8 is an extract of the estimation results of equation [5.1]. It shows the coefficients of the over/under-education variables. Results are also as expected for the covariates in vector X: wages are higher for males and married individuals and for those working for the private sector. They are lower for those on disability benefit, and for those with vocational

Table 5.8 Coefficient on the over/under-education variables of equation [5.1]

	Mean-based	Mode-based
Years adequate education β	0.068	0.071
	(101.18)**	(62.37)**
years over/education γ	0.004	0.026
	(1.14)	(10.21)**
Years under-education δ	−0.007	−0.034
	(2.51)**	(21.90)**

Notes: Robust (to individual clustering) z-statistics (in absolute value) in parentheses in the OLS regressions.
* significant at 5 per cent level;
** significant at 1 per cent level.
The regressions also include a full set of region, sector and firm size dummies, male, married, disable, head of household, on the job training, vocational education and public firm dummies, tenure and its square, age and its square.

education, and, on average, they increase with age and tenure. Regarding the indicators of over/under-education, the main findings are: first, there is a positive return to an additional year of over-education with respect to co-workers who are adequately educated for the job (positive γ); second, δ is around −.034 according to the mode criteria and also negative but quite low in the case of the mean-based index; third, $\gamma - \beta$ is negative in all the cases, around −.04 with the mode criteria and −.06 with the mean one; fourth, $\beta + \delta$ is positive in every case (.057 from the mean and .04 from the mode criteria respectively).

These results show that Poland is not very different from other economies in terms of over-education. Workers who are over-educated for their occupation earn more than their co-workers but less than workers with similar education but who work in occupations that require their level of education (i.e. are adequately matched). On the other hand, under-educated workers earn less than their co-workers, but more than workers with similar education but who are well matched.

5.4.2 Nature of education mismatch in Poland

We will try now to disentangle whether over/under-education in Poland is a long-lasting phenomenon in response to rapid change in the demand or supply of workers' education that cannot be easily satisfied, or whether it is a rather transitory situation at the individual level, while the worker finds a better match (new occupation, promotion, etc.). In doing so, despite the data limitations, we attempt to investigate whether over-education is not a proxy for a more general problem of skill mismatch, as shown above for Western Europe.

One test for this is to see whether over-educated workers eventually change occupation or sector when searching for a better match. For that, we estimate probit models, where the dependent variable takes value 1 if the worker changes occupation. The control variables include a dummy for over- and under-education together with personal- (gender, marital status, education, experience, disability, head of household, etc.) and job-related characteristics (tenure, on the job training, and whether the employer belongs to the private or the public sector). Columns 1 and 2 in Table 5.9 display marginal effects of the expected changes in the predicted probability of changing occupation evaluated at the mean of the covariates. Standard errors are robust to clustering at the individual level. These results confirm that workers with education that differs from the one adequate to perform their job are more likely to change occupation, suggesting that educational mismatch in Poland is coupled with skill mismatch.

We study further the occupational mobility of over/under-educated workers in Poland to see whether (in the case of the over-educated) it responds to career mobility. If this were the case, over-educated workers will be so only transitorily, and will eventually move to occupations that require higher levels of education. To test for this hypothesis we run a probit where now the dependent variable takes value 1 if the movement is into a more demanding occupation in terms of required education. Estimation results, summarized in columns 3 and 4 of Table 5.9, deliver positive and significant estimates of the marginal effects for the over-education dummy; while in the case of under-education, the estimates are not significant or even negative, which indeed confirms the hypothesis of career mobility.

Table 5.9 Occupational/career mobility and education mismatch. Extract of education coefficients

	Mean-based	Mode-based	Mean-based	Mode-based
	Occ. Mobility		Career mobility	
Over-educated	0.012	0.009	0.011	0.013
	(6.74)**	(4.43)**	(9.96)	(12.06)**
Under-educated	0.022	0.028	0.001	−0.004
	(10.69)**	(10.04)**	(1.37)	(−6.03)**

These results suggest that over-education is associated with skill mismatch in Poland and can be thought as a transitory phenomenon at the individual level.[13]

5.5 Overall conclusions

1 There are important differences across countries in the incidence and consequences of educational and skill mismatch. While some of these differences seem to be related to the interplay of institutions and educational choices, the issue deserves further study.

2 Wage penalties in the largest EU-15 countries for over-qualified individuals were found to be small and not always different from zero except perhaps in Spain. In Poland, the wage of over-educated workers is around 8.5 per cent lower than the one of similar workers; while under-educated workers earn between 10 and 14 per cent more.

3 The analysis of the EU-15 sample shows that it is important to distinguish between different categories of over-qualified individuals. A more crucial variable than over-education seems to be whether individuals are properly matched in terms of their formal qualifications. The wage penalty is in fact primarily related to skill mismatch, and there is in general no additional wage penalty from being over-qualified.

4 Our results for Poland indicate that over-education is associated with greater occupational mobility. This suggests that as in the EU-15, over-education is a proxy for skill mismatch. It is also evidence of a transitory situation at the individual level, probably rooted on matching frictions due to imperfect information and mobility.

[13] See Lamo and Messina (2006) for an extensive discussion on over-qualification and mismatch in the new EU countries.

6

Specificity of Skills and Reallocation

6.1 Introduction

In the theory part of Chapter 1, we discussed the issue of the specificity of skill acquisition and notably how institutions such as employment protection induce workers to specialize more in sectors or occupations, as their expected horizon on the job is longer. In the fact part of Chapter 1, we illustrated that European workers on average received more specialized education than workers in the US. Along both dimensions, it appears that European workers have more difficulties in adjusting to transitions and macroeconomic changes, as revealed by the lack of mobility documented in Chapter 4 or skill mismatch as documented in Chapter 5.

Here we want to discuss the implications of the theory from a European perspective. First, we discuss these issues further, starting with a brief survey, and document a few facts (section 6.2). Then we discuss in section 6.3 how one can measure the degree of specificity of skills, and finally, in section 6.4, how one can measure skill obsolescence in periods of reallocation, with a focus on two Eastern European countries, Estonia and Poland.

6.2 Skill specialization in Europe

Krueger and Kumar (2003 and 2004) have developed the view that in Europe, the education system provides a relatively more specialized curriculum, as compared to the US. They argue that this is a source a growth-differential between the two areas, as the US are able to cope with new technologies in a more reactive way. Wasmer (2002, 2006) makes a similar point related to on-the-job skills: as institutions in the labour market tend to raise the relative returns of specific skills, workers over-invest in such skills. They are thus very productive on-the-job, but reallocation of labour is more costly, individually and in terms of aggregate welfare. An implication is that, in a stable macroeconomic environment, the European model with specific skills is rather efficient. In periods of turbulence, when large aggregate and reallocative shocks occur, the European model with specific skills may have troubles because of its lower ability to deal with rapid changes. The picture presented by Krueger and Kumar, and Wasmer, is highly consistent with Blanchard and Wolfers' (2000) view that the interaction of shocks and institutions is at the core of the European unemployment problem.

We now present evidence of the large labour reallocation that Europe has faced, or is currently facing, both in the Eastern and Western countries. We first present empirical evidence that workers in Central and Eastern European Countries (CEEC) were, and still are, concentrated in agriculture and industry. Table 6.1 shows how specific countries (East Germany, former Czechoslovakia, Hungary and Poland) compare to various OECD countries. Here, OECD countries are ranked by quantiles of the income per capita distribution.[1] CEECs and East Germany still have a very large industry compared to the richest OECD countries. The situation is somehow different from the previous enlargements to Southern Europe, where the share of agriculture was dominant. Only Poland can be compared to Southern Europe in terms of the sectoral composition of employment. (See Wasmer (2005) for a longer discussion of these issues.)

Let us now focus on two selected Eastern European countries, Poland and Estonia, and investigate the effect of such macroeconomic shocks (the transition to the market economy in the early 1990s and the Enlargement in the late 1990s). Both countries formally joined the European Union in 2004, but the process was initiated years before, initially in the

Table 6.1 Sectoral composition of employment, OECD and Eastern Europe

	Agriculture (%)	Industry (%)	Service (%)
OECD (top third, 1991)	5.5	29.8	64.7
OECD (mid. third, 1991)	5.8	30.4	63.9
OECD (bottom third, 1991)	17.9	29.5	52.6
East Germany (1989)	10	44.1	45.9
Former Czechoslovakia	11.6	46.8	41.6
Hungary	17.5	36.1	46.4
Poland	27.2	36.3	36.4

Sources: Boeri (2002), Roland (2001).

[1] The bottom third corresponds broadly speaking to Southern European countries such as Spain, Portugal, Greece, and Ireland, the fourth of the 'Cohesion Fund Countries'.

early 1990s when the negotiation for adherence started with the definition of the so-called Copenhagen criteria, and later, when an Accession Partnership was adopted and published in the Official Journal of European Communities in March 1998, after the Luxembourg European Council had adopted the agenda of the Enlargement process.

Figures 6.1 and 6.2 give a good illustration of what can be meant by obsolescence of specific skills. Immediately after the fall of the Berlin Wall and the conversion of Poland to a market economy, the inflow of early retirement peaked at around 160,000 workers; while the subsequent, steady inflows remains at around 40,000 workers a year. In the years preceding the Enlargement, Poland still had a massive recourse to early retirement allowances. Figure 6.2 indicates that the stock of workers under such a scheme is around 800,000 for a stock of unemployed workers of more than 3 millions, which in 2001 represented almost 20 per cent of the labour force. In Estonia, given a very active labour market in which job creation considerably exceeded job destruction, the job separations (lay-offs, retirement etc.) started to increase after 1997, as did the sum of hiring and firing (a measure of labour reallocation). The point we are making here is two-fold: first, the Enlargement, as well as any large transition shock, is associated with more labour turnover. And secondly, as labour is not infinitely mobile across sectors, in some cases labour turnover implies an increase in the inflows into early inactivity. The nature and specificity of

Number of early-retirement pensions in Poland, 1990–96 (thousands)

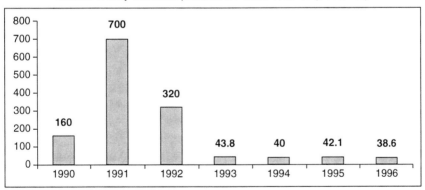

Fig. 6.1 Macroeconomic context during the transition to a market economy, Poland

Primary Source: Kwiatkowski et al.
Secondary Sources: Stastical Yearbook 1997; CSO, Warsaw, 1997, p 137; H. Zarychta, 'A Passive Labour Market Policy in Poland in 1990–1996', in: E. Kryñska, E. Kwiatkowski, H. Zarychta, *The State's Policy on Labour Market in Poland in 1990–1996*, IPiSS, Warsaw, 1998, p 141.

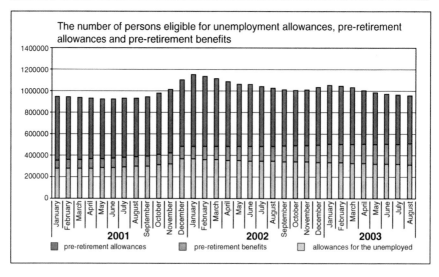

The number of persons eligible for unemployment allowances, pre-retirement allowances and pre-retirement benefits

Fig. 6.2 Macroeconomic context during the adhesion to the European Union, Poland
Source: Ministry of Economy, Labour and Social Policy.

skills are important determinants of the flexibility of the labour force as just argued, and thus might become especially important in periods of rapid reallocation of labour.

6.3 Measurement of specific skills

We have already discussed the need for any theoretical analysis of labour markets to take into account the existence of specific skills among the cross-section of labour market participants: their existence makes labour adjustment slower and more costly. It follows then, at this stage, that we should examine the empirical relevance of such theoretical ideas at the micro-level.

The most direct evidence can be obtained by a careful investigation of returns to seniority. In an earlier paper, Hashimoto and Raisian (1985) demonstrated that Japanese and American workers diverged widely in terms of the number of jobs for life occupied throughout their career. For instance, in the late seventies, they showed that in the US, 15 per cent of male workers aged 40 to 49 had more than 20 years of tenure, while this was the case for 31 per cent of Japanese workers. At age 65, the US worker had occupied on average slightly more than 10 jobs, while the average Japanese worker had occupied only four jobs. Perhaps as a cause, but also as a consequence, they found that, in large firms, returns to tenure were

7 per cent a year (with a quadratic term of $-.03\%$) in Japan, and only 1.2 per cent a year in the US (with an identical quadratic coefficient), controlling for total experience, schooling and several interaction terms. This result has been highly controversial. Subsequent studies for the US found returns to tenure ranging from large positive (Topel, 1991; Kletzer, 1989; see also Kletzer's 1998 survey based on US displaced workers) to zero (Abraham and Farber, 1987; Altonji and Shakotko, 1987). While for Japan, Clark and Ogawa (1992) indicated that returns to tenure were smaller in the mid-1980s, due to changes in the demographic structure of Japan. In France, Lefranc (2003) found evidence of large wage losses after displacement, but not as large as in the US. Interestingly, he argues that wage losses in France are a loss of accumulated human capital, while in the US this is mostly due to the downgrading of occupation. Loewenstein and Spletzer (1999) investigated the content of firms' sponsored training and argued that training is mostly associated with general human capital in the US.

There is also a large literature on workers' displacement, which attempts to investigate in precise detail, the wage loss incurred by workers a few quarters after they were displaced from their previous job.[2] Bender et al. (2002) for instance measured the wage profile of workers before and after plant closure in Germany and France by carrying out standard wage regressions with a full set of dummy variables covering the wage of movers before and after displacement. The comparison group in all the regressions is the group of workers who remained on the job. Contrary to US studies, they do not find important wage losses after displacement. Lamo et al. (2006) extend the approach in Bender et al. (2002) by allowing for different wage profiles for workers with different educational attainment. The key idea is to interact the 'before move' and 'after move' dummies with the degree of specificity of skills, such as measured by the ISCED-1997 classification.

6.4 An application to two accession countries, Poland and Estonia

We borrow from Lamo et al. (2006) and simplify the presentation of their results. In what follows, we attempt to measure the degree of specificity of skills in an economy in investigating the wage profile of workers having moved from one job to another (movers throughout this section). The Bender et al. (2002) method is applied to two countries having faced the

[2] See the compendium of papers included in Kuhn (2002) for a recent study of the issue in different countries.

large reallocation episodes as already discussed: Poland and Estonia. The main data sources are the Polish and Estonian labour force surveys. These surveys follow individuals for a maximum of four quarters within a 1.5 years period.[3] The period of analysis is 1997–2003 covering to a great extent the anticipation of the reallocation shock imposed by the EU Enlargement. Our data set does not distinguish between voluntary and involuntary mobility. Thus, we do not have a priori expectations on the wage consequences of mobility. However, our theoretical discussion suggests that movers with more specific skills should benefit less (or suffer more) from mobility. We distinguish four educational categories: tertiary, secondary vocational, secondary general and lower than secondary. If skill specificity is an important limitation to mobility we should observe workers holding a vocational qualification to suffer higher wage losses (or lower wage gains) than similar workers with more general human capital (secondary general). This is our main hypothesis to be tested.

Table 6.2 presents the main results from the wage regressions in Poland and Estonia. The wage regressions pool information for job movers and job stayers, and include a full set of covariates typically used in this type of analysis. Four dummy variables take Value 1 for movers at different moments in time before and after mobility. Our coefficients of interest are these wage profiles for movers with general secondary education and secondary vocational (thus, the interaction terms between the dummy variables of mobility and the educational dummies). Results for Estonia confirm the predictions of our theoretical insights. Wages of movers with secondary general education before and after mobility are on average 8 per cent lower than wages of stayers. Therefore, there is no difference before and after mobility for movers with general education. Instead, wages of movers with a vocational degree are 4 per cent lower than wages of stayers before mobility, that is, they are in jobs with better pay than movers with general skills, although they are paid less than stayers. Now, the important difference is that the gap after the move is large: wages decrease by 7 per cent compared to stayers in the first quarters after the move to reach -10 per cent one year after mobility. These sizeable differences between both types of workers suggest that human capital specificity can be an important limitation in periods of rapid structural change.

The evidence for Poland, although pointing towards a similar direction, is less clear-cut. In this case, movers with secondary general education benefit

---

[3] For a longer discussion of the main characteristics of the Polish LFS see Chapter 5.

Table 6.2 Human capital specificity and mobility in Poland and Estonia

	Estonia	Poland
	Dep var: Log hourly wages	
More than one year before move (bm_2)	0.09	−0.03
	(3.31)**	(3.15)**
Less than one year before move (bm_1)	0.03	−0.05
	(1.61)	(6.11)**
Less than one year after move (am_1)	0.13	0.03
	(6.77)**	(3.51)**
More than one year after move (am_2)	0.14	0.01
	(6.50)**	(1.67)
Education dummies	Yes (unreported)	Yes (unreported)
Secgen*bm_2	−0.08	−0.06
	(2.27)*	(1.85)
Secgen*bm_1	−0.06	−0.07
	(2.78)**	(2.76)**
Secgen*am_1	−0.09	−0.02
	(3.92)**	(0.73)
Secgen*am_2	−0.08	−0.05
	(3.11)**	(2.02)*
Secvoc*bm_2	−0.04	−0.02
	(0.95)	(1.24)
Secvoc*bm_1	−0.04	−0.01
	(1.58)	(0.81)
Secvoc*am_1	−0.07	0.00
	(2.62)**	(0.14)
Secvoc*am_2	−0.10	0.02
	(3.14)**	(1.14)
Tertiary*(am, bm, etc...)	Yes (unreported)	Yes (unreported)
Number of observations	64,577	254,842
R-squared	0.32	0.29

Notes: z-statistics (in absolute value) in parentheses.
* significant at 5 per cent level;
** significant at 1 per cent level.
Random effects regressions. The regressions include a full set of time and geographical (county) dummies, a male dummy, age, tenure and their squares.

from mobility. There was a 7 per cent gap in wages with respect to stayers before mobility; right after the mobility episode, that is, in the first two quarters, this gap is reduced to −2. This wage gain is somewhat reduced a year after mobility, but not enough to reach the level preceding the job change. Instead, the wages of movers with secondary vocational education do not vary significantly before and after mobility. The massive recourse to early retirement in Poland explains to some extent why we see smaller differences between workers of different education among those who remained in the labour force, an issue further explored in Lamo et al. (2006).

7

Policy implications

This chapter draws on the conclusions of the first six chapters to examine a few policy implications. The main message that emerges from Chapters 1 and 2 is that education systems in Europe have done a good job at supplying basic skills, thus suggesting that their primary and secondary schooling functions relatively well. In contrast, where tertiary education is concerned, both enrolment and funding are substantially lower in Europe than in the US. The share of GDP devoted to higher education is three times less (2 percentage points lower) in Europe than in the US. We believe that one of the highest priorities should be to reduce this gap immediately.

How should this objective be achieved? There are three possibilities. The first one is to re-allocate public spending away from secondary to tertiary education. This move can be justified in various ways, for example, as the size of younger cohorts is reduced over time. But reducing public spending in a given sector, however desirable it might be, is always politically difficult, and it is unlikely that no less than two percentage points of GDP could be transferred from one education sector to another in the short-term. It may not even be desirable, given the evidence that well-financed secondary education may be one reason why Europe has experienced less inequality than the US. A second option is to raise the level of public deficit and public debt in order to reach the objective. This is as unrealistic and undesirable as the first option: European countries already face huge and increased tensions to finance their social security (health and pensions), and are bound to a large extent by the Stability and Growth Pact. So this option can simply be ignored.

Hence, we are left with the third option: to open the doors to the possibility that private money should finance part of the education system. This could come partly from household money, by raising university fees by moderate amounts.[1] Tuition fees in the order of €2000 per year of tertiary education (equal to a quarter of the price of a small car), does not seem beyond the reach of most students with cars. Such a rise should be accompanied by more student loans and student grants being made available to the poorest students. A double dividend of such a reform would be to reduce the allocation of students to inappropriate study fields. Tertiary education that lacks financial backing encourages students to be less than careful in their choice of majors, or degree modules, enhances the consumption of leisure, and reduces student input in terms of effort and success rates, especially during the first years.

Some of these themes were addressed in Dornbusch et al. (2000). For instance, private money could come from firms and foundations. Chairs could be created, financed by endowments in order to keep the private sector from interfering in the nomination of professors. Donors from the private sector might finance university libraries, buildings and various other stock assets. We believe that one of the reasons why European universities cannot attract private money is cultural; another, unfortunately, is that the signal of quality they deliver is insufficient.[2]

We, too, propose reforms at the tertiary level of education. In particular, there is a need to develop strong and clear incentives for teachers both to teach well and to do peer-evaluated research; for universities to allocate resources where it is socially efficient, in a decentralized way; and for students to perform well. The introduction of moderate fees would create such incentives. Furthermore, financing by the private sector should be encouraged, using measures such as fiscal incentives, like tax deductibility of private donations to universities.

A difficult issue, so far left aside, is the extent to which students have to pay for education and to which taxes must finance education. On the one hand, Psacharopoulos (2005) argues that arguments in favour of the public financing of education are often the expression of simple conservatism and are not always corroborated by formal analysis; he gives the example of human capital externalities, which are hard to detect in the data. Further, as noted in Gurgand (2005), free education can be at odds with redistributive ambitions: in fact, families above the median in the income distribution use free education more than those below the

---

[1] In most countries this is a politically sensitive issue but even in France, a high-quality debate has recently started, see e.g. Gary-Bobo and Trannoy (2005).

[2] Europe has only one of the world's top 20 universities; the US has 18 of them according to a recent ranking produced by Tokyo University.

median. On the other hand, Benabou (2005) shows that credit constraints could be an obstacle to investments in human capital and that redistribution through subsidies to human capital accumulation could alleviate this problem. He further notes that there is no obvious connection between growth and redistribution, but that skill-biased technical change might lead the relatively egalitarian European equilibrium to disappear, as incentives for the better-educated to opt out would increase. In other words, the European model may be at risk.

This is why reforms of universities are also necessary. More autonomy and tougher evaluations, with financial rewards for excellence and financial cuts if needed, are a pre-requisite to induce universities to offer better curricula to students. In a centralized system where responsibility is diluted, minimum effort is the rule, and faculties often spontaneously attempt to deliver the same diplomas and the same courses year after year, regardless of market demand. The magnitude of the mismatch problem revealed in Chapter 5 is certainly on a par with this inability of the suppliers of education to react in real time. A couple of anecdotes are illustrative of the state of tertiary education in some European countries. The first one pertains to a very respected and well-liked European professor of economics, at the latest stage of his career. Recently, he distributed lecture notes in which he referred to 'a *recent* colloquium in Portugal, March *1968*'! The other anecdote refers to some advice given to a newly appointed full professor of economics: 'Young colleague, please accept the advice of an old fellow. When you write your lecture notes, you should write big, because over time, your vision will deteriorate.' Neither of these were jokes.

As illustrated in Chapters 1 and 4, sluggish movements of people and labour market frictions within the European Union may slow down the re-allocation of skills, hence labour supply can be inadequate in some locations because of geographical constraints on mobility. It is hard to evaluate the extent to which low mobility figures translates into inefficiencies specific to Europe. Enhanced mobility of workers and optimal allocation of skills to tasks is needed. However, current institutions prevent transition to such an ideal.

In particular, we argue that labour market institutions, in general, tend to reduce mobility, both geographical and between jobs. This shapes the structure of investments, and generates more investments in skills that are specific to sectors and jobs. In a stable macroeconomic environment, this may be a desirable outcome for several reasons: specialization implies efficiency on-the-job, and from the employers' perspective, makes workers relatively attractive. On the other hand, in a world of increased turbulence, for example, in the context of the European Enlargement, general and portable skills are more valuable. In the absence of such general investments in human capital, skills mismatch is a likely outcome (as found in our analysis).

Mismatch should, in principle, generate additional mobility. However, we have the opposite result: mobility rates are low in Europe. European style social insurance probably contributes to the lack of mobility, in that talent is not necessarily rewarded as it should be. Having said this, we should note that wage compression does not seem to impair mobility that much: public and private R&D spending turns out to be more important for mobility than wage dispersion. Another dimension where action is needed is the low attractiveness of Europe to the most talented workers and researchers outside Europe. Although massive injections of both money and incentives in tertiary education would partly remedy this situation, all kinds of bureaucratic barriers, insider privileges, limited labour market competition and poor diffusion of information will still be major obstacles. Even removing these internal barriers it is not clear that highly educated and very talented workers would stay in Europe. Again, the compressed structure of wages (pre- and post-taxes) typical of EU countries (relative to the US) may not provide sufficiently large economic rewards to talent, although our regressions indicate that this is not a major factor.

An important result is that the international mobility of European college-educated workers in Europe itself is lower than that of less educated workers. We think that one of the possible explanations for this phenomenon is the difficulty to harmonize the recognition of diplomas. As a last anecdote, we can cite the example of one of our Ph.D. students in Belgium: he had to validate a bachelor degree (Maîtrise) obtained at the University of Lille I, which is only 100km away from Brussels, in order to become a teaching assistant at the Free University of Brussels. He sent his file to the regional ministry of education, and obtained the following answer (see also the PDF in Appendix A.7):

Sir, (. . .) I transmit your application to the competent instance. For your complete information, I draw your attention to the fact that (. . .) a decision has to be notified to you within four months and fourty days (sic). In the absence of notification after this delay, the case can be brought to the Conseil d'Etat, the silence of the administration being equivalent to a negative answer.

In this case, however, fortunately, the student got his diploma validated and could obtain a salary for his teaching. But the tone of the letter and the mere fact that the validation of the diploma was externalized to a regional administrative committee suggests the magnitude of informal barriers of all kinds.

To conclude, education is relatively egalitarian in Europe, but does not seem to be reactive enough to the macroeconomic context. Although labour market institutions per se explain why mismatch and specific skill investments may arise, we think that an efficient margin for policy is to reform higher education and to consider private sources of financing. It is not our suggestion, however, to privatize the supply of education. There is no evidence that a private sector is more efficient or responsive than a public sector when the latter has motivated, well-paid employees, who have the right incentives. On the other hand, the inability to reform the public system causing its collapse would, *de facto*, induce the market to offer an alternative, at the cost of sacrificing social justice and equality of opportunity.

REFERENCES

Abraham, K. G. and Farber H. S. (1987), 'Job Duration, Seniority, and Earnings', *American Economic Review*, 77(3): 278–97.

Acemoglu, D. (1998), 'Why Do New Technologies Complement Skills? Directed Technical Change and Wage Inequality', *Quarterly Journal of Economics* (November), 113(4): 1055–89.

—— (2002), 'Directed Technical Change', *Review of Economic Studies* (October), 69(4): 781–810.

—— (2003), 'Cross-country Inequality Trends', *Economic Journal*, 113, F121–F149.

—— and Pischke, J. S. (1999a), 'The Structure of Wages and Investment in General Training', *Journal of Political Economy*, vol. 107, Issue 3 (June): 539–72.

—— and —— (1999b), 'Beyond Becker: Training in Imperfect Labor Markets', *Economic Journal Features*, 109, F112–F142.

—— and Zilibotti, F. (2001), 'Productivity Differences', *Quarterly Journal of Economics*, (May), 116(2): 563–606.

Aghion P. and Howitt P. (1992), 'A Model of Growth Through Creative Destruction', *Econometrica*, 60: 323–51.

Albrecht, J. and Vroman, S. (2002), 'A Matching Model with Endogenous Skill Requirements', *International Economic Review*, 43: 283–305.

Altonji, J. G. and Shakotko, R. A. (1987), 'Do Wages Rise with Job Seniority?', *Review of Economic Studies*, LIV, 437–59.

Angrist, J. and Lavy, V. (1999), 'Using Maimonides' Rule to Estimate the Effect of Class Size on Scholastic Achievement', *Quarterly Journal of Economics*, 114: 533–75.

—— and Kugler, A. (2003), 'Protective or Counter-Productive? Labor Market Institutions and the Effect of Immigration on EU natives', *Economic Journal*, vol. 113: 302–31.

Axelsson, R. and Westerlund, O. (1998), 'A panel study of migration, self-selection and household real income', *Journal of Population Economics*, vol. 11, no. 1: 113–26.

Barcelo, C. (2002), 'Housing Tenure and Labour Mobility: A Comparison Across European Countries'. Mimeo CEMFI, December.

Barro R. J. and Lee J. W. (1996), 'International Measures of Schooling Years and Schooling Quality', *American Economic Review*. Papers and Proceeding 86(2): 218–23.

—— and —— (2001), 'International Data on Educational Attainment: Updates and Implications', *Oxford Economic Papers*, 53: 541–63.

Beaton, A., Mullis, I., Martin, M., Gonzalez, E., et al. (1996), 'Mathematics Achievement in the Middle School Years: IEA's Third International Mathematics and Science Study'. Center for the Study of Testing, Evaluation, and Educational Policy, Boston College.

Becker G. (1964), *Human Capital*. The University of Chicago Press, 3rd edn (1993).

Becker, S., Ichino, A. and Peri, G. (2004), 'How Large is the Brain Drain from Italy?', *Giornale degli Economisti e Annali di Economia*, vol. 63, no. 1: 1–32.

Benabou, R. (2000), 'Unequal Societies: Income Distribution and the Social Contract', *American Economic Review*, vol. 90(1): 96–129.

—— (2005), 'Inégalité, technologie et contrat social', keynote speech Banque du Canada-Congrès de la Société Canadienne d'Économie, Charlevoix, May 12–13.

Bender, S., Dustmann, C., Margolis, D. and Meghir, C. (2002), 'Worker Displacement in France and Germany'. In: P. J. Kuhn 'Losing work, moving on: international perspectives on worker displacement', Kalamazoo: Upjohn Institute for Employment Research, 375–470.

Benhabib, J. and M. M. Spiegel (1994), 'The Role of Human Capital in Economic Development: Evidence from Aggregate Cross-Country Data', *Journal of Monetary Economics*, 34: 143–73.

Ben Porath, Y. (1967), 'The Production of Human Capital and the Life-Cycle of Earnings', *Journal of Political Economy*, vol. 75(4): 352–65.

Bertola, G. (1999), 'Microeconomic Perspectives on Aggregate Labor Markets'. In O. Ashenfelter and D. Card (eds), *Handbook of Labor Economics*, vol. 3B, Amsterdam: North-Holland, 2985–3028.

Bertola G. and Ichino, A. (1995), 'Wage Inequality and Unemployment: United States vs. Europe', NBER Macroannuals, 13–66.

Bertola, G. and Rogerson, R. (1997), 'Institutions and labour reallocation', *European Economic Review*, vol. 41, Issue 6, 1147–71.

Bils, M. and Klenow, P. J. (2000), 'Does Schooling Cause Growth?', *American Economic Review*, (December), 90(5): 1160–83.

Björklund, A., Clark, M., Edin, P-A., et al. (2005), *The Market Comes to Education in Sweden*, Russell Sage Foundation.

Blanchard, O. and Katz, L. (1992), 'Regional Evolutions', *Brookings Papers on Economic Activity*, 1: 1–61.

—— and Wolfers, J. (2000), 'The Role of Shocks and Institutions in the Rise of European Unemployment: The Aggregate Evidence', *Economic Journal*, 110, C1–C33.

Blau, F. and Kahn, L. (2001), 'Do Cognitive Test Scores Explain Higher US Wage Inequality?' NBER Working Paper, No. 8210.

Blinder, A. S. and Weiss, Y. (1976), 'Human Capital and Labor Supply: A Synthesis', *Journal of Political Economy*, vol. 84, No. 3: 449–72.

Boeri, T. (2002), *Structural Change, Welfare Systems and Labour Reallocation*. Oxford: Oxford University Press.

—— and Brücker, H. (2001), 'Eastern Enlargement and EU-Labour Markets: Perceptions, Challenges and Opportunities', IZA, dp. 256.

Borjas, G. J. (1987), 'Self-selection and the Earnings of Immigrants', *American Economic Review*, 77(4), 531–53.

—— (1999), *Heaven's Door*, Princeton University Press, Princeton and Oxford.

—— (2003), 'The Labor Demand Curve is Downward Sloping: Reexamining the Impact of Immigration on the Labor Market', *Quarterly Journal of Economics*, vol. CXVIII(4): 1335–74.

—— Freeman, R. and Katz, L. (1997), 'How Much Do Immigration and Trade Affect Labor Market Outcomes?', *Brookings Papers on Economic Activity*, (1): 1–90.

Bound J., Turner, S. and Walsh, P. (2006), 'Internationalization of US Doctoral Education', mss., University of Michigan (April).

Branstetter, L. (2001), 'Are Knowledge Spillovers International or Intranational in Scope? Microeconometric Evidence from the US and Japan', *Journal of International Economics*, 53: 1: 53–79.

Burda, M. (1992), 'A Note on Firing Costs and Severance Benefits in Equilibrium Unemployment', *Scandinavian Journal of Economics*, 94(3): 479–89.

Caballero, R. and Hammour, M (1998), 'The Macroeconomics of Specificity', *Journal of Political Economy*, 106(4): 724–67.

Card, D. (1990), 'The Impact of the Mariel Boatlift on the Miami Labor Market', *Industrial and Labor Relations Review*, XLIII: 245–57.

—— (2001), 'Immigrant Inflows, Native Outflows, and the Local labor Market Impacts of Higher Immigration', *Journal of Labor Economics*, XIX: 22–64.

—— and Di Nardo, J. (2000), 'Do Immigrants Inflow Lead to Native Outflows?', NBER Working Paper, No. 7578.

Caselli F. (2006), 'The Missing Input: Accounting for Cross-Country Income Differences'. In *Handbook of Economic Growth* (eds) P. Aghion and S. Durlauf.

Charlot, Olivier. (2003), 'Education et chômage dans les modèles d'appariement', thése de doctorat, Université d'Aix-Marseille II, Paris I.

Clark, R. L. and Ogawa, N. (1992), 'Reconsidering Tenure and Earnings Profile of Japanese Men', *American Economic Review*, 82: 336–45.

Cole, H. L. and Rogerson, R. (1999), 'Can the Mortensen-Pissarides Matching Model Match the Business-Cycle Facts?', *International Economic Review*, vol. 40, no. 4: 933–59 (27).

Daveri, F. (2002), 'The New Economy in Europe, 1992–2001'. *Oxford Review of Economic Policy*, Oxford University Press, vol. 18(3): 345–62.

Davis, S., Haltiwanger, J. and Shuh, S. (1996), *Job Creation and Job Destruction*, MIT Press, Cambridge, MA.

Decressin, J. and Fatàs, A. (1995), 'Regional Labor Market Dynamics in Europe', *European Economic Review* (December).

De La Fuente, A. and Domenech, R. (2001), 'Educational Attainment in the OECD 1960–1995', Spain, mss. Departamento de Análisis Económico, Universidad de Valencia.

—— and —— (2001), 'Schooling Data, Technological Diffusion and the Neoclassical Model', *American Economic Review*, vol. 91, 2, Papers and Proceedings, 323–7.

DeLong, J. B, Goldin, C. and Katz, L. (2003), 'Sustaining U.S. Economic Growth'. In H Aaron, J. Linday, and P. Nicola, (eds), Agenda for the Nation. Brookings Institution, 17–60.

Devroye, D. and Freeman, R. (2002), 'Does Inequality in Skills Explain Inequality of Earnings in Advanced Countries?' Discussion Paper, no. 552, Centre for Economic Performance.

Dolado, J. J., Jansen, M. and Jimeno, J. F. (2004), 'A Matching Model of Crowding-Out and On-the-Job Search', Mimeo, Universidad Carlos III, Madrid.

Dornbusch, R., Gentilini A. and F. Giavazzi (2000), 'Italian Labor Force Participation: Disguised Unemployment on Campus', Mimeo Uni. Bocconi University.

Duncan, G. and Hoffman, S. D. (1981), 'The incidence and wage effects of over-education', *Economics of Education Review*, 1(1): 75–86.

EEAG (2003), 'Report on the European Economy 2003', European Economic Advisory Group (EEAG) at CESifo, Munich.

Elley, W. (1992), 'How in the World do Students Read? IEA Study of Reading Literacy', IEA, Hamburg.

European Commission (2003), 'Third European Report on Science and Technology Indicators'. Directorate-General for Research, Bruxelles.

Falaris, E. M. (1987), 'A Nested Logit Migration Model with Selectivity', *International Economic Review*, vol. 28(2): 429–43.

Freeman, R. B. (1976), *The Overeducated American*, Academic Press, New York.

Gary-Bobo, R. and Trannoy, Al. (2005), 'Should we Raise Tuition-fees?', *Revue Française d'Économie*, 19(3): 189–237.

Gomez-Salvador, R., Messina, J. and Vallanti, G. (2004), 'Job Flows Dynamics and Firing Restrictions: Evidence from Europe', Mimeo.

Gordon, R. (2004), 'Why was Europe Left at the Station When America's Productivity Locomotive Departed', NBER WP 10661 (August).

Gottschalk, P. and Joyce, M. (1998), 'Cross-national Differences in the Rise in Earnings Inequality: Market and Institutional Factors', *Review of Economics and Statistics*, 80: 489–502.

Gould, E. (2002), 'Rising Wage Inequality, Comparative Advantage, and the Growing Importance of General Skills in the United States', *Journal of Labor Economics* (January).

Gould, E., Moav, O. and Weinberg, B. (2001), 'Precautionnary Demand for Education, Inequality and Technological Progress', *Journal of Labor Economics* (January).

Griliches, Z. (1994), 'Productivity, R&D and the Data Constraint', *American Economic Review*, no. 84(1): 1–23.

Groot, W. and Maassen van den Brink, H. (2000), 'Over-Education in the Labor Market: a Meta-Analysis', *Economics of Education Review*, 19(2): 149–58.

Grossman, G. and Helpman, E. (1991), 'Innovation and Growth in the Global Economy', The MIT Press, Cambridge, MA.

Gurgand, M. (2005), *Économie de l'éducation*, Collection Repères (ed). La Découverte, Paris.

Hanson, G. H. and Spilimbergo, A. (1999), 'Illegal Immigration, Border Enforcement and Relative Wages: Evidence from Apprehensions at the US–Mexico Border', *American Economic Review*, 89: 1337–57.

Hanushek, E. (1997), 'Assessing the Effects of School Resources on Student Performance: An Update', Educational Evaluation and Policy Analysis, 19: 141–64.

—— Kimko D. D. (2000), 'Schooling, Labor Force Quality, and the Growth of Nations', *American Economic Review*, vol. 90: 1184–208.

Hartog, J. (2000), 'Over-education and Earnings. Where Are We, Where Should We Go?', *Economics of Education Review*, 19(2): 131–48.

Hashimoto, M. and Raisian, J. (1985), 'Employment Tenure and Earnings Profiles in Japan and the United States', *American Economic Review*, vol. 75, Issue 4 (Sept.): 721–35.

—— and —— (1985), 'Employment Tenure and Earnings Profiles in Japan and the United States: A Reply', *American Economic Review*, vol. 82, Issue 1, 346–54.

Hassler, J., Storesletten K., Rodríguez Mora, S. and Zilibotti, F. (2005), 'A Positive Theory of Geographic Mobility and Social Insurance', *International Economic Review*, vol. 46, 1: 263–303.

——, —— et al. (2000), 'Unemployment, Specialization, and Collective Preferences for Social Insurance'. In D. Cohen, T. Piketty and G. Saint-Paul (eds), *The New Economics of Inequalities*, CEPR, London and Oxford: Oxford University Press.

Hedges, L., Laine, R. and Greenwald, R. (1994), 'Does Money Matter? A Meta-Analysis of Studies of the Effects of Differential School Inputs on Student Outcomes', *Education Researcher*, 23: 5–14.

Ichino, A. and Riphan, R. (2004), 'Absenteeism and Employment Protection: Three Case Studies', *Swedish Economic Policy Review*, 11(1), 95–114.

Jaffe, A. and Trajtenberg, M. (2002), 'Patents, Citations and Innovations', MIT Press, Cambridge, MA.

Jones C. (2002), 'Sources of US Economic Growth in a World of Ideas', *American Economic Review*, vol. 92(1): 220–39 (March).

Jovanovic, B. (1979), 'Job Matching and the Theory of Turnover', *Journal of Political Economy*, 87(5): 972–90.

Katz, L. and Autor, D. (1999), 'Changes in the Wage Structure and Earnings Inequality'. In O. Ashenfelter and D. Card (eds), *Handbook of Labor Economics*, vol. 3A, 1463–548, North-Holland.

—— and Murphy, K. L. (1992), 'Changes in Relative Wages 1963–1987: Supply and Demand Factors', *Quarterly Journal of Economics*, 107: 35–78.

Kletzer, L. G. (1989), 'Returns to Seniority After Permanent Job Loss', *The American Economic Review*, vol. 79, no. 3: 536–43 (June).

—— (1998), 'Job Displacement', *Journal of Economic Perspectives*, vol. 12, no. 1: 115–36.

Klenow P. and A. Rodríguez-Clare (2006), 'Externalities and Growth'. In *Handbook of Economic Growth*, Philippe Aghion and Steven Durlauf (eds), North-Holland Press, Amsterdam.

Knapp, T. A., White, N. E. and Clark, D. E. (2001), 'A Nested Logit Approach to Household Mobility', *Journal of Regional Science*, 41(1): 1–22.

Kristensen, N. and Westergard-Nielsen, N. (2004), 'Does Job Satisfaction Lead to Job Mobility?', IZA Discussion Paper 1026 (February).

Krueger, A. B. (1999), 'Experimental Estimates of Educational Production Functions', *Quarterly Journal of Economics*, 115: 1239–85.

—— (2003), 'Economic Considerations and Class Size', *Economic Journal*, 113: 34–63.

Krueger, D. and Kumar, K. (2003), 'US–Europe Differences in Technology-Driven Growth: Quantifying the Role of Education', *Journal of Monetary Economics*, vol. 51(1): 161–90.

—— and —— (2004), 'Skill-Specific Rather Than General Education: A Reason for US–Europe Growth Differences?', *Journal of Economic Growth*, vol. 9(2): 167–207.

Krugman, P. R. and Obstfelfd, M. (2000), *International Economics, Theory and Policy*, 5th international edn, Addison-Wesley.

Kuhn (2002), 'Losing Work, Moving On: International Perspectives on Worker Displacement', Kalamazoo: Upjohn Institute for Employment Research.

Kwiatkowski, E., Socha Mieczyslaw, W. and Sztanderska, U, 'Labour Market Flexibility and Employment Security in Poland', Employment Paper 2001/28, ILO, Geneva.

Lamo, A. and Messina, J. (2006), 'Education Mismatch in the New EU Countries', Mimeo, European Central Bank.

Lamo, A., Messina, J. and Wasmer, E. (2006), 'Are Specific Skills an Obstacle to Labor Market Adjustment? Theory and Application to the EU Enlargement', Working Paper No. 585. European Central Bank.

Layard, R. and Nickell, S. (1999). 'Labour Market Institutions and Economic Performance'. *Handbook of Labor Economics*, vol. 3.C, (eds) O. Ashenfelter and D. Card, Amsterdam: North-Holland.

Lazear, E. P. (1990). 'Job Security Provisions and Employment', *Quarterly Journal of Economics*, 105(3): 699–726.

—— (2003), 'Firm-Specific Human Capital: A Skill-Weights Approach', NBER Working Paper No. 9679 (May).

Lefranc, A. (2003), 'Labor Market Dynamics and Wage Losses of Displaced Workers in France and the United-States', The William Davidson Institute, WP No. 614, Michigan University.

—— (2003), 'On the Sensitivity of Returns to Seniority to the Measurement of Earnings', *International Journal of Manpower*, 24(7), 789–811.

Leuven, E., Oosterbeck, H. and Van Ophem, E. (2004), 'Explaining International Differences in Male Wage Inequality by Differences in Demand and Supply of Skills', *Economic Journal*, 114: 466–86.

Ljungqvist, L. and Sargent, T. J. (1998), 'The European Unemployment Dilemma', *Journal of Political Economy*, 106: 514–50.

—— and —— (2002), 'The European Employment Experience', Paper presented at the Center for Economic Performance Conference 'The Macroeconomics of Labor Markets', (May).

Loewenstein, M. and Spletzer, J. (1999), 'General and Specific Training: Evidence and Implications', *Journal of Human Resources*, vol. 34(4): 710–33 (Autumn).

Lucas R. (1988), 'On the Mechanics of Economic Development', *Journal of Monetary Economics*, 22: 3–42.

Malcomson, J. M. (2000), 'Individual Employment Contracts', *Handbook of Labor Economics*, vol. 3. B, (eds) D. Card and O. Ashenfelter, Amsterdam: North-Holland.

Mankiw, N. G., Romer, D. and Weil, D. N. (1992), 'A Contribution to the Empirics of Economic Growth', *Quarterly Journal of Economics*, 107(2): 407–37 (May).

Mendes de Oliveira, M., Santos, M. C. and Kiker, B. F. (2000), 'The Role of Human Capital and Technological Change in Over-education', *Economics of Education Review*, 19(2): 199–206.

Messina, J. (2006), 'Mismatch, Over-qualification and Labour Market Performance'. Mimeo, Università di Salerno.

Ministry of Economy, Labour and Social Policy, Poland (2003), 'Poland 2003. Report Labour Market, and Social Security', Warsaw.

Mortensen, D. T. and Pissarides, C. A. (1994), 'Job Creation and Job Destruction in the Theory of Unemployment', *Review of Economic Studies*, 64: 397–415.

—— and —— (1999), 'Job reallocation, Employment Fluctuations and Unemployment', *Handbook of Macroeconomics*, (eds) J. Taylor and M. Woodford, Amsterdam: North-Holland.

Mundell, R. A. (1961), 'A Theory of Optimum Currency Areas', *American Economic Review*, 51: 657–65.

Munz, R. (2004), 'Migrants, Labor Markets and Integration in Europe: A Comparative Analysis', Global Migration Perspectives, Discussion Paper no. 16. Global Commission on International Migration.

Nathanelsson, K. (2003), 'The Development of the Supply of Skill Across Countries and the Relation to Wage Inequality', mss. Department of Economics, Uppsala University.

Nelson, R. R. and E. S. Phelps (1966), 'Investment in Humans, Technological Diffusion, and Economic Growth', *American Economic Review*, 56: 69–75.

OECD (1993), 'Education at a Glance', Organization for Economic Cooperation and Development, Paris.

—— (1995), 'Education at a Glance', OECD, Paris.

—— (1996), 'Education at a Glance', OECD, Paris.

—— (1999a), 'Employment Outlook', OECD, Paris.

—— (1999b), 'Preparing Youth for the 21st Century: the Transition from Education to the Labour Market', OECD, Paris.

—— (2003), 'Education at a Glance', OECD, Paris.

—— (2004a), 'Education at a Glance', OECD, Paris.

—— (2004b), 'Learning for Tomorrow's World: First Results from PISA 2003', OECD, Paris.

—— and Statistics Canada (1995), 'Literacy, Economy, and Society. Results of the First International Adult Literacy Survey', OECD and Statistics Canada, Paris.

Okun, A. (1975), 'Equality and Efficiency: The Big Tradeoff'. Washington DC: Brookings Institution.

Padoa Schioppa, F. (ed.) (1991), *Mismatch and Labour Mobility*, Cambridge: Cambridge University Press.

Pakes, A. and Griliches, Z (1980), 'Patents and R&D at the Firm Level: a First Report', *Economic Letters*, 5: 377–81.

Peri, G. (2004), 'Knowledge Flows and Productivity', *Rivista di Política Económica*, vol. March–April.

—— (2005), 'Determinants of Knowledge Flows and their Effects on Innovation', *Review of Economics and Statistics*, vol. 87, Issue 2.

Phelps, E. S. (2003), 'Economic Underperformance in Continental Europe: A Prospering Economy Runs on the Dynamism from its Economic Institutions', Lecture, Royal Institute for International Affairs, London, March 18.

Prescott, E. (2005), 'Why Do Americans Work So Much More Than Europeans?' Federal Reserve Bank of Minneapolis Quarterly Bulletin, vol. 28 no. 1.

Psacharopoulos, P. (2005), 'Public versus Private University Systems', CESIfo DICE Report, 4/2004.

Rogerson, R. and Schindler, M. (2002), 'The Welfare Costs of Worker Displacement', *Journal of Monetary Economics*, vol. 49, Issue 6: 1213–34.

Roland, G. (2000), 'Transitions and Economics: Politics, Markets and Firms', The MIT Press.

129

Romer, P. (1990), 'Endogenous Technological Change', *Journal of Political Economy*, 98: 71–102.

Samuelson, P. (2004), 'Why Ricardo and Mill Rebut and Confirm Arguments of Mainstream Economists Supporting Globalization?', *Journal of Economic Perspectives*, vol. 18(3): 135–46.

Saint-Paul, G. (2000), 'The Political Economy of Labour Market Institutions', Oxford: Oxford University Press.

—— (2004), 'The Brain Drain: Some Evidence from European Expatriates in the United States', IZA Discussion Paper, No. 1310.

Serrano, L. (2003), 'Measurement Error in Schooling Data: the OECD case', *Applied Economics Letters*, 10: 73–5.

Sicherman, N. and Galor, O. (1990), 'A Theory of Career Mobility', *Journal of Political Economy*, 98(1): 169–92.

Spence, M. (1973), 'Job Market Signalling'. *Quarterly Journal of Economics*, 87(3): 355–74.

Solow, R. (1956), 'A Contribution to the Theory of Economic Growth', *Quarterly Journal of Economics*, 70: 65–94.

Tatsiramos, K. (2004), 'Geographical Labour Mobility and Unemployment Insurance in Europe', IZA Discussion Paper 1253 (August).

Topel, R. (1991), 'Specific Capital, Mobility, and Wages: Wages Rise with Job Seniority', *Journal of Political Economy*, vol. 99, no. 1: 145–76.

UNESCO (1999), Operational Manual for ISCED-1997 (International Standard Classification of Education), 1st edn (June).

Verdugo, R. and Verdugo, N. (1989), 'The Impact of Surplus Schooling on Earnings: Some Additional Findings', *Journal of Resources*, 24: 629–43.

Wasmer, E. (2002), 'Interpreting Europe and US Labour Markets Differences: the Specificity of Human Capital Investments', CEPR, WP 3780 (Aug.), (under revision).

—— (2005), 'Short-Run Effects of Enlargement, Panel Contribution', Collective volume, ECB-CEPR conference. What explains the pattern of labour supply in Europe? Gomez-Salvador, Lamo, Petrongolo, Ward and Wasmer (eds). Edward Elgar Publishing, CEPR-ECB.

—— (2006), 'General vs. Specific Skills in Labor Markets with Search Frictions and Firing Costs', *American Economic Review*, June, 96(3), 811–31.

Young, A. (1995), 'The Tyranny of Numbers: Confronting the Statistical Realities of the East Asian Growth Experience', *Quarterly Journal of Economics*, 110: 641–80.

APPENDICES

A.2 Appendix to Chapter 2. Data

List of countries in the IALS

Belgium (Flemish community, excluding the city of Brussels), Czech Republic, Denmark, Finland, Germany, Hungary, Ireland, Italy, Netherlands, Poland, Sweden, Switzerland (French and German communities), the United Kingdom (Great Britain and Northern Ireland), and the United States.

Data collection in the IALS

The data in the IALS were obtained via stratified sampling. Whenever using these data we weight the estimates using the sampling weights provided in the survey.

A.4 Appendix to Chapter 4. Data

Data definition

We define the variable *Recentmove* = 1 if the household has moved within 12 months preceding the interview and 0 otherwise; and *Recentmove3* = 1 if the household has moved within 36 months preceding the interview and 0 otherwise. We also define *Bigrmove* = 1 if *Recentmove* = 1 and the household came from another location; *Bigrmove3* = 1 if *Recentmove3* = 1 and the household came from another location; *BigrmoveJob* = 1 if *Bigrmove* = 1 and the move was job-related; *Bigrmove3Job* = 1 if *Bigrmove3* = 1 and the move was job-related.

Selection model

$$E(Y|M = 1) = X\beta + \alpha + Z\delta + E(\varepsilon|M = 1)$$
$$= X\beta + \alpha + Z\delta + \rho\sigma_\varepsilon\phi(W\gamma)/\Phi(W\gamma) \quad\quad [A1]$$

$$E(Y|M = 0) = X\beta + Z\delta + E(\varepsilon|M = 0) = X\beta$$
$$+ Z\delta + \rho\sigma_\varepsilon\phi(W\gamma)/(1 - \Phi(W\gamma)) \quad\quad [A2]$$

and thus the difference is

$$\Delta Y_{E,imp} = \alpha + \rho\sigma_\varepsilon\phi(W\gamma)/\{\Phi(W\gamma)\,[1 - \Phi(W\gamma)]\} \quad\quad [A3]$$

A.5 Appendix to Chapters 4 and 5. ECHP data

More details can be found in Peracchi (2002) and below.

Hourly wages net of taxes are calculated by dividing monthly net wages by monthly hours worked. In order to facilitate cross-country comparisons we use the PPP exchange rates provided with ECHP to convert wages into 2001 PPP units and then deflate them by using the National Consumer Price Indices.

Years of education are not directly observable from ECHP. Instead, education is broadly aggregated into three categories that report the maximum degree obtained by the individual: less than secondary, secondary and tertiary education. It also contains information regarding the year of end of education from which a proxy for the number of years of education can be constructed. We have crossed this information with the above-mentioned three categorical variables of education to minimize the noise, and we corrected for outliers.

Polish data. The Polish Labour Force Survey is a household survey that collects detailed information on individual characteristics. It started in 1992 as a full panel survey and, due to the large attrition, its structure was changed into a rotating panel in 1993. It uses the rotation scheme 2-(2)-2, in which each person is surveyed for two consecutive quarters, excluded for another two quarters, and then included again for two more quarters to be excluded definitively afterwards. Therefore, the maximum number of observations available per individual is 4.[1] The overall sampling fraction is .14 per cent of private households and includes all the members of each surveyed household older than 15.

---

[1] Each quarter, 25 per cent of the sample is interviewed for the first time, 50 per cent were already interviewed in the previous quarter, and the other 25 per cent participated one year ago.

Table A5.1 Definition of variables: EU-15

marry	Dummy Variable, 1 if worker is married
female	Dummy Variable, 1 if worker is female
hhsize	Number of members of the household
yeduc	Years of completed education
exper	Potential experience: age–years of education–6
tend2	Dummy Variable, 1 if worker's tenure is >1 & $<=5$
tend3	Dummy Variable, 1 if worker's tenure is >5 & $<=10$
tend4	Dummy Variable, 1 if worker's tenure is >10
unem	Dummy Variable, 1 if worker is ever unemployed in the last 5 years
nunem	Dummy Variable, 1 if worker is unemployed more than once in the last 5 years
lunem	Dummy Variable, 1 if worker is unemployed for more than a year during the last 5 years
indd2	Dummy Variable, 1 if worker is employed in 'mining, quarrying, and utilities supply'
indd3	Dummy Variable, 1 if worker is employed in 'manufacturing'
indd4	Dummy Variable, 1 if worker is employed in 'construction'
indd5	Dummy Variable, 1 if worker is employed in 'wholesale and retail trade'
indd6	Dummy Variable, 1 if worker is employed in 'transport, storage and communication'
indd7	Dummy Variable, 1 if worker is employed in 'FIRE'
indd8	Dummy Variable, 1 if worker is employed in 'public administration and education'
indd9	Dummy Variable, 1 if worker is employed in 'health, social work and other'
ocud2	Dummy Variable, 1 if worker is employed as 'professionals'
ocud3	Dummy Variable, 1 if worker is employed as 'technicians and associate professionals'
ocud4	Dummy Variable, 1 if worker is employed as 'clerks'
ocud5	Dummy Variable, 1 if worker is employed as 'service workers, shop and market sales workers'
ocud6	Dummy Variable, 1 if worker is employed as 'skilled agricultural and fishery workers'
ocud7	Dummy Variable, 1 if worker is employed as 'craft and related trades workers'
ocud8	Dummy Variable, 1 if worker is employed as 'plant and machine operators, assemblers'
ocud9	Dummy Variable, 1 if worker is employed as 'elementary occupations'
yd2	Dummy Variable, 1 if year is 1995
yd3	Dummy Variable, 1 if year is 1996
yd4	Dummy Variable, 1 if year is 1997
yd5	Dummy Variable, 1 if year is 1998
yd6	Dummy Variable, 1 if year is 1999
yd7	Dummy Variable, 1 if year is 2000
yd8	Dummy Variable, 1 if year is 2001
cd2	Dummy Variable, 1 if country is France
cd3	Dummy Variable, 1 if country is UK
cd4	Dummy Variable, 1 if country is Italy
cd5	Dummy Variable, 1 if country is Spain

The variables definitions are quite harmonized with the European Labour Force Survey; the PLFS follows the international classifications of employment status and of occupations. Information on wages is far from ideal as, apparently, people are quite reluctant to disclose this information. Another peculiarity about wages is that, in fact, the PLFS does not collect information on wages but on monthly net remuneration, although for simplicity we will refer to the monthly net remuneration as wages. Years of education are not available as such, but the levels of education are disaggregated into 7 categories and we have assigned to them the years of education according to the current education system in Poland.

COMMENTS

*Juan J. Dolado**

It is a pleasure to comment upon this thoughtful report on a very important and timely issue: the urgent need for changes in the education systems of many countries, especially those in Europe. If Europe wants to retain its competitive edge in a rapidly changing world, investments and efficiency improvements in education systems are essential in achieving sustainable economic well-being. The idea that Europe still competes mostly with developing countries that are intensive in low-skilled labour at low wages is becoming obsolete. Countries like China or India are increasing the quality of their labour force's skills at a very rapid pace. The combination of higher skills with still reasonably low costs is accelerating the delocalization process of European firms towards these developing countries, giving rise to social alarm among workers. To offset these undesirable consequences, education systems must be made more efficient and flexible in making high skills accessible to a wider range of people.

While the challenges and solutions seem to be clear, it is not always possible to find strong evidence about how the education systems should adapt to a changing macroeconomic environment. The report fills this gap by being both extremely informative and innovative, and hence very useful both for non-specialists and specialists in the field of the economics of education.

Non-specialist readers will appreciate the availability of large statistical information about the characteristics and outcomes of different education systems in OECD countries, where particular attention is paid to the Europe–US differentials. Both this wealth of information and the executive summaries at the end of each chapter will provide them with an excellent overview of the relevant issues that are needed to understand the key educational challenges that European countries face in a global economy ruled by information and knowledge.

* Departamento de Economía, Universidad Carlos III de Madrid.

As regards specialists, I find that a major contribution of this report is that it extends beyond the conventional descriptive content which is typically found in other education reports by international institutions. It does so by developing a broad range of original theoretical hypotheses—together with rich empirical evidence about their plausibility based on a large number of micro-datasets—in order to explain the economic effects of education systems on a wide array of socio-economic outcomes (e.g., wage dispersion, skill accumulation, productivity, within-country and international mobility, over-education and skill mismatch, etc.). Among these new ideas, I find particularly interesting the common theme in several chapters stressing the interaction between the strictness of employment protection legislation in an economy, and the incentives of its workers to invest in specific (rather than in general) skills, and how the education systems in countries with this type of institution reinforce these investments. This idea provides a novel alternative to the better-known agument which relies exclusively upon the interaction between unemployment benefit systems and negative supply shocks as the basic explanation of the unfavourable evolution of the European unemployment rate relative to the US unemployment rate since the late 1970s, in stark contrast to the better European perfomance during the post-war period.[1] To the extent that important reforms of unemployment benefit systems have taken place in several European countries during the 1990s, the latter argument has probably become less relevant and, therefore, this new explanation might make more sense.

The departure point of the report is the assertion that the large investment deficit of the European school system, in relation to the US (and to a number of countries with large investment in education, like Canada, Japan or South Korea), lies in a sizeable unfavourable gap in tertiary education. Whereas in 1960, 5 per cent of the population in Europe had attained a college degree, against 8 per cent in the US, four decades later the corresponding proportions are 22 per cent and 38 per cent, respectively. Thus, despite the strong education drive in both areas, the gap in favour of the US has risen from 3 to 16 percentage points. Moreover, the budgetary effort made in almost equalizing the European enrolments rates in primary and secondary education with those in the US, seems to have produced a chronic fatigue in the investment catch-up process at the tertiary level. In effect, whereas expenditure in higher education as a proportion of GDP in Europe (1.1 percent in 2004) has stagnated or even

---

[1] See, e.g. Blanchard and Wolfers (2000) and Ljungqvist and Sargent (1998, 2004).

fallen over the last decade, it has increased to 2.7 per cent of GDP in the US. As the report stresses, an important factor behind this gap is the much larger contribution of private expenditure to the financing of higher education and R&D in North America than in Europe, a difference which is behind the much larger capacity of the former economy to attract high skill labour.

As a consequence of these enrolment and financing gaps, the less egalitarian and more flexible US school system has been able to produce a more skilled labour force with much higher geographical and occupational mobility, endowing workers with more adaptable (general) skills to bear the risks of the higher turbulence that characterizes modern economies. Further, as a consequence of its more dispersed wage structure, it has become a magnet for talent, attracting the brightest students and researchers in the world to its universities. In contrast, the more egalitarian and rigid European post-school system faces large difficulties in attracting private funding, suffers from an important 'brain drain' phenomenon and has given rise to a slow transition from education to work. Consequently, workers suffer from persistent low mobility and high mismatch, a problem which is further aggravated in those European economies with stringent job protection legislation where two-tier reforms facilitating the generalized use of short fixed-tem contracts has led to excessive workers' turnover and lower productivity.

In view of this carefully documented diagnosis, the report concludes with a call for urgent reforms of higher education in Europe. Despite clear signs of under-financing in some specific countries, in general it is not just a matter of increasing public financing. Rather, what is badly needed is a drastic improvement of its efficiency and competitiveness in order to attract the private funding which exists in the US and is missing in Europe. This requires the elimination of all unnecessary bureaucratic barriers— including the reluctance to raise tuition fees or to eliminate the strong endogamy in the selection process of faculty members—which have drastically reduced the signalling content of education in Europe since the 1980s. More than additional public investments, these barriers are the real obstacles that have prevented a higher growth in the supply of a high-skilled labour force, precisely at a time when skill-biased technical change and trade globalization have led to a large acceleration in the demand for high skill.

Although I strongly agree with most of the analyses and the policy conclusions drawn by the authors, let me just finish these comments by raising a couple of issues that I found missing in the report.

First, the report is, on the whole, silent about the reasons behind some European success stories at the school level, since one should not forget that Europe is far from being homogenous in terms of its education systems. Finland (as Canada and Korea outside Europe) has consistently topped the podium of excellence in the PISA assessments, whereas Germany (as also other major European economies, like France, Italy or Spain, and even the US) has persistently achieved mediocre results. Much has been written in the media and other reports about the Finnish success against the German failure (schools with integrated and individual pathways against dual and tracked systems, 'nationwide' versus 'school' examinations, the role of chartered schools in secondary education, the absortion of immigrants' children in the school system, etc.). However, in my view, most of those discussions are highly rhetorical and it is hard to find any conclusive evidence—besides investment differences in education—about tangible factors behind success. Given the effort made by the authors in providing convincing evidence for other education outcomes, I really found some analysis on this relevant one to be missing.

Secondly, there is a lack of a deeper discussion on what education practices make the US system more conducive to providing a more adaptable (less specialized) curriculum to economic turbulence, as compared to Europe where workers over-invest in specific skills. The authors only devote two lines to refer the reader to previous work by Krueger and Kumar where vocational training studies—much more prominent in Europe than in the US—are identified as the key education programme supplying specific skills. I do not find this assumption too convincing. As stated in Chapter 5, wage penalties arise mainly from mismatch and I do not see why the degree of mismatch should be larger for someone with a vocational training degree (say, an electrician) than with a secondary or tertiary general one (say, in humanities). In countries where an unrestricted access to college education has taken place—either because youth unemployment was high or because tuition rates are very low, as for example, is the case in Italy or Spain—there is evidence that a blue-collar worker with a shorter vocational training degree may have higher wage returns to education and more job offers than a white-collar worker with a mediocre and long college degree. By contrast, I believe that a more important difference with respect to Europe is the availability of college 'majors' in the US. It is often the case when one reads the academic record of American students applying to graduate programmes that they have followed majors in seemingly unrelated issues like, say, history of art and chemistry, a choice that would be unthinkable in the very rigid European curriculum system. Thus, whereas US tertiary-level students really get specialized when they finish college and enter graduate or professional schools, at around 22 years of age, European undergraduates start specializing in a particular discipline (say, physics or humanities) when they are much younger, straight from finishing high school at 18 or 19 years of age. This implies that the more mature American students, who have been able to diversify their preferences in college, are probably much more apt to specialize successfully in a given discipline than their less-experienced counterparts in Europe, a conjecture which is supported by the much higher dropout rate from college in some European countries than in the US (e. g. 60% in Italy against 30% in the US). In this respect, let me point out that, besides the crucial aim of facilitating international mobility, one of the main rationales behind the harmonization of diplomas from different education systems in Europe under the ongoing Bologna Process (which the report ignores) should be to shorten the excessive duration of basic university degrees which still take at least 5 years in countries like Germany, Italy or Spain, as opposed to 3 years in the UK. If agreement on this issue is finally reached, this should facilitate the introduction of a more menu-choice-based system, akin to the 'majors' system in the US. European students will receive more general training during the shorter first-stage (Bachelor) degree before deciding whether they wish to specialize in a particular discipline at a latter stage (Masters and Doctorate programmes), a move which should be welcome in the light of the evidence provided in the report.

Finally, if Europe wants to use the US as a benchmark for its tertiary education reforms, it is important to realize that the American system is also subject to some weaknesses. The comparative advantage of American universities lies in their graduate and professional schools, where competition from European universities is mostly absent. However, as recently echoed by *The Economist*, there are clear signs that the quality of education that undergraduates receive in many American universities is strongly deteriorating.[2] Lectures are typically given by graduate students, rather than by professors, and there is evidence that curricula goes unreformed for a long time. In exchange for this unsatisfactory treatment, in a period of soaring tuition rates, undergraduates get compensated by inflated grades which also reduce the signalling content of higher education in the US. Thus, there seems to be growing evidence that the absence of competition from Europe is making American universities too

---

[2] See the leader in *The Economist* (2006, March 11) entitled 'Remember Detroit'.

complacent and, therefore, that an improvement of the functioning of European universities may start luring talented students away from the US universities sooner than expected.

Education is becoming a win-win investment in terms of efficiency and equality more than ever. The failure of tertiary-level education systems in Europe to encourage social mobility may not be so hard to remedy. The smaller size of the cohorts of students currently entering university and a reduction of the 'parking lot' phenomenon of higher education (i.e., the inverse correlation between college enrolment rates and youth unemployment) as the labour markets slowly improve, will help to achieve reforms. Europeans are becoming increasingly aware that education only pays off if it is properly supplied, and that the existing regressive way of financing tertiary-level education has become ineffective in improving social mobility. Therefore, governments are suffering increasing pressure to make considerable headway in reforming education systems if competition and equality of opportunity are to prevail. It is evident that some countries are more swift to adapt than others that are more complacent with their traditions and past reputation. No doubt, there will be winners and losers, as in any overhaul process, but, overall, I find no option for European countries than to be open to change, except at great cost to their economic well-being, as this report illustrates.

REFERENCES

Blanchard, O. and Wolfers, J. (2000). 'Shocks and Institutions in the Rise of European Unemployment', *The Economic Journal*, 110: 1–33.

Ljunqvist, L. and Sargent, T. (1998). 'The European Unemployment Dilemma', *Journal of Political Economy*, 106: 514–50.

—— and —— (2004). 'European Unemployment and Turbulence Revisited in a Matching Model', *Journal of the European Economic Association*, 2: 456–68.

COMMENTS

Daniel Gros

This is a stimulating paper with a wealth of useful information. Its main message is that Europe lags the US in tertiary education, both in quality and quantity, while there is little difference at the primary and secondary level.

Where does the difference in tertiary education come from? There is little difference between the US and Europe in public spending on tertiary education, but there is a large difference in private spending on tertiary education (specially on Universities), with the US spending almost twice as much in this area. This is an important point to make and it is well documented. The authors also emphasize another, potentially even bigger difference, namely in quality and incentives at the University level. But this factor is much more difficult to document.

The main criticism one may level at this report is that it does not tell us *why* we should care about the transatlantic difference in education, and what we could learn from intra-European differences.

Let me start with the main finding: Where is the EU–US difference in terms of education levels? It seems to exist at both ends of the spectrum: Europe has a much higher proportion of its population below the secondary level and Europe has much lower proportion with the highest level of tertiary education, not just in tertiary education in general. However, this marked difference in the proportion of the population with the highest level of tertiary education is difficult to square with the small trans-Atlantic difference in the overall years of schooling. It would have been helpful if the authors had explained how a year's difference in the length of schooling can lead to such a large difference in the proportion of the population with the highest level of tertiary education.

After this description one is tempted to ask: Why *should* we care about the trans-Atlantic difference in education levels? The authors seem to have three reasons in mind: (i) differences in education levels might lead to differences in growth, (ii) income distribution, and (iii) the contribution a country can make to the advances in science.

The first item is manifestly a problem for Europe at present. Growth is anaemic, but there is little evidence linking the bad performance of the EU economy over the last decade directly to problems with education levels. Given the large differences in educational achievements within Europe a cross-section analysis might have been instructive, but this would have meant writing another paper.

The second reason to care about differences in education, namely its impact on income distribution, might also constitute a reason to worry. But here the stylized facts do not lead to strong conclusions. The income distribution has not really changed that much in Europe over the last years, and Europe remains more egalitarian than the US. So this is not really a problem at present.

The third reason why 'education matters', namely the contribution to the advance to science that Europe might want to make is a 'noble' cause, but it is essentially a luxury good. The broader public does not seem to worry much whether there are enough Europeans to win the Nobel prize.

Let me now turn to two more critical remarks, one more specific, one more general:

(1) The authors put a lot of stress on the lack of mobility in Europe. But is mobility (or the lack thereof) so important? Intra-European mobility of researchers and workers in general is low, but the authors also emphasize the 'brain drain' from Europe, which implies that mobility across the Atlantic is not so low, as it shows that Europeans might move if 'the conditions are right'. I would argue that instead of making a case for more mobility one should make a case for increased competition.

(2) More in general, the wealth of national data that is available for the EU suggests that we should ask ourselves: What can we learn from intra-EU variability? Presumably the answer would not be straightforward, but the fact that intra-European differences are larger than differences between the average EU and the (average) US suggests that intra-EU variability must contain a lot of information. In particular, one should try to see whether differences in educational attainments among EU member countries are linked to economic performance. The next question then would be: What differences matter most?—Quantity measures (i.e., length of schooling, amounts spent by government, etc.) or structure (i.e., type of educational system, e.g., apprenticeship versus general education)?

This brings one back to the key issue, namely, the link between education and growth. The stylized facts do not suggest immediately a strong link in the long term. If one looks over the last 2–3 decades, one sees two developments:

(1) Europe catches up in terms of education.
(2) Europe's growth performance deteriorates, both in relative (EU–US) and absolute terms (Europe today versus Europe twenty years ago).

A first conclusion is thus that an unqualified equation 'more education = higher growth and faster catch-up' does not work without additional elements. To establish this link one has to make additional assumptions. For example: the rate of technological progress has accelerated. Another potential explanation would be that the catch-up potential is simply exhausted now. But the authors do not take a stance on these issues.

I would like to conclude with one clear reason why I think Europe should care about the transatlantic gap that is opening in terms of higher education. This is because it determines our potential to innovate. Our leaders promised in Lisbon more growth through what they called the 'knowledge society'. One intermediate measure that was to be taken on the route to stronger growth was to increase R&D spending from around 2 to 3 per cent of GDP during this decade. Little has been done to achieve this target. But this is not my point here. What I would like to emphasize is that a commitment to more R&D should have implied also a long term commitment to more higher education.

Attaining the Lisbon goal for R and D (EU investment in R&D of 3% of GDP) would imply an increase of 70 per cent. To be effective in terms of translating into a higher output of ideas this requires about 70 per cent more highly qualified researchers, who need to be trained. Training highly qualified researchers takes a decade at least. Thus starting today means that results can be expected only after a decade or so. Moreover, the cohorts ready for University are declining, thus making it more difficult to actually find 70 per cent more highly qualified and gifted researchers. Lisbon should thus have started with a commitment to strengthen higher education, rather than with unrealistic targets concerning more spending on R&D.

PART II

WORKPLACE TRAINING IN EUROPE[§]

Andrea Bassanini, Alison Booth, Giorgio Brunello,*
Maria De Paola, and Edwin Leuven

[§] The views expressed here are those of the authors and cannot be held to represent those of their institutions. We are grateful to two anonymous referees, to our discussants Giuseppe Bertola and Steve Pischke, to Pietro Garibaldi, Michele Pellizzari and the audiences at presentations in Essex, Rome and Venice for comments and suggestions.

* Team coordinator

8

Introduction

A major strategic goal set by the European Heads of Government in the Lisbon summit at the beginning of the new millennium was to make of Europe the most competitive and dynamic knowledge-based economy in the world by 2010. Education and training are key ingredients of the strategy, which recommends to several European countries the modernization of their education systems and the increase in the percentage of individuals participating in lifelong education and training. The emphasis on education and training is common to all advanced industrial societies, because of the widespread belief that the challenges posed by the rise of the new low-cost producers in Asia can only be met if labour attains high levels of skill, in a continuous up-skilling process.[1] Almost halfway through, however, it seems clear that attaining the very ambitious goals of the Lisbon strategy is out of the question for most European countries (see European Commission, 2005).[2]

When macroeconomists talk about human capital, most of the time they focus on education. However, the accumulation of human capital does not end with schools, and training is key to augmenting and adapting existing skills to the changes of technology. Training is particularly important for senior workers, whose skills accumulated at school are likely to be substantially depreciated, and for the less educated, who run the risk of social exclusion.

One could argue that the attention paid to education is justified by the fact that learning begets learning: getting a better educated labour force guarantees that workers and firms invest more in training. But do they

[1] See Crouch (1998).
[2] See Addison and Siebert (1994), for a description of EU training policy before Lisbon.

invest enough? The almost ubiquitous diffusion of training policies seem to suggest the contrary, as these policies often provide subsidies to the parties to encourage more company training. Economists have often pointed out that the market for training is characterized by several market failures, which include imperfections in labour, product and capital markets, and both positive and negative externalities. But what is the evidence? And can we say that the difference in the intensity of training across Europe is due to the different weight of importance given to these failures?

Efficiency is not the only criterion which justifies government intervention in the market for training. The simple observation that learning begets learning suggests that those individuals who are disadvantaged in the education process are also likely to be at a disadvantage in their labour market learning. If access to schooling is not open to all according to talent and effort because of failures in the market for education, the disadvantage accumulated at school is going to be amplified by poor training in the labour market. If individuals mature differently affecting their responses to education, this too could be amplified by subsequent training. A reinforcing factor here is that inequalities of opportunity could affect not only schooling, but also training conditional on schooling.

Even if labour markets were perfectly efficient and equal, government policies which transfer resources from the taxpayer to workers and firms via training subsidies could be explained because of political economy considerations: skilled workers and firms usually are better organized than the ordinary taxpayer, and can lobby politicians for subsidies as a form of redistribution. If the positive effect of training on productivity spills over on the productivity of unskilled workers, the latter too may find it convenient to support training subsidies.

This report examines workplace training in Europe in a comparative perspective. Compared to training in general, workplace training is received while in employment, and is usually, but not exclusively, provided by the employer. This is an important area, not only because company training covers a substantial part of education after labour market entry, but because of the perception—rather widespread in the documents by the European Commissions on the Lisbon Strategy—that European employers do not spend enough in increasing the skills and competences of their employees.

This tension between policy targets at the European level and the behaviour of firms is well described by Colin Crouch (1998) in the following quotation:

Business firms are equipped to maximize, not collective objectives, but their own profitability. In doing this they will certainly provide training and retraining for large numbers of employees; there is however no reason why company decisions and market forces should maximize the level of vocational ability for a whole society except through a largely serendipitous fall-out... (370)

We start by looking at the facts. Figure 8.1 shows the differences in average training incidence across European countries, Anglo-Saxon countries and some countries of Eastern Europe. The figure plots both average training participation and average annual hours of training per employee. We notice that the US—a key competitor—does not perform 'better' than all European countries, because the UK, France and Scandinavian countries have both higher participation and higher annual hours of training. The rest of Europe, including the countries in the 'olive belt' (Greece, Italy, Portugal and Spain), does 'worse' than the US, and is somewhat closer to the new entries from Eastern Europe.[3] While these

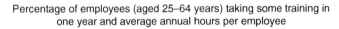

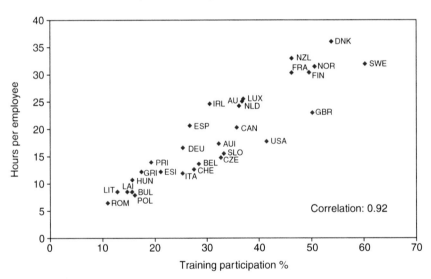

Fig. 8.1 Training participation and training intensity
Source: OECD (2004).

---

[3] The somewhat surprising relative position of Germany in this diagram could be explained with the fact that we are considering only individuals aged 25–64; by so doing, we exclude most apprenticeship training.

indicators need to be considered with care, due to the measurement problems discussed at length in the report, they reveal that Europe is very heterogeneous when it comes to training outcomes.

The figure also suggests that the concern voiced across the Atlantic on the 'poor' performance of US education and training might seem somewhat inflated from the perspective of Southern European countries. In a well-known review of company training in the US, which dates back to the early 1990s, Lisa Lynch, 1994, talks of an emerging consensus that US workers' skills are not on a par with those of European and Japanese workers. She quotes a report by the US Commission on Workforce Quality and Labour Market Efficiency, which concludes that for US firms to compete internationally a reform of the education and training system is in order. An equally pessimistic view has been voiced, almost contemporaneously, by Bishop (1993).

Whether this pessimistic view still holds after the very good performance of US productivity growth since the mid-1990s is an open question. Such performance also throws some doubts on the prevailing mantra—more education, more training—in many policy circles: labour productivity in the business sector grew on average by 2.10 per cent in the US during 1995–2002, in spite of the perception that education and training in that country was not on a par with Germany or Japan, which grew instead at a significantly lower rate. Interestingly, only three European countries have had higher labour productivity growth than the US during the same period: Ireland (3.92%), Greece (3.50%) and Finland (2.42%). Of these, only Finland has an unambiguously higher training participation and better indicators on schooling performance than the US.[4]

We show that most workplace training is done by employers, independently of whether the accumulated skills can be transferred to other employers. On average, the entire cost of three-quarters of the training courses is directly paid by employers, and there is little evidence that employees indirectly pay through lower wages. Large and innovative firms[5] train more than small and non-innovative firms, with the UK being the only European country where this does not hold. Cross-country variation among large and innovative firms is, however, small. Therefore, the lower average training incidence in countries located in the Southern 'olive belt' is correlated both to their larger share of small firms and to the

---

[4] The US does better in advanced education, as detailed in Chapter 1 of this book.
[5] Innovative firms are those which have introduced at least a new product or process during the reference period.

fact that these firms train relatively less than do firms of similar size in Northern Europe.

In Europe, as in the US, training increases with educational attainment and the skill intensity of occupations, and it decreases with age. The age training gap is negatively correlated with the employment rate of older workers, reflecting either the impact of training on older workers' employability, or their incentive to stay on rather than retire and invest in their skills. Women take more training than men, but essentially because they pay for their own training more often, while firms do not appear to accommodate their greater demand for training. Importantly, women tend to receive less employer-sponsored training than men when they are young and have more frequent career interruptions due to childrearing. On average, temporary workers get trained less often.

After netting out observable individual characteristics, country effects account for almost one-half of the explained variation in training participation across Europe—net of Germany.[6] Without doubt, part of this variation reflects measurement error and cross-country differences in definitions and perceptions of training. For instance, since training registered in employer and employee surveys is typically formal, significant episodes of informal training are not counted, which is especially problematic for small firms, where a lot of informal training arguably takes place. However, this residual cross-country variation also includes differences in the institutional and social framework, in government policies and in the macroeconomic conditions.

It is rather difficult to sort out the relative importance of each potential candidate, because some variables are hard to measure, and because of a large host of confounding factors. Yet we find the strong positive correlation between investment in R&D as percentage of GDP and training incidence showed in Figure 8.2 quite suggestive of the interactions between skill development and innovative effort at the country level. While we cannot tell whether this relationship reflects a causal link, we remark that the large difference in average training incidence between Northern and Southern European countries is matched by the large difference in their ability to invest in research and development. An analogous correlation emerges when we measure innovative activity with the share of expenditure in ICT over GDP.

Similarly, Figure 8.3 shows that there is a negative correlation between an index of stringency of anti-competitive product market regulation

---

[6] Germany was excluded because of the quality of the data.

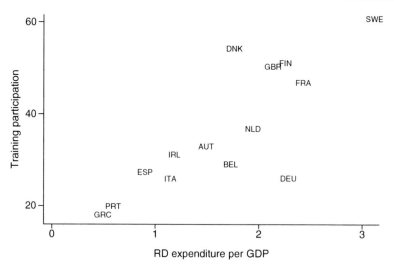

Fig. 8.2 R&D investment and training, by country
Sources: ECHP and Eurostat.

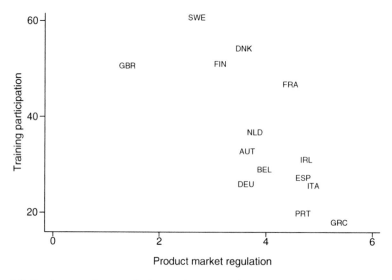

Fig. 8.3 Product market regulation and training, by country
Sources: ECHP and OECD.

(Nicoletti and Scarpetta, 2003) and training incidence. That is to say that training participation is low in Southern European countries, which invest less in R&D and have more regulated product markets. Conversely, no significant correlation exists between training participation—at the country level—and the percentage of workers on a temporary contract. As illustrated by Figure 8.4, if we exclude the case of Spain—an obvious outlier because of the very high share of temporary labour—countries with a similar share of temporary workers have vastly different levels of training participation.

Product and labour market institutions have been changing in Europe under the widespread pressure to develop more competitive markets. Did these changes affect training outcomes? We show that the decrease in product market regulation across Europe has facilitated average training investment. Labour market flexibility, on the other hand, has had mixed effects. That is to say that while the diffusion of temporary work has been associated with a reduction of training incidence, the opposite has occurred with the slow but almost general reduction in the employment protection of regular labour. These results suggest that the progressive deregulation of product and labour markets does not necessarily have a negative impact on the accumulation of human capital in firms, as some have suggested (see Acemoglu and Pischke, 1999a).

Do the cross-country differences in training incidence across European countries also reflect differences in the deviation of the private from the social optimum? This is a difficult question for at least two reasons: First, government policies are in place. Assuming that these policies are effective in changing training participation, the observed outcome is

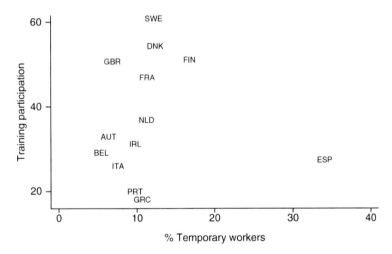

Fig. 8.4 Temporary workers and training, by country
Sources: ECHP and OECD.

different from the one that would prevail without any policy. Secondly, there are other distortions in the labour and product markets, which place us in a second-best environment. When we consider whether government intervention in the training market is desirable, the natural question to ask is how the level of training attained by private agents compares with the socially optimum level of training. While the former is defined by the equality of private benefits and costs, the latter requires that we also consider social benefits and costs.

We argue that answering this question is particularly hard with the statistical data at hand. First of all, we rarely have information on training costs. Secondly, private benefits are related to the increase in productivity after training. Since productivity is measured only in special surveys and case studies, our knowledge of training benefits is also limited.[7]

The closest we can get to the private benefits to training is by looking at the wage returns. Even in this case, however, we need to be aware that wages do not correspond to productivity if labour markets are not perfectly competitive. Broadly, the empirical evidence suggests that these returns are substantial and significantly higher than the returns to education. It also shows that estimated returns are highest in countries where training incidence is lowest, such as Portugal. An implication of this is that cross-country differences in training participation could depend more on differences in supply than in demand. Are these uncovered high returns to training a genuine aspect of the investment in human capital after schooling, or instead a statistical artefact driven by our inability to eliminate confounding factors such as individual talent? It might be too early to provide a definite answer to this question, but there are some signs that the estimated wage returns to training might be overvalued.

While we know a lot about private returns—even though some of what we know may be open to question—we are basically in the dark when it comes to social returns. In theory, we can think of a number of positive and negative externalities affecting training decisions: poaching externalities due to turnover, positive spillovers on unskilled labour, and positive externalities originated by the complementarity between training and innovation. In practice, there is no measure telling us whether such effects exist and how relevant they are. Little help comes also from the large and growing empirical literature on human capital and growth, because the

---

[7] Policy reports have sometimes less blurred views. In a recent report by the European Commission, for instance, it is stated that 'a strong link exists between human capital and productivity in businesses. Investment in human capital increases productivity and is a direct source of innovation and competitiveness' (European Commission, 2005: 3).

standard measures of human capital used in that literature include the quantity and quality of education, but exclude training. In this literature, since education and training are complements, the contribution of education to growth includes also the contribution of training, but we have no way to tell the contribution of each of these two variables apart.

Lack of evidence on under-provision is a reason to be prudent when advocating training measures to eliminate the inefficiencies of private markets. Such measures include regulatory interventions—such as pay-back clauses, apprenticeship contracts, the certification of training and its recognition on a European basis—as prescribed by the Copenhagen declaration, and co-financing measures which fund employers and employees who invest in training.

Training policies, however, can also be motivated by considerations of equity. The European Union gives to equity a prominent role in its Lisbon Strategy, using such keywords as 'equal opportunity' and 'social inclusion' when advocating more education and more training. When individuals cannot attain desirable outcomes because of circumstances that are independent of their actions, policies that try to restore equality of opportunity are warranted even in the absence of efficiency reasons. Examples of such circumstances include family privilege and/or disadvantage, which we capture with measures of family background. We show that, contrary to the case of the United States, training outcomes in Europe depend in a significant way on parental background, even after netting out education, and that this dependence is particularly significant in Southern European countries. Therefore, individuals who come from disadvantaged European households are not only less likely to attain a higher level and better education, but also fail to become recipients of company training. Importantly, differences in family background correlate closely in some countries—Italy and Spain are typical examples here—with regional disparities: poorer regions have both an average poor family background and lower training incidence.

When equity is the issue, training policies should be targeted at the disadvantaged. But are they? Since some co-financing schemes prescribe an active role of the social parties, union concern for equality can help in directing some of these resources to the right targets. An alternative is provided by tax and subsidies to individuals, which include vouchers and learning accounts. Equality as a motivator for policy, however, runs into problems when we consider that the private benefits of the investment may be particularly low among the disadvantaged. Our empirical evidence confirms that workers with lower educational attainment who receive

153

training have significantly lower returns than workers with higher education. This evidence might suggest that an alternative policy which trains the skilled, taxes them, and redistributes to the less skilled, is desirable—see Heckman (1999). The problem, of course, is that such a policy would breed a culture of social exclusion and dependence, which might be less acceptable in Europe than on the other side of the Atlantic.

Since employers, unlike governments and unions, should not be expected to select the recipients of workplace training with an eye to undoing the disadvantages created before labour market entry, policies aiming at the equality of opportunity need also to consider schooling, because of its complementarity with training, and because most of the pre-college schooling in Europe is public. Schooling clearly matters: in the European Union early school leavers—defined as the share of the population aged 18 to 24 with only lower secondary education, and not in education or training—were over 20 per cent in 2004 in Italy, Spain and Portugal, more than twice the percentage in the Scandinavian countries. As shown by Figure 8.5, average training incidence is higher in countries where the percentage of the active population with at least upper secondary education is higher. By increasing the average quantity—and quality—of education, governments can also increase training incidence.

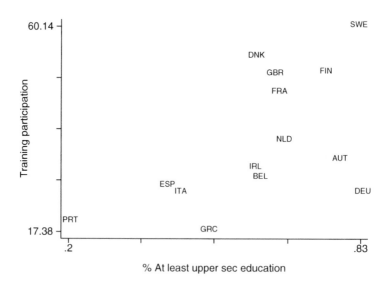

Fig. 8.5 Training incidence and schooling
Sources: ECHP and OECD.

Employers may prefer to respond to technical progress and innovation not by re-training existing employees but by replacing them with new generations of school leavers, who have better and more updated general education. This is clearly a problem for senior employees, especially when they lose their jobs. In these circumstances, government action tends to become associated with the care of social casualties and with failures to cope. Some have also voiced concern that pension reforms in Europe, which reduce the implicit tax on continuing work, and delay retirement age, may damage the prospects of senior workers, who are less employable and more likely to end up in the unemployment pool. Our empirical evidence shows that this concern might be partly inflated, because workers over 50 tend to train more, where the implicit tax on continuing work is lower.

More generally, our evidence suggests that training outcomes can be improved also indirectly. The Lisbon agenda includes among its goals: (a) investments in research and development to be 3 per cent of GDP in 2010 (only Sweden was above the target in the mid-1990s); 55 per cent of the labour force aged 55–64 to be in work in 2010; 70 per cent of the labour force to be in work in 2010. Our empirical results suggest that policies which try to attain these targets are likely to favour investment in work-place training, with reinforcing effects on the targets themselves. For instance, policies increasing female commitment to the labour market—for example, during childrearing years, including childcare policies and maternity leave provisions—should lead to more training. Moreover, measures that help to deregulate the product market and that reduce the incentives to retire are also expected to increase training incidence.[8]

When thinking of policy, it is probably a good idea to realize that Europe is not a homogeneous entity where education and training are considered. Some European countries—most notably the Scandinavian area—are investing more that the US, our key competitor. Others, and typically those in the 'olive belt' area, lag substantially behind. Our report shows that what we know about training in Europe is not yet enough to answer questions of pressing importance for policy design. Many training policies provide resources to employers and employees, but do they work? Do they have a real or a cosmetic effect? What are the deadweight losses? Compared to the US, evaluation studies of training policies in Europe

---

[8] On the other hand, measures that increase the portfolio of available labour contracts can increase labour force participation, with less clear-cut effects on training investments.

are few. More needs to be done, both in terms of access to data and in terms of serious policy evaluation.

To conclude: why is Finland investing in training much more than Italy? While we are aware that the answer to this question is complex, a first try is shown in Figure 8.6. Let the demand for, and supply of, trained employees be a negative and a positive function of the training wage premium w_T, respectively, and let training participation in each country be determined at the intersection of demand and supply. In this report we show that participation is much higher in Finland than in Italy, in spite of the fact that the expected wage premium is similar (see Ch. 12). Our tentative explanation relies on the fact that both the supply of, and the demand for, trained employees is higher in Finland than in Italy. The supply is higher at any price in the former country because the higher quantity and quality of education reduces training costs; the demand is higher in Finland than in Italy because of the substantially higher R&D expenditure and lower product market regulation in the former country, which increase the productivity of trained employees.

Finland turned around the recession of 1990–91 by rapidly converting from natural resources to high-tech production, and so did Sweden. One could conclude that Italy needs another Nokia—or Ericsson. But does it have the right conditions for this to happen? As argued by Blomstrom and

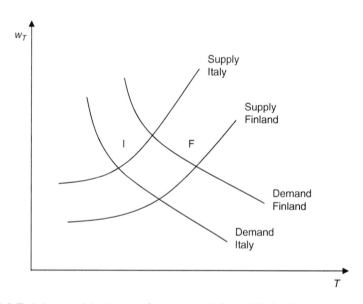

Fig. 8.6 Training participation and returns in Italy and Finland

Kokko (2003), 'in-house training and education have been of central importance for Nokia's ability to absorb new technologies. Both companies—Nokia and Ericsson—have also benefited greatly from public investments in high education and research . . . ' (30). Education policies, which affect both the quantity and the quality of Italian education, might require time but are perhaps a key factor in avoiding economic decline.

This Part is organized as follows. Chapter 9 reviews the basic theory of workplace training in imperfectly competitive—or oligopsonistic—labour markets. Chapter 10 looks at the data we have and at the main facts concerning training participation. Chapter 11 investigates the relationship between average training participation and country-specific labour and product market institutions. Chapter 12 looks at the private and social costs and benefits of training. Finally, Chapter 13 considers policy issues and reviews the main policies adopted in Europe.

9

An Overview of the Theoretical Framework

Introduction

Investments in human capital are central to economic performance and growth. When tastes and technologies are changing rapidly, human capital investments are important in maintaining high levels of competitiveness and of employment. Without a workforce that is continually acquiring new skills, it is difficult to reap all the returns from technological progress. In this second half of the volume, we focus on a particular component of human capital—training. Throughout we use the term *training* to refer to work-related training received while in employment. Thus we exclude from our analysis training received while unemployed or training provided by governments through, for example, active labour market policy.

9.1 The received wisdom

According to orthodox human capital theory, formalized by Becker (1964), and Oi (1962), among others, human capital is an investment that raises expected future productivity, albeit at a cost. Training costs comprise the opportunity costs of foregone earnings as well as the direct costs of training (such as course enrolment costs, materials used while learning, training personnel and the like). Investment in human capital is thus very similar to investment in physical capital but with one crucial distinction. In the absence of slavery, workers retain ownership—and thus control—of their embodied human capital.

Training can be either general or specific in nature (although training is in practice likely to combine a mix of both types, and we will return to this later). In a competitive economy, *general training* represents skills that can be used at countless other firms, and hence the training is general or portable across companies as individuals change jobs. According to human capital theory, general training would therefore be financed by the worker through the receipt of lowered wages during training, although it could be provided by the firm. The reason for this is that training is embodied in the worker, who could leave at any time to go to another job where s/he would be equally as productive. No firm would ever finance such training, since its returns are uncertain and could well be zero. In contrast, *specific training* is by definition only valuable to the firm providing the training. Hence, to reduce potential hold-up problems, both parties would contribute to the financing of training. This sharing mechanism ensures that both firm and worker have the incentive to maintain the relationship after training and thereby to reap the returns. Thus both forms of training—general and specific—are associated with clear predictions, first with regard to their financing, and secondly with regard to who gets the returns. In the general training case, the worker reaps all the returns. In the specific training case, the returns are shared.

For three decades, it was thought that human capital theory, based on the assumption of a perfectly competitive labour market, fully explained who would pay for general training. Any stylized facts diverging from the theory's predictions were believed to be due to imperfections such as credit market constraints. And yet there remained some puzzles that could not be explained within this framework. First, survey evidence showed employers paying for general training in spite of potential poaching of trained workers. And second, there did not seem to be evidence of workers receiving wage cuts during training.[1]

9.2 Challenges to this orthodoxy

More recently, a number of published papers have challenged this orthodoxy. Bhaskar, Manning and To (2002) note that, just as in international trade the introduction of product market imperfections revolutionized our understanding of trade policies and comparative advantage, while in macroeconomics models of monopolistic competition explained

---

[1] For evidence of these puzzles, see for example Bishop (1997); Leuven and Oosterbeek (1999); Acemoglu and Pischke (1999a); Booth and Bryan (2005b).

how small adjustment costs could lead to business fluctuations, so too in labour economics has imperfect competition begun to transform our way of thinking. And this is not just through institutions such as trade unions, which are an obvious labour market imperfection. A growing literature argues that employers actually have market power in setting wages—what we might term the *new oligopsony*. This oligopsony can arise through product differentiation and through imperfect information (rather than through the old definition of a monopsonist as being a single employer in a labour market). And its proponents demonstrate that it can lead to simple and plausible explanations of labour market phenomena that are otherwise regarded as puzzles.

Oligopsony is when the labour supply curve facing a firm is not completely elastic. How can oligopsony arise? There are many potential avenues. Examples include:

- *search frictions* that emerge when there is imperfect information on job opportunities elsewhere;
- *mobility costs* for employees in changing jobs; and
- *heterogeneous preferences over the non-wage characteristics* associated with various jobs (such as their location, work culture, colleague sociability, flexibility of hours, environment, distance from home).[2]

The new training approach uses the insights of new oligopsony theory to generate important new results. Recent papers show that, if the labour market is actually characterized by oligopsonistic wage-setting, some of the predictions of the human capital model are overturned. For example, the wage returns to general training may be less than the productivity returns and firms may find it profitable to pay for training even though it is general.

In the next section, we briefly outline the principal hypotheses regarding training and summarize their predictions as to who pays for general training and the returns to training (at both the training firms and at subsequent firms). For the moment we leave aside the role of institutions, although we will return to this later in the chapter.

---

[2] This can be thought of as horizontal job differentiation. In Booth and Zoega (1999), horizontal differentiation arises because jobs differ in terms of their non-wage characteristics, over which workers have varying preferences. This generates an imperfectly elastic labour supply to the firm. Bhaskar and To (2003), also assume that workers have heterogenous preferences for nonwage job characteristics (and cite various empirical studies supporting this assumption). Bhaskar, Manning and To (2002), note that these can usefully summarize the variety of reasons for imperfect competition in the labour market.

9.3 An overview of the various approaches and their empirical predictions

9.3.1 *General training in a perfectly competitive labour market*

According to standard human capital theory, workers in perfectly competitive labour markets will pay for *general* work-related training by receiving low training wages. They will reap the returns to this investment by receiving higher wages afterwards and their post-training wages will be the same across firms, *ceteris paribus* (Becker, 1964). These predictions are summarized in the first row of Table 9.1, reproduced from Booth and Bryan (2005a).

9.3.2 *Imperfect capital markets and general training*

Workers who cannot afford to accept low wages during general training will be adversely affected by any credit market constraints that disbar them from borrowing to finance their investment. However, should the firm be willing to act as lender, it can pay workers more than their marginal product during training and less afterwards. The firm would only

Table 9.1 Some predictions of human capital theory

Row no.	Model	Who pays	Divergence between wages (w) and net marginal productivity (MP) at training firm	Transferability of training
[1]	Perfect competition, general training	Worker	None	Fully transferable
[2]	As above but with credit constraints	Sharing	$w>MP$ during training and $w<MP$ after training	Transferable but wage returns elsewhere greater than returns at firm providing training
[3]	Perfect competition, specific training	Sharing	$w>MP$ during training and $w<MP$ after training	Non-transferable
[4]	Perfect competition, mix of general and specific training	Sharing	$w>MP$ during training and $w<MP$ after training	Partially transferable; wage returns elsewhere less than returns at firm providing training
[5]	Oligopsonistic labor market, general training	Firm	$w<MP$ during and after training, implying rents for the firm	Fully transferable, wage returns elsewhere greater than returns at firm providing training

Source: Booth and Bryan (2005a).

agree to such a contract if some mechanism can be devised to bind workers to the firm after training until the loan has been paid back (Malcomson, Maw and McCormick, 2003). A binding contract—such as an apprenticeship contract or a minimum employment guarantee—is one means of so doing. The predictions of this model are that firms will pay for general training, and workers' wages will be above marginal productivity during training and below marginal productivity after training. The magnitude of this wedge will reflect the degree of cost-sharing. The training will be transferable across firms, and after changing employers, workers should get a greater return to their training than they received in the firm that provided the training and the loan. These predictions are summarized in the second row of Table 9.1.

9.3.3 *Pure specific training*

Now consider the predictions of the pure *specific* training model. For specific human capital—of value only to the one firm—it is efficient for the firm and the worker to share both the costs and the returns of the training investment to avoid hold-up problems (Hashimoto, 1981; Leuven and Oosterbeck, 2001). Consequently workers' wages will be above marginal productivity during training and below marginal productivity after training. The magnitude of this wedge will reflect the degree of cost-sharing. The training will not be transferable across firms by definition (in contrast to the model of credit constrained workers seeking general training outlined above). These predictions are summarized in the third row of Table 9.1.

9.3.4 *Mixture of training types*

Suppose that, while the labour market is perfectly competitive, training comprises a mix of *general and specific* components. Here workers will finance their general training and firms will share the costs of the specific training. Since there will be some sharing of costs, wages at the training firm will be greater than productivity during training and less than productivity after training. Wages at subsequent firms will reflect returns only to the general component of training, and consequently will be less than wages at the training firm (in which there is some return to the worker to the shared investment in specific training). These predictions are summarized in the fourth row of Table 9.1.

9.3.5 *Oligopsonistic wage setting*

Now consider a labour market characterized by oligopsonistic wage-setting, as in the 'new' training literature.[3] It can be shown that the wage 'compression' associated with imperfectly competitive labour markets may increase the incentive for firms to invest in general training, where we will explain in detail in a subsequent section precisely what is meant by the term 'wage compression'. The necessary condition for this result is that post-training productivity is increasing in training intensity at a faster rate than are wages, as illustrated in Figure 9.1. However, the amount of training provided in equilibrium may be sub-optimal from the viewpoint of society.[4]

In Figure 9.1, reproduced from Acemoglu and Pischke (1999b), $f(\tau)$ denotes a worker's productivity as a concave function of training intensity τ, and w denotes wages. Suppose that Δ represents the costs of moving

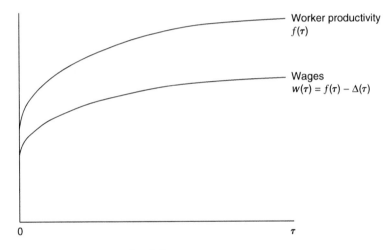

Worker productivity
$f(\tau)$

Wages
$w(\tau) = f(\tau) - \Delta(\tau)$

0 τ

Fig. 9.1 Wage structure and training

[3] See *inter alia*, Katz and Ziderman (1990); Stevens (1994), (1996); Chang and Wang (1996); Loewenstein and Spletzer (1998); Acemoglu and Pischke (1999b); Booth and Zoega (1999).
[4] Acemoglu and Pischke (1999b), isolate four conditions that have to be satisfied for firms to be willing to pay for general training when workers are either credit constrained or would choose a lower level of training. (1) Labour-market frictions making the productivity of a worker exceed his or her outside option and generating economic rents; (2) The propensity to quit is strictly less than one (in discrete time). When the firm is certain that a worker will leave once trained, it is not willing to sponsor the training. (3) The firm's share of the joint surplus due to labour-market frictions is nonzero, i.e. the workers' bargaining power is less than one. If the firm cannot capture a part of the surplus from a job match so that the worker gets all the return to training, it is again not willing to pay for the training. (4) The marginal effect of training on productivity has to exceed (in absolute terms) the marginal effect of training on

between jobs and notice that $f(\tau) - w(\tau) = \Delta$. If Δ were a constant, then $f'(\tau) - w'(\tau) = 0$. Thus the firm would not benefit from training, as profits would be the same at any level of training intensity. However if mobility costs are increasing in the level of training $\Delta'(\tau) > 0$, the wage schedule will be flatter than the productivity schedule, since firms pay workers their outside options. Thus profits change by $f' - w' = \Delta'(\tau) > 0$, and the firm benefits from giving the worker more training.

The predictions of this simple model—and indeed all the models in this genre—are that the firm may finance general training, and that the wages at the training firm will be less than marginal product. However, there are some differences in the other predictions of this class of models. For example, according to the contracting model of Loewenstein and Spletzer (1998), there may be a greater wage return to training in future firms than in the current firm depending on whether or not a minimum wage guarantee binds in the current job. If it does bind, the employer can extract rents from providing general training.

9.3.6 Asymmetric information

Next we consider the impact of asymmetric information on the predictions of the orthodox human capital model. Asymmetry of information about the value of employer-provided training (e.g., where the firm providing general training knows its value but other firms do not) can affect the transferability of training in an otherwise competitive labour market with *identical ability* workers. If outside firms assign a value of zero to the training—as they might if they have no information—such training is in effect specific to the training firm. Consequently, the firm may be willing to share in the costs of its provision and the pay returns in other firms will be non-existent or small. The predictions of this model are as for Row [3] of Table 9.1.

However, a formal qualification associated with a training course is a means of conveying to outsiders the value of the employer-provided general training. For this reason one would expect accredited training to have a larger impact on wages in future firms than non-accredited training *ceteris paribus*. One would also expect it to be financed by the individual, since it is transferable or general. The predictions of the model with

the outside wage. The implication is that the former also exceeds the marginal effect on the firm's own wage, since firms pay workers their outside options. This phenomenon should be referred to as *absolute* wage compression, to distinguish it from the more commonly used definition of the term wage compression that refers to *relative* wage compression.

accreditations for training are therefore the same as for Row [1] of Table 9.1—the individual will pay and will get all the pay returns.

An alternative approach is found in the asymmetric information model of Acemoglu and Pischke (1998), in which workers are characterized by *heterogeneous abilities*. Here training is rewarded more in the current firm than in outside firms because the current firm will pay higher wages to retain high ability workers, whereas low ability workers will be dismissed. Some of the high ability workers who need to leave their jobs will be treated as low ability workers in the outside market. Since training and ability are complements, training will be valued less for workers who have been laid off or who have quit. Consequently in the outside market these workers will receive lower returns to their training. The predictions of this model are as for Row [4] Table 9.1.

9.4 Comparisons of predictions of these models

Of course, the predictions of some of these hypotheses are observationally equivalent. Two models predict that transferable training might have bigger returns to subsequent firms than to the training firm, as inspection of Rows [2] and [5] shows. On the other hand, some predictions are quite distinct. For example, while both models in Rows [1] and [5] predict that training is transferable, the first predicts that workers pay for it while the fifth predicts that firms do.[5]

9.5 A clarification of wage compression

The new oligopsony theory emphasizes that post-training productivity must increase in training intensity at a faster rate than wages in order for firms to be willing to finance general training. In much of the literature subsequent to earlier work by Acemoglu and Pischke—especially in empirical studies—there has been a tendency to use the term 'wage compression' as shorthand for this necessary condition. Following Booth and Zoega (2004), we emphasize that wage compression in the normal usage of the term (Kaldor, 1963; Katz and Murphy, 1992) is not a

---

[5] Booth and Bryan (2005a), distinguished between these hypotheses by (i) using information about who pays directly for work-related training, and (ii) comparing the pay returns to such training at the current and subsequent firms. Booth and Bryan (2005b), analyse survey data about the extent and financing of various types of training in Britain using the newer training questions from the BHPS.

necessary condition for firm-sponsored general training. Now we briefly explain why. In Appendix 1 to this chapter (p. 179). we explain it formally.

Assume that $y(\tau)$ is output of a worker with training τ, $w(\tau)$ is his or her wage, $P(\tau)$ denotes the difference between the two $(y-w)$ and $p(\tau)$ denotes the ratio of the two (y/w).

DEFINITION 1

Absolute wage compression occurs when $P'(0) = y'(0) - w'(0) > 0$. This implies that profits per worker in absolute terms are increasing in τ over some range.

DEFINITION 2

Relative wage compression occurs when $p'(0) > 0$. This implies that the ratio of output to wages is increasing (decreasing) in τ. By taking logs we get

$$\frac{d \log p(0)}{d\tau} = \frac{d \log y(0)}{d\tau} - \frac{d \log w(0)}{d\tau} > 0 \ (< 0) \qquad [9.1]$$

that is the derivative of the log difference with respect to τ is increasing (decreasing) in τ. In this case, training increases output proportionately more (less) than wages.[6]

In Appendix 1 (p. 179), we show that the departure from the Becker framework highlighted in the contribution of Acemoglu and Pischke is more general than implied by their analysis. Their additive formulation of the way that training affects workers' productivity and wages focuses attention on just one set of institutional arrangements—those with absolute wage compression. While such an additive formulation has the attraction of simplicity, it can be interpreted as suggesting that firms will only pay for general training under a rather narrower set of institutional arrangements than is actually the case. The model can also be set up such that training affects productivity and wages in a multiplicative (or log-additive) way. This multiplicative formulation has the advantage of being more plausible, since it assumes that inherent ability and trained productivity are

---

[6] To illustrate the difference between the two definitions, assume that, as a result of increased training, the productivity and wages of every worker doubles. Here there is no change in the ratio of output to wages for any worker and no change in relative wages or relative productivity levels. However, there *is* absolute wage compression, since the difference between output and wages is now higher for those who have received training compared to those who have not. The second definition—*relative wage compression*—comes closer to what is usually understood as wage compression in the macro/labour literature, where what matters is the ratio of the wage income of different income groups. Changes in the income distribution are thus conventionally measured by changes in wage or income ratios.

imperfect rather than perfect substitutes.[7] But more importantly, this formulation also encompasses a wider range of institutional arrangements, including piece rates. In the appendix we show that firms are willing to pay for general training even in the absence of relative wage compression, although the latter does increase the level of training chosen by firms.

9.6 Is there under-provision of training?

According to human capital theory, which assumes perfectly competitive labour markets, there is no role for policy intervention, because the first best allocation is attained by the interaction of market forces and the Invisible Hand leads to optimal provision of general work-related training. Only if there are imperfect capital markets, where workers might be credit constrained and therefore unable to accept lower wages during training, under-provision occurs with respect to the first best and there is a potential role for policy. Here training contracts, pay-back contracts and the like—extensively discussed in Chapter 13—may be appropriate policy tools.

However, if labour markets are not perfectly competitive, there may potentially be an additional role for policy. As we emphasized earlier in this section, provided that the productivity returns from training are increasing in training more rapidly than the wage returns, then firms will be willing to pay for general training. But there is no guarantee that the amount of training they provide will be optimal from society's viewpoint.

The argument here is that firms which bear training costs cannot fully appropriate the benefits of training, which are shared either with trained employees or with future employers. The former type of sharing occurs because workers and firms can bargain over wages after training has taken place, which creates a hold-up problem (Leuven, 2005). The second type occurs when quit rates are positive and new employers pay trained employees less than their productivity. Since their profits are not explicitly considered by training firms when deciding whether and how much to

---

[7] A simple example clarifies the distinction. Suppose that two individuals with different levels of inherent abilities enter a training programme. According to the additive formulation, their productivities will converge the longer they stay in the programme. But according to the multiplicative formulation, the ratio of their productivities will stay constant while their absolute productivities rise. Thus according to the additive formulation, we can put a novice into a computer class and sit him next to Bill Gates, and the abilities of the two will gradually converge since the latter will learn no faster. According to the multiplicative formulation, Mr Gates will maintain his relative lead.

invest, there is a poaching externality which reduces training below its social optimum level (Stevens, 1996).

Other externalities mentioned in the literature—network effects and the spillovers originated by the complementarity between training and innovation (Acemoglu, 1997)—can generate multiple equilibria and private levels of training different from the social optimum (see e.g. Burdett and Smith, 1996; Brunello and Medio, 2001; Snower, 1996; Redding, 1996; Acemoglu and Pischke, 1998). In these environments, under-provision of training is one possible equilibrium, and intervention might be desirable to shift the economy to a high skilled job creation and high training equilibrium.[8]

While poaching and hold-up can produce under-provision of training, they are also consistent with over-provision and with the social optimum, as discussed for instance by Moen and Rosen, 2002. Appendix 2 (p. 182) presents a simple example where this is the case. Unfortunately, as yet, there is generally little guidance from available models as to whether there is under-provision or over-provision of training. And thus these models provide little guidance for policy. The asymmetric information approach is an exception, since accreditation of training programmes is an obvious policy response to imperfect information about the quality of a training course.[9]

To shed further light on the important issue of under- or over-provision of training, we have devised a simple test of the hypothesis of under-provision or over-provision of training in an imperfectly competitive framework. The theoretical basis for this test is shown in Appendix 2 to this chapter. This test aims to establish whether or not voluntary turnover declines with training, and the results of its empirical

---

[8] For example, Snower (1996), models a 'low skill, bad job trap', in which the social returns to posting skilled job vacancies and investing in training are higher than the private returns. This is because a skilled job vacancy increases the probability that a skilled worker finds a good job and consequently raises the expected return to training. On the other hand, investing in training increases the probability of filling a skilled vacancy and therefore raises the returns from creating skilled jobs. This creates the possibility of multiple equilibria—a high equilibrium with high job creation and high levels of training, and a low equilibrium with low job creation and low training levels—the low skills, bad job trap. Laing, Palivos and Wang (1995), develop a model in which the level of education affects economic growth by influencing workers' ability to accumulate skills on the job, and there can be multiple steady-state growth paths.

[9] Some types of training are harder to verify, or to write contracts about, than others. The lack of contractibility of some forms of training, deriving from the sometimes intangible nature of skills investment and the impossibility of complete contracts, may make accreditation difficult, especially for the more informal types of training. See also Acemoglu and Pischke (1998), and Malcomson, Maw and McCormick (2003), who make the case for apprenticeship contracts.

implementation are presented in Chapter 13. If turnover does decline with training, this confirms that we cannot say much about under-provision of training. If it doesn't, then there is under-provision, but we still don't know how far the private optimum is from the first best.[10] This test is not invalidated by the presence of positive externalities.

So far we have discussed only the models in the microeconomic literature, but human capital also plays an important role in affecting growth, as highlighted in the macroeconomic growth literature.[11] The importance of skills acquired on the job, and through training institutions, is emphasized in the learning-by-doing approach developed by Romer (1986); by the human capital approach proposed by Lucas (1988); and by the combination of education and learning on-the-job in Laing, Palivos and Wang (1995). Since skills investments in these models have positive externalities, their financing could in principle involve employers, workers and government. But given the elusive nature of the externalities and the difficulties in their measurement, it is difficult to reach any compelling conclusion. In addition, the more narrowly conceived is the training, the weaker are the social benefits and the less justified is state intervention.[12]

9.7 Is there an equity issue?

Government intervention in the provision of workplace training may be difficult to justify on efficiency grounds, but could be motivated by equity considerations. Following Roemer (1998), equal opportunity policies need to distinguish between differences in outcomes that arise from different individual expenditure of effort, and differences arising from

---

[10] Booth and Zoega (1999), expand the quitting externality approach of Stevens (1994, 1996), by incorporating quits into a continuous time framework with demand uncertainty. They show conditions under which higher quit rates will lead to firms being more willing to finance training. High quit rates can encourage firms to wait less for information about future productivity before training new workers. This effect can offset the usual under-investment effect, in a world of certainty, of quits.

[11] In Acemoglu (1996), firms have constant returns to scale production functions and an interaction between *ex ante* human capital investments and bilateral search, resulting in social increasing returns to average human capital. A similar result is found in Booth and Coles (2005), where the increasing returns to education arise at the participation margin, in a model allowing for the interaction of home and market productivities and the tax system.

[12] So far there is very little growth theory that has looked exclusively at work-related training separately from education. Indeed, the only paper to our knowledge is that of Sepulveda (2002). However, there is a considerable literature looking at externalities associated with general education, as will have been discussed in the first part of this book. Through this avenue there may be a role for policy.

circumstances for which society believes individuals should not be held accountable—such as race, gender, and family background. Since firms can exclude individuals from the provision of workplace training, an important question is whether the recipients of training are favoured because of their higher effort or because of circumstances outside their control. In the latter case, government intervention is warranted.

Carneiro and Heckman, 2003, examine whether the provision of company training in the US is affected by family background, measured by the father's education and family income. Their empirical analysis on the NLSY79 shows that, conditional on ability—measured by the scores of the AFQT test—and education, family background has a negative effect on company training, and concludes that '... private financing arrangements between workers and firms appear to offset family income constraints and partially offset initial disadvantages'. Since the unconditional effect of parental background on company training is in their estimate not significantly different from zero, there is little support for the US for training policies addressing equality of opportunity.

9.8 Institutions

Training outcomes differ significantly across countries, as well as within countries (OECD, 2003a). This heterogeneity relates to differences in institutions—in the labour, product and education markets—affecting marginal benefits and costs. Institutions play an important role in the new training theory, because minimum wages and trade unions—*inter alia*—can affect the wedge between wages and marginal productivity. In Appendix 2 of this chapter (p. 182), we develop an illustrative 'wage compression' model to show how institutions in the labour and product market can affect training provision. In the following discussion we consider the effects of trade unions, followed by minimum wages, product market regulation, and then the tax system. All of these institutions are likely to vary across OECD countries.

9.8.1 *Trade unions*

The channels through which union collective bargaining can affect training and pay are potentially quite complex, and it is not immediately obvious that unionism will be associated with positive or negative returns to training. In this section, we discuss some of the channels through which unions can affect training and training returns, drawing on the survey at the start of Booth, Francesconi and Zoega (2003).

The implications of unionism for training and pay depend, *inter alia*, on the degree of competition in the labour market and on whether the union effect on training is indirect (through the wage structure) or direct (through the negotiation of training). In Appendix 2 we also explicitly incorporate trade unions into our illustrative 'wage compression' model, which produces similar implications to the Booth, Francesconi and Zoega (2005), framework concerning wages, training and turnover.

9.8.1.1 OTHERWISE COMPETITIVE LABOUR MARKETS

We define as 'otherwise competitive' the situation where the labour market is perfectly competitive except for union presence. The benchmark case is a perfectly competitive labour market without any trade union presence. A necessary condition for efficient training investment in competitive labour markets is that wages are set to facilitate such training investments. Some studies (e.g. see Mincer, 1983) therefore argue that, where wages are set collectively by trade unions in an otherwise competitive labour market, wage dispersion is reduced and incentives to invest in general training at the workplace are distorted. This is because union wages cannot be lowered during training and increased after training to allow workers to bear the costs and benefits of general training. Workers and firms will not efficiently invest in such training, and there will be a negative correlation between union presence and work-related training (Duncan and Stafford, 1980; Barron, Fuess and Loewenstein, 1987). In addition, the pay returns to training for union-covered workers will be lower than the pay returns to training for uncovered workers. These predictions are summarized in the first row of Table 9.2.

9.8.1.2 IMPERFECTLY COMPETITIVE LABOUR MARKETS

Next, we define an imperfectly competitive labour market as one characterized by some degree of oligopsony, which may arise through search frictions, workers' stochastic preferences for different firms, and the like. In oligopsonistic labour markets—as we discussed earlier in this section—workers receive wages below their marginal product, and thus workers' incentives to invest optimally in general training will be lowered. Some of the returns to training will accrue to the training firms, whose incentives to invest are increased. But the amount of training provided in equilibrium will be sub-optimal from society's viewpoint.

Table 9.2 Predictions about unions and training

	Model	Description	Empirical predictions for individual-level data
[1]	Otherwise competitive	Unions flatten wage profiles, reducing wage dispersion and distorting workers' incentives to invest in training.	Negative correlation between union presence and training. Training returns lower for union-covered than non-union covered workers.
[2]	Oligopsonistic labour market	[i] Wage compression associated with unions means that firms are more likely to finance training.	Union-covered workers receive sub-optimal levels of training. Ambiguous predictions as to the training returns of union-covered than non-union covered workers.
		[ii] Unions bargain at industry level directly over wages and training.	Union-covered workers receive more training and higher training returns relative to uncovered workers.
[3]	Union concern over the wage and employment package	Unions directly negotiate better training opportunities for covered workers, especially in non-competitive product markets where the available surplus is larger.	Union-covered workers receive more training and higher training returns relative to uncovered workers.
[4]	Turnover	Because unions reduce turnover, they have an indirect effect: union firms train more workers and each worker gets more training.	Union-covered workers receive more training, and also higher training returns relative to uncovered workers, owing to their greater training intensity.
[5]	Union control over supply of labour	[i] Control over the number of trainees reduces the supply of trained workers, lowering incidence but increasing returns.	Negative correlation between unions and training incidence. Training returns for union-covered workers are greater than for non-union workers.
		[ii] Control over the quality of trainees may mean more and better training per worker to sustain occupational standards.	A positive association between unions and training intensity and also higher wage growth.
[6]	Selection models	Union firms more carefully vet new hires who are thus on average of better quality.	More training and greater pay returns for union-covered workers but this reflects their higher unobserved ability/quality. Controlling for unobserved ability should eliminate this effect.

Source: Booth, Francesconi and Zoega (2003).

In imperfectly competitive labour markets, unions will have ambiguous effects on the pay returns to training. Acemoglu and Pischke (1999b), argue that unions cause wage compression in imperfectly competitive labour markets. In their model, unions set wages and the firm determines training. The model predicts that unionism will be associated with increased firm-financed transferable training. However the pay returns to union-covered workers from such training may be lower if the direct (adverse) effect of unions on wages is stronger than the indirect effect through more training. In contrast, Booth, Francesconi and Zoega (2005), model the source of wage compression as workers' stochastic preferences for different firms or heterogeneous mobility costs. In this framework, industry-wide unions that bargain directly over training and wages can extract a share of the surplus and hand it to workers in the form of more training and higher wages. Consequently, industry-wide unionism will be associated with more transferable training and with higher pay returns from training. This is because the union is effectively internalizing the friction.[13] These various predictions are summarized in the second row of Table 9.2.

9.8.1.3 UNION CONCERN OVER THE WAGE-EMPLOYMENT PACKAGE

Assume that union utility is increasing in the wages and job security or employment of its members, as is usual in most models of union behaviour. Unions may ensure that covered workers receive higher wages and greater job security by directly intervening in training provision, for example by making sure that workers' skills are enhanced through more training. Thus training is an instrument through which union goals of increasing employment and job security are attained. Strong unions might therefore be more willing to negotiate better training opportunities for covered workers, especially in non-competitive product markets in which the available surplus is larger. Testable predictions from this hypothesis—summarized in Row [3] of Table 9.2—are that union-covered firms will provide more training and higher returns for such training, relative to uncovered firms.

9.8.1.4 LABOUR TURNOVER

Where unions improve worker morale and organization at the workplace, labour turnover may be reduced (Blau and Kahn, 1983; Freeman and Medoff, 1984). Union-covered firms may therefore have greater incentives to provide training because they are less likely to lose highly productive trained workers.[14] Through this mechanism, unionism may be associated with increased training and productivity, and consequently wages.[15] The testable predictions of this hypothesis are that union-covered firms train a greater proportion of their workers and give each worker more training, because

---

[13] In another context, Booth and Chatterji (1998), show that union–firm wage bargaining can prevent *ex-post* monopsonistic wage-setting by firms and can thereby reduce inefficient quits.

[14] Booth, Francesconi, and Zoega (2005), provide a formal model.

[15] Analysing a panel of British industries between 1983 and 1996, Dearden, Reed and Van Reenen (2000), find that higher training is systematically associated with higher productivity.

covered workers are characterized by lower turnover. Thus the training returns for covered workers will be higher than for uncovered workers because of their greater training intensity (holding tenure and all else constant). These predictions are summarized in the fourth row of Table 9.2.

9.8.1.5 UNIONS' USE OF TRAINING TO CONTROL LABOUR SUPPLY

Union organization in a number of European countries initially developed on a craft (or occupational) basis and only later along industrial lines. A traditional strategy of craft unions in countries such as Britain and Germany was to influence access to training (typically youth access to apprenticeship) as a means of determining labour supply, as well as to monitor the quality of training provided (Ryan, 1994). If this strategy has persisted over time, we may still observe this channel of influence for specific groups of workers such as apprentices or young and inexperienced employees. However, its predictions for training and training returns are ambiguous. For example, union control over the *number* of trainees might result in a negative association between unions and training receipt. Trainee numbers might be restricted to increase labour scarcity, thereby lowering incidence but increasing training returns. Conversely, union control over the *quality* of training might result in a positive association between unions and training incidence and intensity (more and better training per worker to sustain occupational standards) and also for wage growth. These various predictions are summarized in the fifth row of Table 9.2.

9.8.1.6 SELECTIVITY AND OTHER ISSUES

In firms that become unionized, management may respond to higher union wages by more carefully vetting new hires to obtain a better quality workforce. This vetting might also involve induction training. From the supply side, better quality or more motivated workers might self-select into union jobs if the training opportunities and returns are higher in the union-covered sector. If unions bargain directly over training as well as wages, only workers able to benefit from such training will wish to queue for union jobs, or will be offered such jobs. These predictions are summarized in the last row of Table 9.2. They suggest that any observed link between unions, training and training returns may be spurious.[16]

---

[16] This emphasizes the importance in empirical work to control for potential self-selection into training as well as potential self-selection into union coverage. However, in many EU countries union coverage is attached to the job rather than the individual, and thus the issue of selection is somewhat mitigated.

Some of these hypotheses as to the impact of unionism on training and training returns are observationally equivalent, as inspection of the last column of Table 9.2 makes clear. The hypotheses summarized in Rows [2.ii], [3], [4] and [5.ii] all predict that union-covered workers will receive more training and higher training returns relative to uncovered workers. On the other hand, the 'otherwise competitive' model (see Row [1] of Table 9.1) is the only hypothesis predicting a negative correlation between union presence and training and lower training returns for union-covered compared with non-union covered workers. Moreover the hypotheses are not mutually exclusive. Higher job retention of union-covered workers may be at work in imperfectly competitive labour markets. And apprenticeships may go hand in hand with oligopsonistic labour markets.

9.8.2 Minimum wages

With competitive labour markets, human capital theory predicts that the introduction of a minimum wage will reduce investment in training by covered workers who can no longer contribute to training costs through lower wages (see Rosen, 1972). If the labour market for the low paid is competitive and workers are not credit constrained, a minimum wage will reduce training. In the absence of binding training contracts for workers, a minimum wage provides a floor below which wages cannot fall. Thus lower wages cannot be used as a means of allowing workers to finance general training, or to facilitate worker–firm sharing in specific training investments.

But if the labour market for the low paid is imperfectly competitive or workers are credit constrained, a minimum wage can increase investment in the general component of training. Why is this the case? The basic rationale is provided by oligopsonistic models—some of which were outlined earlier in this section—predicting that firms may pay for general training. The oligopsonistic labour market introduces a 'wedge' between wages and marginal product. And it can be shown that the introduction of a minimum wage also acts as a type of wedge between wages and marginal productivity. Thus it can actually increase general training over a range of human capital and induce employers to train their unskilled workers (Acemoglu and Pischke, 2003).

It is an empirical question as to which, if any, of these effects dominates training incidence and volumes in the real world. The answer will depend on the general–specific training mix, the existence of credit constraints on low paid workers, and the degree of imperfect competition in the labour market.

9.8.3 *Taxes and social security systems*

Average income and payroll taxes create a wedge between the gross wage paid by the employer and the pay taken home by employees. The effect of the wedge on training is likely to depend on whether the cost is borne by the employer or by the employee.

9.8.4 *Product market competition and deregulation*

Deregulation increases competition in the product market and can affect training in a number of ways. First, deregulation influences real wages and profits after training, and reduces rents. Secondly, the higher competition induced by deregulation increases productivity by forcing firms to improve efficiency and to innovate. If innovation and skills are complements (see Acemoglu, 1997), firms have a higher incentive to train. By affecting the entry of firms, deregulation also contributes to local agglomeration effects, which encourage the investment in training.[17] Third, the relative bargaining power of workers can fall, because of the higher risk of involuntary turnover and plant closure associated to more product market competition. We illustrate the relationship between training and deregulation by using the model of imperfect competition developed by Blanchard and Giavazzi (2003), in the Dixit–Stiglitz tradition. We use as a measure of product market competition a parameter reflecting the degree of substitutability between available products. The greater this degree, the more competitive the product market.

We show that, in the general symmetric equilibrium with no entry, when the bargaining power of workers is constant and we ignore its effects on productivity, more deregulation reduces the marginal benefits of training by reducing rents. Therefore, training falls. Deregulation, however, affects productivity. By inducing more competition, innovation and a stronger quest for efficiency, deregulation also contributes to increasing the marginal returns to training. Moreover, if the higher risk of dismissal associated to deregulation induces workers to accept wage concessions, then the bargaining power of workers declines. These two effects can compensate the

---

[17] See Brunello and Gambarotto (2004), and Brunello and De Paola (2004a).

negative impact of lower rents and contribute to generate an overall increase of training.[18]

9.8.5 Schooling institutions

The variation of school design—especially of secondary schools—can affect training outcomes, given the complementarity between education and training. Countries differ in the degree of stratification of secondary education and in the importance of tracking. The design of secondary schooling systems varies considerably across European countries, and an important dimension of such variation is the relative importance of vocational and general education. While comprehensive schooling systems which mix general and vocational education are typical of the UK, stratified systems, with a much more marked separation of the vocational and general track, are widespread in Germany. The rest of the major European countries lie somewhere in between.[19] It is an open question as to whether a more stratified schooling system is conducive to higher training outcomes than a more comprehensive system. If vocational schools in stratified educational systems produce very specialized skills that become rapidly obsolete in the presence of technical progress, more training might be required to update existing skills to match the new technical blueprints. On the other hand, comprehensive schools could produce skills that are too general, and which require additional training to become operational.

9.9 Summary

For many years it was thought that human capital theory, based on the assumption of a perfectly competitive labour market, fully explained who would pay for general training. Stylized facts diverging from the theory's predictions were believed to be due to imperfections such as credit market constraints. And yet some puzzles remained that could not be explained within this framework; puzzles such as employers paying for general

---

[18] In contrast, the model in Gersbach and Schmutzler (2004), predicts that training incidence is higher if concentration is high, or competitive intensity is relatively low, or product differentiation is strong. The reason is that they assume that the slope of the outside option function (and therefore of the wage function) increases with product market competition.

[19] See Brunello and Giannini (2004), and Brunello, Giannini and Ariga (2004), for a discussion of these issues.

training in spite of potential poaching of trained workers, and the lack of evidence of workers receiving wage cuts during training.

Over the last decade, new ways of thinking in labour economics have challenged this orthodoxy and begun to transform our ways of thinking about work-related training. A growing literature argues that employers have market power in setting wages—what is termed the *new oligopsony.* This oligopsony can arise through product differentiation and through imperfect information (rather than through the old definition of a monopsonist as being a single employer in a labour market). And its proponents demonstrate that it can lead to simple and plausible explanations of labour market phenomena that are otherwise regarded as puzzles.

In the remainder of this book we use this framework to inform our empirical investigation. We would emphasize that the traditional human capital approach assuming perfectly competitive labour markets forms a useful and powerful benchmark model. However, although the imperfectly competitive approach is still being developed, it offers important new insights about work-related training and conditions under which intervention in the labour market might be justified. In the next chapter, we turn to an investigation of the extent and outcomes of training across a number of countries, and document stylized facts across a number of OECD countries.

APPENDIX 1

In two recent contributions, Acemoglu and Pischke (1999a, 1999b)—AP from now on—argue that it is through wage compression that trade unions and other labour-market institutions induce firms to invest in general training. Using the results in Booth and Zoega (2004), we demonstrate that this condition is satisfied in a much wider range of conditions even including compensation schemes—such as piece rates—that are not commonly associated with wage compression.

Denote a worker's inherent ability or productivity by $\bar{y}$. Then assume that training adds to workers' productivity (y) in an additive fashion where $f(\tau)$ is a strictly concave function:

$$y(\tau) = \bar{y} + f(\tau) \qquad [9A\text{-}1.1]$$

Similarly assume that wages w, in the absence of training, can be denoted by $\bar{w}$ where $\lambda(\tau)$ is again a strictly concave function;

$$w(\tau) = \bar{w} + \lambda(\tau) \qquad [9A\text{-}1.2]$$

and $\bar{y}$ and $\bar{w}$ can take any value. Profits from a worker having received training τ can then be written as

$$P(\tau) = y(\tau) - w(\tau) = \bar{y} - \bar{w} + (f(\tau) - \lambda(\tau)) \qquad [9A\text{-}1.3]$$

Here, absolute wage compression occurs if $P'(0) > 0$. Now denote the probability that a worker stays on after training as $(1 - q)$, where q is the propensity to quit and is taken to be a constant and independent of relative wages. The equality of the expected marginal profit from training—given by $(1 - q)P'(\tau)$—and the marginal training costs $c'(\tau)$—where $c(\tau)$ is a strictly convex function and $c(0) = 0$—gives the optimal level of training τ^*:

$$P'(\tau) = y'(\tau) - w'(\tau) = (1 - q)[f'(\tau^*) - \lambda'(\tau^*)] = c'(\tau^*) \qquad [9A\text{-}1.4]$$

It follows that $\tau^* > 0$ if and only if $P'(0) > 0$ which implies $f'(0) > \lambda'(0)$.

Now, instead of assuming that training adds to both productivity and wages in an additive fashion, suppose that it adds in a multiplicative or log-additive way. We now change equations [1.1] and [1.2] so they become

$$y(\tau) = \bar{y}f(\tau) \qquad \text{[9A-1.1']}$$
$$w(\tau) = \bar{w}f(\tau) \qquad \text{[9A-1.2']}$$

where we have set $f(\tau) = \lambda(\tau)$ to emphasize that $f'(\tau) = \lambda'(\tau)$ for all values of τ. This makes the ratio of output to wages $p(\tau)$ a constant and equal to $\bar{y}/\bar{w}$ and there is no relative wage compression by definition.

Booth and Zoega (2004), argue that it is less plausible for inherent ability (or skills) and acquired productivity through training to appear in an additive (equations [1.1] and [1.2] or a multiplicative fashion (equations [1.1'] and [1.2']). The difference between [1.1] and [1.1'] is simple. The first formulation implies that inherent abilities and trained productivity are perfect substitutes, so that the isoquants in the inherent ability-trained productivity $(\bar{y}, f(\tau))$ space are downward-sloping lines. This is unlikely to be the case. The alternative multiplicative formulation implies that they are imperfect substitutes, so that the upper-contour set becomes strictly convex.

The firm's profits from employing the worker become, under the multiplicative formulation

$$P(\tau) = y(\tau) - w(\tau) = (\bar{y} - \bar{w})f(\tau) \qquad \text{[9A-1.3']}$$

and the first-order conditions with respect to training are now

$$(1 - q)(\bar{y} - \bar{w})f'(\tau^*) = c'(\tau^*) \qquad \text{[9A-1.4']}$$

It again follows that $\tau^* > 0$ if and only if $P'(0) > 0$—there is absolute wage compression as emphasized by AP—but which now only implies $\bar{y} > \bar{w}$. Thus the firm would benefit from increased training in the absence of relative wage compression, and would be willing to pay for it. It follows that absolute wage compression does not imply relative wage compression. Firms may be willing to train in the absence of relative wage compression—relative wage decompression $p'(0) < 0$ not excluded.

We can make this point more succinctly as follows. Relative wage compression is defined as $dp(\tau)/d\tau > 0$ where $p = \frac{y(\tau)}{w(\tau)}$ which implies that

$$\frac{wy' - w'y}{w^2} = \frac{w(y' - w') - w'(y - w)}{w^2} \qquad \text{[9A-1.5]}$$

Since $w'(\tau) \geq 0$ and $y(\tau) \geq w(\tau)$ it follows that relative wage compression implies absolute wage compression: $y' > w'$. However, absolute wage compression does not have to imply relative wage compression.

While relative wage compression increases the level of general training desired by employers, by no means does it constitute a necessary condition. To see this, return to equations [1.1'] and [1.2']. First substitute $\lambda(\tau)$ for $f(\tau)$ in equation (1.2') and then insert the multiplicative functions of [1.1'] and [1.2'] into the expression for profits. This yields the firm's maximand as:

$$\max_{\tau} (1-q)[\bar{y}f(\tau) - \bar{w}\lambda(\tau)] - c(\tau)$$

The first order condition now becomes, after adding and subtracting the term $\bar{w}f'(\tau)$:

$$(1-q)\lfloor(\bar{y} - \bar{w})f'(\tau^*) + \bar{w}(f'(\tau^*) - \lambda'(\tau^*))\rfloor = c'(\tau^*) \qquad \text{[9A-1.6]}$$

where we assume that $\bar{y} > \bar{w}$ and $f'(\tau) > \lambda'(\tau)$. Relative wage compression now appears as the last term on the left-hand side of equation [1.6]. It is clear that, while relative wage compression increases the level of general training desired by employers, it by no means implies a necessary condition. This is because, even when $f'(0) = \lambda'(0)$ and there is no relative wage compression, there will still be absolute wage compression since $P'(0) > 0$ through $(\bar{y} - \bar{w})f'(\tau)$. Therefore the firm will still be willing to pay for general training even with no relative wage compression. However it is clear that, with relative wage compression $f'(0) > \lambda'(0)$, the profitability of paying for workers' training is increased.

Relative wage compression is thus *not* a necessary condition for firms' willingness to pay for general training, but instead a factor affecting how much they are willing to pay. How important this factor is depends on the shape of the training function $f(\tau)$, the level of labour-market rigidity $\bar{y} - \bar{w}$, and the effect of training on wages $\lambda'(\tau)$. In contrast, absolute wage compression does constitute such a necessary condition. However, absolute wage compression is a feature of compensation systems such as piece rates, which one does not usually associate with any form of wage compression.

APPENDIX 2

Consider a static model of training investment with the following sequence of events (see Acemoglu and Pischke, 1998, 1999a): in the first stage the firm decides how much to invest in (general) training τ and bears the training cost; in the second stage the firm and the worker bargain over the wage $w(\tau)$; in the third stage a random event ε occurs, drawn from the distribution $\varepsilon \sim G(0,\sigma)$, which affects the outside option available to the worker, $v(\tau)$. Based on this event and the previous stages of the game, the worker decides whether to quit or stay. If s/he quits, the training firm cannot recoup the training costs. Both the firm and the worker are risk-neutral. Since the labour market is frictional, $f(\tau) > v(\tau) + \varepsilon$, where productivity $f(\tau)$ is concave in training. Turnover can only be voluntary and occurs when $w(\tau) \leq v(\tau) + \varepsilon$. Therefore we have

$$q(\tau) = \xi(\tau)[1 - G(w(\tau) - v(\tau))] \qquad \text{[9A-2.1]}$$

where ξ is the rate of job offers, which we assume to be increasing in training—because training has a positive signalling effect (see Autor 2003).

Using primes for first derivatives, the effect of training on turnover is

$$\frac{\partial q}{\partial \tau} = -\xi g[w'(\tau) - v'(\tau)] + \xi'(\tau)[1 - G(w(\tau) - v(\tau))] \qquad \text{[9A-2.2]}$$

Wages are set by Nash bargaining before the random draw on ε. Since ε is not observed at the time of the bargain, the wage w cannot be indexed to the draw. The worker earns expected wages $w(\tau)$ if employed and has an expected outside option $v(\tau)$ in the event of separation. The outcome of the Nash bargain is

$$w(\tau) = (1 - \beta)f(\tau) + \beta v(\tau) \qquad \text{[9A-2.3]}$$

where β is the bargaining power of the firm, from which we obtain

$$w'(\tau) - v'(\tau) = (1 - \beta)[f'(\tau) - v'(\tau)] \qquad \text{[9A-2.4]}$$

Replacing [2.4] into [2.2], we notice that the first element in the right hand side of [2.2] is negative if $1 - \beta > 0$ and there is absolute wage compression, defined as $[f'(\tau) - v'(\tau)] > 0$. The overall derivative, however, cannot be signed a priori.

Next consider the training decision taken by the firm to maximize expected profits

$$P(\tau) = [1 - q(\tau)]\beta[f(\tau) - v(\tau)] - c(\tau) \qquad [9A\text{-}2.5]$$

where $c(\tau)$ is the total cost of training, which is paid by the firm when there is absolute wage compression. The optimal choice of τ yields

$$(1 - q)\beta[f'(\tau) - v'(\tau)] - q'(\tau)\beta[f(\tau) - v(\tau)] = c'(\tau) \qquad [9A\text{-}2.6]$$

In the absence of positive externalities, the first best is attained if

$$f'(\tau) = c'(\tau) \qquad [9A\text{-}2.7]$$

The private optimum [2.7] corresponds to the first best if[1]

$$-q'(\tau)\beta[f(\tau) - v(\tau)] = (1 - q)\beta v'(\tau) + [1 - \beta + q\beta]f'(\tau)$$

which cannot be excluded if $q'(\tau) < 0$.

Training in the private optimum can be higher than in the social optimum if the left hand side of the above expression is larger than the right hand side. We rule out the case $\beta = 1$, because no firm would invest in training. Since training is often general, we can also exclude $v'(\tau) = 0$. With no externalities, a sufficient condition for under-provision is $q'(\tau) \geq 0$, which can be tested in the data. If $q'(\tau) \geq 0$, the private optimum yields a level of training lower than the first best. How much lower? It depends on the shape of the cost, turnover, productivity and outside option functions.

---

[1] The presence of positive spillovers—due for instance to the complementarity between training and innovation—affects the first best outcome. Letting $f'(\tau) + F'(\tau)$ be the sum of private and social returns to training, the condition above becomes

$$-q'(\tau)\beta[f(\tau) - v(\tau)] = (1 - q)\beta v'(\tau) + [1 - \beta + q\beta]f'(\tau) + F'(\tau).$$

APPENDIX 3

Following Acemoglu and Pischke (1999), consider a frictional labour market where the firm has to decide the investment in training τ. Let $f(\tau)$, $w(\tau)$ and $c(\tau)$ be productivity, the wage and the cost of training, which we assume to be borne by the firm. Let $f(0) = 1$, a useful normalization. Each employee in this firm quits with exogenous probability q and receives in the external labour market the wage $v(\tau)$. With this notation, the firm's profits are

$$P(\tau) = (1 - q)[f(\tau) - w(\tau)] - c(\tau) \qquad \text{[9A-3.1]}$$

A3.1 Unions

Suppose that a union organizes homogenous workers and cares only about its employed members. The representative union member has utility

$$u(\tau) = (1 - q)w(\tau) + qv(\tau) \qquad \text{[9A-3.2]}$$

Let the firm set the optimal level of training in the first step, and let the parties bargain over the wage in the second step. Since training costs are bygones after the investment, profits in the wage bargain are gross of training costs. Let the outside option of the firm be zero and the outside option of the union be $v(\tau)$. Finally, define β as the relative bargaining power of the firm. With Nash bargaining, the bargained wage turns out to be

$$w(\tau) = \beta v(\tau) + (1 - \beta)f(\tau) \qquad \text{[9A-3.3]}$$

Backward induction implies that the (privately) optimal level of training is given by

$$(1 - q)\beta\lfloor f'(\tau) - v'(\tau)\rfloor = c'(\tau) \qquad \text{[9A-3.4]}$$

where the prime is for the first derivative. Training is non-zero if the marginal increase of productivity is higher than the marginal increase in the outside option. This condition is called absolute wage compression (Acemoglu and Pischke, 1999b).

Unions can affect optimal training by influencing turnover and the relative bargaining power of the firm. Stronger unions have higher bargaining power, which reduces β and training. Since they might also reduce turnover via a more effective voice mechanism, the overall effect of stronger unions on (employer-provided) training is not clear-cut.

Next suppose that unions are strong enough to bargain over training investment as well. Compared to the previous case, there is contemporaneous bargaining both over wages and over training. It can be shown that the outcome of the Nash bargain is

$$(1 - q)\lfloor f'(\tau) - v'(\tau) \rfloor = c'(\tau) \qquad [9A\text{-}3.5]$$

Since β is less than one, training is higher when unions bargain over it.

A3.2 Product market regulation

The notation used in this part of the Appendix is slightly different and follows Blanchard and Giavazzi (2003). Consider an economy populated by identical and imperfectly competitive firms. The production function of each firm is simply $y_i = n_i$, where i is the index for firms and n is employment. Profits for each firm are $(p_i - w_i)y_i(\tau) - c(\tau)$, where p are prices, output depends on training and c is the training cost. Let the average price P be normalized to 1. The firm sets training to maximize profits; after training has been set, the firm and the worker bargain over wages and prices (or employment). There is no turnover. The Nash maximand in log terms is

$$\Omega_i = (1 - \beta) \log \left[(w_i - v_i)y_i\right] + \beta \log \left(p_i - w_i\right)y_i \qquad [9A\text{-}3.6]$$

and the relationship between output and prices for each firm is

$$y_i = p_i^{-\sigma} \qquad [9A\text{-}3.7]$$

where σ is elasticity of demand with respect to the price. Deregulation increases σ.

The maximization of [3.8] with respect prices and wages yields

$$p_i = (1 + \mu)v_i \qquad [9A\text{-}3.8]$$
$$w_i = [1 + (1 - \beta)\mu]v_i \qquad [9A\text{-}3.9]$$

where $\mu = \dfrac{1}{\sigma - 1}$. In the symmetric equilibrium prices are equal to the average price. Hence, $v = 1/(1 + \mu)$ and $w = [1 + (1 - \beta)\mu]/(1 + \mu)$.[1] Using these results in the definition of profits before training we obtain

---

[1] Since the equilibrium is symmetric, we drop the subscript from now on.

$$P(\tau) = \left[1 - \frac{[1 + (1 - \beta)\mu]}{1 + \mu}\right] y(\tau) - c(\tau) \tag{9A-3.10}$$

Let $y_{\mu\tau}(\tau)$ be the partial derivative of the marginal productivity of training $y'(\tau)$ with respect to μ, and assume this partial to be negative. Optimal training requires

$$\left[1 - \frac{[1 + (1 - \beta)\mu]}{1 + \mu}\right] y'(\tau) - c'(\tau) = \varphi(\tau, \mu) = 0 \tag{9A-3.11}$$

If the second order conditions for a maximum hold, as we assume, then

$$sign \frac{\partial \tau}{\partial \mu} = sign \frac{\partial \varphi}{\partial \mu} > 0 \tag{9A-3.12}$$

Therefore, deregulation (a decline in μ) reduces training. Next assume that $\beta'(\mu) > 0$, so that the workers' bargaining power increases with regulation. Then

$$\frac{\partial \varphi}{\partial \mu} = \frac{\beta + \mu(1 + \mu)\beta'}{(1 + \mu)^2} y'(\tau) + \left[1 - \frac{[1 + (1 - \beta)\mu]}{1 + \mu}\right] y_{\mu\tau}(\tau) \tag{9A-3.13}$$

can be negative if β' and $y_{\mu\tau}(\tau)$ are large enough.

10

Stylized Facts about Workplace Training

Introduction

The purpose of this chapter is to document stylized facts about the distribution of workplace training in Europe (and, when possible, OECD countries) by looking at the most recent cross-comparable datasets available in the scientific community. When discrepancies come out, we will also compare the picture that emerges from these datasets with previous literature.

In which country are investments in training greater? How large are regional differences within countries? How do employers and employees share the cost of training? At face value, how much do employers invest in training? What type of individual has a greater propensity to take training and/or be trained by his/her employer? And once we control for individual characteristics, how large are differences across countries? These are the questions we address in this section. In order to do so, we will use several large cross-country datasets that are available for OECD countries, such as:

 (i) OECD aggregate training data;
 (ii) the Continuing Vocational Training Survey (CVTS);
(iii) the International Adult Literacy Survey (IALS); and
(iv) the European Community Household Panel (ECHP).

These datasets are briefly described in Appendix 4 (on pp. 216–17).

The datasets we use in this section provide information that is essentially complementary. OECD training data cover 30 OECD and European countries, but provide only aggregate figures. The CVTS is an employer survey covering firms with more than 10 employees in 25 European countries. As such, it provides information on training firms and employer-paid training but little information on trainees and no information on employee-paid training. The International Adult Literacy Survey (IALS) is an individual survey covering many OECD countries. Unfortunately, few European countries fall within the IALS country sample. In addition, the IALS has limited information on the labour market status of trainees (labour market status is measured after the training). None of these three sources, however, has a longitudinal dimension. Whenever necessary, therefore, we will resort to the European Community Household Panel (ECHP), which provides comparable data on training participation for 13 EU countries.[1] The disadvantage of the ECHP is primarily on the fact that additional training information (financing, duration, etc.) is of less good quality—since it is provided only for the last course taken and training refers to a time interval, the length of which can vary from country to country and even from one interviewee to another (cf. Appendix 4). Conversely, its advantage relies in its large set of individual characteristics and its longitudinal dimension.

We start in section 10.1 by discussing measurement issues. Then, in section 10.2, we look at cross-country and cross-region training patterns. Next, we focus on training financing, looking particularly at how large is the share of training investments paid for by the firm (section 10.3), and at how training varies across different types of firms (section 10.4). Finally, in section 10.5 we will turn attention more specifically to the employees and look at the impact of individual characteristics on the probability of taking/ receiving training. The chapter ends with a summary of the key results.

10.1 Measurement issues

Training and, more in general, the stock of human capital is difficult to measure. Initially, studies of training used labour market experience as a proxy for general training and job tenure as a proxy for specific training. In the last two decades datasets containing self-reported measures of training have become increasingly available.[2] These datasets are typically based on household surveys such as the Current Population Survey (CPS) and the National Longitudinal Survey of Youth (NLSY) in the US, in which

---

[1] All the 15 countries that belonged to the EU before enlargement are covered by the ECHP. However, we exclude Germany, since German data exclude short training spells, and Luxembourg, due to sample size.

[2] An early attempt at measuring training more directly is found in the Michigan Panel Study of Income Dynamics (PSID). Respondents were asked: 'on a job like yours, how much time would it take the average new person to become fully trained and qualified?' This seems to measure a characteristic of the job instead of the amount of training the respondent participated in.

respondents are asked whether they participated in some form of training in a specific reference period. In addition to household surveys, employer-based (see Barron et al., 1987) and matched employer–employee surveys (e.g. Black and Lynch, 2001) are also slowly becoming available. Finally there are a few studies that use administrative data from a single firm (e.g. Bartel, 1995).

Most surveys collect flow measures of training, namely: the amount of training over a specified calendar period (e.g. the previous 12 months, or the period since a previous interview). In the CPS the reference period covers the time since the start of the job, which implies that if all reported training is specific this question would measure the stock of training. Logically the amount of training that is reported depends on the period covered by the training questions (e.g. Loewenstein and Spletzer, 1998). The retrospective nature of these self-reported training measures in-troduces, however, measurement errors because of recollection problems. The measurement error is expected to increase both with the span of time between the training spell and the interview, and with the detail of the training questions. It is for this reason that training questions that meas-ure flows are probably more accurate than training questions that attempt to measure stocks. Surveys often ask about training incidence, but increas-ingly try to measure the length of training spells in an attempt to more accurately measure training effort.

Training is almost inherently heterogeneous and some aggregation is therefore inevitable. The aggregation implicit in the training questions varies between surveys. The types of training measured by these surveys therefore vary and are typically derived from the institutional setting, and often combine mode of delivery and provider. The NLSY, for example, asks about: training followed at business schools, apprenticeship programmes, vocational or technical institutes, but also about correspondence courses, formal company training run by the employer, military training, seminars or training programmes run at work by someone other than the employer, seminars or training programmes outside of work, and training given by vocational rehabilitation centres. It is not immediately clear to what extent this is an economically sensible classification.

In particular, the way training is usually defined and classified implies that only information on formal training is collected, and that the data on long initial vocational training (such as apprenticeship training) are inevitably not comparable. Let us look at these two issues in order.

Apart from formal training, there is a growing interest in measuring informal training (e.g. Barron et al., 1997; Frazis et al., 1996; Loewenstein and Spletzer, 1999) but no general dataset has been made available so far for this purpose. The problem is that the definition of informal training is slippery, while formal training can be defined in a very precise way. This explains why data on informal training is often not collected by official statistical offices and researchers focus their analyses on formal training only, with an a priori assumption that the two are correlated. Yet, in the few cases where data on both formal and informal are available, discrepancies among the two can be large, and most training appears to be informal. For instance, the Australian Bureau of Statistics (1990) show that almost 80 per cent of Australian employees received informal training in the 12 months covered by the survey, while participation in formal training turned out to be less than one-third. More worrisome, the distribution of informal training by occupation turns out to be relatively flat, while formal training typically appears to be more frequent among white collar workers.

In certain countries, such as those with a dual system of education, formal initial vocational training plays an important role. This is by and large training undertaken during the employee's working life and it is often paid for, or organized, by the employer. Yet, in contrast with most continuous training, it lasts for a long period (often more than one year) in which both production activity and training are combined in variable quantities. Here, the problem is the following: if training is measured by mere participation (as it is often the case), clearly the amount of initial vocational training will be underestimated whenever we try to aggregate. Conversely, when training is measured in terms of course length (to obtain volume data), the amount of initial vocational training might be exaggerated insofar as effective hours of instruction are usually reported for continuous training and the duration of the period covered by the contract combining instruction and production (measured in weeks, months or even years) is often reported for initial training. The solution adopted by many researchers has been to try to filter out initial vocational training and focus only on continuous training, and we will be no exception here. Such choice enhances comparability and restricts attention to what is clearly measurable, but we warn the reader that, insofar as initial vocational training may represent the largest share of all the training received by an individual during his/her working life, this comes at the price of producing an incomplete picture of the phenomenon of interest, particularly if only formal training is taken into account (see the detailed comments by Steve Pischke on this issue on p. 333).

Related to these problems is the issue of cost. For example, if respondents are employees, they are unlikely to be fully aware of the full opportunity cost of training (i.e. foregone productivity) and, to the extent that the employer paid for training, they are also unlikely to have information on the direct (monetary) cost of training.

The above illustrates the conceptual and practical complexity of collecting information on training. The heterogeneity in training questions introduces problems of comparability between surveys and even within surveys, particularly across countries. For instance, Campanelli et al. (1994), note, from a study of both linguistic and survey data, that the interpretation of the term 'training' varies across groups in the population, in particular employers, employees, and training researchers. Yet, little is known about the extent to which these conceptual measurement problems lead to actual measurement error. The only quantitative study to date hinting at this is Barron et al. (1997). These authors use data from a matched employer–employee survey dataset to see to what extent employer and employee responses are consistent. They find that correlations between worker and establishment measures are less than .5 and that establishments report 25 per cent more hours of training on average than workers do. On average, incidence rates are similar between worker and establishment reports, although 30 per cent disagree on whether on-site formal training occurred. This suggests that training is measured with substantial error.

One of the conclusions that emerges from these measurement problems is that one needs to be particularly careful when trying to document cross-country variation in training, due to the idiosyncratic definition of the concept of training in each specific survey. Early literature (see for instance OECD, 1993; Lynch, 1994; Blinder and Krueger, 1996; Acemoglu and Pischke, 1999b) often resorted to national surveys and compared aggregate training incidence across surveys to infer the cross-country distribution of training. The above discussion suggests that this approach must be handled with care. The extent of the problem is immediately evident by looking at Figure 10.1, which compares training participation rates obtained from the ECHP with OECD aggregate data.[3] ECHP training participation rates are about three-quarters on average of the participation rate in the OECD dataset and this figure is significantly different from 1. In other words, a cross-country comparison of participation rates made by taking some countries from the ECHP and other countries from OECD data, would systematically underestimate the relative training effort of the former countries with respect to the latter.

---

[3] All figures reported in this section refer to employed workers aged between 25 and 64 years, except when differently specified.

Percentage of employees taking some training in one year

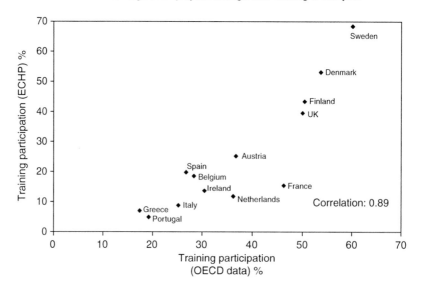

Fig. 10.1 Comparison of training participation rates across datasets
Sources: OECD (2004) and ECHP.

More on the positive side, however, we can observe that the correlation among the two measures is high and the ranking of countries is approximately the same in both OECD and ECHP data (with France and the Netherlands being the only two countries with major differences across datasets),[4] showing that certain cross-country differences are persistent across surveys, and not all the information contained therein is noise. This is reassuring and allows us to meaningfully proceed in our analysis of training patterns using large cross-country datasets. Yet, one caveat regarding cross-country comparability remains necessary. By using a minimum age threshold (typically 25 years), researchers usually eliminate the problem of comparing apprenticeship training with continuous training. This is what we do here. However, the drawback of this approach is that, for countries with large apprenticeship systems (such as Germany, Austria and Australia), training rates and volumes are under-estimated in our figures.

---

[4] Similar correlations are found also between ECHP, CVTS and IALS data. This is not surprising since OECD data are constructed from CVTS and IALS data (cf. Appendix 4 on pp. 216–17).

10.2 The distribution of training across countries and regions

In which country do employees take/receive more training? The most common training measures in the literature are participation rates, that is the share of employees receiving training in a given period, and training hours per employee. On the basis of the OECD datasets, the largest available to us, Figure 1 in the general introduction shows participation rates and hours per employee for 30 European or Anglo-Saxon countries in the second half of the 1990s. Annual training participation varies between 10.8 per cent in Romania and 60.1 per cent in Sweden while average annual hours per employee vary between 6.7 in Romania and 36.1 in Denmark. The two measures are nonetheless strongly correlated. This is due to the fact that training hours per participants are much more homogenous across countries, varying between a low 43 hours in the US to a high 80 hours in Ireland (Figure 10.2) with a coefficient of variation of .16 against .42 for participation rates and .45 for hours per employee.

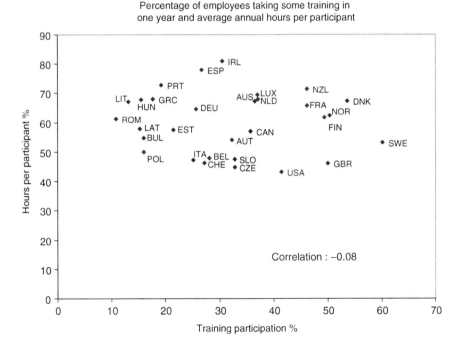

Fig. 10.2 Training participation and training hours per participant in OECD countries

Note: The figures refer to the second half of the 1990s.

Source: OECD (2004).

Hence, with some notable exception, the relative position of countries is the same irrespective to the measure used.

Scandinavian countries as well as France and New Zealand appear to be the most training intensive countries (with participation rates above 45 per cent and more than 30 hours per employee). The United Kingdom could be added to this group as regards participation rate (50%); but it falls behind by more than one standard deviation in terms of hours of training (23 per employee). A similar fate occurs to the US, which is about one standard deviation above the mean in terms of participation rates (41.4 per cent) and just below the mean in terms of hours of training per employee (17.9). At the bottom of the distribution we find several Eastern European countries (Romania, Poland, Lithuania, Latvia, Bulgaria and Hungary) and, just above, the group of Southern European EU countries (except Spain).

Overall, we find that, irrespective of the measure considered, training varies by a factor of 6 between the least and the best performing country. This reduces to 3–3.5, if we focus on the EU before the Enlargement (EU-15 hereafter). But does looking at the distribution of training by country suffice to provide an accurate picture of the geographical distribution of training? To answer this question in a very descriptive manner, Figure 10.3 provides the distribution of training by region for selected EU countries using the 1997 wave of the ECHP and the most disaggregate available decomposition (NUTS 2 for the UK, Portugal, Sweden and Finland; NUTS 1 for all other countries).

Panel A. Nuts 1 regions, selected countries

Regional training participation (average of the country = 100) [a,b]

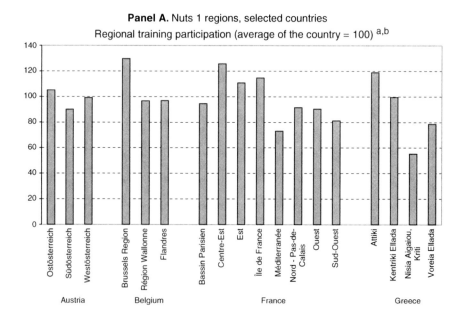

Panel B. Nuts 1 regions, Italy and Spain
Regional training participation (average of the country = 100) [a,b]

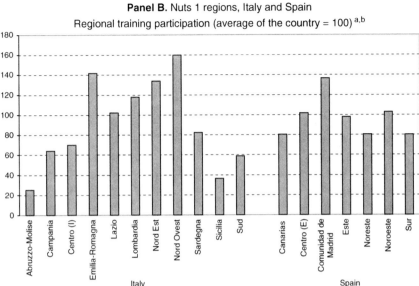

Panel C. Nuts 2 regions, selected countries
Regional training participation (average of the country = 100) [a,b]

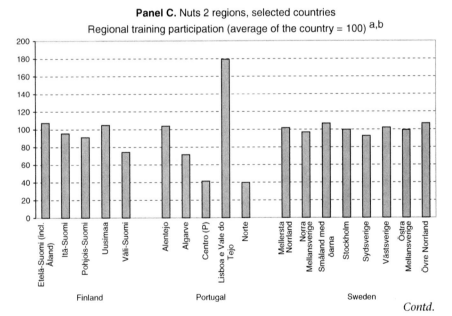

Contd.

Care must be taken in interpreting these figures, since distributions at NUTS 2 level are obviously more disperse than at NUTS 1 level. Taking this into account, however, one fact strikes: regional dispersion of participation rates is somewhat negatively related to the country average. In Finland and,

195

Panel D. Nuts 2 regions, United Kingdom

Regional training participation (average of the country = 100) [a,b]

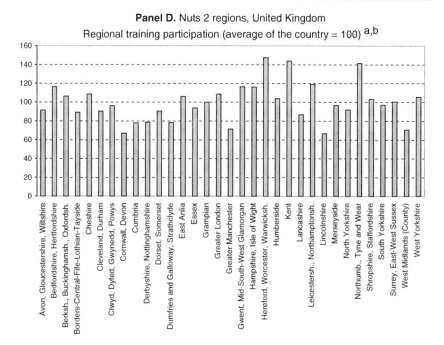

Fig. 10.3 Dispersion of training participation rates in EU countries, by region

[a] Data refer to 1997.

[b] A few regions are not shown due to insufficient data. For the same reason Etelä-Suomi and Åland are aggregated.

Source: ECHP.

especially, Sweden there is in practice no regional variation. Conversely, Italy, Greece and Portugal are by far the countries with the greatest disparities. In Italy, the best performing region (Nord Ovest) trains six times more frequently than the least performing one (Abruzzo-Molise). In Portugal, training varies across regions by a factor of 4 (although these statistics are based on a NUTS 2 classification). These figures are remarkable if compared with the cross-country variation in training participation rates shown in Figure 10.1.

The variation in the distribution of training across regions within a country can be explained at least in part as the result of the interaction between the density of local economic activity and the training decisions of firms. In two separate empirical investigations of the UK and Italy, Brunello and Gambarotto (2004), and Brunello and De Paola (2004a), show that in both countries more agglomerated local areas are characterized by lower training participation. They explain this result as the outcome of the trade-off between turnover and poaching effects and pooling externalities associated to the diffusion of knowledge.

10.3 Who pays for training?

As discussed in Chapter 9, in the standard theory of human capital, employers and employees share the cost and benefits of training when training is firm-specific (and/or training is general but there are multiple skills and each firm employs a specific combination of skills, see Lazear, 2003). When training is perfectly general, employees will pay for the full cost of training if the labour market is competitive, while employers might pay for part or all of it if labour markets are imperfectly competitive.

In Figure 10.4 we decompose the number of training courses according to whether they are (or they are not) partially paid for or provided by the employer (employer-sponsored hereafter) in 16 OECD countries using data from the IALS. Panel A shows that, on average, 80 per cent of vocational training courses are paid for or provided by employers. Although cross-country variation is large, in all countries at least 50 per cent of vocational training courses are employer-sponsored. A similar pattern emerge in the ECHP, where on average 72 per cent of the training courses on which we have information on the source of financing[5] is employer-sponsored (see Table A4.1 in Appendix 4 on p. 218). According to IALS data, a large majority of employer-sponsored training courses (93% on average, with little cross-country variation) is also reported to be entirely financed by employers (see Table A4.2 in Appendix 4).

Decomposing the number of courses by source of finance, however, overstates the share of training investment borne by firms. Employer-sponsored courses are in fact shorter than non-sponsored ones. In the same IALS country sample, non-sponsored vocational training courses are about twice as long as employer-sponsored ones (see Table A4.3 in Appendix 4 on p. 219). Even in the country where the two distributions are less different (Switzerland), employer-sponsored courses are, on average, 25 per cent shorter than non-sponsored ones.[6]

When we decompose the volume of training by source of financing (Figure 10.4, Panel B), it appears, however, that the degree of employer support is still large. On average, two-thirds of employee training is reported to be employer sponsored. Furthermore, in all but three countries (Ireland, Italy and Switzerland) more than half of the training volume is reported to be at least partially financed by the employer.

---

[5] In the ECHP the information on financing is reported for the last course taken only.

[6] A similar pattern is also consistent across surveys: although the ECHP reports information on duration by intervals, it emerges from Table A4.4 that the degree of employer support decreases with course duration (certain countries are excluded due to missing data, see Appendix 4 for the description of the datasets).

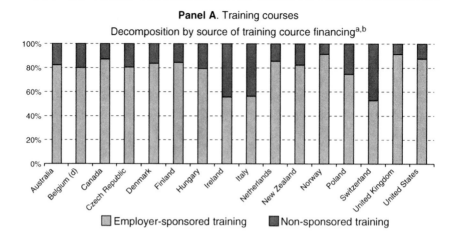

Panel A. Training courses
Decomposition by source of training cource financing[a,b]

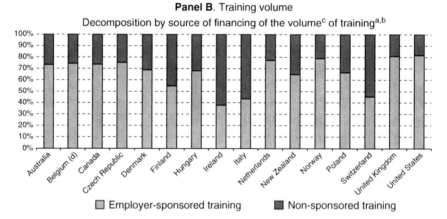

Panel B. Training volume
Decomposition by source of financing of the volume[c] of training[a,b]

Fig. 10.4 Share of employer-sponsored training
[a] Data refer to employed persons aged 26 to 65 years.
[b] Data refer to 1994 for Canada, Ireland, the Netherlands, Poland, Switzerland (German and French-speaking regions) and the United States, to 1996 for Australia, Belgium, New Zealand and the United Kingdom, and to 1998 for the Czech Republic, Denmark, Finland, Hungary, Italy, Norway and the Italian-speaking regions of Switzerland.
[c] Annual hours spent in training undertaken for job or career-related purposes.
[d] Flanders only.
Source: IALS.

When employers only are reported to pay for training, do they really bear the cost of it? Or, are firms simple providers of training services and workers indirectly pay for them by accepting a different wage pattern and accepting to be trained outside normal working hours? Indeed, sharing the cost of training through lower wages does not necessarily imply a nominal wage cut, which is relatively rare, particularly in European countries (see Nickell and Quintini, 2003). Employees can trade-off wage increases in exchange of training, and newly-hired individuals can be offered a contract with lower than usual pay—although possibly steeper tenure-earnings profile—in exchange of current or future training.

The existing empirical literature on training and wages during the training period focuses mainly on the US and, to a lesser extent, the UK. We can distinguish two strands of research on the basis of the source of data. Studies that used employer surveys are generally confined to cross-sections. Autor (2003), using a cross-section of temporary help firms from the 1994 BLS Occupational Compensation Survey, finds that temporary help agencies do provide their workers with nominally free computer skills training, that is inherently general. This notwithstanding, workers share part of the cost of training by not being paid during training: almost without exception, training is given prior to or between assignments during unpaid hours with all direct costs paid by the temporary help supply firm. Barron, Berger and Black (1999), using data from the Employer Opportunity Pilot Project (EOPP), find that initial pay and training are inversely related. However, the effect they found is small (doubling the proportion of time spent on training leads to only 1.8 per cent of wage reduction) and accounted for by the fact that employers do not have a significant propensity to pay lower wages to newly-hired individuals that require more training than normal but are ready to pay higher wages to those who require less training than normal (because of previously accumulated transferable skills that can be used in the new job). The drawbacks of their analysis are that (i) they do not control for employer effects, and (ii) they do not distinguish between general and specific training in their analysis. By contrast, using the same data, Sicilian (2001), makes this distinction and finds a stronger yet small effect (about 5% in the case of fully general training). The limitation of this study is however, that in order to control for firm selection, the sample is reduced to those firms reporting information on at least two workers and therefore estimates are driven by less than 150 individuals.

Recent empirical studies based on employee data have exploited the longitudinal dimension of several individual datasets. For instance, for the US, Loewenstein and Spletzer (1998), consider 5 waves of the National Longitudinal Survey of Youth (NLSY) and estimate a wage level equation that allows for a dummy for job changes to control for match-specific effects on wages. They find that uncompleted spells of training have insignificant effects on wages (even in the case of off-site training courses).

Booth and Bryan (2002), use the same technique to estimate wage level equations for the UK on 3 waves of the British Household Panel Survey and find that next year's training has a positive but insignificant impact on current wage, suggesting that employees do not exchange training against wage moderation before training.

Overall, these studies find little evidence that workers pay for a large share of training costs out of their wages. Obviously, the limit of these analyses is that if workers pay out of their wages only for a small share of training costs, measurement error may suffice to prevent finding a significant effect of current or future training on average hourly wages reported for a given year. Nevertheless, the evidence discussed in this section suggests the following conclusions:

(i) workers do not pay for most of the cost of employer-sponsored training out of their wages;
(ii) the evidence that workers accept lower wages to co-finance training is very limited and not robust;
(iii) there is some evidence that they may accept to be trained outside normal working hours, at least under certain circumstances.[7]

This cautiously suggests that the degree of employer's support that is reported in surveys can be considered an imperfect but not thoroughly unreliable proxy of employer's true investment in training. Hence, from the fact that, at face value, most training is employer-sponsored, we can conclude that employers are major players in the training market.

But how large are their investments in economic terms? As shown in Table 10.1, training expenditures of European employers are reported to have been on average 444 euros per employee (in Purchasing Power Parity, with EU-15 as the base) in 1999, on the basis of CVTS data.[8] In EU-15 countries, this figure is higher, being on average at 603 euros, with Danish firms spending up to 1132 euros per employee. Are these figures significant in economic terms? More often than not, yes. In fact, they correspond to 1.7, 2.3 and 3 per cent of total labour costs, on average, in EU-15 and in Denmark, respectively.

Country rankings by training expenditure follow closely those by participation and hours, except in the case of Italy, which is much closer to the average of EU-15 countries in terms of spending per employee. This

[7] Employer-sponsored training outside normal working hours is however more the exception than the rule in many countries. For instance, Pischke (2001), reports that only 27 per cent of training during leisure hours is at least partially financed by the employer.

[8] Employers are likely to be more precise as regards to firm choices and characteristics than employees. For this reason we rely here on the CVTS.

Table 10.1 Cross-country distribution of training expenditures by firms, European countries

Country	As a percentage of total labour costs (%)	Annual expenditure per employee (eur, in PPPs)
Austria	1.3	365
Belgium	1.6	675
Bulgaria	1.0	134
Czech Republic	1.9	250
Denmark	3.0	1132
Estonia	1.8	197
EU-15	2.3	603
Finland	2.4	698
France	2.4	753
Germany	1.5	506
Greece	0.9	223
Hungary	1.2	144
Ireland	2.4	600
Italy	1.7	563
Latvia	1.1	90
Lithuania	0.8	65
Luxembourg	1.9	592
Netherlands	2.8	875
Norway	2.3	666
Poland	0.8	97
Portugal	1.2	240
Romania	0.5	41
Slovenia	1.3	167
Spain	1.5	385
Sweden	2.8	868
United Kingdom	na	628

Notes: Data refer to training taken in 1999.
The reference for the PPPs is the average of the EU-15 (the values for EU-15 are expressed in current euros).
Initial training is excluded.
Source: CVTS.

might reveal inefficient spending by firms and/or that Italian firms invest in better quality but more expensive training. While available data do not allow us to tell, the Italian experience with apprenticeship training discussed in Chapter 12 suggests that the former explanation goes at least some of the way in accounting for the observed facts.

10.4 The distribution of training investments across firms

Are all firms equal in their propensity to train? And if not, which firms do invest more? And how much do they invest? To investigate these issues Figure 10.5 shows the distribution by firm size of participation rates, hours and the two measures of training expenditure already considered.

Panel A. Training participation

Share of total wage and salary employees who receive employer-sponsored training[a]

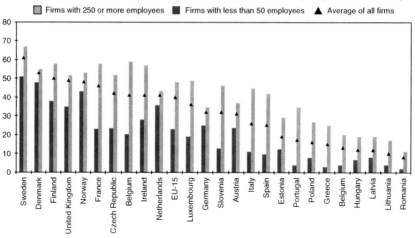

Panel B. Training hours

Average annual hours of employer-sponsored training per employee[a]

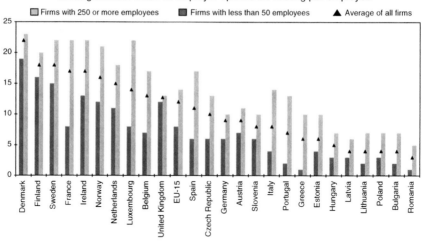

Contd.

The first fact that emerges from the figure is that large firms train more than small ones. This is not surprising for several reasons:

(i) the collection of information, the definition of a training plan and the establishment of a training facility involve fixed costs and scale economies;

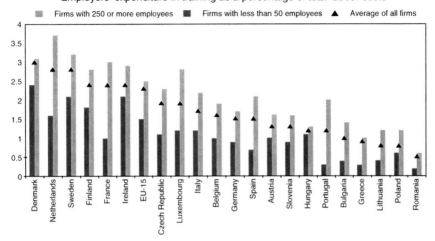

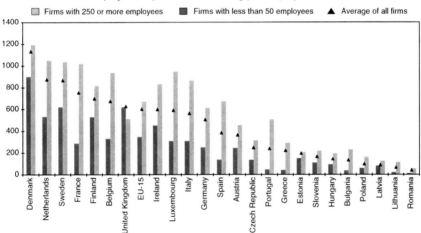

Fig. 10.5 Employers' investment in training: by firm size

[a] Data refer to training taken in 1999. The reference for the PPPs is the average of the EU-15 (the values for EU-15 are expressed in current euros). Initial training is excluded. Labour cost is not available for the UK. The decomposition by size for Estonia, Latvia and Norway is not always available.

Source: CVTS.

(ii) small firms might find it more difficult to replace a worker who temporarily leaves for training; and

(iii) small firms might have fewer opportunities to fully reap the benefits of training through internal reallocation of workers.

Small firm employees receive on average 6.8 hours of training less than their large firm peers and have a participation rate smaller by 20 percentage points. This is reflected in employers' expenditures. On average, expenditures on total labour costs are 1 percentage point greater in the case of large firms. However, the cross-country variation of training is far smaller in the case of large firms than in the case of small firms: in the latter case the coefficients of variation are .71, .68, .56 and .85 for participation, hours, expenditure on labour cost and expenditure per employee, respectively, while in the former they are .38, .42, .39 and .62, respectively. In other words, large firms are relatively similar across countries as regards training, and the difference in training rates across countries is mostly due to the behaviour of small firms as well as to the distribution of firm size within countries. Indeed, countries with the greatest percentage difference between large and small firms (such as Portugal) are concentrated at the bottom end of the cross-country distribution of training, irrespective of the measure of training employed.[9]

The distribution by size in the UK is worth mentioning. In contrast with all other countries, this is essentially flat, especially in terms of hours and spending. As a consequence, the UK ranks below the EU-15 average in the distribution of large firms (except in the case of participation rates) while being at the top in the case of small firms. This is more evident when looking at spending: with an equivalent of 513 euros per employee, the UK ranks just higher than Portugal and Greece, within EU countries, in terms of spending of large firms.

A similar pattern of cross-country distribution of inter-firm differences can be found as regards to innovation and adoption. Figure 10.6 plots training participation rates in firms that introduced new products or processes in the same period. In fact, although innovative firms have on average participation rates that are 15 percentage points higher, innovative and non-innovative firms are not very different in training intensive countries (for instance, in Scandinavian countries, the average difference in participation rates is only 11.8 percentage points). By

---

[9] Interestingly, there is a strong negative correlation between this percentage difference and the average level. Correlation coefficients are $-.90$, $-.82$, $-.71$ and $-.65$ for participation, hours, expenditure on labour cost and expenditure per employee, respectively.

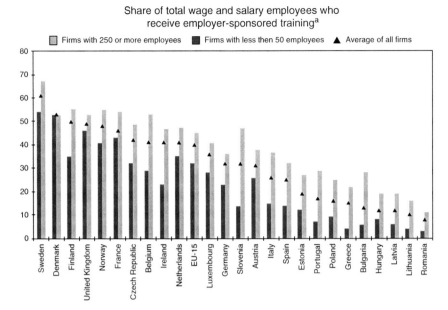

Share of total wage and salary employees who
receive employer-sponsored training[a]

☐ Firms with 250 or more employees   ▨ Firms with less then 50 employees   ▲ Average of all firms

Fig. 10.6 Training participation in innovative and non-innovative firms
[a] Data referring to training taken and innovation introduced in 1999. Initial training is excluded.
Source: CVTS.

contrast, these differences are huge in less training intensive countries (up
to 33 percentage points in Slovenia, and 22 in both Bulgaria and Portugal).
Again, it is mainly the difference across non-innovative firms which is to
be blamed for the dispersion of training rates across countries.[10]

10.5 Training differences across employees

In the previous sections we have treated employees as if they had the
same probability of receiving training. By contrast, in this section, we look
at the distribution of training among employees with different observable
characteristics. In order to do so in a synthetic way we estimate a simple
reduced form model of the probability of training as a function of different
individual, job and firm characteristics on the basis of ECHP data from
1995 to 2001 (see Appendix 4 for details on the selection of the sample).

We characterize the empirical relationship between training and
individual characteristics with the following probit specification:

[10] This relationship between innovation and training is not only due to the fact that large
firms tend to be more innovative than small firms (see Table A4.5 in the Appendix).

$$\text{Prob}\{T_{it} = 1\} = \Phi(\alpha_c + \alpha_{ct} + X_{it}\beta) \qquad [10.1]$$

where T is the training event over the reference period, α_c and α_{ct} are country and country by year effects (for years other than 1997, which is taken as reference), X is a vector of time varying individual, job and firm characteristics, i is the index for individuals, c for the country, t for time, and Φ is the cumulative normal distribution.

Since we pool all available observations over countries and time, we include country and country by time dummies to capture all time varying and country-specific factors, such as those due to institutions (see Chapter 11) and nationwide policies (see Chapter 13), which could affect both covariates and training. These dummies also pick up differences in the interpretation of the training question, which could vary across countries because of language as well as broad cultural and social reasons. Country by year dummies also capture the variation of training over the business cycle.[11]

Table 10.2 presents estimation results for the probability both of taking any training and of receiving employer-sponsored training as a function of educational attainment, gender, tenure, marital status, age (divided in four classes), public/private sector employment, part time/full time status, type of contract (fixed term, casual job and other, with permanent job as the reference), country, industry, firm size and occupation. All time-varying variables are lagged. The table reports average partial effects, that is the deviations in the participation to training from the reference individual (indicated in the table). Percentage point effects can be obtained by multiplying reported figures by 100.

---

[11] A potential drawback of specification [10.1] is that the random error could include an unobserved individual effect. If this is the case, we can distinguish between two alternatives: (i) the individual effect is both independent of the regressors in [10.1] and normally distributed; (ii) independency or normal distribution or both fail to hold. As a first approximation, which seems suitable to simply describe the main patterns, we assume the former to be the case. In fact, any parametric alternative to the pooled probit model remains somewhat arbitrary. First, there is no strong justification for a specific distributional form. Secondly, the individual effect might not be time-invariant (due for instance to unobserved firm characteristics that change from match to match—e.g. innovative firms are more training intensive than non-innovative firms). Finally, parameters might be heterogeneous across several dimensions (see for instance below) and a fully-specified model might require several interactions. For these reasons, we prefer to stick with the simplest model in this descriptive exercise. The probit model applied to pooled data does not estimate partial effects but average partial effects, obtained by averaging partial effects across the distribution of the unobserved individual effect in the population (see Wooldridge, 2002). If we are interested in estimating the partial effects of a regressor on the probability of training at a value $f = 0$ for the individual effect, then the pooled probit does not do the job. However, if we are happy with the average partial effect with respect to the distribution of f, as it is usually the case, the pooled probit does the job.

Table 10.2 Individual characteristics and training incidence. ECHP 1995–2001. Average partial effects

	All training			Emp. spon. training		
Upper secondary education	−.021	***	(.003)	−.011	***	(.002)
Less than upper secondary education	−.076	***	(.003)	−.053	***	(.003)
Female	.006	**	(.002)	.002		(.002)
Tenure	−.003	***	(.001)	−.001	**	(.001)
Tenure squared	.000	***	(.000)	.000	**	(.000)
Married	.004		(.002)	.011	***	(.002)
Age 25–34	.008	***	(.003)	.007	***	(.002)
Age 45–54	−.022	***	(.002)	−.016	***	(.002)
Age 55–64	−.054	***	(.003)	−.041	***	(.002)
Public sector	.068	***	(.004)	.068	***	(.004)
Part time	−.025	***	(.004)	−.027	***	(.003)
Fixed term contract	−.024	***	(.005)	−.034	***	(.004)
Casual job	−.057	***	(.008)	−.063	***	(.005)
Other type of contract	−.026	***	(.008)	−.021	***	(.007)
Denmark	.064	***	(.012)	.031	***	(.010)
Netherlands	−.141	***	(.003)	−.119	***	(.002)
Belgium	−.107	***	(.004)	−.089	***	(.003)
France	−.118	***	(.004)	−.095	***	(.003)
Ireland	−.119	***	(.004)	−.096	***	(.003)
Italy	−.144	***	(.004)	−.118	***	(.003)
Greece	−.146	***	(.003)	−.113	***	(.002)
Spain	−.092	***	(.006)	−.089	***	(.004)
Portugal	−.156	***	(.004)	−.125	***	(.003)
Austria	−.074	***	(.006)	−.072	***	(.004)
Finland	.010		(.009)	−.003		(.007)
NACE C+E	.024	***	(.009)	.036	***	(.008)
NACE DA	−.028	***	(.006)	−.014	**	(.006)
NACE DB+DC	−.069	***	(.006)	−.054	***	(.005)
NACE DD+DE	−.028	***	(.006)	−.016	***	(.006)
NACE DF−DI	−.005		(.007)	.010		(.006)
NACE DJ+DK	−.018	***	(.006)	−.007		(.005)
NACE DL−DN	−.015	***	(.006)	−.001		(.005)
NACE F	−.050	***	(.005)	−.031	***	(.005)
NACE G	−.018	***	(.005)	−.004		(.004)
NACE H	−.049	***	(.006)	−.040	***	(.005)
NACE I	−.015	***	(.005)	−.002		(.004)
NACE J	.055	***	(.007)	.069	***	(.007)
NACE K	.000		(.005)	.011	**	(.005)
NACE L	.004		(.004)	.014	***	(.004)
NACE M	.003		(.004)	.007	*	(.004)
NACE O−Q	−.015	***	(.005)	−.008		(.005)
Firm size: 50–99 employees	.033	***	(.005)	.041	***	(.005)
Firm size: 100–499 employees	.054	***	(.004)	.057	***	(.004)
Firm size: 500 or more employees	.077	***	(.005)	.083	***	(.005)
Legislators, senior officials and managers	.063	***	(.006)	.057	***	(.006)
Professionals	.056	***	(.006)	.047	***	(.005)
Technicians and associate professionals	.057	***	(.005)	.050	***	(.004)
Clerks	.016	***	(.004)	.011	***	(.004)
Skilled agricultural and fishery workers	−.049	***	(.014)	−.049	***	(.012)

(contd.)

Table 10.2 (*Contd.*)

	All training			Emp. spon. training		
Craft and related trades workers	−.033	***	(.004)	−.026	***	(.004)
Plant and machine operators and assemblers	−.038	***	(.004)	−.032	***	(.004)
Elementary occupations	−.067	***	(.004)	−.056	***	(.003)
Pseudo R-squared	0.2014			0.2133		
Observations	165188			163386		

Notes: Each regression includes a constant and country×year dummies. Country dummies shown above refer to 1997.

Observations are weighted by ECHP longitudinal weights.

The reference individual is a male full time single British employee aged 35–44 years with tertiary education, average tenure, tenure, working in 1997 under a permanent contract as a service worker or shop and market sales worker for a private firm with less than 50 employees in the health and social work industry.

*, **, *** One, two and three stars for the coefficients statistically significant at the 10, 5 and 1 per cent level of confidence respectively.

Heteroskedasticity consistent standard errors in parentheses. See Table A4.6 for the list of industries and industry codes.

Results presented in Table 10.2 show that training increases with education and skill intensity of occupations, while it decreases with age.[12] All these results are quite recurrent in the literature (see Asplund (2005), for a recent survey). Consistent with recent evidence (see e.g. Van den Heuvel and Wooden (2000), and Arulampalam et al. (2004)), we find that women have, *ceteris paribus*, a greater probability of taking training than men, although the differences associated with gender are small (.6 percentage points). The same occurs for workers in the public sector. However, their advantage with respect to small-firm workers (6.8 percentage points) is no larger than the advantage enjoyed by workers in firms with more than 500 employees (7.7 percentage points). Conversely, as usually found in the literature (see OECD, 2002), part-time and temporary workers typically take training less often.

Even controlling for this relatively large set of characteristics, cross-country variation remains large: a Danish employee has still a 20 percentage point greater probability of taking training than a Portuguese one. The estimated range of variation among country effects is far greater than that estimated for educational levels (7.6 percentage points), age classes (6.2), firm size classes (7.7), occupations (13) and industries (12.4). Indeed, the analysis of variance reveals that country effects alone explain 45.9 per cent of the fraction of total variance explained by our covariates.[13] Yet, residual

---

[12] As regards tenure, we find a U-shaped curve: training is greater at low tenure and at high tenure, consistent both with the view that initial training is often required at hiring to adapt workers' competences to the specificity of their new job (see e.g. Barron et al., 1999) and with the observation that further training is usually delayed (Loewenstein and Spletzer, 1997). However, tenure is likely to be endogenous and we must be cautious in interpreting these results.

[13] The analysis of variance has been performed on a linear-probability version of model [10.1]. Complete results are available from the authors upon request.

(unexplained) variance remains large. Part of this is due to the persistence of training participation: the analysis of variance reveals that simply including a dummy for training participation in the previous year as an additional regressor raises by up to 28 per cent the fraction of the variance explained by the model.

The comparison of estimates for total and employer-sponsored training is instructive in many respects. When we focus on employer-sponsored training only, the advantage of women disappears. Tenure is a far less important factor. To some extent the same applies to differences by age and education. Conversely, firm size, type of contract and marital status are far more important factors in the case of employer-sponsored training. These patterns suggest that differences across individuals are not homogenous with respect to the source of financing and that certain gaps are concentrated in one form of financing. For instance, it is evident from the estimates reported in Table 10.2 that women are ready to pay for their own training more often than men but firms are not ready to train them more often.

In other words, women's demand in the downstream training market[14] looks greater than that for men but this is not the case for the employers' supply they face. By contrast, this is not the case for older and lower-educated workers, whose poor training rates seem at least equally due to demand and supply factors. Similar patterns are found by Oosterbeek (1998), Leuven and Oosterbeek (1999), and OECD (2003), in IALS data.

To explore this issue further, we estimate several tentative models[15] of the probability of taking non-sponsored training. Results are reported in Appendix 4 (on p. 221). To start, we replicate the probit model [10.1] (p. 206) by substituting non-sponsored for total or employer-sponsored training (Table A4.7, Panel A, first column). However, given that those receiving employer-sponsored training are not a negligible subset of the sample, selection problems are likely to be important for the non-sponsored training equation. For this reason, we estimate also two alternative models

---

[14] The market for training can be broken into two sub-markets (see Stevens, 1994, 1999): upstream, employers buy training services from a training provider; downstream employers re-sell these training services to their employees, with the price for training hidden in wages. The price of the latter transaction might be even zero when the employer bears all the cost. In the case of internal training, training provider and employer are the same institution; in such a case the price of the upstream transaction is not observable and even ill-defined. Conversely, in the downstream market, one can in principle distinguish between a well-defined supply (by the employer) and demand (by its employees). Training outcomes then can be considered as the result of the reaction of supply and demand to market and institutional incentives.

[15] Care must be taken in interpreting the estimates: due to the small incidence of non-sponsored training (see Table A4.2), they are likely to be very imprecise.

that simultaneously consider the probability of employer-sponsored and non-sponsored training. In one of them, we take explicitly into account that employer-sponsored and non-sponsored training are mutually exclusive categories by design[16] and estimate a trinomial logit model, with no training as base category (Table A4.7, Panel B). Next, we assume that decisions about training financing are taken sequentially: first, the employer decides whether or not to pay for training and then, in the case he does not, the employee chooses whether or not to pay for her training.

Under this hypothesis, non-sponsored training can obviously be observed only for those individuals for whom their employers have decided not to pay. With the same distributional assumptions as in [10.1], we can estimate this model as a bivariate probit with censoring (Table A4.7, Panel A, second and third column).[17]

The importance of the selection issue can be seen by looking at the estimated coefficients for firm size. In the probit model without selection, non-sponsored training is estimated to decrease with firm size, pointing to the fact that, on average, employees of small firms tend to pay for their own training more often than employees in large firms do. In the logit model, this pattern is already more ambiguous, while in the bivariate probit model it disappears completely. These results suggest that workers in small firms do not have a greater propensity to pay for their training. They pay more often only to compensate for the lack of employer support. In other words, they have the same demand for training as workers in large firms but they are in short supply. Results from Table A4.7 also confirm that women have a greater demand for training, perhaps due to training needs at re-entry points in the labour market after career interruptions.

Not surprisingly, part-time and temporary workers have the same demand as full time and permanent workers, since these workers might regard their status as temporary and seek to acquire new competences to qualify for better jobs. By contrast, married workers, despite receiving more employer-sponsored training, appear to have a smaller demand

---

[16] The source of financing is reported only for the last course taken in the ECHP (cf. Appendix 4).

[17] The log likelihood of this model for the couple $T_i = (E_i, N_i)$, where E and N stands for employer-sponsored and non-sponsored training, respectively, can be written as follows:

$$l = \sum_{E_i=1} \log \Phi(Z_{it}\beta_E) + \sum_{T_i=(0,1)} \log \Phi_2(-Z_{it}\beta_E, Z_{it}\beta_N, \rho) + \sum_{T_i=(0,0)} \log \Phi_2(-Z_{it}\beta_E, -Z_{it}\beta_N, -\rho)$$

where Z stands for the vector of covariates (including country $\times$ time dummies), Φ_2 stands for the cumulative distribution of the bivariate normal and E and N are indexes for employer-sponsored and non-sponsored training, respectively.

than their unmarried peers, possibly because of liquidity constraints due to family responsibilities.

Finally, even taking selectivity into account, the estimated probability of taking non-sponsored training decreases with age and educational attainment as steeply as the estimated probability of receiving employer-sponsored training does, confirming that employers' discrimination is not, or at least not only, at the origin of downward sloped training-age profiles and upward sloped training-education profiles.

But do women, the educated and younger workers take also longer courses? Do training duration gaps look like training participation gaps? By and large yes, as shown by the results presented in Table A4.9 in Appendix 4 (on p. 226), obtained by estimating Gaussian interval regression models of training duration.[18] The main exceptions are the following: (i) older workers tend to take much shorter courses, when they participate, than their younger peers (workers aged more than 54 years take courses that are on average two weeks shorter than prime-age workers); and (ii) parameter differences between the equation for total and employer-sponsored training are often larger. In particular, the correlation between country effects for total and employer-sponsored training is extremely low (their Fisher and Spearman rank correlation coefficients are only .29 and .12, respectively). Total training durations are longer in Denmark and Finland and shorter in Greece and Portugal. But the latter two countries move up to the third and fourth position, respectively, in the ranking of durations of employer-sponsored training, just after Denmark and Austria, while bottom performers are, in this case, Italy and Spain.

The models considered above assume that the effect of characteristics is invariant across gender, skill groups and age. The discussion of demand and supply patterns already made suggests that this might not be the case. For instance, if greater training participation for women is due to their

---

[18] The ECHP reports information on duration only by intervals (0–2 weeks, 2–9 weeks, and more than 9 weeks). Since cut-off points between classes are known, the Gaussian interval regression model becomes the natural generalization to our data of the probit [10.1]. Its log likelihood can be written as follows:

$$l = \sum_{T_i=0} \log\left(1 - \Phi(Z_{it}\beta/\sigma)\right) + \sum_{\substack{A<T_i\le B \\ [A,B]\subset\{(0,2],(2,9]\}}} \log\left(\Phi((B - Z_{it}\beta)/\sigma) - \Phi((A - Z_{it}\beta)/\sigma)\right)$$
$$+ \sum_{T_i>9} \log\Phi((Z_{it}\beta - 9)/\sigma)$$

where Z stands for the vector of covariates (including country×time dummies) and σ for the variance of the random disturbance.

demand at re-entry points in the labour market, we can posit that this effect should show up especially among the elders. We look for differential effects by estimating separate regressions by gender, skill and age group (results are reported in Table A4.9 in Appendix 4 on p. 226).

We define as high skilled labour those employees who in the year before the survey were classified as professionals, technicians and craft workers; and the rest as low skilled labour, except skilled agricultural and fishery workers who are difficult to classify and therefore are excluded. Furthermore, we define as young individuals those aged between 25 and 40, and the rest as old. Only few estimated coefficients are heterogeneous across groups. Tenure effects are less important for men, for whom, by contrast, age plays a major role. Consistent with previous literature (e.g. Nestler and Kailis, 2002), women receive comparatively less training in certain medium/low-tech manufacturing industries (agro-food, textile, metal products, and machinery and equipment not elsewhere classified, such as household appliances and machine tools). Differences across occupations are larger in the case of women and older workers. Finally, consistent with our conjecture, women's advantage emerges only among the skilled and older workers. By contrast, young women—that is, women at ages when career interruptions are more frequent—get training comparatively less frequently than men. Interestingly, the latter pattern is essentially due to employer-sponsored training:[19] on average, the probability of receiving employer-sponsored training is 1.5 percentage points smaller for young women than for their male peers.

As done before, as regards firm size, we are interested in seeing how training profiles by gender, age, education and type of contract vary across countries. We therefore re-estimate model [10.1] by country and find the following (cf. Table A4.10 in Appendix 4 on p. 228):

- Training-education profiles are always downward-sloped, except in the Netherlands and Portugal.
- The penalty for standard fixed-term contracts that we observed in Table 10.2, seems to be driven by only four countries (Denmark, the United Kingdom, Austria and Finland), where the training gap between permanent and temporary workers is estimated to be above 4 percentage points.[20] In all other countries the penalty, if any, is contained within 1 percentage point.[21]

---

[19] Not shown in the table but available from authors upon request.
[20] Estimates are however very imprecise, pointing to a great heterogeneity.
[21] However, the penalty for atypical contracts is often large.

- The relative position of women varies markedly across countries. In Anglo-Saxon countries, women take training, *ceteris paribus*, more frequently than men by 2.5 percentage points. In Greece, the opposite is true: being a woman in Greece reduces the probability of training by .8 percentage points. Large negative coefficients (below −1 percentage points), although not significant, are also estimated in Austria and Belgium.
- Age-training profiles are downward sloped in all countries. However, the estimated training gap between younger and older workers is smaller than 3 percentage points in Italy, Greece and Portugal, while it is greater than 7 percentage points in Denmark, the UK, and Finland. One would be tempted to conclude that in the least training intensive countries, age discrimination in the access to training is smaller. However, this conclusion would be unwarranted. If we rescale estimated gaps by the average training participation rate of each country (cf. Fig. 10.1), we see that countries such as Italy and Greece appear to be far more unequal.
- The cross-country distribution of 're-scaled' age-training gaps correlates quite well with that of the employment rate of older workers (cf. Fig. 10.7).[22] Of course a bivariate correlation is not a causal relationship and indeed this pattern can be explained in two opposite ways:

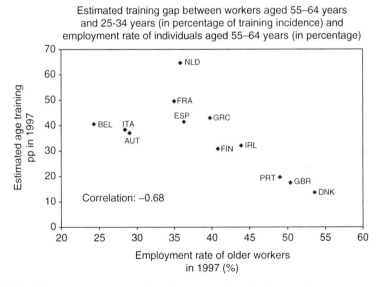

Estimated training gap between workers aged 55–64 years
and 25-34 years (in percentage of training incidence) and
employment rate of individuals aged 55–64 years (in percentage)

Fig. 10.7. Training age gaps and employment rate of older workers
Sources: OECD Database on Labour Force Statistics and own calculations on ECHP data.

[22] Employment rates are from the OECD Database on Labour Force Statistics.

(i) training is a crucial determinant of the employability of older workers, that are therefore more prematurely expelled from employment in countries where they are trained comparatively less frequently; and (ii) the expected age of retirement negatively affects the incentives of older workers to upgrade or maintain their skills through training. Our finding that training-age profiles are equally downward sloped in the case of both employer-sponsored and non-sponsored training, suggests that the second explanation might be valid, at least partially: we can make the conjecture that the greater the incentives to retire early the larger the age-training gap. Chapter 11 will look at this issue in a more systematic way.

Finally, as done before in the business cycle regressions, we check the robustness of our main estimates to using only odd years and eliminating the last three waves for the UK. In addition, in a separate exercise, we retain only individuals who are present in consecutive years, independently of whether these years are two, the minimum; or seven, the maximum. Overall coefficient estimates appear quite robust to these variations.[23]

10.6 Summary

We summarize the results of this descriptive analysis with the following points:

- Cross-country variation of training incidence and intensity in Europe is large, with Scandinavian countries training up to six times more than Eastern countries. Within-country regional variation is also large in countries that are not training intensive, and can be as large as the cross-country variation (in the case of Italy).
- At face value, employers appear to be the main actors in the training market. On average, the entire cost of three-quarters of the training courses is directly paid by employers, and there is little evidence that employees indirectly pay through lower wages. Employers' training investments are not negligible and can be as high as 3 per cent of total labour costs (in Denmark).
- Large and innovative firms train more than small and non-innovative firms, with the UK being the only European country where this does not

---

[23] Results are available from authors upon request.

hold. Cross-country variation among large and innovative firms is, however, small. Therefore, aggregate cross-country differences are essentially due to variation among small and non-innovative firms.

- Training in Europe increases with education and skill-intensity of occupations, while it decreases with age. The age–training gap is negatively correlated with the employment rate of older workers, reflecting either the impact of training on older workers' employability or the incentive of the expected retirement age.

- Women take more training than men, but essentially because they pay for their own training more often, while firms do not appear to accommodate their greater demand for training. Quite the contrary, women tend to receive less employer-sponsored training than men when they are young.

- Even when controlling for observable individual characteristics, country effects account for almost one half of the explained variation in training participation. In fact, differences associated with country of residence remain, *ceteris paribus*, larger than differences associated with industry, occupation, education, age and firm size. Other factors, thus, concur in explaining the difference across countries. In the next chapter, we will turn our attention to the role of labour and product market institutions.

APPENDIX 4

Description of the Datasets and Supplementary Tables

(i) IALS

The *International Adult Literacy Survey* (IALS) is an individual survey that was carried out by the OECD and Statistics Canada in the 1990s (see e.g. OECD and Statistics Canada, 2000). The survey asks whether the workers have received any training or education during the 12 months prior to the survey, but it includes details only about the three most recent courses (purpose, financing, training institution, duration, etc.). Data refer to 1994 for Canada, Ireland, the Netherlands, Poland, Switzerland (German and French-speaking regions), and the United States, to 1996 for Australia, Belgium (Flanders only), New Zealand and the United Kingdom and to 1998 for the Czech Republic, Denmark, Finland, Hungary, Italy, Norway and the Italian-speaking regions of Switzerland.

In the IALS, there is a distinction between job- or career-related training and training for other purposes. Furthermore, education and training courses are divided into seven mutually exclusive categories:

  (i) leading to a university degree/diploma/certificate;
  (ii) leading to a college diploma/certificate;
 (iii) leading to a trade-vocational diploma/certificate;
 (iv) leading to an apprenticeship certificate;
  (v) leading to an elementary or secondary school diploma;
 (vi) leading to professional or career upgrading; and
(vii) other.

In this chapter, only job- or career-related training is considered. Moreover, in order to thoroughly exclude formal education courses, only items iv, vi, and vii are retained in the definition of vocational training courses, while items i, ii, iii and v are subsumed into the category of formal education (used only in Table A4.4).

A limited set of demographic, job and firm characteristics is available in the IALS. However, most of these characteristics have been recorded at the date of the survey, thereby at or after the end of the reported training courses.

216

(ii) CVTS

The second *Continuing Vocational Training Survey* (CVTS), is an enterprise survey covering establishments with at least ten employees. It was carried out by Eurostat in 2000 in EU member states, Norway and nine EU candidate countries (Eurostat, 2000). It provides information on employer-sponsored training, which is taken during the year prior to the survey, for employed persons, excluding apprentices and trainees (this makes figures for countries with a dual education system—such as Austria and Germany—difficult to compare to other countries).

Training is defined as 'courses which take place away from the place of work, i.e. in a classroom or training centre, at which a group of people receive instruction from teachers/tutors/lecturers for a period of time specified in advance by those organizing the course'.

The survey provides a large set of characteristics for the enterprises, but only gender, training participation and total training hours for the employee.

(iii) OECD Aggregate data

OECD aggregate data are obtained by aggregating and merging CVTS and IALS data on both training participation rates and the log of training hours per employee (OECD, 2004). The merging methodology is as follows. First, the aggregate cross-country distributions stemming from surveys were standardized to have zero mean and unit variance. Second, a cross-survey training index was constructed by taking, for each country, the cross-distribution unweighted average of the available standardized values. Third, final measures were reconstructed by multiplying the cross-survey index by the average of the standard errors of the original distributions and adding the average of their means.

Cross-country correlation rates of OECD aggregate data and the original CVTS or IALS measures are very high (greater than .95 in all cases). Moreover, regressing IALS or CVTS participation rates on OECD data without including a constant, the hypothesis that the coefficient of OECD data is not significantly different from 1 cannot be rejected at the 5 per cent level. This holds only at the 10 per cent level in the case of hours.

(iv) ECHP

All the regression analyses are based on the European Community Household Panel (ECHP), waves 2 to 8 (1995 to 2001). As discussed in detail by Bassanini and Brunello (2003), and Arulampalam, Booth and Bryan (2004), the ECHP is an attractive source of information because it covers a significant number of European countries with a commonly designed questionnaire.

The key question on training in the survey is: 'Have you at any time since January in the previous year been in vocational education or training, including any part-time or short-courses?'. While this question is informative on training incidence, it is silent on the duration of training spells as well as their source of financing.

The duration of the last training spell is reported in classes (less than 2 weeks, 2–9 weeks, more than 9 weeks). Unfortunately, the information on the duration of training in the ECHP is completely missing for the Netherlands and Sweden, and largely missing for the UK. Therefore, we exclude these countries in the whole analysis of duration.

In a separate question, the respondent is asked whether the last training spell was paid or provided by the employer. This information is, however, not available for Sweden. For comparability with the previous empirical literature, we select our sample as in Arulampalam, Booth and Bryan (2004). In particular, we only consider individuals (i) aged between 25 and 64 years and working at least 15 hours per week; (ii) not employed in agriculture; (iii) present in at least two consecutive waves; (iv) not in apprenticeships or in special employment training schemes.

Since the reference period of each wave may overlap with the period of the previous wave, we run the risk of double counting training spells. We could try to solve this problem by using the starting dates of any training spell, but this information has a lot of missing values in the data, and is available only for some of the countries in the sample. Rather than losing information or adjusting counts in an ad hoc way, we prefer to ignore double counting in the main regressions and to perform a robustness check which compares our results with those obtained from a reduced sample which only retains odd years, and therefore avoids double counting by definition.

There is also the problem of omitted spells, which appears to be particularly serious in Germany. German data in the ECHP are derived from GSOEP and exclude many shorter training spells. We follow, therefore, Arulampalam, Booth and Bryan (2004), and drop this country from the whole analysis. Finally, in the case of Sweden, no longitudinal information is available for Sweden, which will be therefore omitted in all analyses requiring lagged variables at the individual level.

Table A4.1 Training participation rates by source of financing in the ECHP

Country	Total training	Employer-sponsored training	Ratio
Austria	25.33	20.78	82.05
Belgium	18.76	15.23	81.14
Denmark	53.21	48.55	91.25
Finland	43.50	39.20	90.12
France	15.56	14.20	91.30
Greece	6.96	6.14	88.14
Ireland	13.72	11.30	82.35
Italy	8.79	7.31	83.13
Netherlands	11.75	7.63	64.93
Portugal	5.11	4.10	80.34
Spain	19.98	14.09	70.53
UK	39.67	39.40	99.33
Average	23.97	17.25	71.97

Notes: All figures are in percentages and refer to 1997.
Ratio = Emp.-sponsored training/Total training.

Source: ECHP.

Table A4.2 Percentage of employers-sponsored training courses that are entirely paid by employers, selected OECD countries (IALS sample)

Country	Emp.-sponsored voc. training
Australia	96.3
Belgium (Flanders)	93.2
Canada	89.4
Czech Republic	96.0
Denmark	97.8
Finland	85.4
Hungary	98.3
Ireland	93.5
Italy	91.8
Netherlands	na
New Zealand	92.2
Norway	89.8
Poland	96.5
Switzerland	86.9
United Kingdom	99.0
United States	94.3

Notes: See Chart 2.4 for the year.
na = not available.

Source: IALS.

Table A4.3 Hours of training per participant and source of financing, selected OECD countries (IALS sample)

Country	Emp.-sponsored training	Emp.-sponsored education	Non-sponsored training	Non-sponsored education
Australia	63.2	134.1	110.8	245.5
Belgium (Flanders)	73.5	23.2	102.0	289.3
Canada	61.4	125.8	153.4	411.8
Czech Republic	83.8	92.9	115.8	206.2
Denmark	81.3	273.6	192.2	487.1
Finland	54.2	120.8	246.4	546.6
Hungary	95.2	118.9	177.7	271.7
Ireland	85.1	298.3	179.0	420.8
Italy	55.3	29.7	94.4	356.2
Netherlands	88.9	249.6	166.2	258.8
New Zealand	68.8	180.8	183.2	381.3
Norway	77.9	229.4	226.8	655.2
Poland	75.0	121.1	115.8	304.7
Switzerland	60.9	116.1	83.6	256.1
United Kingdom	50.0	223.4	131.4	288.8
United States	56.0	104.7	92.2	299.3

Notes: See Chart 2.4.

Source: IALS.

Table A4.4 Ratio of employer-sponsored training to total training in the ECHP, by course duration

Country	0–2 weeks	2–9 weeks	>9 weeks
Austria	94.40	83.44	59.34
Belgium	94.69	82.52	51.08
Denmark	93.93	92.00	78.88
Finland	97.15	93.29	60.74
France	94.87	92.35	77.55
Greece	94.63	96.05	64.90
Ireland	95.78	88.38	72.21
Italy	91.52	82.99	62.74
Portugal	94.87	76.76	66.38
Spain	88.27	88.06	48.96

Notes: Data refer to 1997.

Source: ECHP.

Table A4.5 Share of total wage and salary employees who receive employer-sponsored training in innovative and non-innovative firms, by firm size. European countries

Country	10–49 employees		250 and more employees	
	Non-innovative firms	Innovative firms	Non-innovative firms	Innovative firms
Austria	25	40	29	40
Belgium	16	32	49	63
Bulgaria	2	18	10	33
Czech Republic	20	32	45	55
Germany	18	36	30	36
Denmark	48	46	56	54
Estonia	9	19	13	34
Spain	6	14	31	45
Finland	32	47	46	58
France	22	29	57	62
Greece	1	7	5	29
Hungary	5	12	13	23
Ireland	18	33	50	58
Italy	7	18	33	49
Lithuania	3	9	8	20
Luxembourg	15	28	52	48
Latvia	5	15	10	22
Netherlands	34	43	33	47
Norway	39	52	45	56
Poland	5	17	16	32
Portugal	2	10	20	40
Romania	1	3	5	14
Sweden	46	60	61	71
Slovenia	9	23	24	56
United Kingdom	41	48	47	53

Notes: Data refer to training taken and innovation introduced in 1999. Innovative firms are defined as those that introduced new products or processes. Initial training is excluded.

Source: CVTS.

Table A4.6 List of industries used in the regressions

NACE Rev.1 Codes	Industry definition
C+E	Mining and quarrying + Electricity, gas and water supply
DA	Manufacture of food products, beverages and tobacco
DB+DC	Manufacture of textiles, clothing and leather products
DD+DE	Manufacture of wood and paper products; publishing and printing
DF−DI	Manufacture of coke, refined petroleum/chemicals/rubber & plastic products
DJ+DK	Manufacture of metal products, machinery and equipment n.e.c.
DL−DN	Other manufacturing
F	Construction
G	Wholesale and retail trade; repair of motor vehicles, motorcycles and personal/household goods
H	Hotels and restaurants
I	Transport, storage and communication
J	Financial intermediation
K	Real estate, renting and business activities
L	Public administration and defense; compulsory social security
M	Education
N	Health and social work
O−Q	Other community, social and personal service activities; private households with employed persons; extra-territorial organizations and bodies

Table A4.7 Individual characteristics and training. Alternative models for sponsored and non-sponsored training

Panel A: Probits for non-sponsored training with and without selection

	Without selection			With selection (on not receiving employer-sponsored training)					
	Non-sponsored training			Non-sponsored training			Employer-sponsored training		
Upper secondary education	−0.12	***	(0.02)	−0.16	***	(0.02)	−0.06	***	(0.01)
Less than upper secondary education	−0.37	***	(0.03)	−0.46	***	(0.03)	−0.32	***	(0.02)
Female	0.07	***	(0.02)	0.08	***	(0.02)	0.01		(0.01)
Tenure	−0.02	***	(0.01)	−0.02	***	(0.01)	−0.01	**	(0.00)
Tenure squared	0.00	**	(0.00)	0.00	**	(0.00)	0.00	**	(0.00)
Married	−0.12	***	(0.02)	−0.09	***	(0.03)	0.06	***	(0.01)
Age 25–34	0.01		(0.02)	0.02		(0.02)	0.04	***	(0.01)
Age 45–54	−0.07	***	(0.02)	−0.11	***	(0.02)	−0.10	***	(0.01)
Age 55–64	−0.20	***	(0.04)	−0.30	***	(0.04)	−0.28	***	(0.02)
Public sector	−0.02		(0.03)	0.12	**	(0.05)	0.37	***	(0.02)
Part time	0.04		(0.03)	−0.03		(0.04)	−0.17	***	(0.02)
Fixed term contract	0.11	***	(0.04)	0.03		(0.05)	−0.23	***	(0.03)
Casual job	−0.02		(0.07)	−0.18	*	(0.09)	−0.51	***	(0.06)
Other type of contract	−0.05		(0.06)	−0.09		(0.06)	−0.13	***	(0.05)
Denmark	1.49	***	(0.30)	1.55	***	(0.33)	0.16	***	(0.05)

Netherlands	1.45	***	(0.30)	0.72		(0.46)	−1.38	***	(0.05)
Belgium	1.27	***	(0.31)	0.70	*	(0.40)	−0.91	***	(0.05)
France	1.00	***	(0.30)	0.46		(0.38)	−0.90	***	(0.04)
Ireland	1.10	***	(0.31)	0.51		(0.41)	−1.02	***	(0.06)
Italy	1.18	***	(0.30)	0.53		(0.43)	−1.21	***	(0.05)
Greece	0.51		(0.34)	−0.18		(0.43)	−1.41	***	(0.07)
Spain	1.59	***	(0.30)	1.07	***	(0.41)	−0.77	***	(0.05)
Portugal	1.08	***	(0.32)	0.38		(0.45)	−1.45	***	(0.09)
Austria	1.42	***	(0.30)	1.01	***	(0.38)	−0.59	***	(0.05)
Finland	1.29	***	(0.30)	1.20	***	(0.33)	−0.02		(0.04)
NACE C+E	−0.29	***	(0.07)	−0.20	**	(0.08)	0.19	***	(0.04)
NACE DA	−0.24	***	(0.06)	−0.26	***	(0.06)	−0.09	**	(0.04)
NACE DB+DC	−0.29	***	(0.07)	−0.34	***	(0.07)	−0.41	***	(0.05)
NACE DD+DE	−0.23	***	(0.07)	−0.25	***	(0.07)	−0.10	**	(0.04)
NACE DF−DI	−0.27	***	(0.06)	−0.24	***	(0.06)	0.06	*	(0.03)
NACE DJ+DK	−0.17	***	(0.05)	−0.18	***	(0.05)	−0.04		(0.03)
NACE DL−DN	−0.24	***	(0.05)	−0.23	***	(0.05)	0.00		(0.03)
NACE F	−0.32	***	(0.07)	−0.36	***	(0.07)	−0.20	***	(0.03)
NACE G	−0.23	***	(0.04)	−0.22	***	(0.04)	−0.02		(0.03)
NACE H	−0.25	***	(0.06)	−0.32	***	(0.06)	−0.27	***	(0.04)
NACE I	−0.26	***	(0.04)	−0.26	***	(0.05)	−0.01		(0.03)
NACE J	−0.23	***	(0.06)	−0.07		(0.09)	0.34	***	(0.03)
NACE K	−0.21	***	(0.04)	−0.18	***	(0.05)	0.07	**	(0.03)
NACE L	−0.19	***	(0.03)	−0.15	***	(0.04)	0.08	***	(0.02)
NACE M	−0.06	*	(0.04)	−0.04		(0.04)	0.04	**	(0.02)
NACE O−Q	−0.16	***	(0.04)	−0.15	***	(0.04)	−0.04		(0.03)
Firm size: 50–99 employees	−0.11	***	(0.04)	−0.04		(0.05)	0.21	***	(0.02)
Firm size: 100–499 employees	−0.04		(0.03)	0.06		(0.05)	0.29	***	(0.02)
Firm size: 500 or more employees	−0.11	***	(0.03)	0.04		(0.07)	0.40	***	(0.02)
Legislators, senior officials and managers	0.01		(0.04)	0.13	**	(0.05)	0.29	***	(0.02)
Professionals	0.07	*	(0.04)	0.17	***	(0.05)	0.24	***	(0.02)
Technicians and associate professionals	0.05		(0.03)	0.16	***	(0.04)	0.26	***	(0.02)
Clerks	0.06		(0.03)	0.08	**	(0.03)	0.06	***	(0.02)
Skilled agricultural and fishery workers	−0.10		(0.15)	−0.19		(0.15)	−0.37	***	(0.12)
Craft and related trades workers	−0.09	**	(0.04)	−0.14	***	(0.04)	−0.16	***	(0.03)
Plant and machine operators and assemblers	−0.09	*	(0.05)	−0.15	***	(0.05)	−0.20	***	(0.03)
Elementary occupations	−0.16	***	(0.05)	−0.26	***	(0.07)	−0.40	***	(0.03)
Pseudo R-squared	0.0931								
Correlation coefficient				−0.54	**	(0.20)			
Observations	163386			163386					

(Contd.)

Table A4.7 (*Contd.*)
Panel B: Multinomial logit

	Non-sponsored training			Employer-sponsored training		
Upper secondary education	−0.31	***	(0.06)	−0.11	***	(0.03)
Less than upper secondary education	−0.93	***	(0.07)	−0.63	***	(0.03)
Female	0.17	***	(0.05)	0.04		(0.02)
Tenure	−0.05	***	(0.01)	−0.02	***	(0.01)
Tenure squared	0.00	**	(0.00)	0.00	***	(0.00)
Married	−0.26	***	(0.04)	0.10	***	(0.02)
Age 25–34	0.01		(0.05)	0.06	**	(0.03)
Age 45–54	−0.19	***	(0.05)	−0.18	***	(0.02)
Age 55–64	−0.56	***	(0.09)	−0.50	***	(0.04)
Public sector	0.09		(0.07)	0.68	***	(0.04)
Part time	0.03		(0.07)	−0.31	***	(0.04)
Fixed term contract	0.18	**	(0.08)	−0.41	***	(0.05)
Casual job	−0.18		(0.18)	−0.97	***	(0.13)
Other type of contract	−0.15		(0.14)	−0.29	***	(0.09)
Denmark	4.30	***	(1.01)	0.36	***	(0.08)
Netherlands	3.43	***	(1.01)	−2.46	***	(0.10)
Belgium	3.16	***	(1.02)	−1.54	***	(0.10)
France	2.49	**	(1.02)	−1.55	***	(0.08)
Ireland	2.71	***	(1.03)	−1.78	***	(0.11)
Italy	2.87	***	(1.02)	−2.10	***	(0.09)
Greece	1.10		(1.11)	−2.52	***	(0.13)
Spain	3.94	***	(1.01)	−1.24	***	(0.09)
Portugal	2.58	**	(1.05)	−2.60	***	(0.18)
Austria	3.64	***	(1.01)	−0.92	***	(0.08)
Finland	3.66	***	(1.01)	0.01		(0.07)
NACE C+E	−0.61	***	(0.18)	0.34	***	(0.07)
NACE DA	−0.55	***	(0.15)	−0.18	**	(0.07)
NACE DB+DC	−0.68	***	(0.18)	−0.86	***	(0.11)
NACE DD+DE	−0.54	***	(0.17)	−0.18	***	(0.07)
NACE DF−DI	−0.58	***	(0.14)	0.08		(0.06)
NACE DJ+DK	−0.40	***	(0.12)	−0.11	*	(0.06)
NACE DL−DN	−0.55	***	(0.12)	−0.04		(0.06)
NACE F	−0.77	***	(0.16)	−0.42	***	(0.07)
NACE G	−0.51	***	(0.09)	−0.07		(0.05)
NACE H	−0.61	***	(0.14)	−0.57	***	(0.09)
NACE I	−0.60	***	(0.10)	−0.05		(0.05)
NACE J	−0.36	**	(0.15)	0.57	***	(0.05)
NACE K	−0.44	***	(0.10)	0.09	*	(0.05)
NACE L	−0.41	***	(0.08)	0.12	***	(0.04)
NACE M	−0.13		(0.08)	0.06	*	(0.04)
NACE O−Q	−0.34	***	(0.10)	−0.10	*	(0.05)
Firm size: 50–99 employees	−0.22	**	(0.09)	0.37	***	(0.04)
Firm size: 100–499 employees	−0.01		(0.08)	0.53	***	(0.03)
Firm size: 500 or more employees	−0.14	*	(0.08)	0.72	***	(0.03)
Legislators, senior officials and managers	0.11		(0.10)	0.52	***	(0.05)
Professionals	0.23	***	(0.09)	0.46	***	(0.04)
Technicians and associate professionals	0.21	***	(0.08)	0.48	***	(0.04)
Clerks	0.14	*	(0.08)	0.12	***	(0.04)

Skilled agricultural and fishery workers	−0.30		(0.39)	−0.68	***	(0.23)
Craft and related trades workers	−0.28	***	(0.10)	−0.32	***	(0.05)
Plant and machine operators and assemblers	−0.29	***	(0.11)	−0.40	***	(0.05)
Elementary occupations	−0.47	***	(0.12)	−0.78	***	(0.06)
Pseudo R-squared	0.193					
Observations	163386					

Notes: In the Probit model with selection (bivariate probit with censoring), individuals are assumed to be observed paying for training only if they do not receive employer-sponsored training). Each regression includes a constant and country×year dummies. Country dummies shown above refer to 1997. Observations are weighted by ECHP longitudinal weights. The reference individual is a male full time unmarried British employee aged 35–44 years with tertiary education, average tenure, tenure, working in 1997 under a permanent contract as a service worker or shop and market sales worker for a private firm with less than 50 employees in the health and social work industry. *, **, ***One, two and three stars for the coefficients statistically significant at the 10, 5 and 1 per cent level of confidence respectively. Heteroskedasticity consistent standard errors in parentheses. See Table A4.6 for the list of industries.

Table A4.8 Individual characteristics and training duration. ECHP 1995–2001. Interval regression models

	All training			Employer-sponsored training		
Upper secondary education	−0.37	***	(0.11)	−0.20	**	(0.09)
Less than upper secondary education	−2.43	***	(0.15)	−1.70	***	(0.12)
Female	0.27	***	(0.09)	0.11		(0.08)
Tenure	−0.08	***	(0.03)	−0.01		(0.02)
Tenure squared	0.00	***	(0.00)	0.00		(0.00)
Married	−0.04		(0.09)	0.32	***	(0.08)
Age 25–34	0.29	***	(0.11)	0.22	**	(0.09)
Age 45–54	−0.74	***	(0.09)	−0.58	***	(0.08)
Age 55–64	−2.14	***	(0.14)	−1.73	***	(0.13)
Public sector	1.85	***	(0.13)	2.09	***	(0.12)
Part time	−0.50	***	(0.16)	−0.72	***	(0.15)
Fixed term contract	−0.43	**	(0.19)	−1.18	***	(0.18)
Casual job	−1.57	***	(0.41)	−2.62	***	(0.41)
Other type of contract	−0.81	**	(0.34)	−0.77	**	(0.32)
Denmark	0.99	***	(0.25)	5.20	***	(0.31)
Belgium	−4.43	***	(0.34)	0.16		(0.31)
France	−4.87	***	(0.26)	−0.23		(0.41)
Ireland	−4.93	***	(0.40)	−1.50	***	(0.36)
Italy	−6.34	***	(0.33)	−2.67	***	(0.44)
Greece	−8.42	***	(0.45)	1.45	***	(0.34)
Spain	−2.16	***	(0.30)	−2.83	***	(0.56)
Portugal	−7.73	***	(0.56)	1.55	***	(0.33)
Austria	−2.79	***	(0.29)	4.36	***	(0.30)
NACE C+E	0.60	**	(0.27)	0.89	***	(0.24)
NACE DA	−0.84	***	(0.28)	−0.41		(0.26)
NACE DB+DC	−2.15	***	(0.35)	−2.12	***	(0.34)
NACE DD+DE	−0.55	*	(0.30)	−0.30		(0.26)

(*Contd.*)

Table A4.8 (*Contd.*)

	All training			Employer-sponsored training		
NACE DF–DI	0.17		(0.25)	0.63	***	(0.23)
NACE DJ+DK	0.18		(0.23)	0.30		(0.20)
NACE DL–DN	−0.01		(0.22)	0.26		(0.20)
NACE F	−1.86	***	(0.30)	−1.39	***	(0.24)
NACE G	−0.55	***	(0.19)	−0.02		(0.17)
NACE H	−1.80	***	(0.32)	−1.63	***	(0.30)
NACE I	−0.33	*	(0.18)	0.09		(0.16)
NACE J	1.79	***	(0.23)	2.05	***	(0.19)
NACE K	0.17		(0.20)	0.33	*	(0.18)
NACE L	0.27	*	(0.15)	0.51	***	(0.14)
NACE M	0.47	***	(0.16)	0.61	***	(0.14)
NACE O–Q	−0.12		(0.21)	−0.01		(0.19)
Firm size: 50–99 employees	0.93	***	(0.17)	1.31	***	(0.16)
Firm size: 100–499 employees	1.40	***	(0.14)	1.67	***	(0.12)
Firm size: 500 or more employees	1.82	***	(0.15)	2.23	***	(0.13)
Legislators, senior officials and managers	2.10	***	(0.19)	1.92	***	(0.17)
Professionals	2.04	***	(0.18)	1.69	***	(0.16)
Technicians and associate professionals	1.66	***	(0.15)	1.43	***	(0.14)
Clerks	0.78	***	(0.16)	0.54	***	(0.14)
Skilled agricultural and fishery workers	−1.23	*	(0.72)	−1.83	***	(0.70)
Craft and related trades workers	−1.14	***	(0.19)	−0.97	***	(0.17)
Plant and machine operators and assemblers	−1.15	***	(0.20)	−1.09	***	(0.18)
Elementary occupations	−2.27	***	(0.23)	−2.19	***	(0.20)
Left-censored observations	107,734			110,571		
Right-censored observations	4,166			2,690		
Observations	130,565			130,305		

Notes: The dependent variable is the number of weeks of training (or fraction of weeks). Each regression includes a constant and country×year dummies. Country dummies shown above refer to 1997. Observations are weighted by ECHP longitudinal weights. The reference individual is a male full time unmarried Finnish employee aged 35–44 years with tertiary education, average tenure, tenure, working in 1997 under a permanent contract as a service worker or shop and market sales worker for a private firm with less than 50 employees in the health and social work industry. *, **, *** One, two and three stars for the coefficients statistically significant at the 10, 5 and 1 per cent level of confidence respectively. Heteroskedasticity consistent standard errors in parentheses. See Table A4.6 for the list of industries

Table A4.9. Individual characteristics and training incidence. ECHP 1995–2001. Average partial effects, by gender, skill group and age

	Males		Females		Skilled		Unskilled		Young		Old	
Upper secondary education	−.023 ***	(.004)	−.024 ***	(.004)	−.022 ***	(.004)	−.023 ***	(.004)	−.029 ***	(.004)	−.014 ***	(.004)
Less than upper secondary education	−.071 ***	(.004)	−.084 ***	(.005)	−.083 ***	(.005)	−.069 ***	(.004)	−.086 ***	(.004)	−.065 ***	(.004)
Female					.015 ***	(.004)	−.002	(.003)	−.012 ***	(.004)	.025 ***	(.003)
Tenure	−.001	(.001)	−.007 ***	(.001)	−.004 ***	(.001)	−.003 ***	(.001)	−.004 ***	(.001)	−.002 *	(.001)
Tenure squared	.000	(.000)	.000 ***	(.000)	.000 ***	(.000)	.000 **	(.000)	.000 ***	(.000)	.000 *	(.000)
Married	.014 ***	(.003)	−.004 *	(.003)	−.001	(.004)	.007 **	(.003)	.003	(.003)	.011 ***	(.003)
Age 25–34	.023 ***	(.004)	−.008	(.004)	.010 **	(.005)	.006 *	(.003)	.003	(.003)		
Age 45–54	−.028 ***	(.003)	−.011 ***	(.003)	−.019 ***	(.004)	−.023 ***	(.003)			−.019 ***	(.003)
Age 55–64	−.058 ***	(.003)	−.044 ***	(.003)	−.058 ***	(.005)	−.048 ***	(.003)			−.052 ***	(.003)
Public sector	.070 ***	(.006)	.062 ***	(.006)	.074 ***	(.006)	.060 ***	(.005)	.064 ***	(.006)	.067 ***	(.005)
Part time	−.008	(.012)	−.029 ***	(.005)	−.036 ***	(.006)	−.017 ***	(.004)	−.025 ***	(.006)	−.024 ***	(.005)
Fixed term contract	−.025 ***	(.006)	−.019 **	(.007)	−.030 ***	(.007)	−.017 ***	(.005)	−.017 ***	(.006)	−.033 ***	(.007)
Casual job	−.056 ***	(.009)	−.060 ***	(.013)	−.098 ***	(.013)	−.028 ***	(.008)	−.034 **	(.012)	−.079 ***	(.009)
Other type of contract	−.018 *	(.010)	−.038 ***	(.012)	−.041 ***	(.013)	−.013	(.009)	−.033 ***	(.010)	−.027 **	(.012)
Denmark	.087 ***	(.017)	.038 **	(.019)	.102 ***	(.020)	.029 **	(.015)	.065 ***	(.019)	.059 ***	(.016)
Netherlands	−.127 ***	(.004)	−.158 ***	(.005)	−.198 ***	(.005)	−.086 ***	(.005)	−.128 ***	(.006)	−.149 ***	(.003)
Belgium	−.087 ***	(.006)	−.133 ***	(.006)	−.143 ***	(.007)	−.074 ***	(.005)	−.105 ***	(.007)	−.105 ***	(.005)
France	−.102 ***	(.004)	−.140 ***	(.006)	−.154 ***	(.006)	−.084 ***	(.004)	−.115 ***	(.006)	−.118 ***	(.004)
Ireland	−.109 ***	(.004)	−.129 ***	(.007)	−.154 ***	(.006)	−.085 ***	(.005)	−.116 ***	(.007)	−.116 ***	(.004)
Italy	−.131 ***	(.004)	−.158 ***	(.006)	−.167 ***	(.006)	−.116 ***	(.004)	−.146 ***	(.006)	−.137 ***	(.005)
Greece	−.128 ***	(.004)	−.169 ***	(.004)	−.185 ***	(.005)	−.108 ***	(.003)	−.150 ***	(.004)	−.138 ***	(.003)
Spain	−.081 ***	(.007)	−.108 ***	(.009)	−.111 ***	(.010)	−.073 ***	(.006)	−.090 ***	(.009)	−.091 ***	(.007)
Portugal	−.140 ***	(.005)	−.177 ***	(.008)	−.191 ***	(.007)	−.119 ***	(.005)	−.166 ***	(.007)	−.140 ***	(.006)
Austria	−.061 ***	(.008)	−.090 ***	(.010)	−.073 ***	(.011)	−.066 ***	(.006)	−.062 ***	(.010)	−.079 ***	(.007)
Finland	.015	(.012)	.002	(.015)	.013	(.014)	.008	(.012)	.006	(.014)	.009	(.012)
Firm size: 50–99 employees	.033 ***	(.006)	.030 ***	(.009)	.042 ***	(.008)	.021 ***	(.006)	.037 ***	(.007)	.026 ***	(.007)
Firm size: 100–499 employees	.053 ***	(.005)	.054 ***	(.008)	.063 ***	(.007)	.042 ***	(.006)	.056 ***	(.006)	.050 ***	(.006)
Firm size: 500 or more employees	.081 ***	(.006)	.065 ***	(.008)	.087 ***	(.007)	.063 ***	(.006)	.073 ***	(.007)	.082 ***	(.007)
NACE C+E	.027 ***	(.011)	.031	(.021)	.034 ***	(.014)	.016	(.010)	.029 **	(.013)	.019 *	(.011)
NACE DA	−.010	(.009)	−.052 ***	(.011)	.000	(.012)	−.039 ***	(.006)	−.038 ***	(.009)	−.020 **	(.009)
NACE DB+DC	−.039 ***	(.010)	−.080 ***	(.009)	−.087 ***	(.010)	−.051 ***	(.006)	−.070 ***	(.008)	−.064 ***	(.008)
NACE DD+DE	−.023 **	(.009)	−.017	(.012)	−.035 ***	(.010)	−.021 **	(.008)	−.020 *	(.010)	−.040 ***	(.008)

(Contd.)

Table A4.9. (Contd.)

	Males		Females		Skilled		Unskilled		Young		Old	
NACE DF–DI	.008	(.009)	-.019	(.012)	-.004	(.010)	-.005	(.008)	.001	(.010)	-.014	(.008)
NACE DJ+DK	-.005	(.008)	-.046 ***	(.011)	-.031 ***	(.008)	.002	(.008)	-.019 **	(.009)	-.020 **	(.007)
NACE DL–DN	-.005	(.008)	-.017	(.011)	-.017 **	(.008)	-.011	(.007)	-.011	(.008)	-.021	(.007)
NACE F	-.048 ***	(.006)	.011	(.027)	-.065 ***	(.008)	-.028 ***	(.009)	-.056 ***	(.008)	-.046 ***	(.007)
NACE G	.002	(.008)	-.040 ***	(.006)	.012	(.009)	-.030 ***	(.005)	-.020 ***	(.007)	-.020 ***	(.006)
NACE H	-.043 ***	(.009)	-.057 ***	(.009)	-.096 ***	(.014)	-.035 ***	(.005)	-.051 ***	(.008)	-.047 ***	(.009)
NACE I	-.008	(.007)	-.016 *	(.009)	.017 *	(.010)	-.026 ***	(.005)	-.021 ***	(.007)	-.010	(.006)
NACE J	.078 ***	(.011)	.038 ***	(.010)	.071 ***	(.011)	.043 ***	(.009)	.046 ***	(.010)	.062 ***	(.010)
NACE K	.022 **	(.009)	-.024 ***	(.007)	.000	(.008)	.005	(.008)	-.007	(.008)	.005	(.007)
NACE L	.008	(.007)	.005	(.006)	.009	(.007)	.000	(.005)	.013 *	(.007)	-.002	(.005)
NACE M	-.008	(.007)	.008	(.006)	.002	(.006)	.010	(.008)	-.003	(.007)	.004	(.005)
NACE O–Q	-.012	(.009)	-.017 **	(.008)	-.019 **	(.009)	-.011 *	(.006)	-.008	(.008)	-.021 ***	(.007)
Legislators, senior officials and managers	.052 ***	(.008)	.080 ***	(.011)					.058 ***	(.009)	.074 ***	(.009)
Professionals	.043 ***	(.008)	.069 ***	(.008)	.004	(.006)			.047 ***	(.008)	.068 ***	(.008)
Technicians and associate professionals	.052 ***	(.007)	.059 ***	(.007)	-.003	(.005)	.013 ***	(.004)	.050 ***	(.007)	.065 ***	(.007)
Clerks	.008	(.006)	.025 ***	(.006)					.022 ***	(.006)	.012 *	(.006)
Skilled agricultural and fishery workers	-.045 ***	(.014)	-.026	(.050)					-.038	(.023)	-.055 **	(.018)
Craft and related trades workers	-.029 ***	(.005)	-.072 ***	(.010)	-.100 ***	(.005)			-.036 ***	(.006)	-.026 ***	(.006)
Plant and machine operators and assemblers	-.033 ***	(.005)	-.070 ***	(.009)			-.032 ***	(.004)	-.035 ***	(.006)	-.039 ***	(.006)
Elementary occupations	-.057 ***	(.005)	-.079 ***	(.007)			-.056 ***	(.003)	-.059 ***	(.007)	-.073 ***	(.005)
Pseudo R-squared	0.1973		0.2116		0.2003		0.1815		0.1842		0.2278	
Observations	96463		68725		87081		77510		78260		86928	

Notes: Each regression includes a constant and country×year dummies. Country dummies shown above refer to 1997. Observations are weighted by ECHP longitudinal weights. The reference individual is a male full time unmarried British employee aged 35–44 years with tertiary education, average tenure, tenure, working in 1997 under a permanent contract as a service worker or shop and market sales worker for a private firm with less than 50 employees in the health and social work industry, except that in the second column the reference individual is female and in the third one works as legislator, senior official or manager. *, **, *** One, two and three stars for the coefficients statistically significant at the 10, 5 and 1 per cent level of confidence respectively. Heteroskedasticity consistent standard errors in parentheses. See Table A4.6 for the list of industries.

Table A4.10 Individual characteristics and training incidence. ECHP 1995–2001. Average partial effects, by country

	Denmark			The Netherlands			Belgium			France			United Kingdom			Ireland		
Upper secondary education	-.031	*	(.016)	.007		(.008)	-.055	***	(.012)	-.027	***	(.007)	-.090	***	(.013)	-.011		(.010)
Less than upper secondary education	-.145	***	(.022)	-.008		(.009)	-.080	***	(.014)	-.051	***	(.008)	-.160	***	(.011)	-.061	***	(.012)
Female	.012		(.016)	-.006		(.006)	-.013		(.011)	.002		(.006)	.030	***	(.011)	.026	***	(.010)
Tenure	-.010	**	(.004)	-.004	***	(.002)	.002		(.004)	-.002		(.002)	-.015	***	(.003)	-.004	*	(.002)
Tenure squared	.000	**	(.000)	.000		(.000)	.000		(.000)	.000		(.000)	.001	***	(.000)	.000		(.000)
Married	-.001		(.014)	-.017		(.006)	.005		(.011)	-.006		(.006)	.026	***	(.010)	.023	**	(.009)
Age 25–34	-.004		(.019)	.015	**	(.006)	.016		(.013)	.003		(.008)	.016		(.012)	.015		(.010)
Age 45–54	-.014		(.016)	-.038	***	(.005)	-.047	***	(.012)	-.027	***	(.006)	-.021	*	(.011)	-.010		(.009)
Age 55–64	-.077	***	(.021)	-.061	***	(.006)	-.060	***	(.018)	-.074	***	(.007)	-.053	***	(.015)	-.029	**	(.011)
Public sector	.137	***	(.021)	.024	**	(.010)	.061	***	(.018)	.076	***	(.010)	.103	***	(.018)	.026	*	(.014)
Part time	-.063	***	(.023)	-.014	**	(.007)	-.036	**	(.015)	-.017		(.010)	-.145	***	(.024)	-.022	*	(.012)
Fixed term contract	-.051		(.043)	.000		(.016)	-.008		(.023)	.008		(.016)	-.059	*	(.033)	-.007		(.021)
Casual job	-.192	***	(.039)	.049		(.052)	-.128		(.049)	-.113	***	(.028)	-.137	***	(.044)	-.034	*	(.017)
Other type of contract	.022		(.073)	-.015		(.011)	.005		(.031)	.050	**	(.024)	-.211	***	(.044)	-.016		(.023)
NACE C+E	.148	***	(.050)	.068	**	(.033)	.099	**	(.047)	.004		(.023)	-.064	*	(.033)	-.023		(.024)
NACE DA	-.077	*	(.044)	.006		(.018)	-.026		(.035)	-.042		(.023)	-.154	***	(.027)	-.023		(.019)
NACE DB+DC	-.056		(.081)	.010		(.043)	-.033		(.033)	-.012		(.027)	-.267	***	(.025)	-.062	**	(.017)
NACE DD+DE	-.054		(.048)	-.004		(.016)	.022		(.048)	.039	**	(.020)	-.178	***	(.024)	-.046	**	(.019)
NACE DF–DI	-.021		(.046)	.011		(.017)	.073	**	(.034)	.011		(.018)	-.156	***	(.022)	-.046	*	(.030)
NACE DJ+DK	-.041		(.037)	-.011		(.016)	.028		(.032)	.024		(.017)	-.213	***	(.020)	-.038		(.022)
NACE DL–DN	-.027		(.040)	.011		(.015)	.051	*	(.031)	-.040	**	(.015)	-.182	***	(.020)	.011		(.023)
NACE F	-.103	***	(.037)	-.029	**	(.011)	.027		(.037)	.038	***	(.015)	-.082	***	(.029)	-.062	***	(.016)
NACE G	-.016		(.032)	.000		(.011)	-.023		(.026)	-.054	**	(.021)	-.160	***	(.019)	-.056	***	(.013)
NACE H	-.151	**	(.063)	-.005		(.021)	-.053		(.044)	.019		(.014)	-.158	***	(.027)	-.046	**	(.017)
NACE I	-.012		(.034)	-.017		(.012)	.101	***	(.031)	.030	*	(.019)	-.165	***	(.020)	-.010		(.017)
NACE J	.138	***	(.036)	.083	***	(.018)	.117	***	(.029)	-.002		(.013)	-.119	***	(.022)	-.050	***	(.014)
NACE K	.060	*	(.032)	.013		(.011)	.095	***	(.031)	.010		(.011)	-.144	***	(.020)	.001		(.020)
NACE L	.096	***	(.026)	.007		(.010)	.131	***	(.028)	-.044	***	(.009)	-.070	***	(.019)	.061	***	(.021)
NACE M	.088	***	(.028)	.013		(.012)	-.009		(.019)	.043	**	(.019)	-.061	***	(.019)	-.012		(.015)
NACE O–Q	.055	*	(.030)	-.018		(.014)	.061	**	(.027)	.019		(.015)	-.153	***	(.024)	-.043	**	(.017)
Firm size: 50–99 employees	.075	***	(.025)	.013		(.011)	.073	***	(.027)	.081	***	(.014)	.030	*	(.018)	.001		(.016)

(Contd.)

Table A4.10 (*Contd.*)

	Denmark		The Netherlands		Belgium		France		United Kingdom		Ireland	
Firm size: 100–499 employees	.121 ***	(.021)	.023 ***	(.009)	.049 **	(.020)	.067 ***	(.014)	.065 ***	(.018)	.028 **	(.014)
Firm size: 500 or more employees	.109 ***	(.023)	.038 ***	(.009)	.102 ***	(.020)	.060 ***	(.021)	.134 ***	(.014)	.065 ***	(.021)
Legislators, senior officials and managers	.131 ***	(.028)	-.008	(.011)	.116 ***	(.037)	.049 ***	(.017)	.054 ***	(.019)	.068 ***	(.022)
Professionals	.166 ***	(.026)	-.022 **	(.010)	.057 **	(.028)	.083 ***	(.014)	.048 **	(.020)	.079 ***	(.022)
Technicians and associate professionals	.143 ***	(.023)	.005	(.010)	.037	(.026)	.054 ***	(.014)	.038 *	(.019)	.042 **	(.018)
Clerks	.040	(.026)	-.014	(.010)	.015	(.024)	-.075	(.030)	-.031	(.018)	.002	(.015)
Skilled agricultural and fishery workers	-.128	(.142)	-.072 **	(.015)	-.048 *	(.026)	.025 *	(.016)	-.147 *	(.062)	.074	(.079)
Craft and related trades workers	-.038	(.032)	-.036 ***	(.010)	-.050	(.024)	-.011	(.014)	-.036 *	(.021)	-.027 *	(.015)
Plant and machine operators and assemblers	-.028	(.032)	-.020	(.012)	-.074 ***	(.022)	-.043 ***	(.013)	-.086 ***	(.021)	-.024	(.015)
Elementary occupations	-.107 ***	(.031)	-.054 ***	(.009)	-.055 ***	(.012)	-.027 ***	(.007)	-.137 ***	(.022)	-.052 ***	(.014)
Pseudo R-squared	0.1001		0.0614		0.0737		0.0687		0.1012		0.0979	
Observations	10040		19374		8299		15687		14994		9467	

	Italy		Greece		Spain		Portugal		Austria		Finland	
Upper secondary education	-.001	(.006)	-.017 ***	(.004)	-.022 **	(.009)	.007	(.006)	-.026	(.017)	-.079 ***	(.020)
Less than upper secondary education	-.038 ***	(.007)	-.048 ***	(.005)	-.103 ***	(.009)	-.005	(.006)	-.098 ***	(.017)	-.180 ***	(.023)
Female	-.001	(.004)	-.008 **	(.004)	.001	(.008)	.006 **	(.003)	-.017	(.011)	.016	(.017)
Tenure	.002	(.002)	-.002 *	(.001)	.003	(.002)	.002 *	(.001)	-.011 ***	(.003)	-.005	(.005)
Tenure squared	.000	(.000)	.000	(.000)	.000	(.000)	.000 *	(.000)	.001 ***	(.000)	.001	(.000)
Married	-.002	(.005)	-.001	(.004)	-.007	(.008)	-.007 **	(.004)	.011	(.010)	.066 ***	(.015)
Age 25–34	-.009	(.006)	.007	(.005)	.011	(.009)	-.005	(.003)	.031 **	(.013)	.056 ***	(.020)
Age 45–54	-.018 ***	(.005)	-.011 **	(.004)	-.016 **	(.008)	-.003	(.003)	-.032 ***	(.011)	-.027	(.018)
Age 55–64	-.043 ***	(.005)	-.023 ***	(.004)	-.072 ***	(.009)	-.015 ***	(.002)	-.064 ***	(.015)	-.078 ***	(.026)
Public sector	.023 ***	(.008)	.018 ***	(.006)	.079 ***	(.016)	.023 ***	(.006)	.034 **	(.017)	.162 ***	(.026)
Part time	-.001	(.008)	-.010	(.006)	.012	(.022)	-.008	(.004)	-.013	(.016)	-.079 **	(.036)
Fixed term contract	.005	(.013)	-.004	(.008)	-.006	(.012)	-.005	(.005)	-.044 **	(.020)	-.064 **	(.026)
Casual job	-.048 *	(.015)	-.012	(.008)	-.051 *	(.025)	-.004	(.013)	-.084	(.069)	-.070	(.071)
Other type of contract	-.012	(.013)	.001	(.019)	-.056 **	(.021)	-.002	(.006)	-.050	(.032)	-.119	(.098)
NACE C+E	.007	(.016)	.008	(.013)	.031	(.033)	-.007	(.005)	-.007	(.032)	.060	(.064)
NACE DA	-.020	(.013)	.021	(.021)	-.003	(.022)	-.009	(.006)	-.125 ***	(.021)	.001	(.054)
NACE DB+DC	-.046 ***	(.008)	.010	(.018)	-.022	(.024)	-.017 ***	(.003)	-.122 ***	(.024)	-.209 ***	(.064)
NACE DD+DE	-.021	(.012)	-.013	(.011)	-.009	(.028)	-.011	(.005)	-.103 ***	(.021)	.060	(.039)
NACE DF–DI	-.017	(.012)	.019	(.018)	-.005	(.023)	.001	(.009)	-.035	(.030)	-.080 *	(.047)

	(1)	(2)	(3)	(4)	(5)	(6)
NACE DJ+DK	-.016 (.010)	.174 *** (.042)	.025 (.023)	.001 (.011)	-.080 *** (.020)	-.003 (.041)
NACE DL–DN	-.022 ** (.010)	.005 (.017)	.033 (.023)	-.008 (.005)	-.074 *** (.021)	-.054 (.041)
NACE F	-.046 *** (.007)	-.021 * (.008)	-.060 *** (.017)	-.003 (.009)	-.148 *** (.015)	.026 (.043)
NACE G	-.005 (.011)	.015 (.012)	-.014 (.016)	-.009 * (.004)	-.085 *** (.017)	.034 (.034)
NACE H	-.018 (.014)	.004 (.016)	-.036 * (.018)	-.016 *** (.002)	-.107 *** (.021)	-.144 *** (.047)
NACE I	-.001 (.010)	.021 ** (.012)	-.024 (.015)	.001 (.006)	-.040 * (.022)	-.012 (.035)
NACE J	.024 * (.014)	.123 *** (.027)	.127 *** (.034)	.014 * (.010)	.015 (.027)	.146 *** (.044)
NACE K	-.007 (.011)	.008 (.013)	.003 (.021)	-.005 (.005)	-.041 (.023)	.048 (.034)
NACE L	-.013 (.007)	-.002 (.007)	.026 * (.014)	.010 * (.007)	-.042 ** (.018)	.057 (.036)
NACE M	.045 *** (.011)	-.006 (.007)	.003 (.015)	.001 (.005)	.001 (.023)	-.049 * (.029)
NACE O–Q	-.004 (.010)	-.001 (.012)	-.017 (.020)	-.010 (.005)	-.038 (.022)	-.072 * (.039)
Firm size: 50–99 employees	.013 (.011)	.008 (.010)	.056 *** (.016)	.010 (.008)	.072 *** (.023)	.047 (.031)
Firm size: 100–499 employees	.018 ** (.009)	.022 ** (.013)	.069 *** (.014)	.006 (.006)	.080 *** (.018)	.108 *** (.025)
Firm size: 500 or more employees	.046 *** (.012)	.036 ** (.018)	.057 *** (.014)	.038 *** (.012)	.118 *** (.021)	.150 *** (.032)
Legislators, senior officials and managers	.090 *** (.025)	.018 (.015)	.073 *** (.025)	.020 * (.015)	.186 *** (.027)	.057 (.037)
Professionals	.095 *** (.019)	.031 *** (.013)	.051 *** (.017)	.023 *** (.011)	.170 *** (.033)	.040 (.030)
Technicians and associate professionals	.071 *** (.015)	.012 (.010)	.054 *** (.015)	.016 ** (.008)	.104 *** (.020)	.030 (.028)
Clerks	.025 ** (.011)	.000 (.007)	.034 ** (.015)	.008 (.007)	.075 *** (.019)	-.048 (.031)
Skilled agricultural and fishery workers	-.049 ** (.013)	.030 (.055)	-.016 (.054)	-.015 * (.003)	.145 (.115)	-.338 ** (.090)
Craft and related trades workers	-.012 (.011)	-.003 (.008)	-.033 ** (.014)	-.017 *** (.004)	-.059 *** (.018)	-.148 *** (.031)
Plant and machine operators and assemblers	-.011 (.011)	-.003 (.008)	-.046 *** (.014)	-.009 * (.004)	-.087 *** (.018)	-.217 *** (.033)
Elementary occupations	-.034 *** (.008)	-.020 ** (.007)	-.046 *** (.013)	-.011 ** (.004)	-.140 *** (.014)	-.195 *** (.036)
Pseudo R-squared	0.1272	0.1596	0.1203	0.1921	0.126	0.1018
Observations	21452	11571	18546	17215	11001	7541

Notes: Same as Table 10.2, except for the country of residence of the reference individual.

11

Training and Labour Market Institutions

Introduction

Institutional factors affecting the labour and the product market differ significantly among European countries. Product market competition, for instance, is recognized to be stronger in Anglo-Saxon countries, and employment protection to be highest in Southern European countries. There is an extensive literature which investigates how these institutional differences affect unemployment dynamics (see for instance Blanchard and Wolfers (2000); Nickell, Nunziata and Ochel (2005), and the references therein). The bottom line of this research is that the interaction of institutions with economic shocks does a good job in explaining unemployment differences across OECD countries.

Do labour and product market institutions affect training incidence and can they account for part of the variation in training outcomes observed across European countries? The theoretical aspects of this important question were reviewed in detail in Chapter 9. The empirical literature is reviewed in this chapter. We stress that most of the existing evidence is not comparative but country-specific, with a strong emphasis on the US and to a lesser extent on the UK. In this section we take a European perspective by matching data from the European Community Household Panel—a large dataset covering 15 EU countries which we have used extensively in the previous section—with information on time varying institutions—mainly from the OECD database—and provide an empirical investigation of the relationship between training incidence and labour and product market institutions.

We focus on cross-country and time series variations in institutions, because cross-country variations per se cannot be easily disentangled from the host of country-specific effects that characterize European labour markets. By so choosing we hope to be able to answer the first part of the above question as to whether changes in institutions affect training incidence—but acknowledge that it is difficult to answer the second part with these data—how important are institutions in the cross-country variation of training outcomes.

The section is organized as follows. We start in section 11.1 by briefly reviewing the relevant empirical literature. Next, we present the data (in section 11.2), set-up the empirical exercise (in 11.3), and discuss the key empirical findings (section 11.4). The section ends with a summary of the main results.

11.1 Previous empirical literature

We find it convenient to organize this brief review of the empirical literature on institutions and training by discussing in sequence the following institutions: unions, minimum wages, employment protection, product market regulation and school design.

11.1.1 Unions and training

Table 9.1 (p. 161) summarizes the testable predictions on the relationship between unions and training and suggests that this relationship is complex. The empirical papers investigating the different aspects of this relationship provide mixed results. Among the first studies in the US, Duncan and Stafford (1980), and Mincer, 1983, find evidence of a negative union effect on training. Similarly, Barron and co-authors, 1987, use data from a survey of US employers and find that the proportion of non-supervisory workers covered by collective bargaining has a significant negative effect on total training. On the contrary, Lynch, 1992, finds evidence of a positive effect of unions on training in the US National Longitudinal Survey of Youth (NLSY). Similarly, Kennedy et al. (1994), find that Australian firms where unions are actively involved in bargaining have significantly higher training incidence, in spite of the fact that union density does not have statistically significant effects. Green (1993), shows that unions in Britain have significant positive effects on training in small firms but virtually no effect in large firms.

Beside the Lynch's study, additional evidence of a positive union effect is provided by Veum (1995), Booth (1991), Greenhalgh and Mavrotas (1994), Arulampalam and Booth (1998), Green, Machin and Wilkinson

233

(1999), and Booth, Francesconi and Zoega (2003). The latter study investigates the impact of union coverage on work-related training and finds that union-covered British men are more likely to receive training and also receive more days of training than workers with no coverage. A positive union effect is also the key result of a recent investigation of unions and training in German data, by Dustmann and Schonberg (2004). On the other hand, Black and Lynch (1998), find no link between unions and training, as do Green and Lemieux (2001) using Canadian data. These authors find that, everything else equal, unions have little effect on the provision of training.

11.1.2 *Minimum wages and training*

The available empirical evidence on the effects of the minimum wages on training is also rather inconclusive, with recent studies in the US and the UK reporting contradictory findings. Recall that in perfectly competitive labour markets, the introduction of a minimum wage reduces training, because some workers are not capable of financing training by accepting lower wages. Conversely, when labour markets are characterized by monopsonistic power, minimum wages may increase employer-provided training of low-paid workers.

Early research by Leighton and Mincer (1981), and Hashimoto (1982), finds that age-earnings profiles are significantly flatter among workers whose wages are bound by the minimum wage, which is interpreted as suggesting that an increase in the minimum wage significantly reduces on-the-job training. Sharply in contrast, Lazear and Miller (1981), find no statistically significant relationship between the slope of age-earnings profiles and an indicator of whether the minimum wage is binding or not. However, more recent research by Grossberg and Sicilian (1999), shows that the effect of minimum wages on wage growth could be unrelated to the effect produced on training. As suggested by Acemoglu and Pischke (2003), minimum wages eliminate the lower tail of the wage distribution and by so doing flatten the slope of the age-earning profile. This effect is independent of the impact of minimum wages on training. Leighton and Mincer (1981), and Neumark and Wascher (2001), using data on individual workers, consider the relationship between the variation of minimum wages across US states and the investment in training and find that the more binding is the minimum wage, the less likely is a worker to receive on-the-job training. Since the minimum wage variable used by Neumark and Wascher is at a higher level of aggregation than training, the estimated standard errors may understate the inaccuracy of the estimates. This problem is taken into account by Acemoglu and Pischke (2003), who, by focusing on workers affected by minimum wages changes, find no evidence that minimum wages reduce training.

Schiller (1994), and Grossberg and Sicilian (1999), are two relatively recent studies that find opposite results: while Schiller produces evidence that minimum wages reduce training, Grossberg and Sicilian do not. Their approach, however, may be biased because the omitted determinants of training can also be correlated with their indicator of whether minimum wages are binding. Arulampalam, Booth and Bryan (2004), use two different treatment groups, workers stating that they were affected by minimum wages and workers with a wage in 1998 below the minimum. Their study of British Household Panel Survey data finds no evidence that the introduction of the minimum wage in Britain in 1999 has reduced the training of treated workers. If anything, there is evidence that training has increased.

11.1.3 *Flexible labour contracts and training*

A widespread concern with the recent diffusion of flexible employment practices, such as temporary labour contracts, is that these contracts may be detrimental to economic performance because temporary workers are less likely to be trained. Arulampalam and Booth (1998), investigate the relationship between employment flexibility and training using UK data, and find that workers on temporary contracts are less likely to receive work-related training. Quite in contrast, recent work by Autor (2004), on temporary help firms in the US shows that almost one-quarter of temporary help supply firms have received skills training as temporaries. Training in this context not only provides skills but also operates as a screening and a self-sorting device.

11.1.4 *Product market competition, employment protection and training*

The relationship between product market competition and training is significantly less studied in the literature, both theoretical and empirical. In the only empirical investigation we are aware of, Autor (2004), presents evidence of a negative and statistically significant correlation between the Herfindahl index, a measure of product market concentration, and the training provided by temporary help firms in the US. The evidence on the relationship between firing costs, employment protection and training is also rather limited. Bishop (1991), is one study in the area, which reports that the likelihood and amount of formal training are higher at firms where firing a worker is more difficult. Acemoglu and Pischke (2000), argue that there are complementarities between regulation regimes and training systems, and that reducing firing costs and increasing employment flexibility could reduce the incentives to train. Their evidence, however, is impressionistic and focuses mainly on Germany. Clearly, a broader comparison would be more problematic. Take for instance Italy and Japan. The former country has one of the strictest systems of employment protection and very little training, and the latter country is often mentioned as a leading example of a high training equilibrium (see Lynch, 1994), in spite of its having a much lower index of employment protection than Italy.

11.1.5 Schooling and training

There is substantial evidence that the *quantity* of education and training are complements (see Leuven, 2005, for a review), and there is also evidence that the strength of this complementarity depends on whether training is provided on-the-job or off-the-job (see Ariga and Brunello, 2002). To our knowledge, no empirical research has been done so far on the relationship between the *quality* of education and of training. Since quality depends on the design of schooling institutions, an important empirical question is which institutions are more conducive to work-related training.

11.1.6 Training and pensions

The traditional way of looking at the relationship between pension benefits and training is that deferred payments—such as pensions—reduce turnover, increase incentives, and therefore allow firms to recoup the costs of their investments in training (see Lazear, 1979). This view suggests that there is a positive relationship between employer-provided training and the generosity of the pension plans designed by firms.

If we focus on workers approaching retirement age, however, we notice that these employees face the choice of retiring versus continuing work, and investing in further training. The incentive to stay and train is likely to be higher in countries where the implicit tax on continuing work is lower. This tax is defined as minus the change in pension wealth from remaining in the labour market during a given period of time (see Duval,

236

2004). Many European countries have recently changed or are considering reforming the pension system, with the view of increasing its
sustainability in the face of persistent ageing. One concern raised by
these policies is that a postponement of retirement age might increase
the unemployment rate of older workers, who are unlikely to receive the
training needed to stay longer in the labour market. To cope with this,
some countries in Europe have in place early retirement schemes, which
facilitate the transition of older dismissed workers from work to retirement. These systems are expensive for the taxpayer, and do not contribute to increase the participation rate of older workers. In principle,
however, less generous expected benefits from retirement should positively affect the training of senior workers—both employer- and
employee-provided—by increasing the expected length of working life
after the investment, and the time available to recoup the costs of the
investment.

As in the case of the relationship between school design and training, we
are not aware of any empirical research which has investigated whether
the generosity of—mainly public—pension schemes has a significant
effect on the training incidence of senior workers.

11.2 The data

Our data on individual training events are drawn from the European
Community Household Panel (ECHP),[1] waves 1995 to 2001. As discussed
in Appendix 4, the ECHP is an attractive source of information because
it covers a significant number of European countries with a commonly
designed questionnaire. For comparability with the previous empirical literature, we select our sample as in Arulampalam, Booth and Bryan (2004).
In particular, we consider only individuals who are (i) aged between 25 and
60 years and working at least 15 hours per week; (ii) not employed in
agriculture; (iii) present in at least two consecutive waves; and (iv) not in
apprenticeships or in special-employment training schemes.

Since the reference period of each wave may overlap with the period of
the previous wave, we run the risk of double counting training spells.
Rather than losing information or adjusting counts in an ad hoc way, we
prefer to ignore double counting in the main regressions and to perform a

---

[1] The December 2003 release of these data is available at the Department of Economics,
University of Padova, under contract n. 14/99.

robustness check which compares our results with those obtained from a reduced sample which only retains odd years, and therefore avoids double counting by definition. There is also the problem of omitted spells, which appears to be particularly serious for Germany. Since the data for Germany also miss important information on employer-provided training, as well as on industry affiliation, we follow Arulampalam, Booth and Bryan (2004), and drop this country from the sample.[2] A comparison between these training data and those drawn from other sources can be found in Appendix 4.

We consider all training, independently of whether it is defined as general or as firm-specific, or as paid by the employer or by the employee. As documented in the introduction to Chapter 10, average training incidence is higher in countries with a higher percentage of the population having at least a high-school diploma. Not only the quantity but also the quality of education matters. As already discussed, one important area where European secondary schools differ is the degree of stratification or tracking. Compared to the US, where tracking consists of ability grouping within the same comprehensive schooling system,[3] stratification in Europe occurs mainly by separating students into vocational and general tracks, with different degrees of osmosis between tracks. Hannah, Raffe and Smyth (1996), and OECD (2004), classify countries into three groups, depending on the degree of stratification of school curricula: a high stratification group, which includes Germany, Austria, Belgium and the Netherlands; a low stratification group, with the UK, Spain and Scandinavian countries (Sweden, Denmark and Finland); an intermediate group, with the rest of Europe, including France and Italy, which lies between these two extremes. In systems with high stratification, students are divided relatively early into separate tracks, and develop specific and relatively narrow skills in the vocational track. In systems with low stratification, tracking takes place later if ever, and students receive a broader and more versatile education.

We define a dummy equal to 0 for low, 1 for intermediate and 2 for high stratification. Figure 11.1 plots average training incidence in 1997—obtained by the weighted aggregation of the residuals of a linear probability model, where the dependent variable is the individual training event, and the controls are education, gender, age, lagged industry and country

---

[2] The German data in the ECHP are derived from GSOEP and exclude many shorter training spells.

[3] See Epple, Newlon and Romano (2002) for a brief description of tracking in US secondary schools.

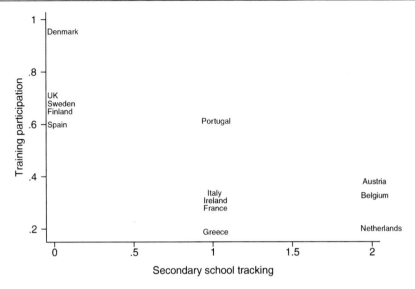

Fig. 11.1 Training incidence and tracking in secondary schools
Note: 1998 for Sweden. Training density is obtained by weighted aggregation of the residuals of a linear probability model, where the dependent variable is the individual training event, and the controls are education, gender, age, lagged industry and country by year dummies. *Sources*: ECHP and OECD.

by year dummies—separately for the three groups of countries. Since training participation depends also on the quantity of education, we divide it by the share of individuals with at least upper secondary education. The figure shows a negative relationship between stratification and incidence. One reading is that more comprehensive education can increase versatility in the presence of unexpected shocks, but requires additional training to transform the general skills it produces into more operational competencies.

The data on labour and product market institutions come from a variety of sources. Time varying union density is from the OECD database. This variable has been used in the literature as a proxy of union influence, mainly because of the availability of time varying data. An important drawback, however, is that the variable of interest in the empirical analysis is union coverage, which might be poorly related to union density. Only in half-a-dozen OECD economies with predominantly company bargaining, do the two go closely together. The case of France, where coverage is high but density low, is a clear example of poor correlation. It follows that, when the extension of union agreements is high, changes in union density are not as informative of union influence on wages, employment and training decisions as when extension is low.

The OECD has developed a measure of the legal or administrative extension of union agreements. Extension makes a collective agreement generally binding within an industrial sector, covering all employees who are not members of its signatory parties. This measure is a dummy equal to one for countries where extension is low (Denmark, the UK and Sweden), two for countries with medium extension (Netherlands, Ireland, Italy, Greece, Finland) and three for countries with high extension (Belgium, France, Spain, Portugal and Austria).[4] Since variations of union density are a good measure of union influence and coverage when extension is low, we define a new variable—the interaction of density with a dummy equal to one for the countries with low extension. This is equivalent to restricting the analysis of the relationship between training and union density to these countries. Since the ECHP measure of training for each year covers the previous year as well, we use the second lag of union density. By so doing, we try to attenuate potential endogeneity problems originated by reverse causality running from training incidence to unionization rates.

We characterize the flexibility of the employment relationship in Europe with three variables—the index of stringency of employment protection legislation (EPL) for regular and temporary workers and the share of temporary workers in the labour force.[5] The data for these variables are also from the OECD database. As in the case of union density, we use the second lag of each variable to reduce potential endogeneity problems. Figures 11.2 and 11.3 illustrate the relationship between the employment protection index for regular and temporary workers in 1995 and training participation in 1997.

Figure 11.2 suggests the presence of a negative correlation between the employment protection of regulars and training incidence, which turns out, however, to be not statistically significant (coefficient: −.055, standard error: .043). The negative correlation is even more pronounced in the case of the index of employment protection for temporary workers. In this case, the estimated coefficient in a linear regression of training on EPL is statistically different from zero (−.060, standard error: .025). The negative correlation between training incidence and either measure of employment protection presumably reflect the fact that the latter is a tax, and that a higher tax reduces profits and the incentive to train.

---

[4] See OECD (2004).

[5] While the index of employment protection for regular workers focuses mainly on firing restrictions, the index for temporary workers considers mainly hiring restrictions.

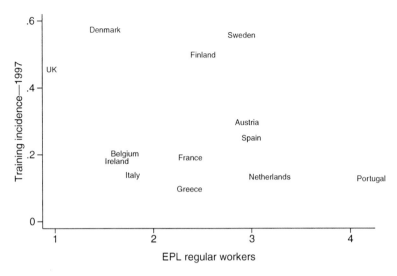

Fig. 11.2 Training in 1997 and the employment protection of regulars in 1995
Note: See Fig. 11.1.

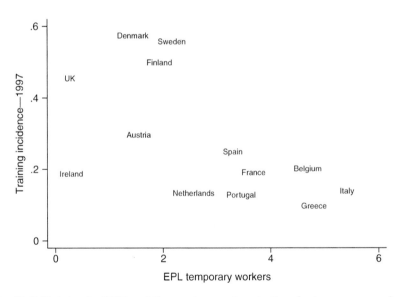

Fig. 11.3 Training in 1997 and the employment protection for temporary workers in 1995
Note: See Fig. 11.1.

The relationship between training participation, the share of temporary workers and the index of product market regulation has already been described in the general introduction of this report. We use the index of product market regulation developed by Nicoletti and Scarpetta (2003), which measures the stringency of anti-competitive product market regulation—varying between 0 and 6 from the least to the most stringent. Since the indicator covers the period from the late eighties to 1998,[6] we minimize the loss of information by associating to training between year *t-1* and year *t* product market regulation in year *t-3*.

Next, we plot in Figure 11.4 the relationship between training participation for workers aged between 50 and 59—relative to participation for the younger age group aged 25 to 49—and the implicit tax rate on continued work. This indicator measures the change in pension or social wealth from remaining in the labour market during the 5 years from age 60 to age 64 and is defined as minus this change divided by length of the interval. Unfortunately, it has been estimated by the OECD only for the year 2003 and does not include Greece (see Duval, 2004). For the purposes of this study, we shall assume hereafter that the indicator proxies in a satisfactory way expected pension benefits during the second part of

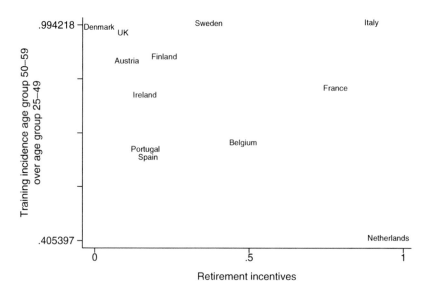

Fig. 11.4 Training of older workers and the implicit tax on continuing work
Note: See Fig. 11.1.

[6] A recent update to include the year 2003 has been produced by the OECD.

the 1990s. With the noteworthy exceptions of Italy and Sweden, a higher value of the implicit tax is associated to a lower relative training participation for workers aged 50 to 59.

Table 11.1 summarizes our data on time varying institutions by classifying countries according to whether the relevant variable has decreased, remained constant or increased between 1993 and 1999. Union density has declined in all the countries with low extension of union contracts; the share of temporary workers has increased in all countries, with the notable exceptions of Denmark, Ireland and Finland, where it has declined.

The index of employment protection of regular employees has remained constant in the large majority of countries, increased in Portugal and declined in Denmark, Spain and Finland; the same index for temporary workers has declined in half of the sample and remained constant in the rest; product market regulation has declined across the board; finally, the expenditure on R&D as a share of GDP has increased in most countries but declined in France, Italy and the UK.

11.3 The empirical set-up

We group individual data by country, year, education (college versus less than college) and age (24 to 49 and 50 to 59)—and estimate by weighted least squares an empirical specification where the dependent variable is the logistic transformation of the proportion of trained employees in each subgroup. Compared to estimates which use individual data, aggregation over groups has the advantage of reducing individual heterogeneity and

Table 11.1 Changes of institutional and other indicators between 1995 and 2001, by country

	Decreased	Constant	Increased
Union density	DK, UK, SW	-	-
Employment protection of regulars	DK, SP, FL	AU, BE, FR, IR, IT, UK, SW, NL	PT
Employment protection of temporary	DK, BE, IT, SP, PT, SW	NL, FR, UK, IR, GR, AU, FL	
Share of temporary workers	DK, IR, FL	-	BE, NL, FR, UK, GR, IT, SP, PT, AU, SW
Product market regulation	All countries	-	-
R&D expenditure on GDP	FR, UK, IT		DK, NL, BE, IR, GR, SP, PT, FL, SW, AU

measurement error in the dependent variable. More in detail, the empirical relationship between training and institutions is

$$\ln \frac{S_{eact}}{1 - S_{eact}} = \alpha_e + \alpha_a + \alpha_c + \alpha_t + \beta X_{eact} + \gamma I_{ct} + \delta Y_{ct} \qquad [11.1]$$

where S is the proportion of trained individuals in the group, α_c, α_t, α_e and α_a are country, year, education and age effects, X is a vector of controls, I a vector of time varying institutional variables, Y a vector of confounding country-specific time varying effects, c is the index for the country, t for time, a for age and e for education.

The introduction of country and time dummies in [11.1] implies that we can estimate the relationship between training and labour market institutions only if the latter vary both across countries and over the available time span. Notice, however, that the variation of training across countries and over time can also be due to confounding factors, which operate at the same level of aggregation of the selected institutional variables. Failure to control for these factors could seriously bias our results. To illustrate, suppose that training incidence is affected by country-specific technical progress, and let this variable change over time. By excluding measures of technical progress from the regression, we run the risk of attributing its effects to time varying institutions.

An important feature of specification [11.1] is that the institutional variables are at a higher level of aggregation than the dependent variable. The combination of years and countries generates a number of clusters, and we shall assume that errors are independent between clusters but correlated within clusters. This implies that standard errors need to be adjusted to take into account the different levels of aggregation of the dependent variable and of the institutional variables.

11.4 The empirical results

We estimate equation [11.1] on ECHP data for 13 countries[7] and the period 1995–2001,[8] and take into account the fact that training covers both the year of the survey and the previous year by using the latter as reference for the selected controls. The vector of institutions I includes union density

---

[7] These countries are: Austria, Belgium, Denmark, Finland, France, Ireland, Italy, Greece, the Netherlands, Portugal, Spain, Sweden and the UK.
[8] We exclude 1994, the first wave, because it does not contain data on Austria, Finland and Sweden and is slightly different from the other waves in the availability of data on training.

interacted with a dummy equal to 1 if the extension of union contracts is low, the index of employment protection for regular and temporary employees, the index of product market regulation,[9] the interaction between age in the range 50 to 59 and the implicit tax on continued work and the interactions between the share of R&D expenditure on GDP, no college education—a dummy equal to 1 for individuals with less than college education—and no tracking—a dummy equal to zero for countries with a comprehensive secondary school system. These two dummies are interacted both separately and jointly with R&D expenditure.

The first interaction is expected to capture the disincentive effects on training of higher expected returns from retirement. The second set of interactions investigates whether the effects of technical innovations— captured by the share of R&D expenditure on GDP—vary with the level of educational attainment and with the degree of tracking in secondary schools. Technical change is likely to make narrowly specialized skills obsolete, and it might be necessary as a consequence to re-train more individuals with a less versatile and narrower education than individuals with general skills. If this is the case, we expect the relationship between technical progress and training to be positive and stronger in countries where schooling is more stratified.

In so doing, we also need to take into account the fact that the degree of secondary school stratification has changed over time in some countries, most notably Italy and the UK. In the UK, stratification was fairly radical before 1965, when individuals were tracked into grammar and secondary schools.[10] In Italy, a sweeping reform unified lower secondary school in a single comprehensive track in 1963. We take this into account by assigning to the high tracking group the individuals born before 1995 in the UK and before 1952 in Italy.

There is a substantial literature on skill-biased technical change (see Katz and Autor, 1999 for a review), showing that new technological developments and higher education are complements. Complementarities between innovations and educational attainment imply that new innovations increase the relative demand for college graduates. If training and education are also complements, an implication is that the effect of

---

[9] This index ranges from 0 to 6 and measures the intensity of regulation with respect to: economic and administrative regulation, tariff and other barriers, state control and public ownership, barriers to entrepreneurship, impediments to trade and investment. See Nicoletti and Scarpetta, 2003.

[10] See Galindo-Rueda and Vignoles (2004).

technical progress, captured by R&D expenditure, is likely to be stronger for individuals with higher education.

The vector Y of confounding factors consists of the country and time-specific unemployment rate, the share of temporary workers in the labour force and the share of R&D expenditure on GDP. The first two variables are expected to capture cyclical effects and changes in the composition of labour contracts, and the latter variable to proxy technical progress. Ideally, we would also like to include indicators which capture changes in training policy, but the only closely related indicator—the share of expenditure on active labour market policies on GDP—includes almost entirely training subsidies paid out to the unemployed.

Table 11.2 presents the summary statistics of the key variables used in the regressions, and Table 11.3 reports our results from estimating model [11.1]. About 20 per cent of the workers aged 24 to 59 in our sample get trained at least once during the sample period. Close to 71 per cent of sampled individuals have less than college education, and about 56 per cent are males. Table 11.3 consists of three columns: in the first column we present a parsimonious specification which excludes all institutional variables; in the second column we include all institutional variables except the interaction of age with the implicit tax on continuing work, which is not available for Greece; in the last column we add the latter variable and restrict our sample to 12 countries.

Our results do not vary significantly when we restrict our sample only to odd years, in order to remove the risk of double counting training events.[11] We can compare the goodness of fit of the less parsimonious

Table 11.2 Summary statistics

	Mean	Standard dev.	Minimum	Maximum
Training	.207			
Less than college	.713			
Percentage females	.434			
Union density × low extension dummy	.116	.251	0	.822
Share of temporary workers	.126	.768	.049	.350
Employment protection index for regular workers	2.394	.896	.950	4.330
Employment protection index for temporary workers	2.608	1.532	.250	5.380
Product market regulation	3.907	1.127	1.024	5.665
Implicit tax on continued work	.421	.344	−.014	.920
R&D expenditure as share of GDP	1.606	.763	.470	3.800
Unemployment rate	.086	.037	.024	.188

[11] Results available from the authors upon request.

Table 11.3 Employer provided training and time varying institutions. ECHP 1995–2001. Dependent variable: logistic transformation of the proportion of trained individuals. Weighted least squares.

	Full sample	Full sample	Full sample
Unemployment rate	5.298***	3.309**	2.682
	(1.555)	(1.632)	(1.678)
Total R&D expenditure on GDP	0.726***	0.605**	0.706***
	(.178)	(.260)	(.265)
Share of temporary workers in total	−1.370	−1.410	−1.408
employment	(1.032)	(1.179)	(1.071)
Union density × low extension		−0.003	0.005
dummy		(.029)	(.028)
Product market regulation		−.422***	−0.423**
		(.159)	(.178)
Employment protection index for		−0.250**	−0.259**
regular workers		(.099)	(.101)
Employment protection index for		−0.053*	−0.051
temporary workers		(.032)	(.033)
[Aged between 50 and 59 /100] ×		-	−0.500***
implicit tax rate on continued work			(.131)
at age 60–64			
Total R&D expenditure on GDP × no		0.448***	0.471***
college dummy		(.061)	(.064)
Total R&D expenditure on GDP × no		−0.010	−0.168
tracking dummy		(.349)	(.346)
Total R&D expenditure on GDP × no		−0.177***	−0.171***
tracking × no college		(.049)	(.049)
Year dummies	Yes	Yes	Yes
Country dummies	Yes	Yes	Yes
R Squared	.938	.952	.958
Nobs	319	319	292

Notes: Each regression includes a constant, the percentage of females, college and age group dummies.
*, **, *** One, two and three stars for the coefficients statistically significant at the 10, 5 and 1 per cent level of confidence respectively. Heteroskedasticity consistent and cluster adjusted standard errors.

model in the second column, which includes time varying institutions, with the fit of the parsimonious model in the first column, which excludes them. Since the decline in the adjusted R Squared turns out to be quite small, from .952 to .938, we conclude that the contribution of time varying institutions to explaining the time series and cross section variation of training outcomes is rather limited. Clearly, cross-country differences in the level of institutions are likely to be important, as suggested by Figures 11.1–11.4, but cannot be identified in these data because of the impossibility to control for the full set of confounding country-specific effects.

We find that training incidence increases with the unemployment rate, which supports the view that firms and individuals engage more frequently in training activities when the opportunity cost of training—in terms of foregone production—is lower (Hall, 2000). Training participation also increases with total expenditure on R&D—measured as share of GDP—and this effect is significantly lower for college graduates, which suggests that the latter require less training when innovations occur.

The effect of union density on training—limited to the countries with low extension of union contracts—is very small and imprecisely estimated. Training turns out to be lower when the share of temporary workers in total employment increases. Therefore, an increase in the flexibility of the employment relationship associated to the introduction and diffusion of temporary labour contracts reduces the incentives of both parties to train. This effect, however, is imprecisely estimated.

At the same time, training incidence is lower when the degree of employment protection of both regular workers and temporary workers increases, although this effect is statistically different from zero at the 5 per cent level of confidence only for the former. How do we explain this? It is well known that employment protection is associated to firing costs, and that these costs have both a transfer and a tax component. While the transfer part could be undone by properly designed labour contracts, the tax component is difficult to undo (see Garibaldi and Violante, 2002). A common view in this literature is that firing costs increase wages (see Mortensen and Pissarides, 1999). According to Lindbeck and Snower (1988), these costs increase the bargaining power of insiders by sheltering them from the competition of outsiders. How could this affect training? Using the simple illustrative model in Appendix 3 (A3.2), suppose that wages of regular workers—the insiders—are the results of Nash bargaining and let

$$w(\tau) = \beta(\theta)v(\tau) + [1 - \beta(\theta)]f(\tau) \qquad [11.2]$$

where the notation is w for wages, β for the bargaining power of the firm, f for productivity, v for the outside option, θ for the firing tax and τ for training. If training is employer-provided and the firm bears its costs, optimal provision satisfies the following condition

$$(1 - q)\beta(\theta)[f'(\tau) - v'(\tau)] - c'(\tau) = 0 \qquad [11.3]$$

where q is the exogenous rate of turnover. If a higher firing tax reduces the bargaining power of the firm, and the second order conditions for a local maximum hold, then it follows that

$$\frac{\partial \tau}{\partial \theta} < 0 \text{ if } (1-q)\frac{\partial \beta}{\partial \theta}[f'(\tau) - \nu'(\tau)] < 0 \qquad [11.4]$$

which holds when there is wage compression and the bargaining power of insiders increases in the firing tax.

An alternative explanation is selection. When firing costs are high, employers cannot easily dismiss less able or less suitable regular employees and therefore end up with a more heterogeneous regular labour force than employers who can more easily dismiss unsuitable employees. If training and ability are complements, or if labour force heterogeneity imposes a negative firm-specific externality on individual productivity, employers with a more homogeneous regular labour force should train more.[12]

Giuseppe Bertola, in his discussion of this chapter, suggests yet another explanation, which builds on the observed positive correlation between stringent EPL and poorly developed households—finance markets. He shows that, conditional on a borrowing conditions indicator, there is no residual correlation between EPL and training, and argues that the association we uncover between EPL and training simply reflects the correlation between training and borrowing conditions. We find this argument interesting and worth further exploration, but not wholly convincing, because Bertola's evidence is based on the correlation between the *level* of training and the *level* of the borrowing conditions indicator. Our evidence, instead, is on the relationship between the *change* of EPL and the *change* of training incidence over time. Since our regression explicitly controls for all country-specific level effects with unrestricted country dummies, our findings cannot be affected by the inclusion of time invariant measures of borrowing conditions. Clearly, a more convincing argument would require that we associate the variation of training with the variation of borrowing conditions over time.

Conditional on employment protection, training incidence is lower when product market regulation is higher. Therefore, liberalizing product markets do not damage training incentives, quite the contrary. This evidence does not support the view expressed by Gersbach and Schmutzler (2004), that training should be higher when industrial concentration is

---

[12] One could object that employers facing higher employment protection select their employees more carefully, and therefore reduce heterogeneity. If labour quality can only be learned over time, however, hiring policies cannot fully undo heterogeneity.

high and /or competitive intensity is comparatively low, but is in line with the finding by Autor (2004), that temporary help firms operating in more concentrated markets train more.[13]

Overall, these results provide an interesting picture. On the one hand, product market liberalization does not reduce training. On the other hand, more flexible labour markets have contrasting effects on the incentive to train. If higher flexibility is obtained by reducing the employment protection of regular workers, training increases. If this flexibility is the consequence of the diffusion of temporary work in two-tier systems, training incentives are reduced.

We find that the interaction of age and the implicit tax on continued work is negative and statistically significant. Therefore, the age-training profile of workers in the 50–59 age group is reduced by the expectation of better retirement benefits. An implication of this finding is that pension reforms which reduce the implicit tax on continuing work during age 60 to 64 are likely to increase the training of senior employees. Thus, the concerns about the labour market prospects of senior workers which often accompany these reforms might be exaggerated to the extent that these workers receive further training. As shown by Bassanini (2005), additional training of senior workers increases their employability.

Finally, the interaction between R&D expenditure on GDP and lack of secondary school tracking yields a negative and statistically significant coefficient for individuals with less than college education, suggesting that technical progress has for these individuals a positive effect on training where schooling is stratified and a negative effect where schooling is comprehensive. This result points to the possibility that the vocational skills developed in stratified schools require more training and updating in the face of technical innovations. Therefore, countries with less stratified schooling systems have endowed workers with more versatile skills and need less training to match newly developed techniques than countries with more stratified education systems.

How big are the effects discussed above? Going by the results in the last column of the table, a 10 per cent increase in the share of R&D expenditure is expected to raise the probability of training for college graduates by 5.54 per cent.[14] The Lisbon Strategy sets at 3 per cent the target share of R&D expenditure on GDP, to be attained by 2010.

---

[13] The evidence does not confirm the view that more stability increases the incentives to train, a point raised by Giuseppe Bertola in his discussion of this chapter.

[14] The elasticity of training to R&D is given by $\frac{\partial S}{\partial (R\&D)} \frac{1}{(1-S)'(R\&D)}$.

According to our estimates, this would require an increase from the current European average of 1.4 percentage points, close to 50 per cent from the baseline. If such an increase could be attained, we expect training participation to increase by 28 per cent—a substantial amount. The expected increase in the probability of training is even higher for individuals without a college degree, and depends on the nature of the secondary school.

When evaluated at the sample mean values of employment protection, a 10 per cent increase in the degree of product market regulation reduces the probability of training by 1.37 per cent. Conversely, a 10 per cent increase in employment protection reduces training incidence by 1.36 in the case of regular workers and by 0.24 per cent in the case of temporary workers.

11.5 Summary

We summarize the results of this empirical investigation with the following points:

- product market regulation affects training negatively and significantly. Therefore, more competition in the product market is conducive to higher investment in training;
- labour market flexibility affects training in a less straightforward manner: on the one hand, the diffusion of temporary contracts reduces the investment in training; on the other hand, the reduction in the degree of employment protection for regular workers increases the provision of training. Therefore, labour market reforms that accelerate the diffusion of temporary contracts and at the same time increase the protection of a limited core of permanent employees produce negative effects on the accumulation of human capital taking place mainly in firms;
- training incidence declines with age and is lower than average for workers who have reached age 50. The decline is higher, *ceteris paribus*, in countries with a more generous pension system, because the higher implicit tax on continuing work at age 60 to 64 reduces the expected time horizon required to recoup the costs of the investment. Therefore, pension reforms which reduce the implicit tax are likely to have as a by-product an increase in the training of senior workers;
- there is little evidence that union density matters significantly for training. One reason could be that our measure of unionism does not

allow us to fully capture the complexity of this relationship. We have restricted union density to affect training only in those countries where the extension of union contracts is low, and cannot say much on the effects of unions on training in the remaining countries;

- training and investment in research and development are complements, but the degree of complementarity is lower for college graduates, possibly because the latter have sufficient skills and do not need to be trained or re-trained to be able to cope with innovations;
- secondary school design matters in the relationship between innovative activity and training: when schooling is more comprehensive, high school graduates require less training to adapt to technical progress.

12

The Costs and Benefits of Workplace Training

Introduction

In our review of the basic theory of workplace training in Chapter 9, we have remarked that efficient provision requires that the marginal private and social benefits of training be equal to marginal private and social costs. We have also argued that employers in imperfectly competitive labour markets are willing to bear the costs of general training if the increase in productivity after training is higher than the increase in wages. Since the costs and returns to training play an important role in both statements, the natural question to ask is what do we know about the effects of training on wages and productivity, and about training costs?

This chapter documents that the answer to this question is: 'not enough'. While there is an extensive literature on the social returns to schooling (see De La Fuente and Ciccone, 2002), little is known on the size of externalities associated to training. The extensive literature that has documented the relation between human capital and income, both at the individual and at the national level, leaves little doubt that investments in human capital are crucial for economic well being. Many of these investments take place both in the household and in the educational system but, as documented in Chapter 9, substantial investment in human capital takes place after entry into the labour market. However, most of the existing literature that considers returns to human capital has focused on schooling.

To the extent that the determinants of individual wage growth over the life-cycle (i.e. after entry into the labour market) have been considered, the literature has estimated returns to experience and tenure. Although experience and tenure are considered to be proxies for human capital, it is well known that economic mechanisms other than human capital alone can generate upward sloping wage profiles. One mechanism that generates wage growth is job search and matching (Jovanovic, 1979a; Mortensen, 1978), a second mechanism is contract based: upward sloping wage profiles that by postponing rewards can provide an incentive for workers to exert effort early on. Distinguishing between these alternative explanations of life-cycle wage patterns has proven to be a daunting task. That there is a direct relation between these returns and training investment is suggested by the analysis of Brown (1989), who finds that firm-specific wage growth occurs mainly during periods of on-the-job training. This illustrates the importance of studying the incidence and effects of more direct measures of training.

In the last two decades an increasing number of studies has attempted to estimate returns to training using more direct measures. In this chapter we discuss the fundamental problems that arise in the context of such estimations, including measurement and identification problems, and show that the interpretation and comparison of return estimates is not always straightforward.

12.1 Estimating the private returns to training

Let wages w and productivity y be functions of training τ. Most of the empirical literature estimates parametric specifications of $w(\tau)$ that in turn give estimates of $\partial w/\partial \tau$, the marginal impact of training on earnings. If labour markets are perfectly competitive, wages are equal to (the value of) marginal product, $w(\tau) = y(\tau)$.[1] As discussed in Chapter 9, labour market imperfections can drive a wedge $\Delta(\tau)$ between wages and productivity, so that $w(\tau) = y(\tau) - \Delta(\tau)$. If $\Delta(\tau) \neq \Delta$, the partial $\partial w/\partial \tau$ traces the impact of training not on productivity alone, but on productivity net of the marginal return to the employer, $\partial \Delta/\partial \tau$. With absolute wage compression, $\Delta'(\tau) > 0$ and the marginal effect of training on productivity is higher than the effect on earnings.

12.1.1 *Identification*

The fundamental problem that one encounters when estimating returns to training (either $\partial w/\partial \tau$ or $\partial y/\partial \tau$) is treated extensively in the evaluation

---

[1] Except when workers finance training by taking a wage cut. Costs then drive a wedge between wages and productivity: $w(\tau) = y(\tau) - c(\tau)$.

literature (see Heckman et al., 1999, for an overview). It is an omitted variables/selectivity problem and can be conveniently illustrated by considering the prototypical wage equation that is estimated in the literature:[2]

$$\ln w_{it} = x'_{it}\beta + \gamma\tau_{it} + \varepsilon_{it} \qquad [12.1]$$

where w_{it} is the wage of individual i at time t, x_{it} is a vector of control variables and ε_{it} the residual/error term. The first studies estimated [12.1] by ordinary least squares (OLS). Without covariates x_{it} and with τ_{it} defined as mere participation, the OLS estimate of the effect of training is simply the difference in mean earnings between those who participated in training and those who did not. Participation in training must therefore be random and the important shortcoming of OLS is that γ is unbiased only if training is uncorrelated with the error term: $E[\tau_{it}\varepsilon_{it}|x_{it}] = 0$. Ordinary least squares therefore ignores the possibility that there are unobserved individual characteristics, such as ability, that affect wages and correlate with training.

The current state-of-the-art in this literature is to estimate fixed effect versions of [12.1], where it is assumed that $\varepsilon_{it} = c_i + u_{it}$, so that the estimation equation now becomes

$$\ln w_{it} = x'_{it}\beta + \gamma\tau_{it} + c_i + u_{it} \qquad [12.2]$$

This method effectively estimates [12.2] using deviations from individual means and is comparable to estimating [12.1] in first differences.[3] The fixed effects estimator takes into account any confounding influence of unobserved individual characteristics that correlate both with wages and training, as long as these are fixed over time (they are picked up by c_i). Thus, the crucial identifying assumption here is that participants would have experienced the same wage growth as non-participants in the absence of training.

Some studies (OECD, 2004; Lowenstein and Spletzer, 1998, 1999) have estimated equations that control for match-specific effects. These fixed effects estimates are within-job estimates and therefore do not capture returns to training in the form of mobility to better jobs. Return estimates

---

[2] We will discuss the main estimation issues in the context of the estimation of $w(\tau)$, but the same problems arise in analyses based on firm level data that relate training to output instead of wages.

[3] With $T = 2$ first differencing and fixed estimation are equivalent. With $T > 2$ they are not. Which of the two is more efficient depends on the properties of u_{it}. If u_{it} is i.i.d. FE is more efficient and if u_{it} follows a random walk first differencing is more efficient.

from these types of studies are therefore expected to be lower than returns estimates from standard fixed effects models.

A few studies (Pischke, 2001; Frazis and Loewenstein, 1999) have recognized that training participants may experience higher wage growth in the absence of training than non-participants. If this is the case, then standard fixed effect estimates are biased. To take this into account Pischke (2001), estimated fixed effect growth equations by adding individual specific growth rates of earnings $\delta_i t$ to equation [12.2].

As an alternative to fixed effect based approaches a number of papers have estimated γ using selection models or instrumental variables (IV). The outcome equation [12.1] is now augmented with a participation equation

$$\tau_{it}^* = w_{it}' \eta + \nu_{it} \qquad [12.3]$$

Selection models specify a joint parametric distribution for (ε, ν) and can be estimated using maximum likelihood. An alternative is a 2-step method where in the first step a control function $\hat{\lambda}_{it} = \lambda(w_{it}' \hat{\eta})$ is estimated such that $E[d_{it}(\rho \lambda_{it} + \varepsilon_{it})] = 0$. Equation [12.2] is then augmented in a second step with the control function, and OLS gives a consistent estimate of the effect of training on wages γ.

It has been pointed out that selection models and control function methods can be very sensitive to misspecification of the joint distribution of (ε, ν) and are identified exclusively on functional form and distributional assumptions unless w_{it} includes variables that are not included in x_{it}. Unfortunately not any variable will do. What is needed is a variable z_{it} that affects participation but is orthogonal to the error term in (12.2): $E[z_{it} \varepsilon_{it}] = 0$. This is commonly referred to as an exclusion restriction, and to z_{it} as an instrumental variable. In addition z_{it} will need to have a significant effect on participation. With an instrument a common approach is to estimate γ using two-stage least squares (2SLS). The obvious challenge is to find variables that arguably affect training participation but are independent of wages or productivity.

12.1.2 Rates of return

To estimate rates of return we need information on costs: $r = b/c$, with b for benefits and c for costs. The benefits for the employee equal $b = h \cdot w(\tau + \Delta\tau) - h \cdot w(\tau) \equiv h \cdot \Delta w$, where h is hours worked. To see how wage return estimates relate to rates of return, assume that training is measured in hours and that there are no direct costs. In this case the cost of training equals $c = \Delta\tau \cdot w$ and the rate of return is

$$r = \frac{b}{c} = \frac{\Delta w/w}{\Delta\tau/h} \qquad\qquad [12.4]$$

Equation [12.4] estimates $\gamma = \Delta \ln w/\Delta\tau \approx (\Delta w/w)/\Delta\tau = r/h$. If training is measured as incidence, then it estimates $\gamma = \Delta \ln w \approx (\Delta w/w) = r \cdot \Delta\tau/h$.

This discussion assumes that there are no direct costs. Almeida and Carneiro (2004), find for Portugal that it is in fact direct costs which represent the bulk of training costs, as opposed to opportunity costs. With direct costs, total training costs now become $c = \Delta\tau \cdot w + f$, and returns $r' = (\Delta w/w)/(\Delta\tau/h + f/(wh)) > r$.

12.2 Returns to employees

As mentioned in the introduction, the initial literature that estimated wage returns to training was based on indirect training measures. These studies regress wages on labour market experience and job tenure (seniority). The coefficient on labour market experience is then interpreted as the return to general training, whereas the coefficient of job tenure is interpreted as the return to specific human capital. Abraham and Farber (1987), Altonji and Shakotko (1987), and Topel (1986), are early attempts to estimate the return to seniority up and above the return to experience. They find only small effects of seniority on wage growth. Topel (1991), re-examined the data and concluded that the findings in these studies are biased because of measurement error and selectivity issues. He finds that 10 years of current job seniority raises the wage of a typical male worker in the US by 25 per cent.

Human capital theory predicts upward sloping productivity profiles, and wage profiles are assumed to proxy these productivity profiles. There are several other theories (e.g. deferred compensation, self-selection, and matching theories) besides human capital theory that predict upward sloping wage profiles, and as such it is hard to argue that this is a definitive test. One would like to know to what extent wage growth correlates with productivity growth. Medoff and Abraham (1980, 1981) use performance ratings among professional and managerial employees in three US corporations, but do not find any statistically significant correlation between these ratings and wage growth. They conclude that the on-the-job training model explains only a small part of the observed return to labour market experience. This result rests on the assumption that these ordinal performance ratings are unbiased measures of productivity.

12.2.1 *The US evidence*

Table 12.1 contains a summary of the main empirical studies on the wage returns to training. For the US training returns have been estimated using a number of datasets. Some of these, such as the Panel Study of Income Dynamics (PSID) or the Current Population Survey (CPS), have very limited information on training. The most widely used datasets are the Employment Opportunity Pilot Project Survey (EOPP) and especially the National Longitudinal Survey of Youth Cohort (NLSY) which has arguably the most precise and comprehensive information on training.

Lynch (1992), is one of the first studies that uses the early waves of the NLSY (1981 and 1983) to estimate wage returns. The sub-sample she considers includes those who did not graduate from college and finished schooling by the 1980 interview date. She presents return estimates using both Heckman two-step selectivity corrections and fixed effects regressions. In the estimations she controls for tenure, experience and personal and job characteristics. The two-step estimates show that a week of company training (completed or uncompleted) is associated with a .2 per cent higher wage. This estimate is significant for uncompleted training. The fixed effect estimates do not show a significant impact on wages. One drawback of these early NLSY data is that training is only reported if it lasted longer than one month. It seems likely that many training spells are left unreported. Of the 12,686 individuals in the NLSY only 3,064 are used in the analysis. Of these 128 report on-the-job training, which is 4.2 per cent of the sample.

Veum, 1995, uses the NLSY for the years 1986 to 1990. After 1986, the training questions changed and also covered training lasting less than a month. Respondents could report information for up to four training programmes. Veum considers those who had completed formal schooling by the 1986 interview. About 18 per cent report having participated in company training, while the average time spent on this training was 135 hours. This does indeed suggest that many company training programmes are of short duration. Veum finds that one hour of company training increases wages by .7 to .9 per cent.

Parent (1999), uses the NLSY for the longer period of 1979 to 1991. About 16 per cent of the individuals report having participated in on-the-job training. He estimates both simple OLS regressions and IV

Table 12.1 Wage returns studies

Country	Study	Dataset	Period	Traindef	Method	b	se
United States	Lynch (1992)	NLSY	1980–1983	weeks of OJT	OLS+SC	0.0020	−0.0012
					FE	−0.0002	−0.0399
	Veum (1995)	NLSY	1986–1990	hours of OJT	OLS	0.0073	−0.0392
					FE	0.0090	−0.0255
	Parent (1999)	NLSY	1979–1991	years of OJT	OLS	0.1692	−0.0372
					HT	0.1216	
	Loewenstein and Spletzer (1998)	NLSY	1988–1991	Formal company training	FE	0.0346	−0.0193
Canada	Daniel Parent (2003)	FSLS, Men	1995	career of job-related training	FE	0.1034	−0.0311
		FSLS, Women			FE	0.0168	−0.0292
United Kingdom	Booth (1991)	BSAS, Men	1987	incidence, formal job-related	OLS	0.1060	−0.0380
	Booth (1993)	BSAS, Women	1986/87	weeks in 1st year, employer provided	OLS	0.1660	−0.0400
		BNSG, Men			OLS+SC	0.0100	−0.0020
		BNSG, Women			OLS+SC	0.0100	−0.0030
		BNSG, Men			FE	−0.0020	−0.0030
		BNSG, Women			FE	0.0100	−0.0040
	Blundell et al. (1996)	NCDS, Men	1981–1991	incidence, on-the-job empl. provided	quasi-difference	0.0360	−0.0180
		NCDS, Men			quasi-difference	0.0660	−0.0170
		NCDS, Women				0.0030	−0.0320
		NCDS, Women				0.0460	−0.0320

(Contd.)

Table 12.1 (*Contd.*)

Country	Study	Dataset	Period	Traindef	Method	b	se
	Blundell et al. (1999)	NCDS, Men	1981–1991	empl. prov. course without qual.	OLS	0.0830	−0.0170
		NCDS, Men			FE	0.0500	−0.0190
		NCDS, Men			IV	0.0650	−0.0440
		NCDS, Women			OLS	0.1420	−0.0220
		NCDS, Women			FE	0.1100	−0.0260
		NCDS, Women			IV	0.0270	−0.0560
	Arulampalam and Booth (2001)	NCDS	1981–1991	incidence, work related	Selection model	0.3420	−0.1740
France	Goux and Maurin (2000)	FQP	1988–1993	participation, firm provided	OLS+SC	−0.0570	−0.0680
		FQP			OLS	0.0710	−0.0200
	Denis Fougère et al. (2001)	FQP, Job switchers	1993	participation, firm provided	Switching Regr.	0.2930	−0.1210
		FQP, Non switchers			Switching Regr.		
Germany	Pischke (2001)	GSOEP	1986–1989	years, work related	FE, growth	0.1280	−0.0910
						0.0380	−0.0270
	Kuckulenz and Zwick (2003)	BIBB/IAB	1998/99	incidence, work-related	FE	0.0260	−0.0190
					Selection model	0.1500	−0.0400
Norway	Pal Schoene (2002)	NSOE	1989/1993	incidence, employer provided	OLS	0.0530	−0.0070
Netherlands	Leuven and Oosterbeek (2002)	EPIO	2000	incidence, work related	FE	0.0110	−0.0060
					OLS	0.0980	−0.0290
Switzerland	Gerfin (2003)	SLFS	1998–2000	incidence, work-related	SC	−0.0050	−0.0560
					Matching	0.0200	

regressions with Hausman–Taylor type instruments that are orthogonal to the individual fixed effects.[4] The OLS estimate of the return to one full-time year of training is 18 per cent. This estimate drops slightly in his partial fixed effect estimation to 12 per cent.

Frazis and Loewenstein (1999), estimate various specifications using the NLSY data for the years 1979 to 2000. They focus on rates of return— instead of wage returns, and find that at median training of 60 hours the rate of return is in the 150–175 per cent range, while their preferred estimate that takes into account heterogeneity in wage growth (fixed effects wage growth regressions) is a rate of return in the region of 40 to 50 per cent for one full-time week of training.

Finally, Parent (2003), uses data for Canada from a Follow-Up to the School Leavers Survey (FSLS). He estimates fixed effects models for men and women separately. For men, participation in employer-supported training increases hourly wages by more than 10 per cent. For women the effects are much more modest, about 2 per cent, and not statistically significant. Parent also reports returns to weekly earnings. These returns are higher, both for men (.1364) and for women (.0564), suggesting that there might be employment effects.

With the exception of Lynch (1992), (and to some extent Parent, 1999), return estimates for the US are high. There are various possible explanations for Lynch's results. First, her sample is made up of less educated individuals. Secondly, the data are for the early 1980s, while it is widely documented that returns to skill increased substantially over the 1980s. A more likely explanation for her relatively low return estimates is the fact that training spells that lasted less than a month are not reported in her data (the same holds for most of the data used in Parent, 1999). This not only suggests that there are quickly decreasing returns to training, but is also suggestive that the high returns that subsequent studies found are largely due to relatively short training spells.

12.2.2 The European evidence

There are numerous studies that estimate wage returns for the UK. An early study is Greenhalgh and Stewart (1987), that uses 1975 data from the

---

[4] Hausman and Taylor (1981), observed that for time-varying variables the deviation from their time mean can be used as instruments. They also showed that the time means of the exogenous time-invariant variables can be used as instruments for the time-invariant endogenous variables. This requires that there are at least as many exogenous time-invariant variables as endogenous time-invariant variables.

British National Training Survey. The outcome variable they consider is occupational status. It is found that training, defined as anything that may have helped an individual to learn/do his work, has a significant effect on occupational status, but the marginal benefit is zero after four weeks. Booth (1991), uses data from the 1987 British Social Attitudes Survey (BSAS). The outcome variable that Booth considers is annual earnings. She finds high returns, 11.2 per cent for men and 18.1 per cent for women. Potential selectivity into training is not taken into account. Booth (1993), improves on this using the 1980 British National Survey of Graduates and Diplomates (BNSG). This study reports estimates using both selectivity corrected OLS and fixed effect estimates. She finds that one week of training in the first year on the job increases earnings by one per cent both for men and women. Unfortunately, her exclusion restriction in the training probit lack explanatory power so that her Heckman two-step procedure is basically identified on functional form only. Turning to fixed effect estimates, there are no longer non-zero returns for men, while the point estimate for women remains the same.

A number of studies have used the National Child Development Survey (NCDS) to estimate the wage returns to training. These studies look at training incidence and wage growth over the period 1981 to 1991. Blundell et al. (1996), use a quasi-differencing approach that allows unobserved heterogeneity to affect wages differentially over time. In addition, the remaining transitory shocks are instrumented using individual first job characteristics and wages, observed ability, family background, pre-1981 training and post-school qualification variables other than a degree. They find that participation in employer-provided on-the-job training increases wages by 3.6 per cent for men. For women there is no significant effect on wages. Participation in off-the-job training has higher returns, about 7 per cent for men and 5 per cent for women.

Blundell et al. (1999), report OLS, fixed effect and instrumental variable estimates using the same data but for a somewhat larger sample, and consider employer-provided training courses. For men, OLS gives a wage return of 8.3 per cent, the fixed effect estimate is lower at 5 per cent while the IV estimate is 6.5 per cent. Returns to training courses that do lead to a qualification are of similar magnitude. For women, the returns are somewhat less clear cut, but still considerable. The OLS estimate of the return to an employer-provided training course that does not lead to a qualification is about 15 per cent, the estimated return from the fixed effect specification is about 12 per cent, and the IV estimate drops to about 3 per cent. Returns are higher for training courses that do lead to a qualification. Here the fixed effect estimate is over 17 per cent and the IV estimate about 8 per cent.

Finally, Arulampalam and Booth (2001), estimate a hurdle model on the NCDS data, where the number of training occurrences is instrumented with the local unemployment rate in 1981, marital status, the presence of children, early ability measures and pre-1981 training courses. It is found that participation is associated with a 41 per cent higher wage growth between 1981 and 1991. This study only finds significant returns to incidence, but not to the number of training courses.

For countries other than the US or the UK, evidence on training returns is more scant. Goux and Maurin (2000), estimate wage returns to employer-provided training for France. While their OLS estimate is 7.1 per cent and significant, it drops to −5.7 with a large standard error after correcting for selectivity. This finding is somewhat at odds with the results of Fougère et al. (2001), who find returns to training participation for job-switchers close to 30 per cent. For non-switchers the point estimate is still a sizable 13 per cent, but no longer statistically significant. Pischke, 2001, is a careful study using the German Socio-Economic Panel (GSOEP). He presents both fixed effect estimates and is the first to estimate fixed effect wage growth regressions. He finds that one year of full-time work-related training increases wages by 2.6 to 3.8 per cent. These estimates are however not significant. Kuckulenz and Zwick (2003), have access to the 1999 'Qualification and Career Survey' (BIBB/IAB), a .1 per cent sample of all employed Germans. They find that participation in work-related training is associated with more than 15 per cent higher wages after correcting for the endogeneity of training. Their exclusion restriction includes self perceived training needs and dummy variables indicating whether the employer went through a period of downsizing or workplace restructuring. Schøne, 2002, finds that training participation is associated with 1 per cent higher wages in Norway. Gerfin (2003), finds effects twice that size for Switzerland using matching methods, where it is worthwhile to note that the average training course lasted 17 hours (median 8). Finally, Leuven and Oosterbeek (2002), find cross-sectional returns to training in the Netherlands of about 10 per cent, but this return drops to almost zero after narrowing down the comparison group of non-participants.

12.2.3 Evidence from the ECHP

Cross-country comparisons of private returns to training are difficult because of the different definitions of training, different empirical specifications and econometric methods. Some comparative perspective can be gained for European countries if we estimate the same specification—model [12.2]—using the European Community Household Panel, a dataset explicitly conceived for international comparisons, and focusing on the effects of training incidence. Since we are interested in the stock rather than in the flow of training, we cumulate this variable from the initial year of the sample, which we choose to be 1995, to the final year, 2001. Because of the problems associated with the definition of the reference period— discussed in some detail in Chapter 10—we only use odd years. We select the sub-sample of workers aged 25 to 59 who are employed full-time in the private sector and work between 15 and 70 hours per week. Table 12.2 presents the results by country, using both ordinary least squares and fixed effects.

Ordinary least square estimates of the impact of training incidence on log hourly earnings range between 3.7 and 21.6 per cent, and are higher in the countries with lower incidence, especially Greece and Portugal. Since we have defined training incidence as a stock variable ranging between 0 and 4, this impact is the expected return to receiving at least one training course in one year of the sample.

When we turn to fixed effects, however, estimated returns are considerably lower and often not statistically different from zero, with the noteworthy exception of Denmark, the UK, Italy, Greece, Finland, Portugal and Belgium. Fig. 12.1 plots these estimated returns against training incidence, and shows some evidence of a negative relationship.

Table 12.2 Private returns to training. ECHP 1995/97/99/2001

	OLS	FE
Denmark	.042*** (.005)	.020*** (.007)
Netherlands	.037** (.019)	−.030 (.031)
Belgium	.055*** (.011)	.026* (.016)
France	.072*** (.007)	.000 (.013)
UK	.079*** (.005)	.019* (.010)
Ireland	.081*** (.010)	.005 (.022)
Italy	.097*** (.013)	.038*** (.014)
Greece	.216*** (.027)	.060* (.032)
Spain	.072*** (.007)	.017 (.012)
Portugal	.180*** (.013)	.105*** (.025)
Austria	.103*** (.006)	.004 (.012)
Finland	.055*** (.008)	.038** (.018)

Notes: Each regression includes age, age-squared, country, year, education, gender, marital status and industry dummies.

*, **, *** One, two and three stars for statistical significance at the 10, 5 and 1 per cent level of confidence.

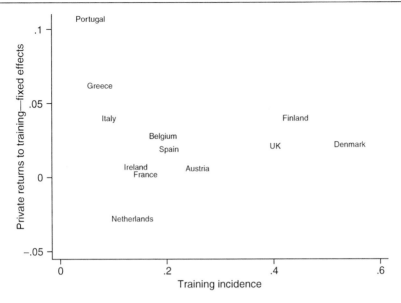

Fig. 12.1 Returns to training and training incidence, by country
Source: ECHP.

Overall, the returns to private-sector training are high compared to the
returns to schooling. Since over 65 per cent of the training courses in the
ECHP data are shorter than 2 weeks, our estimates suggest that a relatively
short training spell administered to a worker during a year could increase
log hourly earnings by close to 2 per cent in Denmark and the UK, 4 per
cent in Italy and Finland, and a hefty 10 per cent in Portugal. For these
countries, one additional year of education yields—for men—6.4 per cent
in Denmark, 6.2 per cent in Italy, 9.7 per cent in Portugal, 8.6 per cent in
Finland and 9.4 per cent in the UK (see Harmon, Walker and Westergaard
Nielsen, 2001).

12.2.4 *Are the wage returns to training really high?*

These high returns raise the question of whether the estimates reviewed
(on p. 258) are indeed causal effects. To illustrate this point, consider the
recent work by Leuven and Oosterbeek (2004), who exploit a provision in
the Dutch tax system that allows employers to deduct an extra 40 per cent
of the training cost of employees who are 40 years or older from
their taxable profits. The structure of the age-dependent tax deduction
is therefore discontinuous at age 40. All workers younger than 40 are

excluded from this additional deduction, while all workers aged 40 or older are included. This structure constitutes a perfect example of a so-called regression discontinuity (RD) data design. While the IV point estimates do not provide evidence of substantial returns to employer-provided training, they are too imprecise to warrant firm conclusions.

Although IV seems promising, and a few studies previously discussed have followed this approach, it is very difficult to come up with variables that affect wages only through training. An alternative approach is followed by Leuven and Oosterbeek (2002). The idea is to narrow down the comparison group to those non-participants who did not participate due to some random event. This is achieved by using the information obtained through two especially designed survey questions in the Netherlands. The first is whether there was any training related to work or career that the respondent wanted to follow but did not do so. The second asks whether this non-participation was due to some random event such as family circumstances, excess demand for training places, transient illness, or sudden absence of a colleague. Respondents who give an affirmative answer to both questions are arguably a more appropriate comparison group.

It turns out that OLS estimates based on these data are similar in magnitude to those found for the studies cited above, and equal to 12.5 per cent for those participating in one training course (with median duration of 40 hours) during the past 12 months. Restricting the comparison group to workers who wanted to participate in training but did not do so reduces the estimated return to 8.7 per cent. When the comparison group is further restricted to those workers who wanted to participate in training but did not do so due to some random event, the point estimate of the return to training is .6 per cent. Although the sample size does not allow precise estimation of the latter effect, the credibility of the proposed strategy is supported by the fact that on each subsequent narrowing down of the comparison group, the participants and comparison individuals are increasingly similar on observed characteristics. In line with this increased similarity of trainees and non-trainees, the point estimate of the return to training consistently drops.

While instructive, these results are based on a small sample. The question is whether they can be generalized to the relevant population. Under some homogeneity assumptions, they measure the average treatment effect on the treated. However, if these assumptions do not hold, they capture a local average treatment effect. It is the former which has policy relevance, not the latter (see Angrist, 2004). Furthermore, in all the studies reviewed here, the effect of training on wages is estimated by restricting the sample to employed workers; therefore, estimated returns might also be biased downward, due to exclusion from the control group of those that are expelled from employment between two observations (or during the time period covered by the survey). For instance, consistent with the IV estimates of Leuven and Oosterbeek (2004), OECD (2004), and Bassanini (2005), find non-significant wage returns for workers aged 35 years or more, using ECHP data; training, however, is found to enhance job security of this category of workers, so that once foregone income due to unemployment spells is taken into account, training appears to increase earnings at any age.

12.2.5 Summary

The bottom line of the discussion in this chapter can be summarized as follows:

- Estimated private returns to training are high, especially in the countries where training incidence is rather low—Portugal and Greece are good examples;
- These estimates could be over-stated by the failure to control in an adequate way for the spurious correlation of training with confounding factors that affect wages;
- Recent research based on the identification of credible instruments for training participation finds much lower returns. It is still an open question, however, whether these results can be generalized.

12.3 Returns to employers

Returns to employers depend on the effects of training investment on productivity and wages, as well as on training costs. Due to measurement problems, there are relatively few studies on the productivity effects of training. These studies are usually based on firm level data, because of the issues surrounding the measurement of individual productivity. The papers in this line of research typically regress some measure of output on a vector of inputs which includes training. As with the wage return studies, the comparison of results between studies is hampered by the differences in training definitions. In addition, there is a large variety of functional form specifications and output measures, which further complicates comparison.

There are basically two types of quantitative studies: survey-based studies, and case studies—sometimes company-sponsored. Survey-based studies have the potential advantage that the results are representative for a particular population of firms, and that the findings can be generalized. The disadvantage is that they usually lack information on the cost of training, and it is therefore in general not possible to estimate rates of return using survey data. Case studies have the advantage that they more often have information on cost.

Dearden et al. (2000), combine British data from various sources and construct a panel of industries covering the period 1983–96. Training information comes from the Labour Force Survey. They find that increasing the proportion of trained workers in an industry by 5 percentage points leads to a 4 per cent increase in value added per hour, and a 1.6 per cent increase in hourly wages. Barrett and O'Connell (2001), analyse a sample of Irish firms and find that training which provided 'broad skills and knowledge' had a positive impact on sales growth between 1993 and 1995. In particular, increasing the number of training days per employee by 1 per cent increased productivity by 3 per cent. On the other hand, they find that training 'directly related to the operation of the company' did not have an impact on productivity.

Zwick (2004), uses German IAB data to study the impact of participative work practices on firm productivity and finds that training positively affects productivity. Brunello (2004), uses survey data for 97 Italian large enterprises, and estimates by fixed effects the relationship between value added per head and alternative measures of training. He finds that a 10 per cent increase in the average number of hours of training per head increased productivity in his sample by 1.32 per cent. Similar results are obtained by Ballot et al. (2001), (2006), on French and Swedish data, and by Conti (2005), on Italian data.

Most studies that consider the productivity effects of training are, however, for the US. Bartel (1994), uses a survey dataset consisting of 495 business lines, and compares businesses that implemented formal training programmes (in 1983) with those that did not. She finds that the former experienced a 6 per cent higher annual productivity. Holtzer et al. (1993), use data on firms that applied for training grants between 1988 and 1989 in Michigan. They estimate fixed effect regressions of hours of training on the scrap rate and found that doubling training reduced the scrap rate by 7 per cent (worth about $15,000). This effect, however, halved in the next year, and it seems likely that this dissipation would have continued in subsequent years.

Black and Lynch (2001), use a nationally representative sample of businesses to estimate a production function with sales as the dependent variable. They are able to estimate fixed effects regressions, but do not find any effect of training on productivity. Bartel (2000), provides a comprehensive review of the literature measuring the employer's rate of return, including case studies. As already discussed, cost data are necessary to calculate rates of return. She concludes that large scale survey studies are uninformative on rates of return because of missing cost data, and that econometric studies more often than not fail to solve endogeneity issues. She also reviews 16 company case studies (published between 1987 and 1997) that measure rates of return on training investments. With the exception of two studies, Bartel argues that this research is plagued by serious methodological flaws, including inappropriate evaluation design, lack of attention to selection bias, a focus on short term outcomes, and using self-reports from trainees as information on productivity gains from training. The two studies that were well conceived found high rates of return on investment, ranging from 100 to 200 per cent. Although these studies get rid of within-company selectivity, they do not solve between-company selectivity issues and it is unclear to what extent the results from these two companies can be generalized to the population of enterprises as a whole.

The limited information on productivity hampers the possibility of developing a direct test of the absolute wage compression hypothesis advocated by Stevens (1994), and Acemoglu and Pischke (1999b), and discussed at length in Chapter 9. In a recent attempt to probe the standard Beckerian view of general training against this hypothesis, Bassanini and Brunello (2003), develop an upper bound estimator of the relationship between wage compression and training, which does not require measures of productivity. Under the maintained hypothesis that wages and productivity are positively correlated, they estimate for a sub-sample of European country the relationship between training incidence and training wage premia. Their evidence is that this relationship is negative. Since most of the training is general in nature, they conclude that only the wage compression view is consistent with their results.

The combined findings on the productivity and wage effects of training begs the question whether training has a positive effect on the profitability of training firms. Blundell et al. (1999), review this literature and conclude that ' . . . not all the productivity gains resulting from training are compensated through a corresponding increase in individual remuneration, so that the investment in training remains profitable for firms...' (13). Importantly, the profitability of the investment appears to extend to future employers, who hire already trained employees. This evidence confirms that poaching externalities may be an important component of the training decision.[5]

12.4 Training and growth

As mentioned in the Introduction to this chapter, most of the empirical literature on the relationship between human capital and growth finds that human capital matters. Unfortunately, human capital is typically measured with the average number of years of schooling, and no attempt has been made, so far, to investigate the importance of training, mainly because of lack of suitable data. In a recent review of the empirical literature, De La Fuente and Ciccone (2002), find that the contribution of years of schooling to productivity growth in the OECD between 1960 and 1990 has been equal to 15.36 per cent. Our evidence in Chapter 10, as well as most of the empirical literature, shows that education and training are complements in the production of human capital. We infer from this that schooling affects growth both directly and indirectly, by accelerating the accumulation of human capital.

12.5 Summary

We summarize the discussion in this chapter as follows:

- Traditional wage return studies, that depend on differencing (fixed effect) methods where non-participants are used as a comparison group, often find high wage returns. Studies that exploit arguably exogenous variation in training participation are in their infancy. They find much lower wage effects of training. These estimates, however, are imprecise, and rely on small and somewhat specific samples.
- Compared to the numerous studies on wage effects of training, there are relatively few studies on the impact of training on productivity. This is mainly explained by the lack of data on productivity. If such information is available then it is either at the industry or, in the best case, at the

---

[5] Collier, Green, Peirson and Wilkinson (2003), show that training increases company survival.

firm level. These studies do not give a consistent picture of the impact of training on output.

- Rates of return estimates are even scarcer than productivity studies. This is because data on cost are even more difficult to find than data on output. When such data are available (in company case studies) it is unclear to what extent we can generalize the results.

13

Is There Scope for Policy?

Introduction

In the European Employment strategy designed in Lisbon, more and better education and training are considered as key factors to increase the competitiveness of European countries or to avoid social exclusion. The view is that training and lifelong learning are especially valuable for those workers—the old and low-skilled—who face the highest risk of being negatively affected by the ongoing economic changes.

Public training policies can be justified either on efficiency or on equity grounds. Both of them are crucial. Perhaps surprisingly, even if there is a large consensus in the economic literature on the importance of training, there is less agreement on whether the observed levels of investment in training are inefficiently low and, consequently, on the necessity of policy interventions. In spite of the many theoretical reasons for under-investment, discussed in Chapter 9, it is difficult to come up with convincing empirical evidence that workplace training is under-provided, and even more difficult to know how far the private optimum deviates from the first best. The key reason, we have argued in Chapter 12, is that training costs and returns—on which efficiency evaluations are based—are not well measured.

Apart from efficiency arguments, equity considerations can be relevant to justify training for groups of workers in disadvantaged economic conditions. If equity is interpreted as equality of opportunities—as in Roemer (1998), low participation in training activities by some disadvantaged categories of workers may be not socially desirable, even if efficient. A key issue here is whether economic policy should try to correct outcomes—differences in training—or to modify initial conditions—for instance differences in educational attainment. In addition, since it is often very costly to increase the human capital of low skilled and older workers, cost-effectiveness considerations have to be taken into account.

We start this final chapter with a brief discussion of how the design of training policies is strictly related to the type of potential market failures conducive to under-provision. Next we turn to consider the empirical evidence on the relevance of efficiency and equity issues. We then propose a political economy view of training subsidies. The last two sections of the chapter are devoted to examining the key features of the training policies in place and the implications for training of labour and product market reforms. Appendix 6, describing existing policies in some detail, concludes.

13.1 Policy responses to market failures in training provision

Since market failures in the provision of training can originate both in the labour and in the capital market, the appropriate policy intervention depends on the nature of the problem at hand, as illustrated in Table 13.1. With perfectly competitive capital and labour markets, there is little role for policies pursuing efficiency. If capital and labour markets are characterized by imperfections, however, training investment may be lower than the efficient level and a natural policy approach is to try to eliminate the sources of inefficiency. Credit constraints may be relaxed both by interventions, which make credit markets more competitive, and by subsidies paid out to constrained individuals. When labour markets are imperfect and there is absolute wage compression, firms are involved in general training and bear the costs. In the case of under-provision, training subsidies should be targeted at individuals and firms. An additional role for policy is to reduce asymmetric information in the market for training and improve contractibility by removing the problems which emerge when the worker and the firm have different information on the contents of training.

Since the identification of market failures and unequal circumstances are prerequisites to sensible public intervention, we turn to examine the empirical case for the under-provision of workplace training and for inequality of opportunity in the investment.

13.2 Under-provision: what is the evidence?

As shown in Chapter 10, the empirical literature on training shows that there is substantial variation across countries and across socio-economic groups in training participation rates, with Nordic European countries

Table 13.1 Different types of market failures and policy interventions aimed at restoring efficiency

	Perfectly competitive capital markets	Policy interventions	Capital market imperfections	Policy interventions
Perfectly competitive labour markets	Efficient investment		Training investment can be inefficient	Subsidies to individuals
			Workers are not able to accept a sufficiently low wage or are unable to insure against uncertain training returns	
Labour market imperfections	Training investment can be inefficient	Policies that reduce contractibility problems	Training investment can be inefficient	Policies that reduce contractibility problems
	Contractibility problems are less relevant since part of the training is financed by the firm	Subsidies to firms	Investment higher than with perfectly competitive labour markets accompanied by capital market imperfections	Subsidies to firms and individuals

showing higher participation than Southern European countries and low-educated and older workers generally participating less than other groups in training activities. These differences reflect individual incentives to train, which are affected by labour and product market institutions—as discussed in Chapter 11—and by training and education policies already in place.

When considering workplace training policy, one would like to know first of all whether training outcomes produced by economic agents in the absence of policy would have attained the first best allocation. If yes, there would obviously be no role for policy on efficiency grounds. To do that, however, we would need to observe training outcomes in the absence of policy, obviously a difficult task given that such policies are quite widespread. Nor can we infer inefficiency by observing how ubiquitous training policies are, since many of these policies may be ineffective and not altering private outcomes.

Another difficulty with assessing the presence of under-investment is that such an evaluation would require that we compare social and private benefits with social and private costs. Again, the discussion in Chapter 12 has shown that we know very little about costs. Some have claimed that evidence of under-investment is the combination of high private rates of return to training and low training incidence, and have quoted in support several studies suggesting that private rates of return to training are considerably higher than the real rate of return of other investments with similar risk. Even if we take such evidence at face value, we question whether one can infer from high returns to training and low investments the existence of under-provision. Assuming that the marginal returns to training decrease with the stock invested, high observed returns are consistent both with the presence of liquidity constraints, which prevent some individuals from investing, and with high marginal costs of training. While the former explanation supports under-provision, the latter explanation is perfectly in line with efficient provision.

A reason for under-provision is that private and social returns to workplace training do not coincide, because of the positive externalities generated by the complementarity of training on innovation (see Acemoglu, 1997) and of the positive spillovers on the productivity of unskilled employees (see Johnson, 1984). As briefly reviewed in Chapter 12, however, we have little empirical evidence of the positive external effects of human capital, and what we have refers exclusively to the impact of schooling.

As discussed in Chapter 9, models of workplace training in imperfectly competitive labour markets do not suggest that private outcomes in the absence of policy are necessarily inefficient. The observation that employers who invest in general training are forced to share some of the revenues with employees—the hold-up problem—or the fact that some of the returns to training are captured by future employers—the poaching externality problem—can both be causes of under-provision, but do not necessarily produce it, as Bishop (1997), concludes. Appendix 2 (to Chapter 9) shows that, when turnover is endogenous, a negative relationship between training and turnover can undo the negative effects of hold-up and poaching externalities and even produce over-investment.

In the next two sub-sections, we examine the evidence on the effect of training on turnover, and review the limited evidence on the importance of credit constraints. To anticipate our conclusion, the evidence at hand is not sufficient to claim the existence of under-provision, or, even more difficult, to measure the gap between the socially optimal allocation and the outcomes produced by private agents. We conclude that one needs to be prudent when designing public policies aimed at raising the provision of workplace training.

13.2.1 *Training and turnover*

We investigate the empirical relationship between training and turnover using ECHP data and focusing on voluntary quits. The ECHP dataset includes two interesting questions on turnover behaviour, which can be used to study whether (voluntary) turnover is affected by employer-provided training: first, workers are asked to indicate the year when they stopped working in their previous job. Secondly, they are asked to indicate the reason of separation. If we focus on individuals who were trained by the employer between year $t-1$ and year t and compute the percentage of those who quitted between year $t+1$ and year $t+2$—conditional on staying in the job in year t—we find that the percentage of workers who leave for a better job is on average 6.94 per cent in the sample of 11 European countries with available data.[1] This percentage increases to 9.88 per cent when we add voluntary turnover due to non-economic reasons—such as childbearing, moving, marriage and else. Therefore, a European employer who is considering training a worker can expect—based on this data, that 7 to 10 trained workers out of 100 quit between one and two years after training.

Does turnover decline among trained employees? We investigate this question by selecting the individuals who had received employer-provided training from January in the year $t-2$ to t, the time of the survey, and by asking whether they have quitted their last job in the year $t+1$, conditional on no turnover in year t. We choose to focus on turnover one year after the survey, rather than in the same year, to avoid the risk of having separations taking place before the training event, and to reduce endogeneity issues. The empirical model is

$$q_{it} = \alpha + \beta X_{it} + \gamma \tau_{i,t-1} + f_i + \varepsilon_{it} \qquad [13.1]$$

where q is turnover—a dummy equal to 1 in the event of turnover and to 0 otherwise; X is a vector of time varying controls, τ is the training dummy, c is an individual fixed effect and ε is a random error orthogonal to training. If more able individuals are less likely to quit and more likely to receive training, failure to account for unmeasured individual fixed effects could seriously bias downwards our estimates. To take this into account, we estimate a linear probability model using fixed effects. The vector X includes age, age squared, year dummies and five dummies representing the time varying degree of job satisfaction. Table 13.2 reports the estimates

[1] These countries are Denmark, Belgium, France, the UK, Ireland, Italy, Greece, Spain, Portugal, Austria and Finland.

Table 13.2 Estimates of the probability of separation in year t+1 as a function of employer provided training in years t−2 to t. Linear probability model. Fixed effects. 1996–2000

	Quitted because of a better job	Quitted for different reasons
Trained by employer	−.002	−.004
between year t−2 and t	(.004)	(.003)
Age	−.029***	−.020***
	(.005)	(.004)
Age squared	.0003***	.0002***
	(.000)	(.000)
Job satisfaction at time t: level 2	−.012	−.009
	(.012)	(.007)
Job satisfaction at time t: level 3	−.017*	−.014
	(.010)	(.008)
Job satisfaction at time t: level 4	−.027***	−.026***
	(.011)	(.007)
Job satisfaction at time t: level 5	−.049***	−.043***
	(.010)	(.008)
Job satisfaction at time t: level 6	−.057***	−.046***
	(.010)	(.009)
Nobs	55154	55154

Notes: Standard errors in parentheses with $p < 0.10 = {}^\wedge$, $p < 0.05 = \sim$, $p < 0.01 = *$.
Each regression includes a constant and year dummies.

separately for turnover to a better job—column 1; and for any voluntary turnover—column 2.

In these estimates, we consider the period 1996–2000 and restrict our attention to individuals aged 25 to 54. As expected, our estimates show that turnover declines with age and with the index of job satisfaction. Conditional on these factors, the relationship between training and turnover is negative, small and not statistically different from zero. Therefore, our results lack sufficient precision to reach any firm conclusion. Ambiguous results emerge also from the few papers in the literature which address this issue. Lynch (1991), using US data on young workers (National Longitudinal Survey of Youth), finds that while on-the-job training (more firm-specific) reduces the probability of job separations, workers participating in off-the-job training (more general) are more likely to leave their current employer. Veum (1997), using the same source of data, concludes that trainees are equally likely to quit than non-trainees. Similar results are obtained by Krueger and Rouse (1998), by focusing on personnel files from two large US companies. On the other hand, Parent (1999), using data from the NLSY, shows that on-the-job training reduces the probability of job separations.

13.2.2 *Credit constraints*

Even when the labour market is perfectly competitive, there could be under-provision if workers investing in general training are credit constrained. The importance of these constraints is a very investigated topic in the economics of education literature. According to Kane and Rouse (1999), for instance, the presence of these constraints is confirmed both by the fact that pupils from poor households invest less in education in spite of the higher returns from the investment, and by the higher impact that an increase in tuition costs produce on their choices. On the contrary, Carneiro and Heckman (2004), and Cameron and Taber (2000), argue that there is no relationship between family income and educational outcomes and that, after controlling for ability, differences in returns among groups of individuals vanish. Some attempts to study the effect of credit constraints on training are Greenhalgh and Mavrotas (1994), and Chapman (2002), who show that the training decisions of low-income workers may be negatively influenced by financial restrictions.[2]

13.3 Is there an equity issue?

With scant evidence on market failures and efficiency, we can justify widespread policy intervention in the market for training because of equity reasons. As discussed in Chapter 9, policies aimed at equal opportunities need to be grounded in the distinction between differences arising from variations in the individual expenditure of effort, and differences arising from circumstances for which society believe individuals should not be held accountable—such as race, gender, and family background.

In this chapter, we replicate the empirical study by Carneiro and Heckman (2004), on the relationship between family background and training provision using data for Europe drawn from the European Community Household Panel. Unfortunately, this dataset has not been designed to collect information on family background, which precludes a straightforward investigation of the role played by parental variables in educational choice. As a gross approximation, however, we focus on individuals aged between 18 and 30, and link up these individuals with the households of their parents to recover as much as possible the necessary

---

[2] In his study, Chapman considers job losers. After controlling for a large number of characteristics, he shows that having liquid assets at the time of the job loss is very important in determining investment in self-financed training.

information on parental background. Since the ECHP includes both a personal and a household file, this is clearly possible as long as the young individual is still living with his/her parents. When this is not the case, one can still retrieve to an extent the relevant parental background information by tracking young individuals as they leave their parents to form their own households.

Clearly, our ability to connect household information to young individuals is higher for the 'olive belt' countries of Southern Europe, because young individuals in these countries tend to live in their parents' household much longer than in Northern and Continental Europe. Since individuals in these countries are over-represented in the final sample, we need to be careful in interpreting our results as suggestive of, rather than representative of, the European situation.

We select individuals working at least 15 hours per week. To connect these individuals with the households of their parents, we start by selecting a sub-sample of households with one of the following characteristics: (i) one-person household aged less than 30; (ii) single parent with at least one child aged 16 or more; (iii) couple with at least one child aged 16 or more; and (iv) couple without children, with both members aged less than 65.

The household types (ii) and (iii) clearly include our target group of young individuals, and for these individuals it is easy to construct the relevant parental background variables. Conversely, the household types (i) and (iv) include those youngsters who have recently moved out of their parents' household to start their own families. For this sub-group of individuals, we use longitudinal information. To illustrate the idea, consider a young individual aged 24 in 2001 who moved out of his parents' household at 20 to live on her own or with a partner. The ECHP associates a time invariant personal identification number to each individual, but updates the household identification number when the individual moves out. Therefore, in our example, we should find that the household identification number in 1997 is different and typically lower than the newly assigned household number.[3] In such a case, we assign to the individual her old household number and the attached parental background variables. By so doing, we are able to retain in the final sample many—but not all—young individuals who are living on their own.

Parental background information includes the attained education of parents at the time of the survey. Information on the education of each

---

[3] We are grateful to Simona Comi for a clarifying discussion on this point.

parent is categorized as a dummy equal to 1 for upper secondary or college education and to 0 otherwise. Since we pool all available observations over countries and time, we include time and country dummies to capture time effects and all time-invariant and country-specific institutional differences, which could affect both labour market outcomes and training. Country dummies also pick up differences in the interpretation of the training question, which could vary across countries because of broad cultural and social reasons.

Table 13.3 focuses on workplace training and presents the estimates of two alternative specifications: in columns (1) and (2) we include two dummies for educational attainment—high school and less than high school, a gender dummy, age, household size and two dummies for parental background, the education of the father and the mother. In the remaining two columns we add interactions of these two dummies with a dummy for the countries belonging to the 'olive belt'. For each specification, we report the average marginal effect of parental background on participation in workplace training, both conditional and unconditional on attained individual education.

Inspection of the table shows that parental background has a statistically significant positive effect on workplace training, independently of whether we control for individual education or not. As expected, this effect, and particularly the father's education, is more relevant for young

Table 13.3 Enrolment in education. 1996–2001. Average partial effects. Weighted estimates. Dependent variable: workplace training

	(1)	(2)	(3)	(4)
High school education	−.029***	–	−.028***	
	(.006)		(.006)	
Less than high school	−.110***	–	−.108***	
	(.005)		(.006)	
Father with high school or college	.011**	.025***	−.000	.008
	(.005)	(.005)	(.006)	(.006)
Mother with high school or college	.021***	.034***	.022***	.033***
	(.006)	(.006)	(.006)	(.006)
Father with high school or college × olive belt dummy	–	–	.038***	.051***
			(.013)	(.014)
Mother with high school or college × olive belt dummy	–	–	−.002	.003
			(.012)	(.013)
Nobs	37492	37492	37492	37492
R Squared	.146	.131	.147	.132

Notes: Each regression includes a constant, age, gender, year and country dummies.
Robust standard errors within parentheses.
*, **, *** One, two and three stars for statistical significance at the 10, 5 and 1 per cent level of confidence.

individuals in the countries of Southern Europe. We conclude that employer-provided training in Europe is not neutral to family background, contrary to the evidence for the US presented by Carneiro and Heckman. Table 13.4 confirms these results when we restrict attention to employer-provided training. With the caution required by the quality of the data at hand, our results suggest that workplace-provided training in Europe, rather than offsetting the differences associated to initial circumstances, increases such differences. A tentative explanation of the uncovered difference is that family and social networks are more pervasive and more important in Europe than in the US, and that these networks extend beyond the schooling stage—especially in Southern Europe—to influence the likelihood of finding a good job and therefore receiving company-provided training.

How big is the estimated impact of family background? A switch of father's education from less than high school to higher education is estimated to increase—on average—participation to workplace training by .011 when controlling for education and by .025 without controls. This effect increases to .038 and .059 when we consider Southern European countries. Since the average participation rate in the sample at hand is .180, this increase is between 10 and 30 per cent of mean participation—a significant effect.

Table 13.4 Enrolment in education, 1996–2001. Average partial effects. Weighted estimates. Dependent variable: employer provided training

	(1)	(2)	(3)	(4)
High school education	−.024***	−	−.023***	
	(.004)		(.004)	
Less than high school	−.050***	−	−.048***	
	(.004)		(.004)	
Father with high school or college	.010**	.017***	.000	.004
	(.004)	(.004)	(.004)	(.004)
Mother with high school or college	.010**	.016***	.010**	.014***
	(.003)	(.004)	(.004)	(.004)
Father with high school or college × olive belt dummy	−	−	.038***	.046***
			(.012)	(.013)
Mother with high school or college × olive belt dummy	−	−	−.001	.001
			(.009)	(.004)
Nobs	35826	35826	35826	36075
R Squared	.127	.119	.129	.121

Notes: Each regression includes a constant, age, gender, year and country dummies.
Robust standard errors within parentheses.
*, **, *** One, two and three stars for statistical significance at the 10, 5 and 1 per cent level of confidence.

We conclude that there is some evidence of an equity issue in the distribution of training outcomes in the European young population, especially the one residing in the Southern part of the Continent. The uncovered differences in training outcomes by parental background partly reflect the within-country differences remarked in Chapter 10. A good example here is Italy: average parental education is much lower in the South than in the North of the country, with consequences both on educational attainment (see Brunello and Checchi 2005), and on the distribution of training within the country.

13.4 What do we learn from the empirical evidence?

The discussion in the previous two sections suggests that it is difficult to make a strong case for under-provision of workplace training: measurement problems and estimation issues concur to the conclusion that more needs to be done in order to provide a satisfactory answer to this crucial question. We need more research on externalities, more information on costs, and to verify whether the existing estimates, especially those on the private returns to training, are robust to more adequate estimation techniques.

We are more optimistic when it comes to the distributional implications of training. We have presented evidence which clearly suggests that differences in training outcomes may be due to a significant extent to differences in circumstances which are partially out of the control of individuals. If more training means better earnings and higher job security, there is ground for training policies which reduces social exclusion.

Given the status of our knowledge to date, which training policy should be recommended? And which kind of intervention is more likely to produce satisfactory results? What are the expected effects on training investment of policies and reforms which affect the rules and institutions of European labour markets? Before attempting to answer these questions, we suggest an alternative justification of training policies, which does not rely on efficiency, but is based on a political economy approach.

13.5 A political economy approach

The scant empirical evidence that market failures exist and are important is in striking contrast with the great attention lavished by many policy-makers on lifelong learning policies. In the absence of efficiency issues, one can claim the need to redistribute and provide equal opportunity as a firm ground for public training policy. There are two problems with this view, however. First, as we shall argue later, training is not a very good redistributive instrument, since its returns to disadvantaged workers are not particularly high. Secondly, firms are concerned with profitability and may pay little attention to the need of compensating disadvantaged individuals, even in the presence of subsidies.

We posit that a consensus on training policies could emerge even in the absence of efficiency or equity considerations when firms and employed workers, which are generally better organized than the average individual in the population, succeed in influencing political decisions in favour of redistribution to their advantage.

In the very simple model illustrated in Appendix 5, we consider a majority voting equilibrium involving firms, trained and untrained employees. In the absence of training subsidies and taxes, there is a socially optimal provision of training. Suppose now that firms receive a training subsidy funded by a proportional payroll tax on all workers, and that workers receive wages that are proportional to productivity. Because of the subsidy, there is over-provision of training. We show that firms generally favour the policy and argue that skilled workers may also support it if firms redistribute part of the subsidy. If these two groups have sufficient political power, they can promote this policy independently of efficiency or equity considerations. Notice that such a policy could even be supported by unskilled labour if there are strong complementarities between skills and unskilled labour, as discussed by Johnson (1984), with reference to education subsidies.

13.6 Policies offering financial support to workplace training

European policies offering financial support to individuals and firms usually consist of government sponsored co-financed schemes. In the last years the policy approach has shifted from direct subsidization of external (public or private) providers of training services to co-financing schemes. The emphasis on the increase of the contribution of firms and trainees to financing training schemes responds both to shrinking government budgets and to the need of providing adequate incentives for training quality.

Co-financing schemes in Europe are oriented both to firms (levy/grant schemes, train or pay and tax deduction systems) and to individuals (subsidies, vouchers, individual learning accounts, grants from specific funds, etc.). In spite of the diffusion of these systems, rigorous empirical evaluations of their effectiveness are uncommon, and many investigations provide only descriptive statistics with no counterfactual for the assessment of the policy impact. As a consequence, it is not possible at this stage to tell whether these policies have determined sufficiently high gains to compensate for their costs.

The main characteristics of each scheme are described and discussed in some detail in Appendix 6. Here we focus on the key aspects that are relevant for the design of effective policies. First, it is important to avoid subsidizing training investments that would have been realized in any case by the parties involved. To do this, the subsidy component of a policy package should compensate only the gap between marginal costs and marginal private benefits that may arise at the socially desirable investment level, leaving to firms or workers the responsibility of financing the rest. As discussed in the appendix, while some of the implemented policies respect these principles, others do not and tend to generate large dead-weight losses.[4] Since little is known on the relevance of informal training processes, these policies may also produce inefficient substitution between informal learning processes and formal training. This risk is especially relevant for policies directed to firms, since informal training is usually aimed at imparting specific competencies and is generally paid by the employer.

It is important to stress that co-financing schemes directed at firms do not address the low training participation of particular groups of workers. As shown in Chapter 10, firms generally prefer to involve in their training programmes better educated workers who are involved in more complex jobs, and the targeting of public support in favour of particular groups of workers is likely to produce relevant substitution effects. As a consequence, when training policy is aimed at reducing perceived inequalities, it is necessary to adopt co-financing schemes focused directly on individuals (such as loan and individual subsidy schemes). These policies should be accompanied by complementary measures which favour the diffusion of information on training opportunities, the quality of the training schemes on supply and the portability of the acquired skills.

In markets that are rapidly changing, the access to training opportunities might be improved by government policies which establish informa-

---

[4] According to the survey of large Italian firms by ISFOL, (see Brunello, 2004), close to 53 per cent of the 185 surveyed firms declared that they would have invested in training even in the absence of the training subsidies.

tion systems with data on 'the availability, cost, subsidies and markets for trained personnel in a variety of occupations as well as individual data on providers' (Levin, 1998). A number of countries have experimented with models for forecasting employment by occupation (in the Netherlands, Canada, USA and Australia this work has been enhanced by estimates of labour demand for newcomers or re-entrants in the workforce). However, governments often do not have any advantage over the private sector in anticipating training needs and their contribution is therefore that of collecting information and creating systems incorporating data about training providers.

An additional role for governments is that of increasing the individual benefits of training via qualification systems that make potential employers aware of the skills and competences acquired by learning experiences. Such systems are being developed on a European scale by the European Union under the Lisbon Strategy and in several countries—including Australia, Austria, Denmark, Hungary, Italy, Netherlands, New Zealand, Norway and UK. The goal of a transparent system of reliable vocational qualification is, however, difficult to achieve, since the definition of 'skill standards' poses many measurement problems (Greenhalgh, 1999; OECD, 2003a; Colardyn, 2002).

Some countries (for example the UK) rely on locally administered vocational qualification systems, which use different methods of assessment, with greater risk for employers, and consequently lower wages for trained workers (Conlon, 2000). More satisfactory results are obtained in countries such as Finland, France and Germany, where social partners contribute in deciding the content of training and in supervising its provision. This suggests that unions may play an important role both in solving hold-up problems and in helping workers to obtain a share of training benefits, and by so doing in avoiding poaching problems. A role for the government can also be that of creating a framework and a legal condition that ensures that private parties are willing and able to finance training. Contracts, such as pay-back clauses, apprenticeships and working-time accounts, go in this direction and are reviewed in the appendix of this chapter.

There is little agreement on the effectiveness of training policies in addressing equity issues, and one matter of debate is whether these issues have to be posed in terms of income redistribution or in terms of better access to training opportunities. One view is that while public assistance might undermine self-reliance, training helps individuals in finding jobs that assure a decent standard of life.

An alternative view casts doubts on the fact that providing more human capital will enable disadvantaged workers to get jobs that meet their expectations or that such efforts can be cost-effective. Training may not be an effective way to redistribute income when disadvantaged workers obtain relatively low returns from it. To better illustrate this point, we have replicated the fixed effects estimates in Table 12.2 by adding an interaction term between the stock of training and low education, which is expected to pick up the differential in the return to training for the poorly educated. Our results are presented in Table 13.5.

As expected, we find that the wage returns to workplace training are lower for those with less than secondary education, a result which confirms existing evidence from the US. The gap is particularly significant in the UK, Portugal and Austria. These findings suggest that a more effective strategy for improving the income of the poor could be to invest more in the highly skilled, tax them, and redistribute to the poor. A relevant problem with this approach, however, is that it would breed a culture of poverty and helplessness (see Heckman, 1999).

More agreement exists on the role that can be played by policies targeted at increasing the educational attainment of disadvantaged groups. As shown in Chapter 10, there is broad support of the fact that education and training are complements, and that learning begets learning. By increasing the basic skills of the work force, in terms of literacy, numeracy and cognitive and communication abilities, policy can contribute both to directly raising the standard of life of disadvantaged individuals, and to

Table 13.5 Private returns to training by education

	Average return to training	Deviation from average for the poorly educated
Denmark	.023***	−.034**
Netherlands	−.015	−.017
Belgium	.029*	−.025
France	−.002	.031
UK	.028**	−.053***
Ireland	.010	−.030
Italy	.041***	−.026
Greece	.066**	−.114
Spain	.020*	−.032
Portugal	.143***	−.080**
Austria	.010	−.121**
Finland	.040**	−.016

Notes: See Table 12.2.

increase the private incentive to train. We illustrate the potential relationship between cognitive abilities and training by plotting in Fig. 13.1 average training participation in 2001 for the age group 25–30 and the average score in the maths tests taken by 15-year-old children at school in OECD (2003). The picture is only meant to be suggestive, but the message is clear: countries where children at school perform better in their maths are also the countries with the higher workplace training incidence.

13.7 Labour market policies and training

Labour and product market policies that aim at reducing regulation, and increasing competitiveness, have implications for training. A recurrent theme in policy debates is, for instance, the potentially negative effects that reforms which increase labour market flexibility may have on training incentives. Clearly, these reforms affect many economic variables and a general equilibrium approach would be necessary to fully investigate the issue. According to many, the success of market reforms is strictly related to a different type of flexibility, which refers to the individual ability to perform multiple tasks and operations, and to continuously acquire the skills required to move from old to new jobs. Clearly, understanding

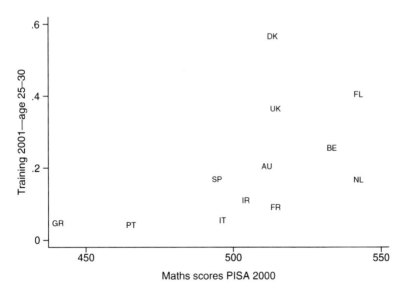

Fig. 13.1 Training and PISA scores
Sources: ECHP and OECD.

whether higher product and labour market flexibility increases or reduces the incentives for workers and firms to invest in skill acquisition is a key issue.

As shown in section 13.4, there is evidence that European policies which increase product market competition are positively correlated with the incidence of workplace training. Less straightforward, however, is the relationship between increased labour market competition and workplace training. Reforms which increase labour market flexibility tend to produce several effects both on employers' and employees' incentives to invest in training. For example, measures which favour the reduction of a compressed wage structure by affecting minimum wages and the rules of collective bargaining are expected to have opposite effects on employees and employers.[5]

A less compressed wage structure, on the one hand, increases the returns to training reaped by workers but reduces the gains obtained by firms: training increases if the higher incentives to invest for workers compensates the lower incentive for firms. As discussed by Stevens, 1998, this is unlikely to happen when workers are liquidity constrained, or in the presence of contractibility problems and poor information on training opportunities and returns.

The common strategy followed by European countries of liberalizing atypical/temporary/part-time employment contracts for new entrants in the labour market (Golden and Appelbaum, 1992; OECD, 1993; OECD, 1996) also has implications for training. The higher flexibility in the adjustment of the labour force, on the one hand, helps firms to deal with the risk of negative shocks, and on the other hand, reduces the incentive to provide skills and knowledge to workers. As shown in Chapter 11, the empirical evidence suggests that training incidence in Europe declines with the increase in the relative importance of temporary contracts. In many European countries, higher labour market flexibility has also extended to reducing the employment protection of regular workers. Again, the evidence in Chapter 11 suggests a negative correlation between the degree of protection of regulars and training. It follows that the reduction of employment protection for regulars, combined with the diffusion of temporary contracts, has an overall ambiguous effect on average training incidence.

Finally, the common European concern on the ageing society, and the need to reform pension policies—widely perceived by European citizens

---

[5] A compressed wage structure should not be confounded with the concept of absolute wage compression.

(see Boeri, Boesch-Supan and Tabellini, 2002)—raises worries that a reduction of expected benefits and/or an increase in retirement age could reduce the training incentives of senior employees. Our evidence in Chapter 11 suggests the opposite, and shows that senior employees are more likely to train where the implicit tax on continuing work is lower.

13.8 Summary

We summarize the key points of this section as follows:

- The design of public policies for workplace training should vary with the type of problem that needs to be tackled, be it a particular market failure or inequality of opportunity;
- There is no clear-cut evidence that the level of workplace training produced by firms and employees is significantly lower than the socially efficient level;
- Compared to the US, the distribution of training opportunities is significantly affected by circumstances which are usually considered as beyond the individual control, such as parental education;
- Policies addressing perceived market failures should affect marginal benefits and costs in order to minimize deadweight losses;
- Since firms care about profits rather than social inclusion, training policies addressing equality of opportunity should be targeted at individuals rather than at firms;
- Since the returns to training to the disadvantaged are low, one should consider complementary policies, such as those which improve access to good quality education; these policies clearly work in the long run;
- Governments have an important role to play in improving information about training opportunities, setting appropriate legal frameworks and ensuring portability of skills. The European Employment Strategy, especially after the Copenhagen declaration, is rightly investing efforts in developing a European-wide system of recognition of skills;
- Product and labour market reforms do affect training participation. While less regulation in the product market encourages skill formation at work, less clear-cut is the impact of deregulation in the labour market. Pension reforms which reduce the implicit tax on continuing work may increase the willingness to invest in skills by senior workers, who have a longer time horizon to reap the associated benefits.

APPENDIX 5

A Simple Political Economy Model of Training Subsidies

Consider a simple economy populated by a given number of workers and firms. Let the measure of each be equal to 1. Each firm can hire at most one worker. Workers differ in their ability A, which is uniformly distributed in the support $A \in [0,1]$. Let output without and with training be Ay and $A(y + \sigma)$. Wages are set after the training decision taken by each firm and are equal to a share $1 - \beta$ of output. Training costs c are borne by the firm.

After training, workers can quit and exit the labour force. Let the quit rate of trained and untrained workers be q_1 and q_0, with $q_1 < q_0$. Therefore, training reduces turnover by increasing the attachment of each worker to the firm. We normalize *ex-post* profits and earnings in the event of quits to zero.

If there are no subsidies, training firms are those for whom

$$(1 - q_1)A(y + \sigma)\beta - c \geq (1 - q_0)Ay\beta \qquad \text{[A5.1]}$$

which yields

$$A \geq \frac{c}{[(q_1 - q_0)y + (1 - q_1)\sigma]\beta} = A^* \qquad \text{[A5.2]}$$

Efficiency requires that training occurs if

$$A^b \geq \frac{c}{\sigma} \qquad \text{[A5.3]}$$

Since we want to start from a situation where subsidies are not required because of efficiency reasons, we assume that

$$[(q_1 - q_0)y + (1 - q_1)\sigma] = \frac{\sigma}{\beta} \qquad \text{[A5.4]}$$

which yields the first best allocation.

Next assume that the government pays to training firms a subsidy s as a percentage of training costs. Let this subsidy be funded with a payroll tax on all workers. The percentage of training firms and workers becomes

$$A \geq \frac{c(1-s)}{\sigma} = A^\wedge \qquad [A5.5]$$

and the budget constraint is

$$sc(1 - F(A^\wedge)) = \delta(1-\beta)\sigma \int_{A^\wedge} AdA + \frac{\delta(1-\beta)y}{2} \qquad [A5.6]$$

Since A has a uniform distribution, we have $1 - F(A^\wedge) = 1 - A^\wedge$ and $\int_{A^\wedge} AdA = \frac{1-A^{\wedge 2}}{2}$, so that

$$\delta = \frac{2sc[\sigma - c(1-s)]}{(1-\beta)\left\{\sigma y + \sigma^2 - c^2(1-s)^2\right\}} \qquad [A5.7]$$

Suppose that each firm and worker votes on the introduction of the training subsidy. There are three groups of workers: the always untrained, the always trained and those who are trained because of the subsidy. We examine them in turn. The always untrained are against the subsidy because they need to pay payroll taxes without any change in gross income; the always trained are also against the subsidy, because they would be trained anyway, even without paying the payroll tax. Finally, the workers in the ability range $\lfloor A^b, A^\wedge \rfloor$ are trained only with the subsidy. They are better off if

$$(1-\delta)(1-q_1)(1-\beta)A(y+\sigma) > (1-q_0)(1-\beta)Ay \qquad [A5.8]$$

that is, if the increase of productivity and the reduction of turnover are sufficient to compensate the payroll taxes needed to fund the subsidy. Suppose this is the case. Then the percentage of workers supporting the subsidy is $A^* - A^\wedge$. Next consider firms. The firms which were training before the subsidy are better off because they receive the subsidy. On the other hand, the firms that do not train—independently of the subsidy— are as well off, since the burden on the measure is on workers and they receive no subsidy. Finally, the firms which train because of the subsidy are gaining because of [A5.2]. It follows that the percentage of firms voting in favour of the subsidy is $F(A^*) - F(A^\wedge) + 1 - F(A^*) = 1 - A^\wedge$. If each worker and firm have one vote and vote independently, majority voting in favour of the subsidy requires

$$1 + A^* - 2A^\wedge > 1 \qquad\qquad [A5.9]$$

or

$$A^* > 2A^\wedge \qquad\qquad [A5.10]$$

which holds if the subsidy is higher than a half. In this case, there might be a political equilibrium in favour of a positive training subsidy even if the private training outcome is by construction equivalent to the social optimum. Notice that in our illustrative simple model most workers vote against the subsidy. It is clear, however, that this is not necessarily the case. In his discussion of educational subsidies, Johnson (1984), shows that unskilled workers may support such subsidies—or training subsidies—if there are complementarities between skilled and unskilled labour. In this case, an increase in skilled labour would increase the productivity of unskilled workers, who would be better off and might vote for the subsidy if the payroll tax is not too high.

In our simple model, training firms which receive the subsidy have a windfall profit gain, which they can share with trained employees by offering them higher wages. Such redistribution from profits to wages could induce trained employees to favour the subsidy. Yet another variation is that training subsidies are financed by a tax on payroll and on profits. This would imply that some firms would not favour the subsidy anymore.

APPENDIX 6

Training Policies in Europe

In this appendix we review the main training policies adopted in the OECD countries, and discuss their advantages and drawbacks. First, we review the institutional arrangements that create adequate incentives for employers and individuals to invest in skill development. Secondly, we turn to policies which provide financial support to firms and individuals investing in training.

A6.1 Regulation: pay-back clauses, time working accounts and apprenticeship contracts

Firms may not invest efficiently in training because of the risk of turnover, and workers may not be able to finance the investment because of liquidity constraints. If contracts were fully enforceable, these problems could be solved by agreements that force workers to stay with the current firm after training a period of time sufficient to recoup training costs. Pay-back clauses, working-time accounts for employees and apprenticeship contracts operate in this direction. Since these systems are widespread in OECD countries, we shall now discuss the main advantages and problems encountered in their application, which are summarized in Table A6.1.

Pay-back clauses are essentially devices that encourage firms to undertake the costs associated with training programmes by imposing a penalty on workers who quit within a certain period. These schemes help in reducing the risk of poaching, since workers are induced to stay with the firm providing training. Legal frameworks, which establish and permit pay-back clauses in individual contracts or collective agreements, are present in many European countries (see OECD, 2003a). Their practical diffusion, however, is limited, because it is difficult to contract upon the contents of training.[1] The reason is that the worker's promise to pay may

[1] Moreover, the penalty imposed on the trainee in the event of exit needs to be neither too low, otherwise quits cannot be discouraged, nor too high, otherwise workers will not accept the training contract.

Table A6.1 Regulation: pay-back clauses, time working accounts and apprenticeship contracts

	Diffusion	Main advantages	Main problems
Pay-back clauses			
	Legally admitted in many OECD countries (for example Luxembourg, Germany, Italy)	Reduce the risk of poaching and help credit constrained workers	Difficulties due to training contractibility
	Limited practical diffusion		
Apprenticeship contracts			
	Several OECD countries (for example Germany, Italy, UK, Spain, France)	Facilitate the sharing of training costs and the school-to-work transition	When publicly financed likely to produce deadweight losses and substitution effects. Low training quality—it requires an adequate length and certification system
Time working accounts			
	Several OECD countries (for example Denmark, the Netherlands, France)	Overcome time related constraints	Difficulties due to training contractibility

not be credible if, s/he is constrained by liquidity, and the contract does not require the poaching firm to pay.

On the other hand, since training is hardly verifiable, firms may require workers to pay even if the training provided was of poor quality and scarcely valuable in the labour market. These problems imply that pay-back clauses are adequate for training programmes with content and quality that can be easily assessed and certified, but less useful for other types of training (OECD, 2003a).[2]

The sharing of training costs among firms and workers is facilitated by working times accounts, diffused in many OECD countries (for example in Denmark, the Netherlands, and France, see OECD 2003a for details). These systems allow workers to accumulate working time credits, for example through overtime hours, which can be used for undertaking training

---

[2] Enforcing such kinds of legal devices may result in difficulties also for certified training. Story and Redman (1997), do not find many cases of enforced payments, suggesting that firms use this instrument more as a deterrent than as a cost recovery practice.

activities. Clearly, as for other sharing costs systems, a crucial issue is represented by training contractibility: the worker will anticipate the cost of training, working additional time before the training programme, only if he can trust the firm to provide general and high quality training.[3]

Another contractual form that has an important role in the training system of many European countries is apprenticeship, which combines training and employment in a way that enables people to enter an occupation and develop skills valuable to many firms. With perfectly competitive labour markets, the firm cannot reap the benefits deriving from general training, and the cost of the investment is shifted onto the apprentices, who accept a sufficiently low wage in the expectation of earning a higher wage once they have qualified. This expectation depends on the value that acquired skills have in the labour market. In the case of large markets where information is not easily available, the worker is interested in investing in skills only if there is a system that certifies his/her competences, making them recognizable in the market. As a consequence, as already noticed, the state may have a role in defining an adequate certification system even in the case of training being financed completely by workers.

The importance of state regulation increases when firms lend part of the training cost to workers or when they share the investment with workers. Since it is often the case that the worker's contribution to production net to training costs during the apprenticeship period is very low, paying a wage equal to the net productivity of the worker may prevent liquidity constrained individuals from investing. This problem can be solved with a contractual arrangement such that the trainee is required to stay with the employer providing training for a defined period of time. Agreements of this type can be based either on explicit rules, such as pay-back clauses, or on systems that implicitly make early quits inconvenient for workers, such as apprenticeship contracts. Under the latter, the worker is overpaid during the first period of the training and underpaid during the final part of the training spell (in this way the firm is allowed to recover training costs). The length of the contract is a key element to give adequate incentives to both parties: on the one hand, the incentives for the worker to invest in training decrease with the length of the apprenticeship, as s/he is paid a

---

[3] In many countries, statutory or contractual training leave schemes guarantee employees the right to return to their jobs after training periods. In some countries, training leave subsidies are available, allowing workers to cover living expenses or partially replace foregone income (see Bassanini, 2004).

lower wage for a longer period; on the other hand, incentives for the firm increase, as the return of its investment amplifies with the length of the apprenticeship contract.

Nevertheless, the definition of an optimal contract length is not an easy task, since public authorities do not have full information on training costs and how they are shared between the parties. Information provided by firms and employees may turn out to be distorted by their own interests in increasing or reducing the contract length respectively (Brunello and De Paola, 2004b).

In order to discourage workers from leaving before expected, the design of the contract usually implies that the (certified) qualification is awarded only at the end of the apprenticeship period. Clearly, the cost of leaving is higher when the qualification awarded at the end of the apprenticeship is highly valued in the labour market, which is strictly related to the effectiveness of the certification system.

However, in the case of firms not only lending the cost of the training to trainees, but also contributing to the financing of the investment, the certification system may produce some problematic outcomes. While on the one hand, this system generates adequate incentives for workers, on the other hand it reduces asymmetric information, increases turnover, and discourages firms from investing. As a consequence of these adverse effects, training should ideally be financed mainly by workers.

This prediction does not find support in the experience of some countries, however, notably Germany, where, in spite of a well structured certification system, which increases the portability of acquired skills, firms contribute in a substantial way to training expenses (Pischke, 2000). As argued by Acemoglu and Pischke (2000), this can be explained by taking into account that the effectiveness of training is strictly influenced by the active participation of recipients. Certification, guaranteeing workers a higher wage, induces them to put a high level of effort into the skill acquisition process, thus making training convenient also for firms.

Apprenticeship contracts are diffuse in many OECD countries even though the regulation system varies considerably. Table A6.2 summarizes the main features in terms of overall governance, educational and training content, duration, and finance. Some important differences emerge in relation to the length of the apprenticeship period and the level of the youth wage. While in Germany, France and the Netherlands, the contract length is defined by law and the average duration is of 2–3 years, in Britain and Spain the contract duration is defined by the firm and the average

	Germany	Austria	Denmark	Netherlands	Ireland	UK
Principal national statutes	Vocational Training Act 1969 1981 1984	Vocational Training Act 1969 1993 1997	Apprenticeship Act 1937, 1956, 1989	Apprenticeship Act 1966, 1992, 1995	Apprenticeship Act 1993	Industrial Act 1937
Target group	No upper limit	No upper age limit. Advantages for older people	Age 15 or 16. Special shorter programme for older than 25	At least 16, no upper limit	At least 16, no upper limit	16–25
Social parties involved						
Employers	Yes	Yes	Yes	Yes	Yes	Yes
Trade unions	Yes	Yes	Yes	Yes	Yes	No
Teachers	Yes	Yes	Yes	Yes	Yes	No
Training duration	2–4	2–4	3–5	2	4	Unspecified
Mand. educational content		4/5 of the training time is spent in the firm				
Share of:						
Off-job ed.	20–25	16	40	20–40	21	0
General ed.	33	25	33	33	2	0
Train. certification						
Employers	Yes	Yes	Yes	Yes	Yes	Yes
Vocational teaching	Yes	na	No	Yes	No	No
Public subsidies						
Train. outside workplace	Full	Full	Full	Partial	Full	Partial
Workplace train.	None	Some groups of workers. Tax reductions for training companies and reductions of social security contributions for apprentices.	Intermittent	Tax relief	None	Grants
Relative pay	20–45%	40–60%	51–54%	na	na	60%

(Contd.)

Table A6.2 (*Contd.*)

	Finland	Belgium Flemish	Belgium Walloon	Spain	France	Italy
Principal national statutes			Decree dated 3/7/91, decree dated 4/5/95	Decree 5281 1977. Royal decree law 18/1993	Law on apprenticeship 1971, 1992 1993	Law N. 25/1955 and N. 6/1987, Decree n.276, 2003
Target group	At least 15, no upper limit	15–18	At least 15, no upper limit	16–21. In some cases 16–24	16–25	15–24
Social parties involved						
Employers	Yes	Yes	Yes	No	Yes	Yes
Trade unions	Yes	No	No	No	Yes	Yes
Vocati. Teach.	Yes	Yes	No	No	No	No
Training duration	2–3 years	1–3 years	3 years	6 months; 3 years	2–3 years	2–6 years
Mand. educational content		1 or 2 days a week	12 hours/week in the first year and 8 hours/week in the second and the third years		400 hour for year	120 hours of formal training both inside and outside the firm
Share of:						
Off-job ed.	70–80			0–15%	1/4	
General ed.	20			0	3/4	
Train. certification						
Employers	Yes	Yes	Yes	No	Yes	To be defined
Vocational teaching	Yes	Yes	Yes	No	Yes	
Public subsidies						
Train. outside workplace	Full	Full	Partial	Partial	Partial	Tax relief
Workplace train.	Partial	None	None			Tax relief
Relative pay	80%			60–80%	na	

Sources: Ryan (2000); Linderholm and Parker (2000); Marhuenda Fluirà (2000); Brunello and Topo (2004).

duration is of less than a year. In Italy, the apprenticeship period lasts three years but can be completed in different firms (Brunello and Topo, 2005). As far as the apprentice's wage is concerned, Marsden and Ryan (1990) report that the youth manual workers' wages in Germany were 46 per cent of adult level, compared to 62 per cent and 85 per cent in the UK and Italy, respectively.

The availability of young German workers to accept a low wage during the apprenticeship period is probably due to the good career prospects ensured by a certification system that makes their competences also recognizable outside the training firm. In Germany, apprenticeships end with an examination conducted by a committee including representatives of local Chambers of Commerce, trade unions, sectoral employers' organizations and vocational teachers. Formal tests, conducted by organizations external to the firm, are also used in Austria and Denmark, while Britain, Spain and Italy rely on the evaluations of employers. In Spain, it is the company that provides the training certificate, which lacks any professional value, as it does not have the recognition of either the Employment or the Education Authorities (Steedman, 2001a, 2001b).

In many European countries, apprenticeship is treated as part of upper secondary education, and apprentices are required to attend part-time formal education. For example, in France the apprentice attends the *Centres de formation d'apprentis* for 400 hours a year and a quarter of this time is devoted to general training, with the remaining three-quarters dedicated to technological specific training. In Germany, off-the-job training is provided in public educational institutions. Formal training is required also in Austria, Ireland, the Netherlands and Denmark, while, in Spain, the UK and Italy there is less attention to the educational side. In Spain, as argued by Marhuenda Fluixà (2000), even if formal training should account for at least 15 per cent of the agreed working hours, there is not, to date, any control over the educational content, and apprenticeship contracts may be signed without covering any educational requirement, as long as the company pays the 'Minimum Inter-professional Wage' to the apprentice. In the UK, as argued by Ryan (2000), off-the-job training attended in a company training centre is often sufficient to satisfy legal requirements.

These differences in the legislative framework translate into differences in training quality. In Italy and Spain, apprenticeship contracts are mainly a low cost labour contract. Problems related to training quality seem relevant also in the UK where—according to Gospel (1995, 1997)—there are few companies offering good quality apprenticeship slots. The low quality of training provided through apprenticeship in some countries, apart from being related to regulation systems that do not provide adequate incentives to parties, may depend also on particular institutional settings. As argued by Gospel (1997), poaching problems hinder firms from offering high quality training. In order to solve these problems, it is necessary to define the formal arrangements that support the system and help to share the training costs. For example, in countries such as Germany, Austria and Switzerland, a crucial role is played by intra-firm organizations and industry-wide arrangements (Pischke, 2000). These systems facilitate implicit agreements among firms aimed at restraining poaching behaviour. But at the same time, the influence of intra-firm training arrangements is low in countries where the apprenticeship system is not strong, as in Britain and Italy.

In many countries, public intervention in the apprenticeship system is not limited to designing formal rules, but also provides financial support. In Germany, Denmark, Austria, and the Netherlands the state pays for formal education while the firms and apprentices pay for training on-the-job. The role of firms as financiers is very important in these countries. According to Berger and Walden (2002), employers in Germany provide over 75 per cent of funding for the operation of the apprenticeship system.

In France, firms pay an apprenticeship tax that dates back to 1925 and is mainly used by enterprises for financing—together with the state, local communities and professional organizations—the cost of apprentice training in the Apprenticeship Training Centres. In other countries, for example Italy, the state contribution is considerable and firms that offer these contracts are exempted from paying nearly 100 per cent of payroll taxes. On the other hand, training content and quality is subject to low monitoring (Croce, 2005b).

The evaluation of the effects of public financial support to apprenticeship systems needs to consider the effects of deadweight losses and substitution. The point being that these policies might fail to substantially increase the number of apprentices—due to the fact that part of the financial support goes to investments that would have been realized anyway—or might reduce the supply of other types of job opportunities. In the case of deadweight losses, both the efficiency and the equity arguments usually employed to back up the policy are undermined, since the final beneficiary of the subsidy is not the worker, but the employer, who would have delivered the training anyway, even without the public policy.

A6.2 Co-financed schemes directed at firms

Co-financing systems directed at firms can be based on a compulsory or on a voluntary approach. The poaching problem motivates the former approach: with all firms contributing to training through the payment of a levy, the free-riding problem becomes less relevant. The levy schemes take different forms: traditional schemes tax all firms and finance training provided by the public sector or by sectoral training funds;[4] there are other schemes that reduce training costs through tax arrangements or grants.[5] In this sub-section we review these systems and discuss their main advantages and drawbacks, which are as summarized in Table A6.3.

The most widespread compulsory schemes aimed at increasing employers' investments in training are levy schemes which require firms to pay a tax and obtain resources to award grants to support training (levy-grant schemes), or which impose on firms to pay a tax if they do not meet a pre-determined level of training (train-or-pay schemes).

Levy/grant schemes, which combine a tax levied on all firms—normally on payroll—with grants awarded to training projects presented by some firms, are fairly widespread within the European Union. Some countries, in particular Belgium, Spain and Italy, have defined compulsory financing schemes at a national level and others, such as the Netherlands and UK, have opted for contributions at a sectoral level (see Ok and Tergeist, 2003; Croce, 2005a).

In these systems, grants can be allocated to priority training programmes, and some levy-paying firms may not obtain training grants if their training activity is not in line with national standards and objectives. Since a set of conditions has to be respected by training projects eligible for financing by levy-based funds, it is possible to control, to some extent, the content and the quality of training provided by firms. Employers have to be consulted and involved to avoid the system being perceived as an additional tax which further reduces competitiveness.[6]

---

[4] Revenue generating schemes that tax firms to finance training provided by the public sector, while still used in many developing countries, are present in industrialized countries only in the form of employment insurance funds to finance training of the unemployed.

[5] In countries where governments do not regulate firms' training expenditure, an important instrument for financing training is represented by collective labour agreements, establishing training clauses and the creation of training funds. Besides, governments offer tax-related incentives for training through different types of tax arrangements.

[6] In the UK, the abandonment of the levy/grant systems is partly attributed to employers' bad perception (Gasskov, 2001).

Table A6.3 Co-financed schemes directed at firms

	Diffusion	Main advantages	Main problems
Train-or-pay schemes	France and Canada	Low cost of administration Effective in increasing training investments	Low training quality High expected deadweight losses
Levy-grant schemes	Belgium, Spain, Italy	Training quality controlled to some extent Opportunity for the development of national or sectoral training policies	Employers may perceive it as an additional tax reducing competitiveness Demanding in administrative terms and likely to generate abuses
Tax deductions	Austria, Italy, Luxembourg	Low expected deadweight losses Low costs of administration	Work only as long as there are positive profits. When financed through general tax revenues, taxpayers are required to pay for the training obtained by a small portion of the workforce

The management of this scheme requires the definition of administrative bodies which decide priority training programmes and grants. In some countries a crucial role is played by the government, while in others, for example Spain and Italy, grants are decided by social parties. In the second case, the active role of unions can help to monitor training quality and the design of training curricula with an eye to the portability of skills (see Ok and Tergeist, 2003).

This system involves many case-by-case decisions and management competences, is demanding in administrative terms, and is likely to generate abuses. An alternative to the combination of levies and grants is 'train or pay' schemes, with levies payable only if the training investment falls below a legal minimum. Train or pay schemes (or levy-exemption mechanisms), used in France and Canada,[7] allow firms to reduce their levy obligations by the amount of training they provide or purchase. Since these systems operate through the individual actions of employers, they do not require special and costly organizations to be established and, as a

---

[7] In the Province of Quebec, Canada, a training levy of the French type has been introduced by the law, known as the *Loi favorisant le developpement de la formation de la main-d'oeuvre*, which requires firms to devote one per cent of their payrolls to training or submit an equivalent amount to the Quebec Minister of Revenue.

consequence, imply low administration costs. Where bureaucratic costs are high and public procedures slow, this could be an important advantage. Levy exemption schemes, on the other hand, in contrast to levy-grant schemes, leave full autonomy to employers in training decisions, provide less opportunity for the development of national or sectoral training policies. Besides, firms could use training as a perquisite with cosmetic rather than substantial effects on skill development.

Other countries, such as Austria (in 2000), Italy (in 2001), Luxembourg (in 1999) and the Netherlands (introduced in 1998 and abolished in 2004), have opted for tax deductions from revenues, which allow firms to deduct some or all training costs and thereby reduce corporate taxes. Tax deductions are generally higher than 100 per cent of total expenses, implying a training subsidy (extra-deductions amount to 10 per cent of training expenditures in Luxembourg, 20 per cent in Austria and the Netherlands and up to 50 per cent in Italy). Since deductions work only as long as there are positive profits, some countries allow firms to carry forward these expenses to fiscal years where profits are positive (see OECD, 2003a, 2004).[8]

In spite of the diffusion of tax arrangements and levy-grant schemes, rigorous evaluations of their effectiveness are uncommon. In particular, the substitution between formal and informal training has not been evaluated. An open issue is related to the most appropriate source of funding. Schemes diffused in OECD countries in some cases are based on general tax revenues, such as tax arrangement schemes, while in other cases they are financed with funds collected through levies imposed on firms, such as train-or-pay and levy-grant schemes.[9] In the first case,

[8] In many countries, governments participate in funding training programmes. In European countries there are also available resources from the European Community training policies, operating both through the concession of funds into national programmes (European Social Funds) and through separate training initiatives. An important community policy instrument is represented by the subsidization of member state programmes. These interventions aim to increase training to a level higher than that chosen by national governments, under the assumption that training produces a public benefit that has not been considered by national government. Clearly a first relevant issue is whether a supra-national institution can decide a level of training that is better than that decided by each state. Another problem is represented by the displacement effect of existing national expenditure by community subsidies. This effect may be avoided following a principle of additionality establishing that the member state has to maintain its public assistance at least at the same level as it was before the obtainment of the Community subsidies. However, as argued by Addison and Siebert (1994), since in practice there are problems in enforcing even minimal principles of additionality, displacement effects are very likely to occur. Moreover, it is also to be considered that whether an additionality form was enforced or not, there would be the risk of devoting too many resources to training (Addison and Siebert, 1994).

[9] See also Whalley and Ziderman (1990), who discuss these schemes referring to developing countries.

taxpayers are required to pay for the training obtained by a small portion of the workforce, which can be considered fair only if training is expected to produce large externalities or when training is offered to disadvantaged workers. Otherwise, if externalities take place mainly among firms, and workers obtaining training are not in need, systems based on levies imposed on firms seem more adequate. Nevertheless, redistributive considerations are important also in this case. With levies on payroll, even if taxes to finance training are paid by the enterprise, the real burden may be passed onto workers in the form of lower wages. If the burden of the tax is entirely on employees, net wages fall to compensate for the tax. On the other hand, the subsidy received by firms reduces in the same proportion the share of the training costs borne by trainees. As suggested by Stevens (1996), this policy has no impact on employers, but affects the training decisions of employees, with some redistribution from employees not receiving training to employees receiving it. Since most training is obtained by skilled workers, this poses an equity issue because even if all workers are contributing to the scheme, only workers in better positions benefit from training.

The conclusion that levies on payroll do not influence the supply-side of the training market change if employers are not able to shift the burden of the tax entirely onto employees, and if employees are not able to entirely appropriate the advantages of the subsidy in terms of a lower training price. The incidence of the levy depends on the relative market power of firms and workers. The share of tax borne by the worker increases as the elasticity of labour demand becomes higher and the share of the tax borne by the employer is larger when the elasticity of labour supply is high. On the other hand, workers will respond to the price reduction of training depending on their preferences. As a consequence, evaluating the impact of these schemes requires information on the responsiveness of wages and training prices to changes in payroll taxes and training grants. The impact of taxes levied on profits are more straightforward, since they directly influence the marginal decision between training and poaching by reducing the profits from poaching. Tax deductions financed through corporate taxes may attain a similar objective.

Another open issue is whether levy or tax deduction rates should be uniform or vary across sectors and whether firms of different dimensions should be treated in a different way. Training under-investment—if it exists—may vary among industries, and small firms generally require less training since they adopt less sophisticated technologies. Whether levy and tax deduction rates should reflect these differences is a matter for debate. Even if they should, it is questionable whether a differentiated policy can be implemented when some of the costs are not verifiable. If efficiency were the issue, a sector-specific policy would require that the government has information on the sector-specific efficient level of training.

A related problem is represented by the definition of training expenses eligible for tax deduction and of training programmes suitable for grants. On the one hand, expenditures and programmes have to be defined in a clear and transparent way in order to avoid abuses and, on the other hand, it is necessary to avoid substitution between different forms of training. Allowing for the deduction of any training expense, either internal or external, or financing any training programme, avoids the second problem but imposes a risk, as firms may implement low quality training programmes. Alternatively, when only external expenses are deductible, firms may substitute informal training programmes with more formalized ones. Similarly, since levy-grant and train-or-pay schemes are generally directed to formal training, it is likely that firms react substituting informal training with formal courses.

Finally, an important question, already discussed in this section, is that fiscal policy to encourage training may end up subsidizing programmes that would have been provided by firms in any case. For the employer's decision to invest in training, the difference between marginal expected benefits and marginal training costs is relevant. As a consequence, in order to avoid large deadweight losses the subsidy component of a policy package must seek to compensate only the gap between marginal costs and marginal private benefits that may arise at the socially desirable investment level, leaving to employers the responsibility of financing the rest. Any subsidy that does not change the employer marginal costs and benefits will not modify his investment decisions, but end up in financing the training that would have been done anyway.

Tax deduction and grant schemes respecting this principle are likely to produce efficient results. However, some of the schemes discussed above are not based on these principles and tend to generate large deadweight losses. A typical example is represented by train-or-pay schemes used in France and Canada, which combine a payroll tax of a given percentage, independent of training expenditures, a 100 per cent automatic subsidy of training expenditures up to that percentage of payroll and an additional grant funded by the resources collected through the levy and awarded through case-by-case analysis of training projects. By covering total costs up to a predetermined ceiling, and then leading the marginal cost to zero, train-or-pay schemes do not provide a matched contribution to firms that would have spent less than the legal minimum in the absence of the scheme and, therefore, 'overpay' any increase in training investment they induce. Conversely, firms that would have spent up to the legal minimum anyway enjoy a windfall, which does not increase their incentives to invest in training (Bassanini, 2004).

Finally, these systems, even if they increase training participation, do not address the low participation of particular groups of workers. As a result, participation of unskilled workers, women and minority groups in co-financed training programmes is low (Veeken, 1999). On the other hand, targeting public support in favour of particular groups of workers is likely to produce relevant substitution effects. As shown by Leuven and Oosterbeek (2004), the 40 per cent extra-deduction to train workers aged 40 years or older, introduced in the Netherlands in 1998 and recently abolished, induced significant substitution effects. As a consequence, when training policy is aimed at reducing inequalities, it is necessary to adopt co-financing schemes focused directly on individuals (such as loan and individual subsidy schemes). As we shall discuss later, their effectiveness depends on the availability of sufficient and reliable information by workers.

A6.3 Co-financed schemes directed to individuals

In OECD countries the upgrading of skills of disadvantaged categories of workers is pursued by funding the supply of training by public and private institutions, and by financing demand with subsidies, tax deductions and loan schemes.

Traditional systems targeted at supply are widespread in those countries where public sponsored training, directly provided by public agencies, is offered to disadvantaged categories of workers. These policies are part of wider active labour market measures aimed at encouraging individual self-support through programmes which facilitate job search and human capital accumulation.[10] While in the US the main objective of these programmes is to increase the earnings of the working poor, in European

[10] The European Union and the OECD-countries have in recent years emphasized these programmes as an important means to reduce long-term unemployment and promote growth. Nevertheless, public expenditure on training programmes varies considerably among OECD countries, with countries such as Czech Republic, Japan, Luxembourg, Poland and the USA spending less than .05 per cent of GDP and Scandinavian countries (Denmark, Finland and Sweden) with an expenditure of around 0.5 per cent of GDP (OECD, 2000).

countries, characterized by high rates of unemployment, these programmes are mainly aimed at increasing working opportunities of the
unemployed or other groups facing a high risk of job loss. As our report
does not consider training programmes directed to unemployed subjects,
we will not discuss these schemes. We concentrate instead our attention
on schemes opened to employed workers, who finance their demand for
training with tax deductions, loan schemes and subsidies to individuals.
The diffusion of these schemes in OECD countries and their main characteristics are discussed below and summarized in Table A6.4.

While loans financing tertiary education are diffuse among OECD countries, loans financing adult learning have been introduced only in a few
countries (UK and US).[11] Similarly, even if in several countries the expenditure for formal education can be deducted from personal income taxes,
training expenses usually cannot be deducted. Only recently some countries have launched initiatives aimed at allowing individuals to deduct
training expenses (e.g. Austria). However, these systems are more likely to
be effective for high-wage employees, because low-wage workers are
scarcely responsive to tax deductions and reluctant to finance learning
through loans (Bassanini, 2004).

An alternative system to promote training investments, experimented
with by a growing number of countries, is represented by different types of
subsidies (such as vouchers and individuals' training accounts), which
directly offer financial support to individuals belonging to a target
group who undertake training activities. Training vouchers are used in
certain regions of Austria, Italy and Switzerland, while individual learning
accounts, consisting in saving accounts that can be opened by individuals
to fund training activities, with contributions from third parties (government and employer), are being tried out in Canada, the Netherlands, the
Basque region of Spain, the UK and the US (for a review see OECD, 2003c).

In Italy, training vouchers were introduced in 1993 (Law n. 236). During
the period 1999 to 2001, regions which introduced this system received
about 15 000 requests and granted 9,000 vouchers (Croce, 2005b). A first
look at this data shows that workers participating in the system are
mainly those with high skills and high education, while the demand by
disadvantaged categories of workers is low (ISFOL, 2001).[12] A similar result

---

[11] Career Development Loans, allowing adults to borrow from GBP300 to GBP8000 to pay
for training at special conditions, were launched in the UK in 1988. However, the number of
borrowers was much lower than expected.
[12] Moreover, due to the lack of a well-defined certification system (there is only a certification of attendance), it may be difficult to make potential employers aware of the acquired skill.

Table A6.4 Co-financing schemes directed to individuals

	Diffusion	Main advantages	Main problems
Tax deductions	Austria	Encourage training investments reducing their cost and making them convenient also in case of low and uncertain rates of return	Since individuals can only make use of these deductions if they earn enough in a fiscal year to be liable to pay taxes, they are more effective for short and/or part-time training and for training investments realized by high-wage employees
Loan schemes	UK, US	Help in solving individual difficulties in financing training through borrowing	They may generate high levels of debt and workers, in face of uncertain returns to training, may not be able to repay the loan. Adults tend to be reluctant to finance learning processes through loans
Vouchers	Austria, Italy, Switzerland, US	Increase competition on the supply side with positive expected effects on training quality	Large dead-weight losses in case of vouchers that cover training costs or consisting in a fixed contribution. To be effective require sufficient information about the variety and the quality of training programmes offered by providers. The available evidence suggest that they are mainly used by high skilled workers
Individual learning accounts	Canada, the Netherlands, UK, US, Spain	The available empirical evidence suggests that they are widespread among disadvantaged categories of workers	Risk of abuses and frauds
Leave schemes	Austria, Belgium, Finland, France, Italy, Japan, Korea, Norway, Spain, Sweden	Help at overcoming time constraints	Low participation rates

emerges from the training voucher system experimented by the Swiss canton of Geneva, where only 16 per cent of total applicants were persons with only compulsory schooling.

To avoid these problems, some countries offer subsidies targeted at particular categories of workers. For example, in Germany the government subsidizes the training expenditures of workers aged over 59, with no qualification or employed in semi-skilled or unskilled occupations for more than four years. According to the available evidence, a large diffusion among disadvantaged categories of workers has been attained also by systems combining tax arrangements or loans with subsidies, such as individual learning accounts. Different types of such schemes have been introduced in Canada, the Netherlands, the Basque region of Spain, the United Kingdom and the United States (for a review see OECD, 2003b). In many of these countries the aim of these schemes has been that of establishing accounts for the payment of direct training and education costs, while only in a few cases their objective has been that of replacing the income of individuals undertaking full-time learning activities. The risk of abuse and fraud is very high in the case of direct contribution from third parties.

Usually, to preserve accountability, the co-financing partner matches individual contributions at the time of the transaction to purchase education or training services, but also in this case it is not always possible to prevent funds from being spent for purposes other than those allowed. As for the financial incentives to firms, in the absence of rigorous evaluation, it is difficult to compare the different types of schemes that have already been discussed. However, as argued in Chapter 13, subsidy schemes are more likely to be efficient when they are matched contributions that reduce marginal costs of training for any subsidy recipient.

In many countries, leave schemes guarantee workers the right to return to their jobs after training spells (for a discussion see OECD, 2003a). As foregone income may depress employees' incentives to participate in training programmes, these schemes are more effective when accompanied by subsidies covering living expenses and replacing foregone income (such as those offered by the German government).

Independently, on their specific form, systems financing demand are expected to generate a larger competition among providers with gains in terms of efficiency and innovation. Nevertheless, the use of subsidies directed at individuals does not necessarily stimulate competition. Without sufficient information about the variety and the quality of training programmes offered by providers, consumers are not in a condition to stimulate a high quality and cost-effective supply. Individuals need information that identifies job vacancies and the skills necessary for in-demand jobs, information on local, regional and national employment trends, and on the performance of training providers in preparing people for jobs. Only if sufficient information is available to the demand-side would it be possible to enhance a high quality system. On the contrary, in a context of asymmetric information, adverse selection problems may lead to a low quality market. In fact, on the one hand, providers may not be able to prove the quality of their services and, on the other hand, consumers may not be able to make adequate cost–benefit evaluations.

Generally, since this information system is very costly and difficult to implement, subsidy schemes do not allow total freedom of choice to individuals, but leave them free to choose within courses offered by accredited training providers with training programmes meeting a minimum standard of performance. If the supply-side does not expand, subsidies that increase the demand for training may lead to higher prices and produce a small increase in training participation.

REFERENCES

Abraham, K. G. and Farber, H. S. (1987), 'Job Duration, Seniority, and Earnings', *American Economic Review*, 77(3), 278–97.

Acemoglu, D. (1996), 'Microfoundation for Social Increasing Returns in Human Capital Accumulation', *Quarterly Journal of Economics*, 111, 779–804.

—— (1997), 'Training and Innovation in an Imperfect Labor Market', *Review of Economic Studies*, 64, 445–64.

—— and Pischke, J. (1998), 'Why do Firms Train? Theory and Evidence', *Quarterly Journal of Economics*, 113, 79–119.

—— and —— (1999a), 'Beyond Becker: Training in Imperfect Labor Market', *Economic Journal*, 109 (February), F112–F142.

—— and —— (1999b), 'The Structure of Wages and Investment in General Training', *Journal of Political Economy*, 539–72.

—— and —— (2000), 'Certification of Training and Training Outcomes', *European Economic Review*, 44, 917–27.

—— and —— (2003), 'Minimum Wages and On-the-Job Training', *Research in Labor Economics*, 22, 159–202.

Addison, J. and Siebert, W. (1994), 'Vocational Training and the European Community', *Oxford Economic Papers*, Oxford University Press, vol. 46(4), 696–724.

Agell, J. and Lommerud, K. (1997), 'Minimum Wages and the Incentives for Skill Formation', *Journal of Public Economics*, Elsevier, vol. 64(1), 25–40.

Alba-Ramirez, A. (1994), 'Formal Training, Temporary Contracts, Productivity and Wages in Spain', *Bulletin of Economics and Statistics*, Oxford: Blackwell Publishing, vol. 56(2), 151–70.

Almeida, R. and Carneiro, P. (2004), 'On-the-Job Training: Estimating Costs and Returns Using Firm Level Data', *Working Paper*, UCL.

Almeida-Santos, F. and Mumford, K. (2004), 'Employee Training and Wage Compression in Britain', IZA Discussion Papers, 1197.

Altonji, J. G. and Shakotko, R. (1987), 'Do Wages Rise with Job Seniority?' *Review of Economic Studies*, 54, 437–59.

Andrén, T. and Gustafsson B. (2004), 'Income Effects from Labor Market Training Programmes in Sweden during the 80s and 90s', *International Journal of Manpower*, vol. 25, Issue no. 8.

Angrist, J. (2004), 'Treatment and Heterogeneity in Theory and Practice', *Economic Journal*, C52–C83.

Ariga, K. and Brunello, G. (2006), Do the Better Educated Receive More Training? Evidence from Thailand', *Industrial and Labor Relations Review*, (July), 245–68.

Arulampalam, W. and Booth A. (1998), 'Labour Market Flexibility and Skills Acquisition: Is There a Trade-off?', *British Journal of Industrial Relations*, 36(4), 521–36.

—— and —— (2001), 'Learning and Earning: Do Multiple Training Events Pay? A Decade of Evidence from a Cohort of Young British Men', *Economica*, 68, 379–400.

——, —— and Bryan, M. (2004), 'Training in Europe', *Journal of the European Economic Association*, 2(2–3), 346–60.

——, —— and —— (2004), 'Training and the New Minimum Wage', *Economic Journal*, March, C87–C94.

Asplund, R. (2005), 'The Provision and Effects of Company Training: A brief review of the literature', ETLA Discussion Paper no. 907.

Australian Bureau of Statistics (1990), *How Workers Get Their Training, Australia 1989*, ABS, Canberra.

Autor, D. (2003), 'Why Do Temporary Help Firms Provide Free General Skills?', *Quarterly Journal of Economics*, MIT Press, vol. 116(4), 1409–48.

Ballot, G., Fakhfakh, F. and Taymaz, E. (2001), 'Firms' Human Capital, R&D and Performance: A study on French and Swedish firms', *Labour Economics* 8(4), 443–62.

——, —— and —— (2006), 'Who Benefits from Training and R&D: The Firm or the Workers? A Study on Panels of French and Swedish Firms', *British Journal of Industrial Relations*, 44(3), 473–95.

Barrett A. and O'Connell P. (2001), 'Does Training Generally Work? The Returns to In-Company Training', *Industrial and Labor Relations Review*, 54(3), p. 647–62.

Barron, J. M., Berger M. and Black D. (1997), *On-the-Job Training*, W. E Upjohn Institute for Employment Research.

—— ,—— and —— (1999), 'Do Workers Pay for On-the-Job Training?', *Journal of Human Resources*, 34(2), 236–52.

Barron, J. M., Berger M. and Black D. (1997), 'How Well Do We Measure Training?', *Journal of Labor Economics*, 15(3), 507–28.

——,—— and Loewenstein, M. A. (1987), 'Employer Size: The Implications for Search, Training, Capital Investment, Starting Wages, and Wage Growth', *Journal of Labor Economics*, 5(1), 76–89.

—— Fuess, S., and —— (1987), 'Further Analysis of the Effect of Unions on Training [Union Wages, Temporary Layoffs, and Seniority]', *Journal of Political Economy*, University of Chicago Press, vol. 95(3), 632–40.

Bartel, A. (1994), 'Productivity Gains from the Implementation of Employee Training Programs', *Industrial Relations*, 33(4), 411–25.

—— (1995), 'Training, Wage Growth, and Job Performance: Evidence from a Company Database', *Journal of Labor Economics*, 13, 401–25.

—— (2000), 'Measuring the Employer's Return on Investments in Training: Evidence from the Literature', *Industrial Relations*, 39(3), 502–24.

Bassanini A. (2004), 'Improving Skills for More and Better Jobs? The Quest for Efficient Policies to Promote Adult Education and Training', *European Economy: Special Report*, 3, 103–37.

—— (2005), 'Training, Wages, and Employment Security: an Empirical Analysis on European Data', *Applied Economics Letters*, 13(8), 523–7.

—— and Brunello G. (2003), 'Is Training More Frequent when Wage Compression is Higher? Evidence from the European Community Household Panel', IZA Discussion Papers, n. 839.

Bhaskar, V. and To, T., (2003), 'Oligopsony and the Distribution of Wages', *European Economic Review*, Elsevier, vol. 47(2), 371–99.

——, Manning A. and —— (2002), 'Oligopsony and Monopsonistic Competition in Labour Markets', *The Journal of Economic Perspectives*, 16(2), 155–74.

Becker, G. S. (1964), *Human Capital: A Theoretical and Empirical Analysis, with Special Reference to Education*. New York, National Bureau of Economic Research.

Berger, K. and Walden, G. (2002), 'Trends in Public Funding for In-Company Training in Germany: From a Dual to a Plural System'. In G. Burke and J. Reuling (eds), *Vocational Training and Lifelong Learning in Australia and Germany*, Adelaide, NCVER.

Bishop, J. (1991), 'On-the-Job Training of New Hires, in Market Failure in Training?' (eds) David Stern and Jozef M. M. Ritzen, 61–98. New York: Springer Verlag.

—— (1993), 'Underinvestment in Employer Training: a Mandate to Spend?' *Human Resources Development Quarterly*, 4(3), 223–41.

—— (1997), 'What We Know about Employer-Provided Training: A Review of the Literature'. In Polachek, S. and Solomon, W. (eds), *Research in Labor Economics*. London, JAI Press, 19–87.

Black S. and Lynch L. (1998), 'Determinants of Employer-Provided Training', *Industrial and Labor Relations Review*, vol. 51: 365–81.

—— and —— (2001), 'How to Compete: The Impact of Workplace Practices and Information Technology on Productivity', *The Review of Economics and Statistics*, 83, 434–45.

Blanchard, O., and Giavazzi, F. (2003), 'Macroeconomic Effects of Regulation and Deregulation in Goods and Labor Markets', *The Quarterly Journal of Economics*, 879–907.

—— and Wolfers, J. (2000), 'The Role of Shocks and Institutions in the Rise of European Unemployment, the Aggregate Evidence', *The Economic Journal*, 110, C1/33.

Blau, F. and Kahn, L. (1983), 'Job Search and Unionized Employment', *Economic Inquiry*, Oxford: Oxford University Press, vol. 21(3), 412–30.

Blinder, A. and Krueger A. (1996), 'Labor Turnover in the USA and Japan: A Tale of Two Countries', *Pacific Economic Review*, vol. 1, 27–57.

Blomstrom, M. and Kokko, A. (2003), 'Natural Resources to High-Tech Production: The Evolution of Industrial Competitiveness in Sweden and Finland', CEPR Discussion Paper, no. 3804.

Blundell, R., Dearden L. and Meghir C. (1996), 'The Determinants and Effects of Work-Related Training in Britain', Institute for Fiscal Studies, London.

——, —— and —— (1999), 'Work-Related Training and Earnings', Mimeo, Institute of Fiscal Studies.

——, ——, —— and Sianesi B. (1999), 'Human Capital Investment: The Returns from Education and Training to the Individual, the Firm and the Economy', *Fiscal Studies*, 20(1), 1–23.

Boeri T., Boersch-Supan A. and Tabellini G. (2002), 'Pension Reforms and the Opinions of European Citizens', *American Economic Review*, 1 May 2002, vol. 92, no. 2, 396–401(6).

Booth, A. (1991), 'Job-Related Formal Training: Who Receives It And What Is It Worth?', *Oxford Bulletin of Economics and Statistics*, 53, 281–94.

—— (1993), 'Private Sector Training and Graduate Earnings', *Review of Economics and Statistics*, 76, 164–70.

—— and Bryan M. (2002), 'Who Pays for General Training? New Evidence for British Men and Women', IZA Discussion Paper no. 486 (April).

—— and —— (2005a), 'Testing Some Predictions of Human Capital Theory: New Training Evidence from Britain', *Review of Economics and Statistics* (May) (forthcoming).

—— and —— (2005b), 'Who Pays for General Training in Private Sector Britain?', IZA Discussion Paper no. 486, *Research in Labor Economics* (forthcoming).

—— and Chatterji M. (1998), 'Unions and Efficient Training', *Economic Journal*, 108, 447, 328–43.

—— and Coles M. G. (2005), 'Increasing Returns to Education and the Skills Under-Investment Trap'. Mimeo, Australian National University.

——, Francesconi, M. and Zoega G. (1999), 'Training, Rent-Sharing and Unions', CEPR Discussion Paper Series, no. 2200.

——, —— and —— (2003), 'Unions, Work-Related Training and Wages: Evidence for British Men', *Industrial and Labor Relations Review*, vol. 57, no. 1, 68–91.

Booth, A., Francesconi, M. and Zoega G. (2005), 'Oligopsony, Institutions and the Efficiency of General Training', forthcoming Ch. 2 of *Proceedings of the 2004 ECB/CEPR Labour Market Workshop*, Edward Elgar Publishers, (eds) J. Messina, C. Michelacci, J. Turunen and G. Zoega.

—— and Zoega G. (1999), 'Do Quits Cause Under-Training?', *Oxford Economic Papers*, 51, 374–86 (February).

—— and —— (2000), 'Why do Firms Invest in General Training? "Good" Firms and "Bad" Firms as a Source of Monopsony Power', *Institute for Labour Research*, Working Papers no. 058, University of Essex.

—— and —— (2004), 'Is Wage Compression a Necessary Condition for Firm-Financed General Training?', *Oxford Economic Papers*, 56, 88–97.

Brown, J. N. (1989), 'Why do Wages Increase with Job Tenure? On-the-Job Training and Life-Cycle Wage Growth Observed Within Firms', *American Economic Review*, 79(5): 971–91.

Brunello, G. (2003), 'On the Complementarity between Education and Training in Europe'. In Checchi and Lucifora (eds), *Education, Training and Labour Market Outcomes in Europe*, Palgrave, McMillan.

—— (2004), 'La formazione continua nelle grandi imprese italiane: un'analisi dei risultati della seconda indagine ISFOL', ISFOL, Rome.

—— and Checchi, D. (2005), 'Family Background and School Quality in Italy', *Economics of Education Review*, 24(5), 145–63.

—— and De Paola, M. (2004a), 'Training and the Density of Economic Activity: Evidence from Italy', IZA Discussion Paper 1073. (Forthcoming in *Labour Economics*.)

—— and —— (2004b), 'Market Failures and the Under-Provision of Training', OECD and European Commission (processed).

—— and Gambarotto, F. (2004), 'Agglomeration Effects of Employer Provided Training: Evidence from the UK, final revision', *Regional Science and Urban Economics*.

—— and Giannini, M. (2004), 'Stratified or Comprehensive? The Economic Efficiency of School', *The Scottish Journal of Political Economy*, 2004, 156–73.

——, —— and Ariga, K. (forthcoming), 'The Optimal Timing of School Tracking', in Petersen, P. and Woessmann, L., (eds), *Schools and Equal Opportunity*, MIT Press.

—— and Medio A. (2001), 'An Explanation of International Differences in Education and Workplace Training', *European Economic Review*, vol. 1, 307–22.

—— and Topo A. (2005), 'Dalla formazione apparente alla formazione effettiva? Il nuovo apprendistato professionalizzante', *Rivista Italiana di Diritto del Lavoro*, 33–58.

Bruyneel, D. (1999), 'Tax and Accounting Treatment of Vocational Training', OECD, Paris.

Cameron, S. and Taber, C. (2000), 'Borrowing Constraints and the Returns to Schooling', NBER Working Paper no. W7761.

Burdett, K. and Smith E. (1996), 'Education and Matching Externalities'. In A. L. Booth and D. J. Snower (eds), *Acquiring Skills. Market Failures, their Symptoms and Policy Responses*, Cambridge: Cambridge University Press, 65–80.

Campanelli P. and Channell J., with contributions from L. McAulay, A. Renouf and R. Thomas (1994), 'Training: An Exploration of the Word and the Concept', Employment Department Research Series No. 30, July.

Card, D. (1999), 'The Causal Effect of Education on Earnings', in *Handbook of Labor Economics*, (eds) O. Ashenfelter and D. Card, vol. 3A, ch. 30, 1801–63, Elsevier, Amsterdam.

—— (2000), 'Estimating the Return to Schooling: Progress on Some Persistent Econometric Problems', NBER Working Paper No. 7769, Cambridge, MA.

Carneiro P. and Heckman J. (2003), 'The Evidence on Credit Constraints in Post-Secondary Schooling', *Economic Journal*, 112, 705–34.

—— and —— (2004) 'Human Capital Policies'. In A. B Krueger, J. Heckman, B. Friedman (eds) *Inequality in America: what role for human capital policy?* MIT Press, Cambridge, MA.

Caroli, E. and Van Reenen, J. (2001), 'Skill-Biased Organizational Change? Evidence from a Panel of British and French Establishments', *Quarterly Journal of Economics*, vol. 116, Issue 4, 1449–92.

Chang, C. and Wang Y., (1996), 'Human Capital Investment under Asymmetric Information: The Pigovian Conjecture Revisited', *Journal of Labor Economics*, 14, 505–19.

Chapman. B. (2002), 'Credit Constraints and Training after Job Loss', Mimeo.

Colardyn, D. (ed.) (2002), 'Lifelong Learning: Which Ways Forward?', Kenniscentrum EVC, Utrecht: Lemma Publishers.

Collier, W., Green, F., Perison, J. and Wilkinson, D. (2003), 'Training and Establishment Survival', Mimeo, Kent University.

Conlon, G. (2000), 'The Marginal Effect of Vocational Qualifications on Labour Market Performance and Earnings', D.Phil. Thesis, Nuffield College, University of Oxford.

Conti, G. (2005), 'Training, Productivity and Wages in Italy', *Labour Economics*, 12(4), 557–76.

Croce, G. (2005a), 'An Economic Evaluation of "Interprofessional" Funds as Training Policies', University of Rome La Sapienza.

—— (2005b), *Limiti e prospettive della formazione continua in Italia*, in Economia & lavoro, 2.

Crouch, C. (1997), 'Skills-Based Full Employment: the Latest Philosopher's Stone', *British Journal of Industrial Relations*, 367–91.

—— (1998), 'Skills-Based Full Employment: the Latest Philosoper's Stone', *British Journal of Industrial Relations*, 35(3), 267–91.

Currie, J. and Fallick, B. (1996), 'The Minimum Wage and the Employment of Youth', *Journal of Human Resources*, 31, 404–28.

315

Dearden, L., Reed H. and Van Reenen J. (2000), 'Who Gains when Workers Train? Training and Corporate Productivity in a Panel of British Industries', *Centre for Economic Policy Research*, Discussion Paper, no. 2486.

De La Fuente, A. and Ciccone, A., (2002), 'Human Capital in a Global and Knowledge-Based Economy', The European Commission.

Duncan, G. and Stafford, F. (1980), 'Do Union Members Receive Compensating Differentials', *American Economic Review*, 70(3), 355–71.

Dustmann, C. and Schonberg, U. (2004), 'Training and Union Wages', Mimeo, UCL.

Duval, R. (2004), 'Retirement Behaviour in OECD Countries: Impact of Old-Age Pension Schemes and Other Social Transfer Programmes', *OECD Economic Studies*, 37.

Epple, R., Newlon, E. and Romano R. (2002), 'Ability Tracking, School Competition and the Standardization of Educational Benefits', *Journal of Public Economics*, 83, 1–48.

Eurostat (2000), Continuing Vocational Training Survey (CVTS2): European Union Manual, Eurostat Population and Social Conditions Working Paper 3/2000/E/N°17, Luxembourg.

European Commission (2005), 'Progress Towards the Lisbon Objectives in Education and Training', Commission Staff Working Paper.

Fougère, D., Goux, D. and Maurin, E. (2001), 'Formation continue et carriers salariales. Une évaluation sur données individuelles', *Annales d'Économie et de Statistique*, 62: 49–69.

Frazis, H., and Loewenstein, M. A. (1999), *Reexamining the Returns to Training: Functional Form, Magnitude, and Interpretation*, Working Paper no. 367, US Department of Labor, Bureau of Labor Statistics, Washington, DC.

——, Gittleman, M., Horrigan, M. and Joyce, M. (1996), 'Formal and Informal Training: Evidence from a Matched Employee–Employer Survey', Paper prepared for the conference 'New Empirical Research on Employer Training: Who Pays?' held at Cornell University, November 15–17.

Freeman, R. and Medoff, J. (1984), '*What Do Unions Do?*' New York: Basic Books.

Galindo-Rueda, V. and Vignoles, A. (2004), 'The Heterogeneous Effect of Selection in Secondary Schools: Understanding the changing role of ability', Mimeo.

Garibaldi, P. and Violante, L. (2002), 'The Employment Effects of Severance Payments with Wage Rigidities', New York University.

Gasskov, V. (2001), 'Government Interventions In Private Financing Of Training', ILO, Geneva.

Gerfin, M. (2003), 'Work-Related Training and Wages—an Empirical Analysis for Male Workers in Switzerland'. Mimeo, Volkswirtschaftliches Institut, Universität Bern.

Gersbach, H. and Schmutzler, A. (2004), 'A Product Market Theory of Training', IZA Discussion Paper 327.

Golden, L., and Appelbaum, E. (1992), 'What was Driving the 1982–88 Boom in Temporary Employment?', *American Journal of Economics and Sociology*, 51(4), 473–93.

Gospel, H. (1995), 'The Decline of Apprenticeship Training in Britain', *Industrial Relations Journal*, 26(1), 32–44.

—— (1997), 'The Revival of Apprenticeship Training in Britain?' Centre for Economic Performance, Discussion Paper, no. 372.

Goux, D., and Maurin E. (2000), 'Returns to Firm Provided Training: Evidence from French Worker–Firm Matched Data', *Labor Economics*, 7, pp. 1–19.

Green, D., and Lemieux, T. (2001), 'The Impact of Unionization on the Incidence of the Sources of Payment for Training in Canada: a study based on the adult education and training survey', Mimeo.

Green, F. (1993), 'The Determinants of Training of Male and Female Employees in Britain', *Oxford Bulletin of Economics and Statistics*, 55(1), 103–22.

——, Machin, S. and Wilkinson D. (1999), 'Trade Unions and Training Practices in British Workplaces', *Industrial and Labor Relations Review*, 52(2), 179–95.

Greenhalgh, C. (1999), 'Adult Vocational Training and Government Policy in France and Britain', *Oxford Review of Economic Policy*, Oxford University Press, vol. 15(1), 97–113.

—— (2002), 'Does an Employer Training Levy Work? The Incidence of and Returns to Adult Vocational Training in France and Britain'. IFS Working paper, no. 23.

—— and Mavrotas, G. (1994), 'The Role of Career Aspirations and Financial Constraints in Individual Access to Vocational Training', *Oxford Economic Papers*, 46, 579–604.

—— and Stewart, M. (1987), 'The Effects and Determinants of Training', *Oxford Bulletin of Economics and Statistics*, 49(2) 171–90.

Grossberg A. J. and Sicilian P. (1999), 'Minimum Wages, On-the-Job Training and Wage Growth', *Southern Economic Journal*, 65(1).

Håkanson, C., Johanson S., Mellander E. (2003), 'Employer-Sponsored Training in Stabilisation and Growth Policy Perspectives', IFAU Working Paper 2003: 8.

Hall, R. E. (2000), 'Reorganization', *Carnegie-Rochester Conference Series on Public Policy*, vol. 52, 1–22.

Hannah, F., Raffe, K. and J. Smyth, (1996), 'Cross-National Research in School to Work Transition: an Analytical Framework', OECD, Mimeo.

Harmon, C., Walker, I. and Westergard Nielsen, N. (2001), *Education and Earnings in Europe*. UK: Edward Elgar.

Hashimoto, M. (1981), 'Firm-Specific Human Capital as a Shared Investment', *American Economic Review*, 71, 475–82.

—— (1982), 'Minimum Wage Effects on Training on the Job', *American Economic Review*, 72, 1070–87.

Hausman, J. A. and Taylor, W. (1981), 'Panel Data and Unobservable Individual Effects', *Econometrica*, 49, 1377–98.

Heckman, J. (1999), 'Policies to Foster Human Capital', NBER Working Paper, no. 7288.

Holzer, H. J., Block, R. N., Cheatham, M. and Knott, J. H. (1993), 'Are Training Subsidies for Firms Effective? The Michigan Experience', *Industrial and Labor Relations Review*, 46(4), 625–36.

ISFOL (2001), *Rapporto 2001*, F. Angeli.

Johnson, G. (1984), 'Subsidies for Higher Education', *Journal of Labor Economics*, 2(3), 303–18.

Jovanovic, B. (1979a), 'Firm-Specific Capital and Turnover', *Journal of Political Economy*, 87, 1246–60.

—— (1979b), 'Job Matching and the Theory of Turnover', *Journal of Political Economy*, 87, 972–90.

Kaldor, N. (1963), 'Capital Accumulation and Economic Growth', in Friedrich A. Lutz and Douglas C. Hague (eds), *Proceedings of a Conference Held by the International Economics Association*, London, Macmillan.

Kane T. and Rouse C. (1999), 'The Community College: Training Students at the Margin Between College and Work', *Journal of Economic Perspectives*, vol. 13, no. 1, 63–84.

Katz, L. and Autor, D. (1999), 'Changes in the Wage Structure and Earnings Inequality', in *Handbook of Labor Economics*, (eds) O. Ashenfelter and D. Card, vol. 3A.

—— and Murphy K. (1992), 'Changes in Relative Wages, 1963–1987: Supply and Demand Factors', *Quarterly Journal of Economics*, 107, 35–78.

Katz, E. and Ziderman, A. (1990), 'Investment in General Training: The Role of Information and Labour Mobility', *Economic Journal*, vol. 100, pp. 1147–58.

Kennedy, S., Drago, R., Sloan, J. and Wooden, M. (1994), 'The Effect of Trade Unions on the Proand Humanities Research Council of Canada. Vision of Training: Australian Evidence', *Journal of Industrial Relations*, 32(4), 565–80.

Krueger, A. (1993), 'How Computers Have Changed the Wage Structure: Evidence from Micro Data, 1984–1989', *Quarterly Journal of Economics*, vol. 108, no. 1, 33–60 (February).

—— and Rouse, C. (1998), 'The Effect of Workplace Education on Earnings, Turnover, and Job Performance', *Journal of Labor Economics*, 16(1), 61–94.

Kuckulenz, A. and Zwick, T. (2003), 'The Impact of Training on Earnings–Differences between Participant Groups and Training Forms'. Mimeo, ZEW Mannheim.

Laing, D, Palivos T. and Wang P. (1995), 'Learning, Matching and Growth', *Review of Economic Studies*, 62, 115–29.

Lazear, E. (1979), 'Why is There Mandatory Retirement?', *Journal of Political Economy*.

—— (2003), 'Firm-Specific Human Capital: A Skill-Weights Approach', NBER Working Paper, no. 9679 (May).

Lazear, E. and Miller F. (1981), 'Minimum Wages Versus Minimum Compensation', in *Report of the Minimum Wage Study Commission*, vol. 5, Washington, DC: US Government Printing Office.

Leighton, L. and Mincer, J. (1981), 'The Effects of Minimum Wages on Human Capital Formation', in Rottenberg, Simon (ed.), *The Economics of Legal Minimum Wages*, American Enterprise Institute, Washington, DC, 155–73.

Leuven, E. (2005), 'The Economics of Private-Sector Training', *Journal of Economic Surveys*, 19(1), 91–111.

——, Oosterbeek H., Sloof R. and Van Klaveren C. (2003), 'Worker Reciprocity and Employer Investment in Training', *Economica* (forthcoming).

—— and —— (1999), 'The Demand and Supply of Work-Related Training: Evidence from Four Countries', in S. Polacheck and J. Robst (eds), *Research in Labor Economics*, 18, 303–30.

—— and —— (2001), 'Firm-Specific Human Capital as a Shared Investment: Comment', *American Economic Review, 91*, 342–47.

—— and —— (2002), 'A New Method to Estimate the Returns to Work-Related Training'. Unpublished Working Paper, Department of Economics, University of Amsterdam.

—— and —— (2004), 'Evaluating the Effects of a Tax Deduction on Training'. *Journal of Labor Economics*, 22(2), 461–88.

Levin, H. (1998), 'Financing a System of Lifelong Learning', *Education Economics* 6, 201–18.

Lindbeck, A. and Snower, D. (1988), *The Insider-Outsider Theory of Employment and Unemployment*, Cambridge: Cambridge University Press.

Linneman, P. (1982), 'The Economic Impact of Minimum Wage Laws: A New Look at an Old Question', *Journal of the Political Economy*, 90(3), 443–69.

Loewenstein, M. and Spletzer, J. (1997), 'Delayed Formal On-the-Job Training', *Industrial and Labor Relations Review*, vol. 51, Issue 1, 82–99.

—— and —— (1998), 'Dividing the Costs and Returns to General Training', *Journal of Labor Economics*, 16(1), 142–71.

—— and —— (1999a), 'Formal and Informal Training: Evidence from the NLSY', *Research in Labor Economics*, vol. 18, 403–38.

—— and —— (1999b), 'General and Specific Training: Evidence and Implications', *Journal of Human Resources*, 34(4), 710–33.

Lucas, R. (1988), 'On the Mechanics of Economic Development', *Journal of Monetary Economics*, 22, 3–42.

Lynch, L. (1991), 'The Role of Off-the Job vs. On-the-Job Training for the Mobility of Young Women Workers', *American Economic Review*, 81, 151–6.

—— (1992), 'Private Sector Training and the Earnings of Young Workers', *American Economic Review*, vol. 82, 299–312.

—— (1994), 'Training and the Private Sector: International Comparisons', Chicago, University of Chicago Press.

Malcomson, J., Maw, J. and McCormick B. (2003), 'General Training by Firms, Apprentice Contracts, and Public Policy', *European Economic Review*, vol. 47, no. 1, 197–227.

Marhuenda Fluixà F. (2000), 'The Rebirth of Apprenticeship in Europe: Linking Education to Work?' Leonardo SPES-NET. Final report.

Marsden, D. and Ryan P. (1990), 'Institutional Aspects of Youth Employment and Training Policy in Britain', *British Journal of Industrial Relations*, 28(3), 351–70.

Medoff, J. and Abraham, K. (1980), 'Experience, Performance, and Earnings', *Quarterly Journal of Economics*, 85, 703–36.

—— and —— (1981), 'Are those Paid More Really More Productive? The Case of Experience', *Journal of Human Resources*, 16(2), 186–216.

Middleton, J., Ziderman A. and Adams A. (1993), 'Skills for Productivity', New York: Published for the World Bank by Oxford University Press.

Mincer, J. (1983), 'Union Effects on Wages, Turnover and Job Training', *Research in Labor Economics*, 2, 217/52.

—— (1996), 'Training: Costs, Returns, and Wage Profiles', *in The Economics of Training, Theory and Measurement*, (eds) Ashenfelter, O., LaLonde, R., Elgar Reference Collection, International Library of Critical Writings in Economics, vol. 65, 105–23, Cheltenham, UK.

Moen, E. and Rosen, A. (2002), 'Does Poaching Distort Training?', CEPR Discussion Paper no. 3468.

Mortensen, D. T. (1978), 'Specific Capital and Labor Turnover', *Bell Journal of Economics*, 9, 572–85.

—— and Pissarides, C. (1999), 'New Developments in Models of Search in the Labour Market', in *Handbook of Labor Economics*, (eds) O. Ashenfelter and D. Card, vol. 3A.

Nestler, K. and Kailis, E. (2002), 'Disparities in Access to Continuing Vocational Training in Enterprises in Europe', Eurostat Statistics in Focus no. 22/2002.

Neumark D. and Wascher W. (2001), 'Minimum Wages and Training Revisited', *Journal of Labor Economics*, vol. 19, no. 3, 563–95.

Nickell, S., Nunziata, L. and Ochel, W. (2005), 'Unemployment in the OECD Since the 1960s. What Do We Know?', *The Economic Journal*.

—— and Quintini, G. (2003), 'Wage flexibility and the rate of inflation in the UK', *The Economic Journal*, 458–76.

Nicoletti, G. and Scarpetta, S. (2003), 'Regulation, Productivity and Growth: OECD Evidence', *Economic Policy*, 9–72.

OECD (1993), *Employment Outlook*, Paris.

OECD (1999), *Employment Outlook*, Paris.

OECD (2002), *Employment Outlook*, Paris.

OECD (2003), *Employment Outlook*, Paris.

OECD (2004), *Employment Outlook*, Paris.

OECD and Statistics Canada (2000), *Literacy in the Information Age*, Paris and Ottawa.

OECD (2001), *The Economics and Finance of Lifelong Learning*, Paris.

OECD (2003), *Learning for Tomorrow's World: First Results from PISA 2003*, OECD Paris.

OECD (2003a), 'Upgrading Workers' Skills and Competencies', ch. 5, *Employment Outlook*, Paris.

OECD (2003b), 'Beyond Rhetoric: Adult Learning Policies and Practices', Paris.

OECD (2003c), 'Descriptions and Evaluations of Recent Experience with Mechanisms for Co-financing Lifelong Learning': Reports Prepared by National Authorities and Members of the ELAP Network, prepared for the 'Second International Seminar: Mechanisms for the Co-finance of Lifelong Learning', London, 27–29 November, OECD, Paris.

OECD (2004a), *Learning for Tomorrow's World. First Results from PISA 2003*, Paris: OECD Publications.

Oi, W. (1962), 'Labour As a Quasi-Fixed Factor', *Journal of Political Economy*, 70, 538–55.

Ok W. and Tergeist, P. (2003), 'Improving Workers' Skills: Analytical Evidence and the Role of the Social Partners', OECD *Social, Employment and Migration Working Papers*.

Oosterbeek, H. (1998), 'Unravelling Supply and Demand Factors in Work-Related Training', *Oxford Economic Papers*, vol. 50, no. 2, 266–83.

Parent, D. (1999), 'Wages and Mobility: The Impact of Employer-Provided Training'. *Journal of Labor Economics*, 17(2), 298–317.

—— (2003), 'Employer-Supported Training in Canada and its Impact on Mobility and Wages'. *Empirical Economics*, 28, 431–59.

Piore, M. (1968), 'On-the-Job Training and Adjustment to Technological Change', *Journal of Human Resources*, vol. 3, 435–49.

Pischke, J. (2001), 'Continuous Training in Germany', *Journal of Population Economics*, 14: 523–48.

Redding S. (1996), 'The Low-Skill, Low-Quality Trap: Strategic Complementarities between Human Capital and R&D', *The Economic Journal*, 106, 458–70.

Roemer, J. (1998), *Equality of Opportunity*, Cambridge: Harvard University Press.

Romer, P. (1986), 'Increasing Returns and Long Run Growth', *Journal of Political Economy*, n. 94.

Rosen, S. (1972), 'Learning and Experience in the Labor Market', *Journal of Human Resources*, 7, 326–42.

Rubenson, K. and Schuetze H. (1999), 'Lifelong Learning for the Knowledge Society: Demand, Supply and Policy Dilemmas', in K. Rubenson and H. Schuetze (eds), *Transition to the Knowledge Society: Policies and Strategies for Individual Participation and Learning*, Human Resources Development Canada and The Institute for European Studies, Vancouver, British Columbia.

Ryan, P. (1994), 'Training Quality and Trainee Exploitation'. In R. Layard, K. Mayhew and G. Owen (eds), *Britain's Training Deficit*, Aldershot: Avebury.

—— (1998), 'Is Apprenticeship Better? A Review of the Economic Evidence', *Journal of Vocational Education and Training*, 50(2), 289–325 (Summer).

Ryan, P. (2000), 'The Institutional Requirements of Apprenticeship: Evidence from Smaller EU Countries', *International Journal of Training and Development*, 4(1), 42–65.

Schiller, B. R. (1994), 'Moving Up: The Training and Wage Gains of Minimum Wage Entrants', *Social Science Quarterly*, 75(3), 622–36 (September).

Schøne, P. (2002), 'Why is the Return to Training so High?' Mimeo, Institute for Social Research, Olso, Norway.

Sepulveda, F. (2002), 'Training and Business Cycles', Michigan State University, Mimeo.

Sicilian, P. (2001), 'On-the-Job Training and Starting Wages', *Journal of Labor Research*, 22(4), 809–16.

Snower, D. (1996), 'The Low-Skill, Bad-Job Trap, 1996'. In *Acquiring Skills* (ed. with A. Booth), Cambridge: Cambridge University Press, 109–24.

Steedman, G. (2001a), 'Five Years of the Modern Apprenticeship Initiative: An Assessment Against Continental European Models', *National Institute Economic Review*, no. 178.

Steedman, H. (2001b), 'Benchmarking Apprenticeship: UK and Continental Europe Compared', CEP Discussion Papers 0513, Centre for Economic Performance, LSE.

Stevens, M. (1994), 'A Theoretical Model of On-the-Job Training with Imperfect Competition', *Oxford Economic Papers*, vol. 46, no. 4, 537–62.

—— (1996), 'Transferable Training and Poaching Externalities', in A. L. Booth and D. J. Snower (eds), *Acquiring Skills: Market Failures, Their Symptoms and Policy Responses*, Cambridge University Press, Cambridge, UK.

—— (1999), 'Human Capital Theory and UK Vocational Training Policy', *Oxford Review of Economic Policy*, 15(1), 16–32.

Story, A. and Redman, T. (1997), 'Training Agreements: Resolving Under-Investment in Training?', *International Journal of Training and Development*, 1(3), 144–76.

Topel, R. (1986), 'Job Mobility, Search, and Earnings Growth: A Reinterpretation of Human Capital Earnings Functions', *Research in Labor Economics*, 8, 199–233.

—— (1991), 'Specific Capital, Mobility, and Wages: Wages Rise with Job Seniority', *Journal of Political Economy*, 99(1), 145–76.

Van den Heuvel, A. and Wooden, M. (2000), 'Causalities of Workplace Change', *Australian Training Review*, 6–10.

Veeken, N. (1999), *Industrial social funds in the Netherlands*. Paper for the ILO, Geneva.

Veum, J. (1995), 'Sources of Training and Their Impact on Wages', *Industrial and Labor Relations Review*, 48(4), 812–26.

—— (1996), 'Gender and Race Differences in Company Training', *Industrial Relations*, 35, 32–44, Vocational Training in France and Britain, *Fiscal Studies*, 23(2), 223–63.

—— (1997), 'Training and Job Mobility among Young Workers in the United States', *Journal of Population Economics*, 10(2), 219–33.

Whalley, J. and Ziderman A. (1990), 'Financing Training in Developing Countries: The Role of Payroll Taxes', *Economics of Education Review*, 9(4): 145–58.

Winkelmann, R. (1994), 'Apprenticeship and After: Does it Really Matter?', CEPR Discussion Papers 1034.

Wooldridge, J., 2002, *Econometric Analysis of Cross Section and Panel Data*, Cambridge, MIT Press.

Zwick, T. (2002), 'Continuous Training and Firm Productivity in Germany', ZEW Discussion Paper.

—— (2004), 'Training – A Strategic Enterprise Decision? Modern Concepts of the Theory of the Firm – Managing Enterprises of the New Economy', (eds) G. Fandel, U. Backes-Gellner, M. Schluter, and J. Staufenbiel, 355–66. Springer, Heidelberg.

Comments

Giuseppe Bertola

The nice report reproduced in this book is motivated by issues that currently are extremely important in European countries worried about low productivity and growth. To appreciate its approach and results, it is useful to go back again to Becker's classic insights. Markets and contracts in general cannot provide appropriate levels of 'general' training because it is difficult to make credible promises in two different respects. On the one hand, young workers, whose income and wealth status may already be insufficient to fund desired consumption flows, cannot easily borrow in order to pay for their own training, because the financial market will not necessarily believe that such loans will be repaid. On the other hand, it is also difficult for workers to obtain training from their employers, because if training is at least partly 'general' and therefore useful to other firms, there is no guarantee that workers will keep their promise to continue to work at the current wage for the employer who trained them, after their productivity has been increased by training.

The report also outlines theoretically a variety of other, possibly relevant market imperfections besides the basic ones just recalled. Its value-added, however, lies in its assessment of the extent to which such problems hamper training in Europe. In order to observe whether structural market features influence training, the interesting empirical specifications proposed and discussed in the report regress observed training on individual and job characteristics (such as age and industry) that are in principle relevant to the first-best amount of training; and these interact with structural and policy features that may in practice prevent training levels from achieving the first best. This is a potentially fruitful approach inasmuch as it can exploit differences in the 'forcing' features when assessing the relevance of the 'constraints': to estimate a slope, such as the effect on training on, for example, more, or less, severe financing problems, one needs to exploit the differences in exogenous instrumental variables.

The difficulty, of course, lies in identifying and defending exogeneity assumptions for specific forcing variables. Variation in microdata of individual and job characteristics is a suitable candidate. In the relevant data, the relevant variables covary with training in sensible ways: more educated people working in more skill-intensive jobs receive more training. Older people receive less training, especially when pension-system characteristics imply that they (and their training) will inevitably stop producing in the near future. This is eminently sensible, as market imperfections may well imply that training is inefficient, but not really that it takes place so late in life as to be unproductive from the point of view of both workers and employers. It is similarly unsurprising, and a good test of the data's quality, to find that women receive less training at those ages when their labour force participation is most likely to be interrupted. But if microeconomic characteristics tend to distribute training across workers in roughly sensible ways, is it possible to tell whether financial market imperfections reduce its overall intensity? The report makes a valiant attempt to answer this crucial question, but it focuses perhaps too soon and too narrowly on the possible financial difficulties of firms. It is true that data indicate that most training is 'employer-provided'. But survey data offer an admittedly imperfect measure of 'total training', and especially of 'general training', whose provision is potentially problematic. It is also true that in different countries and in different cyclical phases employers may find it more, or less, difficult to finance investment in their employees' training. However, it is far from clear that training, rather than physical investment, should be particularly affected by cash-flow problems. To assess the relevance to training of firms' access to finance, it would be interesting to control for physical investment when regressing training expenditure on cash-flow indicators. But of course training, even when it is provided by employers, can be financed by workers should they accept to be paid less than their productivity. This possibility is not observed in the data, making it impossible (as is clearly stated in the report) to tell whether observed training is financed by employers rather than by the compression of the workers' wage income, consumption, or leisure, and to what extent.

It is similarly difficult to interpret other statistics, such as the partial correlation (controlling for age, job satisfaction, and many other observables) between training and turnover across individual observation in survey data. If the partial correlation were found to be negative, as implied by a theoretical model in which more training is provided when exogenous turnover is low, it would be fair to wonder which unobservable variation across surveyed individuals drives the empirical correlation. Perhaps fortunately, however, the correlation is small and not statistically significant, confirming the difficulty of estimating empirical effects in the absence of clearly identified instruments.

To this end, it is natural to try and exploit as a forcing (and hopefully exogenous) force the wide cross-country variation in market structure and institutions. It is interesting, if unsurprising, to find that across countries the intensity of training is correlated with that of R&D activity. But it is hard to formulate a structural, causal interpretation: is the evidence in the report's Figure 10.5—reflecting some underlying forcing variable—some feature of countries that makes them likely candidates for high-tech, training-intensive industries? Or is it shaped by institutional features?

Answers may be sought in other cross-country scatterplots (and country-level interactions coefficients in microdata regressions, which tend to confirm the impression conveyed by simpler bivariate correlations). Some are as unsurprising as the R&D–training relationship just discussed, but others need to be interpreted carefully. It may be surprising to find that product market regulation is negatively correlated to training: recalling the praise lavished on the Japanese and German economic systems in the 1980s, one might have thought that the stability fostered by regulation would foster the kind of forward-looking behaviour that, in the standard Becker framework, is hampered by contractual incompleteness.

Of course, more competition can foster innovation and investment if it threatens inefficient firms with failure and disappearance, so one might interpret the bivariate correlation between training and regulation as evidence that this is the case in reality. But other bivariate correlations are confusing: across countries, temporary contracts are reasonably associated with less training, but also more stringent employment protection legislation (EPL) appears to reduce training. This is surprising for those who argue that, in an environment where contractual incompleteness prevents general training, EPL may strengthen job attachment and training incentives. But while it is true that EPL implies longer tenures, this need not lengthen the planning horizon for general training investments: EPL cannot force workers to remain with employers who have financed their general or specific training, so it is hard to see why such financing and training should be more intense if EPL is tightened in that realistic situation. EPL may of course force employers to retain workers they would otherwise fire, so training would indeed possibly increase with EPL if workers were, rather unrealistically, in a better position than their employers to finance specific training.

The report makes a valiant attempt to rationalize the fact that tighter EPL is associated with less training, as in Figures 11.2 and 11.3, making ad hoc assumptions as to the relationship between EPL and workers' bargaining power, and discussing whether selection effects might (or might not) lead to the observed correlation. It might be more insightful, however, to acknowledge that the cross-country association between EPL and training should not be interpreted on a *ceteris paribus* basis. The same countries where EPL is stringent also tend to feature poorly developed household-finance markets (Fogli, 2000; Bertola and Koeniger, 2004). This is not surprising, since a stable labour income is more desirable when poor borrowing opportunities make it difficult to smooth consumption. It is very intriguing to find (in Fig. C1) that the Jappelli–Pagano (1994) index of household borrowing conditions is tightly correlated with the OECD index of training participation analysed in the report.

This is of course just a cross-sectional, bivariate correlation. But it is readily interpretable in terms of the Becker insights recalled at the beginning of this discussion: if workers are liquidity constrained, then they cannot easily finance their (general) training, not even by accepting lower wages (and compressing their consumption) in exchange for employer-provided training. This establishes a direct channel for financial market imperfections to bear on training opportunities and outcomes. The bivariate correlation between EPL and training can from this perspective be a spurious effect of correlation between EPL and borrowing conditions, both of which may help workers achieve a desirably smooth consumption path. After controlling for

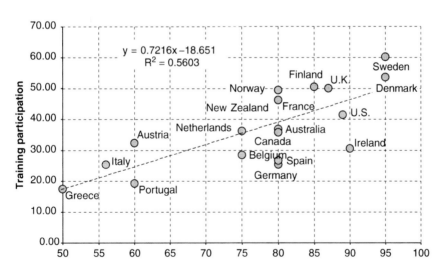

Fig. C1 Mortgage loan-to-value (1980s)

the borrowing conditions indicator, in fact, there is no relationship between EPL and training (as shown by the residuals in Fig. C2). Hence, there may be no need to invoke elaborate theories of why regulating dismissals might encourage employers to fund their employees' training.

Better data would of course be needed to make this multivariate perspective more precise; it might be worthwhile to try and bring to bear on it the access-to-credit indicators available in the ECHP dataset. The relevant mechanisms may also be relevant to the correlation between the incidence of temporary employment and that of training. Individuals with insecure jobs naturally find it difficult to access the credit market and, to the extent that general training must be financed by their own current consumption, will of course be trained less than would be implied by efficient forward-looking investment decisions.

An interpretation of the evidence along these lines does not deny the wisdom of the report's policy punchline. Training should not be targeted by subsidies, because there is no clear theoretical argument or empirical evidence establishing that the intensity of training is too low in a *laissez faire* economy, and because it is only too easy for politically attractive subsidies to be influenced by lobbying activities. I very much agree with this recommendation and I wonder whether the rich institutional information in Appendix 5 could be used to test it—for example, seeing

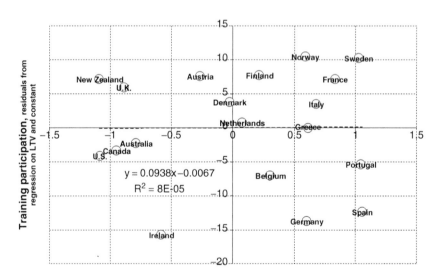

Fig. C2 EPL, residuals from regression on LTV and constant

whether subsidies are more prevalent in countries with more lobby-prone policy decision processes. I also wonder about the applicability in this context of the standard—if currently less fashionable—argument that favours delegation to the European Union of policies which, at the national or lower levels, are likely to suffer from political shortsightedness or regulatory capture. In the training area, the EU role might in fact not be that of a facilitator and funding agency, but rather that of a policeman against lobby-induced market distortions, more along the lines of State Aid enforcement than along those of the Social Fund.

To the extent that the world is imperfect, of course policy is important. But instead of targeting training directly, it would seem advisable to work on the fundamental failures that may underlie under-provision of training. The structure of education systems and of financial and labour markets should be reformed so as to offer workers and their employers more and better incentives and opportunities to train. Better enforcement of contracts and property rights and appropriate rewards for skills are in theory the key to resolving Becker's under-provision problem. Countries with insufficient training and growth could benefit from a market-driven, skills-oriented reorganization of economic interaction, which may well deliver the training (as a means) and growth (as a goal) that citizens and politicians currently yearn for in Europe.

REFERENCES

Fogli, Alessandra (2000), 'Endogenous Labor Market Rigidities and Family Ties', New York University, Mimeo.

Jappelli, Tullio and Marco Pagano (1994), 'Saving, Growth, and Liquidity Constraints', *Quarterly Journal of Economics*, vol. 109, 83–109.

Bertola, Giuseppe and Winfried Koeniger (2004), 'Consumption Smoothing and the Structure of Labor and Credit Markets', IZA DP no. 1052, Bonn.

Comments

Jörn-Steffen Pischke*

The report reproduced in this book brings together a wealth of material on workplace training: it surveys a wide literature, both theoretical and empirical, and it provides some new data and empirical results for a large number of European countries on training. In my discussion, I would like to touch on four of the areas highlighted in it: measurement and data issues, estimates of the returns to training, theoretical issues, and training policy. I feel what I have to say more often compliments the report, than criticizes it. In fact, where I am critical, it is more about the shortcomings of the work done in this area, and this includes my own work.

1 Measurement of training

Thirty or fourty years ago, the economics of human capital used to be comparatively simple. The human capital model was the work horse model to explain wage growth of individuals, as well as a variety of wage differentials between individuals. Since wages reflected marginal products in the models of Gary Becker and Jacob Mincer, many measurement problems were absent because much could be said without measuring training directly.

Things have become much more complex since. In addition to human capital, labour economists now entertain a myriad of other models to explain wage growth and wage differentials. Many labour economists feel that wages do not reflect marginal products. Hence, in order to say something about training, we need to measure training directly, which is difficult. The report does an excellent job in bringing together and presenting some cross-country measures of training from the best data sources we have available, and the authors are experts on these data. Nevertheless, I feel that even the best data in this area are likely to miss something, and I would like to point to two areas where I see particular problems. The first is the interplay of institutional features of vocational

* These comments were prepared for the fRDB conference 'Education and Training in Europe', June 11, 2005.

training systems and the resulting measurement of training, and the second is the role played by informal training.

I shall discuss the case of Germany in order to illustrate some of the problems, which may arise due to particular national institutions. I pick Germany simply because it is a country I know a lot about. Germany is not included in many of the statistics in the report because of data problems. However, according to Figure 8.1, training participation in Germany is below the mean, and towards the bottom end of the range found in the old EU members. Is Germany a low training country? Much workplace training in Germany takes place in apprenticeships, but apprentices are not counted in the surveys these data are based on. As the authors also note, this will understate the training level in Germany if apprenticeships are a substitute for workplace training later during workers' lives. I shall show some evidence that this is likely to be the case.

What happens if we count training in the German apprenticeship system? Take the numbers in Figure 8.1 again. The average participation rate in training in a year is about 35 per cent, and average hours per trainee are about 60. Extrapolating these numbers, an average worker receives about half a year of training during a 40-year working life. Compare this to the training in the German apprenticeship system. About 60 per cent of a cohort participate in apprenticeship training, and an apprenticeship lasts 3 years on average. This works out to 1.8 years of training for the average worker. Not all the time spent in the apprenticeship is actual workplace training, some is productive work. But even if only half of it is training, apprenticeship training alone would move Germany to the top of the list, without counting any of the other workplace training, which takes place.

But this is a rather specific problem, and it may well be special to the apprenticeship systems run in the German-speaking countries. The more important problem lies with initial vocational training more generally. In vocational training, the divide between school and firm-based training is somewhat fluid. German apprentices spend one day a week in schools. Someone training as a plumber would be classified as an apprentice, hence firm-based training. Someone training as a nurse would be classified as learning in a school, although the trainee spends most of his/her time in a hospital. I suspect similar classification problems arise in other countries, and classifications will differ across countries. This makes comparisons difficult.

Why does this matter? Take one example. An important stylized fact in this literature is the observed correlation between formal schooling and participation in workplace training observed at the individual level.

This has typically been interpreted as schooling and training being complementary, or explained as some individuals being better learners than others. But the German apprenticeship system is a prime example that the correlation may well be negative: the typical apprentice gets 9 or 10 years of schooling, the typical non-apprentice gets far more formal schooling. Firm-based vocational training clearly seems to be a substitute for school-based academic training.

Let me demonstrate some numbers on Germany in order to convince you that initial vocational training is quite important for individuals, long into their working lives. The numbers come from two waves of the German Qualification and Career Survey in the 1990s. Workers in the survey were asked where they obtained the skills they use most on their job, and they could mention two sources. Table C1 shows sources of workplace skills. About 60 per cent of respondents say that the most important avenue for acquring their skills was from school or in an apprenticeship. Apprenticeships are far more important than any formal training later on in life: only 6 per cent mention these avenues as most important, and they are not mentioned as a major category the second time either. The table also breaks down the source mentioned first by age of the respondent. Schooling and initial vocational training declines in importance with age, but it does so surprisingly little.

If formal company training is not a major source of workplace skills, what is it? The responses clearly point out that it is informal on-the-job training or learning, either instruction by colleagues, or learning through experience. In fact, such informal training is mentioned about five times as often as formal training. Informal training is notoriously hard to measure, and, of course, the numbers I have just presented do not tell us the

Table C1 Sources of job-relevant skills in Germany (in percent)

Source of skill	First mention	Second mention	First mention Age ≤ 40	Age > 40
School	3	4	3	4
Apprenticeship/vocational school	40	11	43	37
Technical school	6	4	6	6
University	12	3	11	12
Instruction by colleagues	17	21	18	17
Formal company training	4	11	4	4
Formal training outside company	2	5	2	2
Self-study	2	6	2	1
Experience on the job	14	35	12	15

amount of resources that are being spent on informal training. But they suggest that informal training may be quite important.

The typical argument in empirical analyses of training is always to look at formal training, which we can measure with some degree of accuracy, and argue that formal and informal training are most likely correlated. This would imply that looking at formal training is enough. I have made this argument myself but the only piece of evidence I know is the paper by Loewenstein and Spletzer (1999) based on the US NLSY data, which asked respondents directly about informal training.

Table C2 casts a shadow of doubt on this conclusion. I have tabulated some numbers by firm size from the same data, counting any mention of formal or informal training as a source of skills. Not surprisingly, formal training is a more important source of skills in larger firms. However, this is at least partially offset by informal training being more important in small firms. The nature of the data I have used has a tendency to produce this type of result, because individuals had to name *some* source for their skills, so if it was not formal training that was named, then automatically it was more likely to be informal training. Nevertheless, the result is far from mechanical. Ignoring informal training could well lead to some incorrect conclusions.

Another piece of evidence on the importance of formal training, which has struck me while working in this area, has been an analysis I did on the returns to training. In the traditional human capital model, on-the-job training is *the* source of wage growth over the life-cycle. However, including measures of training in a standard wage regression hardly attenuates the estimates of experience and tenure effects at all. This could mean various things. Maybe training simply is not responsible for a large part of wage growth over the life-cycle. But if that is so, then we ought to understand what else it is, and we really do not have much of an idea. An alternative is that training is important, but is measured very poorly. To the extent that the unmeasured training is informal, and it is correlated with measured formal training, the formal training should simply pick up the effect of the informal training. Hence, this interpretation is only viable

Table C2 Sources of job-relevant skills and firm size (in percent)

Source of skill	Firm size < 100	Firm size ≥ 100
Any mention of formal company training	11	18
Any mention of informal training	72	68

if much informal training is uncorrelated with the formal training we measure.

Taking these pieces of evidence together it seems that informal training, and learning by doing, may be quite important ingredients in understanding skill formation in the workplace. But measurement of informal training will be difficult, and I have no miracle cures for the measurement problem.

Before concluding the thoughts on measurement, let me add a few remarks about human capital more generally. Training is just one type of human capital. Human capital investment can take a variety of forms, through search and matching between workers and employers, for example, or migration. This is important to realize, because it may change how we judge what is happening in labour markets. Turnover of workers generally tends to be bad for skill accumulation and often reduces the value of these skills. But turnover can bring about better matches between workers and employers, and therefore be productive as well. In addition, human capital itself is not enough to make workers productive, because the skills are embodied in humans. They must put forth effort, and hence incentive systems complement skills in the labour market. Different labour markets may put different emphases on these different facets of human capital, and this might be particularly important in comparing the low turnover labour markets in continental Europe with the more fluid ones in Anglo-Saxon countries.

2 *Returns to training*

The second topic I would like to talk about is the estimates of returns to training. The authors of the report show some estimates for various European countries. The most striking feature of these results, and others in the literature, is that the returns are huge. The estimates in the report are for the incidence of training. Converting the median fixed effects estimate (for Denmark) to an annual return (similar to how we measure returns to schooling) yields 58 per cent. Returns to schooling are typically thought to be in the range of 5 to 10 per cent a year. Of course, the duration of training is far from a year on average. In fact, most incidents of workplace training are rather short in duration: a week or less. Studies which have looked at returns to the duration of training have consistently found a pattern of very high returns to short training spells, and low returns to long spells.

How can we make sense of large estimates of the returns to training? I can basically see five potential explanations. The first is that the marginal returns to training are truly very high, and expanding training would yield large rewards to employees. This would imply that workers and firms are leaving large investment opportunities unexploited. Workers should be shifting large chunks of their education from schools to workplaces. The fact that this does not happen may be a result of the externalities discussed in the report (and I will comment on these later). I think that this is unlikely, simply because the numbers are too large to be plausible. I also think that the pattern of the empirical evidence points towards other explanations.

The second possibility is that very short training spells indeed have high returns, but long training spells have low returns. This strikes me as a quite plausible possibility. Imagine someone being promoted to a managerial position. The worker receives a week of management training. The pay-off to learning that it is not a good idea to constantly shout at your employees is probably quite large. However, after the week is over, there is probably little material left that would make the individual a better manager. At this stage, it might be much more productive to go off and apply the material that has been learned. After, say, a year, there may well be an opportunity to participate in another short training spell, where something new could be taught. I think a lot of workplace training, particularly formal training, could be of this type.

The third possibility is that there is a lot of selection taking place as to who gets trained, and the standard methods do not deal with it properly. The standard procedure is to account for fixed personal characteristics by looking at changes in wages due to training. But this may not be enough. I quite like the following idea. Individuals tend to have different rates of wage growth, at least over short horizons. Individuals, who have high wage growth, are more likely to participate in short training spells, and individuals, who lave low wage growth, tend to participate in long training spells. The high-wage-growth, short-training-spell individual is our manager from before. S/he has high wage growth, because s/he got promoted to manager. Now s/he receives a week of management training which has a fairly normal rate of return. However, we see her/his training spell being correlated with the wage increase from her/his promotion, and erroneously attribute the wage growth to training.

The low-wage-growth individual is someone who is doing poorly in their occupation. S/he takes a long duration course in order to retrain for a new, and hopefully better paying, occupation. But the pay-offs to this training often only materialize after years, when the individual has found a suitable new job. Hence, the data will show exactly the pattern we see: high apparent returns to short training spells, and low returns to long training spells. In my paper on workplace training in Germany (Pischke, 2001), I show some evidence that accounting for individual level wage growth indeed leads to rather modest estimates of the returns to training, and the strong difference between short and long spells disappears. The report discusses other empirical evidence that attempting to control for selection into training tends to lead to lower estimates of the returns, which is also consistent with this explanation. Unfortunately, these estimates, including mine, are rather imprecise, and it would be good to have more replication of these types of results on different data sets.

The last two explanations for high returns are related to measurement problems. The first is the presumed complementarity of formal and informal training. Let's say for the sake of argument, we ignore informal training completely (this is basically true), there is about four times as much informal training than formal training (this is plausible from the numbers I demonstrated earlier), formal and informal training are perfectly correlated (which is a strong assumption), and have the same return (we have no idea on this whatsoever). Then, the returns estimates we get by only using formal training should be five times the true return. The 58 per cent return for Denmark would now be in the order of 12 per cent, a much more plausible number. I could see that this explanation is indeed part of the story, but as I described before, I am not really convinced that formal and informal training are as positively correlated as is often assumed.

The last explanation is measurement error in the training variables which get recorded in surveys. Without going into the details, let me say that it is possible that the measurement error is such that it yields the observed pattern of high returns to short training spells. I am certainly happy to accept that there is likely to be a lot of measurement error in training variables, particularly the duration variable. However, the consensus seems to be that this is unlikely to be a large part of the explanation for the pattern of estimated returns (see Pischke, 2001, and Frazis and Loewenstein, 2005).

My tentative conclusion from the available evidence is that the true returns to training are probably overstated, and that the marginal returns to training are more likely to be in a sensible range. It may well be true that some short training spells have higher returns than longer ones. All this is consistent with the idea that the returns to training may still be higher than what we observe elsewhere, and hence with the idea that there are externalities and under-investment in training. This is particularly true because some of the returns are likely to accrue to firms, and the returns discussed here are purely those for the employees. I shall now turn to the theoretical issues, and the externalities next.

3 Theoretical issues and externalities

The authors of the report have done a good job in giving a flavour of the more recent theoretical research on training, and the main insights emerging from this research. While there is much that we have learned, the theoretical research has often been of the type: 'Theoretically, it is possible that x happens' with x being an ever expanding set. But in the end, it is important to know what is going on in the world, not what is theoretically possible. Unfortunately, often there is not enough of a link between the theoretical research and the empirical analysis to come to a good assessment of which theories are useful and which ones are not.

One reason for this is that the predictions of the theory in the new training literature are often not directly on observables. Much of this literature is on general training. However, many of the implications for general training are similar to those of the Becker model for specific training. Unfortunately, empirically, we do not have good ways of distinguishing general and specific training. Hence, in interpreting the data we are often at a loss to distinguish between specific training in the Becker model, and general training in the new training literature. For example, the Becker model predicts that specific training (but not general training) and turnover should be negatively correlated, while the new training literature predicts that general training and turnover are negatively correlated. The fact that observed training and turnover are negatively correlated does not help in distinguishing the models if we cannot make the distinction between specific and general training in the data.

A second problem is that the new training literature emphasizes imperfect labour markets. In the Becker model, where wages equal marginal products, looking at the wage is enough to learn everything about the pay-offs of training (general at least). In imperfect labour markets, we learn nothing about productivity by looking at wages. In fact, the difference between the two is an important driving force in these models but it is not a quantity that has an obvious empirical analogue since productivity is notoriously difficult to measure.

A third problem arises from the literature to which I have contributed. This literature has been concerned with the question of whether it is theoretically possible for firms to pay for the investment in general skills, and under what conditions this would happen. Hence, the goal of the research was to say something about the financing of training. But financing is not something we observe directly. Workers may pay implicitly for training through lower wages, even when the direct outlays are born by the firm. The typical short cut is to look at whether training takes place at all. The problem is that the firm paying is not necessarily the same as more training taking place: this only happens under rather stringent conditions. For example, in Acemoglu and Pischke (1999), we have shown that under complete contracting over training between firms and workers the firm will pay for a larger share of training if there is more wage compression. But the amount of training will be less.

So the great challenge here is to link the robust implications of the models more directly to observables in the data. This is important because we need to learn which class of models describes training more closely, and in what circumstances. This in turn, just as importantly, will tell us something about the efficiency of provision of training in the market. These issues are at the core of evaluating training policy.

What are the possible sources of external effects of training, and how large are these externalities likely to be? There are basically three classes of externalities: those between the training firm and the worker (will the worker and firm agree on the optimal level of training for them?); those affecting future employers of the worker (often dubbed the poaching externality); and spillovers on other workers outside the firm. Let me discuss these three externalities in turn.

There are two complications why the training firm and worker may not agree on the optimal level of training. The first is credit constraints of the workers. This strikes me as a small obstacle for employed workers. Since the average worker trained receives about 60 hours of training a year, this means that a full-time worker has to give up about 4 per cent of annual earnings to finance the training, regardless of the direct costs of training. This strikes me as a fairly small amount. I would expect that even someone who wants to spend a lot of resources now, might be willing to forgo some present consumption if the returns to the training are indeed substantial. And they could be substantial for the types of short training spells which we commonly observe. Credit constraints may be more of a problem for initial vocational training, like apprenticeships, where the investment is much higher.

The second complication relates to contracting possibilities. Can the worker and the firm agree *ex-ante* on the level and content of training and the necessary monetary transfers between themselves? That seems much less likely since the training process may be highly idiosyncratic. This should be a particular problem for informal training, which depends on the quality of the co-workers of a trainee. Hence, contracting problems may well be a major obstacle and could prevent the provision of large amounts of profitable training. This would happen, for example, if the training decisions which are made in practice are optimal for either the firm or the worker individually, but not necessarily for the pair taken together. This problem could be overcome were it possible to write complete contracts over future wages, rather than over the training, for the employee at this firm. This mechanism might allow the pair to vest all the incentives for the investment in one of the parties, for example the firm. Again, such contracts are unlikely to be possible in practice. Employment relationships often last for many years, and it would be difficult for workers to commit to be underpaid compared to their outside options for many years.

The second type of externality is the poaching externality. If labour markets are imperfect, and employers earn rents on their employees, then future employers might gain by being able to hire a more skilled worker. The initial training firm and the worker will not take the gain of these third parties into account when they decide over the level of training. Therefore, too little training may be provided. The size of this externality depends on two things: how much turnover there is for skilled workers, and how much of the returns to training go to outside firms (the degree of wage compression in the market). In general, we would expect these two to be negatively correlated across economies: a high turnover economy is likely to have less wage compression. This suggests that this externality is unlikely to be extreme. On the other hand, at least one of the components might be high, so that the size of the externality could be more than negligible. For example, continental European countries may have relatively little turnover, but future employers gain a lot whenever they do hire a skilled worker. It is important to note that not all turnover necessarily leads to this type of externality. Moen and Rosén (2004) point out that there is turnover, which is efficient in allocating workers across firms, and even labour markets with a lot of frictions may be organized in a way that they do not lead to a poaching externality. Nevertheless, this argument does not negate the fact that the poaching externality is likely to exist in practice.

But the poaching externality may be relatively unimportant for another reason. Lazear (2003) suggests that much training which looks general may really be firm specific. This is because individuals' skills may well be rather general, but there are many skills, and the mix used in a particular firm could be very specific. If skills are highly specific, the poaching externality is not much of a problem since the training pays off only in the current job. Turnover does not matter directly for the optimal choice of training then: the training firm and the worker will choose less specific training when there is more turnover but this choice is optimal. Of course, the turnover in the economy itself may be inefficient. But this is unlikely to be a problem which should be addressed with training policy.

The third externality results from human capital spillovers across workers in different firms. This would happen if more training in one firm lead other firms to be more productive, through channels other than the poaching externality. An example of this could be that a supplier firm might operate more efficiently if the agent at the buying firm is more knowledgeable in specifying the product requirements, and in understanding the capabilities of the supplier. Such spillovers have been discussed in the growth and agglomeration literatures a lot, and there is some investigation of whether there are spillovers from formal schooling. The conclusions of this literature are still up in the air, and I have seen no work yet considering such spillovers in the context of workplace training.

In summary, are any of these externalities likely to be important? My hunch is that contracting possibilities between training firms and workers are at the heart of what is preventing them from reaching the optimal level of training. I doubt that credit constraints are very important. The poaching externality may matter but is probably not the major part of the story. Spillovers to workers in other firms may exist, but it is again difficult to imagine that they are huge. However, these are at best informed guesses, or more likely, rather uninformed ones. The only way to tell is to test the implications of specific models which imply different externalities. This is a complex undertaking. There are certainly no simple tests, like looking at the relationship between training and turnover, as suggested in the report. This is only informative about the under-provision of training in a specific and simple model, but many other factors need to be taken into account simultaneously.

4   *Training Policy*

So is there a role for training policy? Obviously, if there are inefficiencies in the market for training, and it is quite likely that there are, there is a potential case for some government intervention. On the other hand, as I said, our understanding of the importance of the externalities is still rather limited, and there is basically nothing yet to show by how much training provided by the market is falling short of the optimal level. Given that we do not fully understand the nature of the externalities, it is difficult to know how the optimal policy should look. Even if we did, should we expect government to implement that policy? It is more likely, given the political process, that actual policy would at best be a rough approximation—possibly something falling short by quite a bit. But if we are willing to settle for rather imperfect government policies, should we expect them to actually improve matters? At this stage, I am sceptical that this is the case.

Here is an additional point, which complicates policy: I have argued that informal training may be quite important empirically, and possibly account for much more investment than formal training. Informal training may be more difficult to contract on, so it may be subject to larger externalities. This suggests that policy should be directed primarily towards informal training. But what policy would actually raise informal training? If private parties have problems contracting over such training, it is difficult to see how the government could write laws regulating it.

The second role for training policy pointed out in the report is for equity reasons. Can and should training policy be used to redistribute income? Here I am even more sceptical. Why? First, workplace training, at least formal training, is not important enough to have a big impact on wages. Going by my earlier calculation, an average European worker receives half a year of training over their life-time. Say policy can raise this by 50 per cent for some workers, which certainly would require substantial intervention: at a 10 per cent return to training for workers, this would mean 2.5 per cent higher wages—a very modest amount.

The second reason why I am sceptical about government policy in this area is because it is already going on, on a reasonably large scale. Many government-run or subsidized training programmes are focused on workers who are unemployed or at the bottom end of the wage distribution. Some of these programmes are rather expensive. There is a large literature evaluating their effectiveness, and the conclusions are not particularly promising. Many of them seem to have no effect, and any positive returns are certainly not out of the ordinary (see Heckman et al., 1999). This contrasts rather sharply with the evaluation of some interventions in formal schooling. It seems to me that an appropriate design of the formal schooling system is the much more effective route to redistribute income.

REFERENCES

Acemoglu, Daron and Jörn-Steffen Pischke (1999), 'The Structure of Wages and Investment in General Training', *Journal of Political Economy*, 107, 539–72.

Frazis, Harley and Mark Loewenstein (2005), 'Reexamining the Returns to Training: Functional Form, Magnitude, and Interpretation', *Journal of Human Resources*, 40, 453–76.

Heckman, James (1999), 'The Economics and Econometrics of Active Labor Market Programs', in Orley Ashenfelter and David Card (eds), *Handbook of Labor Economics*, vol. 3C, Amsterdam: Elsevier, 1865–2097.

Lazear, Edward (2003), 'Firm-Specific Human Capital: A Skill-Weights Approach', NBER Working Paper no. 9679.

Loewenstein, Mark and James Spletzer (1999), 'Formal and Informal Training: Evidence from the NLSY', in Solomon Polachek (ed.), *Research in Labor Economics*, vol. 18, Greenwich, CT: JAI Press.

Moen, Espen and Åsa Rosén (2004), 'Does Poaching Distort Training?' *Review of Economic Studies*, 71, 1143–62.

Pischke (2001), 'Continuous Training in Germany', *Journal of Population Economics*, 14, 523–48.

Final Remarks

John P. Martin

I would like to concentrate my remarks on three topics. First, I would like to highlight some issues around the efficiency/equity trade-off in secondary education drawing on the results from the OECD's PISA surveys of educational achievement among 15-year-olds in 2000 and 2003. Secondly, I would like to reflect on some of the public policy implications for training policy flowing from the very rich survey by Bassanini et al. Finally, I would like to draw your attention to some new data initiatives by OECD in the fields of education and training and international migration.

1 *The efficiency/equity trade-off in secondary education*

Publication of the PISA results has provoked considerable discussion about the impact of different ways of structuring schools. PISA measures the performance of students at age 15 and also obtains other relevant background information about them and their families. This allows comparisons across countries of the average reading, maths, science (and in 2003, problem-solving) test scores and the dispersion of test scores across students and schools. It also allows an analysis of the relationship between students' social backgrounds (measured by a composite index of socio-economic status) and their performance.

The text score averages provide a basis for comparing the efficiency/quality of performance across countries. The dispersion of scores provides a good basis for comparing the equity of outcomes. Countries with a wide spread of performances are leaving weaker students further behind.

The relationship between students' social background and their performance provides a much more relevant basis for judging equity of outcomes. In all countries, students from more privileged backgrounds tend to do better in education than those from disadvantaged backgrounds. But it is very important to note that there are considerable differences among countries in how much better socially advantaged students do.

The PISA results show that there are countries which achieve high average results (high quality), but also have only a relatively weak relationship between the social background and performances of their students (high equity). Finland is a well-known example of a relatively good performer in Europe on the maths scores in 2003 in both the efficiency and equity dimensions, whereas the so-called 'olive belt' countries (Greece, Italy, Portugal and Spain) are examples towards the other end of the spectrum—below-average performance combined with relatively high inequality.

The results from both PISA 2000 and PISA 2003 show that, in countries that stream students at an early stage into schools of different types, students' social backgrounds tend to be relatively strongly related to their performance. Disadvantaged students are more likely to be placed in low-status schools with less demanding curricula and so lower expectations of their learning. It is hardly surprising that they end up with relatively poor performance. Socially advantaged students are more likely to be placed in high-status schools with demanding curricula and to end up with relatively high quality performance. In that sense, schools tend to reproduce the existing social arrangements.

In countries that keep students together in comprehensive schools, the relationship between social background and educational performance is weaker. This suggests that schools are able to make a real difference to the performance of their students rather than having it entirely determined by parental/social background.

A comparison of the results from PISA with those of other studies strengthens this interpretation. In countries that differentiate students early into schools of different types, the spread of performances and the strength of the relationship between social background and performances are much smaller in primary education than in secondary education after the separation has taken place.

It is not for nothing that many politicians and educational policy markers are visiting Finland these days to get some insights into how the Finns apparently do so well in terms of efficiency/equity performance, as measured by PISA test scores, while only spending a bit more than the EU average (in 2001 they spent 5.8% of GDP on education). It is worth noting that almost 98 per cent of that spending in 2001 was public spending. It is also worth noting that Finnish teachers are relatively well paid and enjoy high status in Finland.

In sum, I would not agree with the conclusion in the paper by Wasmer et al. that investment in secondary education can only help the equity objective, whereas further investment in the tertiary sector will tend to enhance growth prospects. The PISA evidence suggests there is much scope in many OECD countries to improve both the efficiency and equity objectives associated with current spending on secondary education.

2 *The scope for public intervention in the training market*

The massive survey by Bassanini et al. makes very sober reading for any policymaker. These days, calls for investing in the knowledge economy, upgrading skills and competences and lifelong learning for all are dime a dozen in speeches by politicians and commentators in almost all OECD countries. So much so that the case for more investment in training is taken as Holy Writ by many.

But Bassanini et al.'s careful survey should be required reading for them. It is a masterful 'two-handed economist' survey. It reviews the theory, tests the predictions against available cross-country evidence and explodes many myths. For example, it concludes that the available empirical evidence for under-investment in on-the job training is not strong. This knocks one of the planks of the lifelong learning agenda out of joint. It is true that there may still be a case for public investment on efficiency grounds if there are positive externalities associated with training—along the lines of some of the 'new growth' theory stories. But as Bassanini et al. point out, there is little evidence on such externalities.

They are prepared to drop one hand and plump for a case for public intervention on equity grounds. But even this good news for policymakers is less reassuring than it seems because they go on to argue that training is not a very effective redistributive tool since training returns to disadvantaged workers are not very large, and firms do not appear to be very willing to invest more in training the disadvantaged. The latter presents a particular challenge for policymakers: How to overcome firms' preference for what I call 'the Matthew Principle' based on the well-known quotation from St Matthew's Gospel—'to them that hath shall be given'.

As they rightly point out, the track record of policies to encourage firms to invest more in training the disadvantaged is not encouraging, even in the absence of many rigorous evaluations. It is possible that schemes which target individuals, for example, co-financing schemes such as loans, individual learning accounts, vouchers, might be more cost-effective. But we are very hampered by the lack of rigorous evaluations of such schemes. There is also more than a suspicion that highly-skilled/highly educated workers are more likely to avail of such co-financing schemes, once again demonstrating the ubiquity of the Matthew principle in the training field.

I conclude that we need much more evaluation in this field to establish what works, for whom, why and in what circumstances. It is rather ironic that we know a lot more about the effectiveness of public training targeted to the unemployed (there are many surveys of the evaluation literature, e.g. Heckman et al. (1999); Martin and Grubb (2001)). But this is not a major area of public investment: on average, EU countries spent around one quarter of 1 per cent of GDP on training for the unemployed in 2003. In the meantime, it behoves us all to adopt a more two-handed approach to the issue of lifelong learning and more investment in training, otherwise we might perpetuate the great training robbery! And we should always remember that early intervention is best, echoing a mantra of Jim Heckman, so public intervention needs to get early childhood development and basic education right.

3 New and planned OECD data sets on education and training and international migration

Both parts of the report reproduced in this book make extensive use of OECD data sets, namely IALS, PISA and EAG. I would like to inform you about three new initiatives at OECD on the data front. The first might be called the 'son of IALS': the Adult Literacy and Life Skills Survey (ALL). The first results from ALL have just been released by OECD and Statistics Canada.[1] Unfortunately, only five OECD countries opted to participate in it—Canada, Italy, Norway, Switzerland and the United States. The main reason for the low participation is that most other countries felt that ALL did not offer sufficient value-added over and above IALS. Note it is possible to link the ALL results with those in IALS for the reading and document literacy scores for four of the countries—Italy is the exception because of quality problems with its IALS data set.

We at OECD are now engaged in an intensive discussion with member countries to see if they would be willing to launch a new international adult skills assessment survey—what we call the Programme for International Assessment of Adult Competences (PIAAC). This would add extra value to IALS by adding problem-solving and ICT literacy to the skill domains. We are also considering how to incorporate an employer perspective on skills into the assessment since many countries have expressed a keen interest in this. A key decision will have to be taken at the end of this year by countries as to whether they are willing to proceed to pilot testing some of the new instruments. If they do give the green light, and all proceeds well, the tentative schedule would have the first

---

[1] See OECD and Statistics Canada (2005), *Learning a Living: First Results of the Adult Literacy and Life Skills Survey*, Paris and Ottawa.

cycle of PIAAC being undertaken in 2009, with a second cycle in 2012, and so forth. We are keeping our fingers crossed that sufficient countries will be willing to buy into this ambitious new OECD venture.

The final data set I will mention is a new comparable data base on the 'foreign-born population' in OECD countries in 2000. The concept of 'foreign-born' is more suitable for comparisons of the stock of immigrants in OECD countries than the concept of foreigner. We have collected these data from the 2000 round of population censuses and they are disaggregated by key demographic characteristics and level of educational attainment. This is a very rich data base, for example, for 15 countries, it contains data on the number of Ph.D.s, which countries they come from and where they have moved to. In this way, it can be used to throw new light on the 'brain drain/brain exchange' debate which is discussed in the Wasmer et al. paper. It can be accessed using the OECD website and there is a detailed description of it in the latest issue of our annual publication, *Trends in International Migration*.

INDEX

Appendices, figures, notes and tables are indexed in bold, e.g. 295**ap**. More than one table etc per page is indicated by **(a)** and **(b)**.

Abraham, K. G. 115, 257
Acemoglu, D. 14, 52**n**, 58, 151, 159**n**, 163, 163**n**, 166, 168, 168**n**, 169**n**, 172, 175, 179**ap**, 191, 234, 235, 236, 269, 275, 296**ap**, 338
Addison, J. 145**n**, 303**apn**
Adult Literacy and Life Skills Survey (ALL) 346
Africa 63
age-earnings profiles 234
age-training profiles 213–214, 250
ageing society 288–289
Aghion, P. 59
Albrecht, J. 92
ALL see *Adult Literacy and Life Skills Survey*
Almeida, R. 257
Altonji, J. G. 115, 257
Anglo-Saxon countries 147, 193
  labour markets 334
  product markets 232
  schooling, years of 39**f**
  skills 40–41
Angrist, J. 51, 61**n**, 266
Appelbaum, E. 288
apprenticeships 141, 153, 162, 174, 175, 189, 192, 201, 216**ap**, 218, 237, 285, 292**ap**, 293**t**, 295–296**ap**, 296**apt**–299**apt**, 338;
  see also Germany, apprenticeships

Ariga, K. 177**n**, 236
Arulampalam, W. 208, 217**ap**, 218**ap**, 232, 233, 235, 237, 263
Asia:
  low-cost producers 145
  migrants to USA 59
Asplund, R. 208
asymmetric information 164–165, 273
Australia 190
Austria 211, 212
  females 213
  literacy 48, 50
  mobility 33
  schooling 238
  trade unions 240
Autor, D. 199, 235, 245, 250
Axelsson, R. 74, 79, 86

Ballot, G. 268
Barcelo, C. 76**n**
Barrett, A. 268
Barro, R. J. 20**n**, 57, 58
Barron, J. M. 171, 189, 191, 199, 208**n**, 233
Bartel, A. 189, 268, 269
Bassanini, A. 217**ap**, 250, 267, 269, 295**apn**, 306**ap**, 307**ap**, 345
Beaton, A. 47**n**
Becker, G. S. 10, 13, 63, 166, 269
Becker, S. 9, 74, 158, 346

Belgium 31
  educational attainments 41
  females 213
  literacy 48
  mobility 77
  schooling 238
  skills 42f(a), 51, 96
  trade unions 240
  training, returns 264
Ben Porath, Y. 13
Benabou, R. 12, 120
Bender, S. 115, 116
Benhabib, J. 56
Berger, M. 189, 191, 199, 208n, 233,
    300ap
Bertola, G. 9, 74, 96n, 327
Bhaskar, V. 159, 160n
binding contracts 162
Bishop, J. 148, 159n, 236, 275
Björklund, A. 47
Black, S. 189, 191, 199, 208n, 234, 269
Blanchard, O. 112, 232
Blau, F. 52n, 53, 173
Blinder, A. S. 13, 191
Blomstrom, M. 156, 157
Blundell, R. 262, 269
Boeri, T. 289
Boesch-Supan, A. 289
Booth, A. 159n, 160n, 163n, 165, 165n,
    169n, 171, 173, 173n, 179ap,
    180ap, 199, 208, 217ap, 218n,
    233, 234, 235, 237, 262, 263
Borjas, G. J. 62n
borrowing conditions 327–328
Bound, J. 65
brain drain 66, 347
Branstetter, L. 68, 69
Britain see UK
British Household Panel
    Survey 199–200, 235
British National Survey of Graduates and
    Diplomates 1980 (BSNG) 262
British National Training Survey 262

British Social Attitudes Survey (BSAS) 262
Brown, J. N. 254
Brunello, G. 168, 177n, 196, 217ap,
    236, 268, 269, 282, 296ap, 299ap
Bryan, M. 159n, 165n, 199, 208,
    217ap, 218n, 235, 237
Bulgaria 194, 205
Burdett, K. 168

Caballero, R. 14
California (USA) 61
Cameron, S. 278
Campanelli, P. 191
Canada 18, 234, 261, 346
  emigration 67, 68n
  employment rates 28–29
  female 31
  unemployment 31
capital markets, perfectly
    competitive 273
Card, D. 62n
Carneiro, P. 170, 257, 278
Caselli, F. 58
Central Europe 112
Chang, C. 163n
Channell, J. 191
Chapman, B. 278, 278n
Charlot, O. 13
Chatterji, M. 173n
Checchi, D. 282
children, in school 47–49
China, migration 63, 65
Ciccone, A. 253, 270
citations 69
Clark, M. 47
Clark, R. L. 115
class size 50–51
co-financed schemes:
  firms 283–284, 301ap–302apt,
    303ap–306ap
  individuals 306ap–308apt,
    309ap–310ap
cognitive abilities 286, 287

Colardyn, D. 285
Coles, M. G. 169n
collective bargaining 170–171, 233
Collier, W. 270n
competitiveness 158, 159, 272
comprehensive schools 177, 238,
    250, 344
Conlon, G. 285
Conti, G. 268
Continental Europe 22
  households 279
  labour:
    markets 334; turnover 339
  schooling 41
  skills 41, 52
Continuing Vocational Training Survey
    (CVTS) 187–188, 189, 200,
    217ap–217ap
contracts 285, 288, 326, 338–339, 340
costs:
  firing 96, 235–236, 248, 249
  human capital, increase 273
  opportunity 257
  of training 167, 175, 202, 253, 257,
    267, 268, 272
    general 253; through lower
      wages 198–199
  rates of return 256–257
  under-investment 274–275
craft unions 174
credit:
  constraints 177, 273, 278, 338
  markets 273
Croce, G. 300ap, 301ap, 307ap
Crouch, C. 145n, 147, 148
Current Population Survey (CPS) 188, 258
CVTS see *Continuing Vocational Training
    Survey*
curriculum 111–112
Czech Republic:
  schooling 43, 44f(a)
  skills 44f(b), 45
Czechoslovakia 112

Daveri, F. 59
De La Fuente, A. 20n, 22n, 58, 253, 270
De Paola, M. 196, 296ap
Dearden, L. 173n, 262, 268, 269
DeLong, J. B. 39
Denmark 18, 31, 193, 200, 208, 211,
    212, 213, 214, 336
  employment protection 243
  literacy 48
  mobility 33, 34, 77
  schooling 41, 42f(b), 238
  skills 43f
  trade unions 240, 243
  training 334
    wages returns 264, 265
Devroye, D. 52n, 53
Di Nardo, J. 62n
disadvantaged individuals 283,
    285–287, 289, 344, 345
distributional implications (of
    training) 282
Dolado, J.-J. 92, 104
Domenech, R. 20n, 22n, 58
Dornbusch, R. 119
Drago, R. 233
Duncan, G. 171, 233
Dustmann, C. 115, 116, 234
Duval, R. 236, 237, 242

earnings 26, 27t, 54, 54t, 55, 74, 254,
    262, 265, 282; *see also* wages
East Asia 57
Eastern Europe (CEEC) 43, 60, 112,
    147, 194, 214
  labour market, reallocation 112, 112t
  skills 52, 111
East Germany 112
ECHP see *European Community
    Household Panel*
economic growth 56, 59, 158
economic policy 272
Edin, P.-A. 47
education, costs 10–13

educational attainments 19t, 20, 21t,
    29t, 30t, 31, 37, 39–40, 43, 46,
    54, 56, 58, 149, 153–154, 206,
    211, 272, 280, 282
  and skills 40f, 45
  social background 344
educational systems 96, 111, 118,
    253, 329
  modernization 145
  private finance 118–119
Elley, W. 47n
employees 249
  training participation 192f, 193,
    155, 328
    costs 187–188, 190–191, 196–197;
      effects on wages 267
  unskilled 275
Employer Opportunity Pilot Project
    (EOPP) 199, 258
employers:
  competitive markets, imperfectly 253
  returns to 267–270
  skills 346
  training 215, 247t, 337–338
    costs 187, 190–191, 196–197, 200,
      204–205;
    non-sponsored/sponsored 207,
      210–213, 219t(a), 220t(a),
      220t(b), 234, 236, 238, 276, 284
employment 28, 96, 158
  female 31
  flexible 235
  levels of 158
  probabilities 26–27
  protection 14, 15, 35, 111, 233,
    235–236, 240f(a), 240f(b), 245,
    245t, 248, 249, 251, 288
  legislation 97f, 240, 326–328, 327f;
  rates 29t, 31
  older workers 213, 213f, 214
  regulations 294t
  sectoral composition 112t
  trade unions 173, 238

enrolment in education 24t, 280t, 281t
emerging economies 58
Epple, R. 238n
equal opportunities 170, 272, 278,
    283, 289
equity 272, 278–283, 285, 341, 343, 345
Ericsson 156, 157
Estonia:
  human capital, specificity 117t
  labour markets 111–116
  wages 116
EU 20, 25, 112, 194
  education attainments 47, 70, 92
  employment 28–29
    female 31
  foreign-born residents 60t(a),
    61–62, 70
  immigration to 59–63
  labour markets 72–73
  literacy 37, 50
  mobility 34, 71, 73–74, 88, 90
  schooling, years of 39, 39f
  skills 47
  wages 67
EU Enlargement 116, 121, 194
EU-12 72
EU-15 75, 91, 110, 200, 204, 232
  skills, mismatch 93–95f, 96f,
    104, 106
European Community Household Panel
    (ECHP) 33, 75–76, 76n, 80, 91,
    93, 187, 188, 191, 192, 194, 205,
    217ap–218ap, 232, 237, 240, 244,
    263–265, 267, 276, 278, 279, 328
European Employment
    strategy 272, 289
European Labour Force Survey 61
European Union (EU) 329
exogeneity 324, 325, 326
expenditure:
  level of education 24t
  per GDP 23t
    public 24, 26f

private 25, 25t
public 25
on training:
    per employee 203f(b), 204; by
    firms 201, 201t; as percent of
    labour costs 203f(a)
externalities 338, 345

Fakhfakh, F. 268
family background 278–279
Farber, H. S. 115, 257
females 208, 209, 210, 211–212, 325
  access to education 18, 212, 213, 215
  commitment to labour markets 155
  employment rates 31
  wages 262
finance 22–25, 324
  of courses 198f(a), 210
  markets:
    imperfections 327; reforms 329
  firms, difficulties 325
financial imperfections 9–12
Finland 18, 31, 156, 156f, 194, 195,
    211, 212, 213, 285
  educational attainments 344
  employment protection 243
  labour productivity 148
  mobility 33, 34, 77
  schooling 41–42, 42f(b), 43, 238
  skills 43, 43f, 47, 96
  trade unions 240, 243
  training, returns 264, 345
firing costs see costs, firing
firms see employers
Fogli, A. 327
foreign-born residents 89
  distribution 65
  by skills group (EU-12) 65f
  by skills group (USA) 64f, 65
  wage differentials 64t(a)
foreign skills 71
formal training 333, 332t, 334, 335,
    336, 341;

see also informal training
Fougère, D. 263
France 147, 194, 268, 285
  higher education 61
  immigration 61–62
  literacy 48
  mobility 33, 34, 72–73, 77, 85, 88
  schooling 238
  R&D 243
  skills 51, 93
  trade unions 239, 240
  wages losses 115
Francesconi, M. 171, 173, 173n, 234
Frazis, H. 189, 256, 261, 336
Freeman, R. 52n, 53, 92, 173
Fuess, S. 171

Galindo-Rueda, V. 245n
Galor, O. 92
Gambarotto, F. 196
Garibaldi, P. 248
Gary-Bobo, R. 119n
Gasskov, V. 301apn
GDP 56
  higher education 118
  R&D 149, 155
  unemployment, training for 346
GDP per capita 22, 56
gender 25
general human capital 13
  payment for 14
general training 159–162, 164–167,
    171, 175, 188, 197, 238, 273,
    324, 325, 337
  costs 253
  payment by employers 177–178
  wage returns 257
Gentillini, A. 119
geographical mobility see mobility,
    geographical
Gerfin, M. 263
German Qualification and Career Survey
    (Germany) 332

German Socio-Economic Panel
    (GSOEP) 263
Germany 148, 268, 285, 337
  apprenticeships 299**apt**, 331–332
  economic systems 326
  educational attainments 41
  employment 236, 238
  higher education 61
  migrants 63
  mobility 33, 34, 77, 85, 88
  over-qualification 98
  schooling 331
  skills 42**f(a)**, 93, 96, 332**t**
  schooling 177, 238
  wages:
    growth 263; losses 115
Gersbach, H. 177**n**, 249
Giannini, M. 177**n**
Giavazzi, F. 119
Gittleman, M. 189
Golden, L. 288
Goldin, C. 36
Gordon, R. 56, 59
Gospel, H. 299**ap**, 300**ap**
Gottschalk, P. 52**n**
Goux, D. 263
government intervention 169
government policies 151–152, 284,
    340–341
Greece 195, 211, 213, 242, 246
  educational attainments 344
  females, training 213
  labour productivity 148
  mobility 33
  skills 96
  trade unions 240
  training incidence 264, 267
Green, D. 234
Green, F. 233, 270
Greenhalgh, C. 233, 261, 262, 278, 285
Greenwald, R. 50
Griliches, Z. 69, 69**n**
Groot, W. 92

Grossberg, A. J. 234, 235
Grossman, G. 59, 234
Gurgand, M. 119

Hall, R. E. 248
Hammour, M. 14
Hannah, F. 237
Hanson, G. H. 61**n**
Hanushek, E. 50, 58
Harmon, C. 265
Hartog, J. 107
Hashimoto, M. 114, 234
Hausman, J. A. 261**n**
Heckman, J. 154, 170, 255, 258, 262,
    278, 341, 345, 346
Hedges, L. 50
Helpman, E. 59
Herfindahl Index 235
higher education 18, 58, 67–68, 154, 246
  costs vs. returns 74–75
  growth 56–70
  higher employment 31
  mobility 74
Hong Kong 57
Horrigan, M. 189
households 75–76**t**, 77, 77**t**, 78, 78**f**,
    78**t**, 79, 79**t**, 86, 87**t**, 279, 327
Howitt, P. 59
human capital 9, 32, 37, 74, 145, 151,
    153, 169, 188, 251, 254, 275,
    286, 334
  costs 15
  economics 330
  growth 57–58, 152–153, 270
  and income 253
  inequality 12**f**
  investments 120, 121, 152, 253, 334
  labour spillovers 340
  migration 56
  specificity 116
  theory 16. 159, 161, 161**t**, 164, 167,
    175, 177–178, 196–197, 257;
    see also specific human capital

human resources 28
Hungary 194
   labour markets 112
   literacy 48
   schooling 43, 44f(a)
   skills 44f(b), 45

IALS see *International Adult Literacy Survey*
Ichino, A. 9, 74
immigration 34, 37–38, 67, 71
   USA and EU 33t
income gain 85–87t, 88
income per capita 57, 70, 112
India, migration 63, 65, 68
individual characteristics 324–326
industries 222apt(a)
informal training 189–190, 284,
   332–333, 333t, 334, 336, 341;
   see also formal training
information systems 284–285
information technologies 56, 58–59
innovation 66, 152, 155, 245, 275
   firms, training participation 167–169,
   205f, 214–215
   talents and 68–69t, 70
institutions 96, 243t, 244, 247–248
   training 170–177, 233
International Adult Literacy Survey
   (IALS) 37, 38, 39–40, 45, 187,
   188, 197, 209, 216ap, 346
International Reading Literacy Study 48–49
investments:
   training 171, 175, 187, 200, 201–205,
   269–270, 273
Ireland 183, 197, 268
   employment protection 243
   labour productivity 148
   literacy 48, 50
   mobility 33
   skills, variations 51
   trade unions 240, 243

ISCED-97 Classification
   (UNESCO) 15–17, 17f, 18, 115
Italy 18, 31, 156, 156f, 195, 195f(a),
   196, 197, 200–201, 211, 213,
   214, 265, 268, 346
   education:
     attainments 344; parental 282;
     policies 157
   employment 236
   higher education 61
   mobility 33, 85, 88
   over-qualification 98, 99, 104
   R&D 243
   schooling 43, 44f(a), 154, 238, 245
   skills 44f(b), 93, 96
   trade unions 240
   training participation 243

Jaffe, A. 69n
Jansen, M. 92, 104
Japan 148
   economic systems 326
   employment 236
   jobs for life 114–115
Jimeno, J. F. 92, 104
jobs:
   characteristics 258, 324–325
   non-wage 160
   search 254
   separations 276, 277, 276t
Johnson, G. 275, 283
Jones, C. 57
Jovanovic, B. 92
Joyce, M. 52n, 189

Kahn, L. 173
Kailis, E. 212
Kaldor, N. 165
Kane, T. 278
Kahn, L. 52n, 53, 173
Katz, E. 163n
Katz, L. 36, 52n, 53, 165
Kennedy, S. 233

Kimko, D. D. 58
Klenow, P. J. 56
Kletzer, L. G. 115
knowledge-based economy 145
Koeniger, W. 327
Kokko, A. 157
Krueger, A. 50, 51, 111, 112, 191
Kuckulenz, A. 263
Kugler, A. 61n
Kuhn, P. J. 116n
Kumar, K. 111, 112

labour:
  contracts 246
    flexible 235; temporary 248, 251
  costs 200, 204, 249
  economics 160, 178
  experience 253–254, 257–258
  flexibility 114, 250, 251, 287, 288
  frictions 13–14, 120, 160
  institutions 9, 122, 151, 157, 215,
      232, 239, 244, 274, 282
  learning 146
  markets 54, 56, 57, 96, 114, 152, 160,
      162, 163, 178, 188, 234, 246, 280,
      334, 337
    competitive 159, 167, 171–173,
      175–177, 197, 273, 275,
      278, 339
  policies 287–289
  reallocation 9, 17, 35, 96–97,
      111–112, 114
  reforms 273, 289, 329
  turnover 171, 173–175, 196,
      275–277, 277t, 325, 334,
      337, 340
Labour Force Survey (UK) 268
Laine, R. 50
Laing, E. 168n, 169
Lamo, A. 110n, 115, 117
Latin America 59
Latvia 194
Lavy, V. 51

Layard, R. 9
Lazear, E. 197, 234, 236, 339
learning 286
  decreases with age 13, 15
Lee, J. W. 20n, 57, 58
Lefranc, A. 115
Leighton, L. 234
Lemieux, T. 234
Leuven, E. 52n, 53, 159n, 162, 167,
      209, 236, 263, 266, 267, 306ap
lifelong education 145, 272, 282, 345
Lindbeck, A. 248
liquidity constraints 275, 288, 327
literacy 37, 286
  test scores 48t
Lithuania 194
Loewenstein, M. 115, 163n, 164, 171,
      189, 190, 199, 208n, 233, 255,
      256, 261, 333, 336
Lucas, R. 57, 169
Luxembourg 18, 76
  mobility 33
Lynch, L. 148, 189, 191, 233, 234,
      236, 258, 261, 269, 277

Maastricht Treaty 34
Machin, S. 233, 234
Malcomson, J. 162, 168n
Mankiw, N. G. 57
Manning, A. 159, 160n
Margolis, D. 115, 116
Marhuenda Fluixà, F. 299ap
market:
  failures 273, 274t, 278, 282, 289
  imperfections 324, 325
  liberalization 250
  structures 326
Martin, M. 47n
mathematics:
  skills 50t
  tests 51, 287, 287f, 344
Maurin, E. 263
Mavrotas, G. 233, 278

Maw, J. 162, 168**n**
McCormick, B. 162, 168**n**
measurement, training 188–192,
    330–334, 336
Medio, A. 168
Medoff, J. 173, 257
Meghir, C. 115, 116,
    262, 269
Mendes de Oliveira 104
Messina 102**n**, 110**n**
migration 57, 74
  income gain 85–88
  internal 71
  international 59–66
  model 78–79
  between US states 72
Miller, F. 234
Mincer, J. 234, 235
minimum wages 170, 175–176,
    233, 288
  and training 234–235;
  see also wages
mobility 14, 82**t**, 83**t**-84**t**, 92, 111,
    116, 121, 255
  costs 81, 160, 164
  and education 72–75
  geographical 31–32**t**, 33–35, 74,
    75–76, 76**t**, 77**t**, 78, 78**t**, 79,
    79**t**, 90, 120
    by education 32**t(b)**, 33;
    internal 73**t**; by reason and
    country 32**t(a)**
  highly educated workers 89**t**
  house-related 75–76, 80
  internal 71–72, 90
    USA and EU 33**t**, 34, 72–73;
  job-related 34, 78**f**, 80–85, 86, 87**t**, 90
  occupational 109, 109**t**
  residential 32, 85
  skills and 7
  between states (US) 34
Moen, E. 168, 339
mortgage loan-to-value 327**f**

Mortensen, D. T. 248, 254
Mullis, I. 47**n**
Mundell, R. A. 71
Munz, R. 61**n**
Murphy, K. 53, 165

National Child Development Survey
  (NCDS) 262, 263
National Longitudinal Survey of Youth
  (NLSY) (USA) 188–189, 199, 233,
  258, 259, 261, 277, 333
Nelson, R. R. 57
Nestler, K. 213
Netherlands 213
  educational attainments 41
  literacy 48, 50
  mobility 33
  participation (in training) 263
  schooling 237
  skills 42**f(a)**, 45
  tax systems 265–266
  trade unions 240
networks 168
Neumark, D. 234, 235
New York 61
New Zealand 194
Newlon, E. 238**n**
Nickell, S. 9, 232
Nicoletti, G. 150, 242, 245**n**
Nobel laureates 63–65
Nokia 156–157
Nordic countries 18, 22
  educational attainments 41
  employment rates 31
  literacy 43
  participation (in training) 274
  skills 512
North Africa 60
North America:
  education figures 18
  employment rates 31
Northern Europe 149
  households 279

Norway 346
 literacy 48, 50
 schooling 41, 42f(b)
 skills 43f
 numeracy 286
 training participation 263
Nunziata, L. 232

occupations 13, 208, 215, 262, 285, 335
Ochel, W. 232
O'Connell, P. 268
Ogawa, N. 115
Oi, W. 158
Ok, W. 301ap, 302ap
oligopsony 160, 171
 theory 165
 wage setting 163–164, 171, 178
on-the-job:
 skills 13, 14, 111–112, 169
 training 234, 236, 254, 257–258,
  262, 277, 332, 345
Oosterbeek, H. 159n, 162, 209, 263,
  266, 267, 306ap
over-investment 275
over-provision (of training) 283
over-qualification 91–99t, 100–110

Pakes, A. 69
Palivos, T. 168n, 169
Panel Study of Income Dynamics (PSID)
  (USA) 258, 287f
Parent, D. 258, 259, 261, 277
patents 69
pay-back clauses 293ap–294ap
pensions 236–237, 242–243, 251,
  288–289
Peri, G. 9, 69, 74
Perison, J. 270n
Ph.Ds 69–70, 89, 94, 121, 347
Phelps, E. S. 56, 57
piece rates 167
PISA see Programme for International
  Student Assessment

Pischke, J. S. 14, 151, 159n, 163,
  163n, 166, 168, 168n, 172, 175,
  179ap, 191, 200n, 234, 235, 236,
  256, 262, 269, 296ap, 300ap,
  336, 338
Pissarides, C. 248
poaching externalities 270, 275, 339
Poland 194
 human capital specificity 117t
 labour market, reallocation 112–113
 literacy 37
 mobility 116–117, 117t
 over-education 105–106, 106t, 107,
  107t, 108, 108t, 109–110
 retirement pensions, early 113f
 schooling 43, 44f(a)
 skills 44f(b), 45
  mismatch 91–92, 102, 104–110;
  obsolescence 111;
  specificity 115–116
 unemployment allowances 114f
 wages 106, 107, 116–117
Polish Labour Force Survey (PLFS) 91,
  104, 105
political economy 282
 training subsidies
  model 290ap–292ap
Portugal 18, 26, 152, 194, 195, 196,
  205, 208, 211, 212, 213
 costs, direct training 257
 educational attainments 344
 employment protection 243
 mobility 33
 schooling 154
 skills 51
 trade unions 240
 training incidence 264, 267
 wages returns 265
pre-primary education 23
Prescott 56
primary education 23, 33, 36, 118
private benefits 275
private returns 152–154

to training 254–257, 264t, 265, 265f,
    267, 275, 286t, 287
product markets 151, 152
    competition 235–236
        deregulation 176–177
    flexibility 288
    institutions 157, 215, 232, 239, 274
    liberalization 250
    policies 287
    reforms 273, 289
    regulations 150f(b), 170, 233, 242,
        243, 245, 251, 326
productivity 56, 59, 67, 152, 158, 162,
        163, 164, 165, 166, 167, 170, 173,
        253, 257–258, 267, 268, 269,
        270, 271, 324, 337
profitability 269–270, 283, 289
Programme for International Student
        Assessment (PISA) 47, 48, 51,
        55, 343–345, 346
Psacharopoulos, P. 119
PSID see Panel Study of Income Dynamics
public finance 119
public intervention 345
public spending 118
public training 346
    policies 272, 283, 289

Qualification and Career Study
        (Germany) 263
qualification systems 285
quality of education (residual
        skills) 46t, 46–47, 174, 236, 238
quantity of education 236, 238, 239
Quintini, G. 198

R&D 58, 69, 70, 72, 88, 89, 90, 121,
        149, 150, 156, 251, 326
    investment per GDP 150f (a), 243,
        245, 246, 246t, 250–251
Raffe, K. 238
Raisian, J. 114
reading literacy 51, 346

Reading Literacy Study 47
Redding, S. 168
Redman, T. 294apn
Reed, H. 173n, 268
research see R&D
retirement:
    age 236–237
    incentives 242f
Riphahn, R. T. 9
Rodríguez Clare, A. 56
Roemer, J. 169, 170, 272
Rogerson, R. 9
Romania 193
Romano, R. 238n
Romer, P. 59, 169
Rosen, A. 168, 339
Rosen, S. 175
Rouse, C. 277, 278
Ryan, P. 174, 299ap

Saint Paul, G. 63
Scandinavia 147, 155, 194, 204, 214
    schooling 154, 238
Scarpetta, S. 150, 242, 245n
Schiller, B. R. 235
Schindler, M. 9
Schmutzler, A. 177n, 249
Schøne, P. 263
Schonberg, U. 234
schooling 154, 236, 245, 253, 275
    access to 146
    by cohort 39, 39f, 40–47
    design 233, 237, 341
    and employment rates 31
    growth effects 58
    institutions 177, 236
    levels 11f(a), 11f(b)
    returns to 334
    years of 16, 20t, 21, 22, 36–37, 39,
        41f, 45, 51, 54, 58, 270
secondary education 2, 20, 23, 36,
        118, 343
    general 116

secondary education (*Cont.*)
  lower 31, 55, 116, 154
  mobility 33
  schools 177, 238, 239f, 250, 251, 252
sector-specific skills 13, 14, 15
senior workers:
  skills 289
  training 237, 250, 251, 325
  wages 257
Sepulveda, F. 169n
Serrano, L. 20n
Shakotko, R. A. 115, 257
Sicherman, N. 92
Sicilian, P. 234, 235
Siebert, W. 145n, 303apt
Singapore 57
skill-biased technology 58–59, 93,
      120, 245
skills 35, 36–55, 118, 289
  chosen by individuals 14
  by cohort 36–39t, 40–47
  general 15, 239, 245
  immigrants 62t
  inequality 51
  investments 9–10, 169, 288
  mismatch 91–100t, 101–110, 121
    taxonomy 95t
  in school 47–49
  specificity 111–117
  unskilled 283
  variations in 37, 38t, 51–52
    and quality of education 53
Sloan, R. 233
Slovenia 205
Smith, E. 168
Smyth, J. 238
Snower, D. 168, 168n, 248
social benefits, of training 253, 275
social exclusion 282
social inclusion 289
social returns 152
  to schooling 253
  to workplace training 275

Solow, R. 59
South Korea 57
Southern Europe 18, 22, 31, 34, 43,
      148, 149, 150, 153, 194, 195f(a),
      211, 282
  employment protection 232
  households 279
  mobility 77
  higher education 61
  mobility 33
  over-education 110
  over-qualification 98, 99, 104
  participation in training 274
  schooling 154
  skills, mismatch 93, 96, 103–104
  temporary labour 151
  tertiary education 104
Spain 93, 137, 138, 211, 244, 299
  apprenticeships 296, 299
  educational attainments 18, 344
  employment 31
    protection 244
  family background 153, 344
  finance 301, 302, 305, 309
  foreign-born residents 61, 73
  human capital 37
  mobility 33
  over-qualification 98, 103, 104, 106,
      110
  training participation 151, 195f(a)
  schooling 154, 238
  trade unions 240
specific human capital 13, 14, 257;
    see also human capital
specific training 159, 162, 188, 197,
      238, 337, 339–340
Spence, M. 92
Spiegel, M. M. 56
Spilimbergo, A. 61n
spillovers 168, 274
Spletzer, J. 115, 163n, 164, 189, 190,
      199, 208n, 255, 333
Stafford, F. 171, 233

Statistics Canada 37, 346, 346**n**
Steedman, G. 299**ap**
Steedman, H. 299**ap**
Stevens, M. 163**n**, 168, 169**n**, 209**n**, 269, 288, 304**ap**
Stewart, M. 261
Story, A. 294**apn**
student loans, subsidised 26
student/teacher ratios 51
  lower secondary schools 49, 49**t**
study grants 26
subsidies 146, 273, 283, 284, 328, 329
Sweden 18, 22, 76, 193, 194, 195, 268
  high-tech production 156
  literacy 37, 48–49
  mobility 33
  schooling 42**f(b)**, 238
  skills 43, 43**f**
  trade unions 240
  training participation 243
  wages, inequality 53
Switzerland 197, 346
  educational attainments 41
  skills 42**f(a)**
  training participation 263

Tabellini, G. 289
Taber, C. 278
Taiwan 57
talents 59, 63–66, 88, 121
  and economic well-being 66–70
Tatsiramos, K. 76**n**
taxes 26–28, 155, 245, 248–249, 283, 289
  education, finance 119
  employment, protection 240
  social security system 176
  system 170
Taylor, W. 261
Taymaz, E. 268
technological innovations 57, 58, 90, 145, 245
temporary agencies 199

temporary contracts 235, 288
temporary workers 243, 246
  and training 151**f**, 248, 250, 251
tenure 114–115, 174, 209, 211, 253–254, 257, 258, 326
Tergeist, P. 301**ap**, 302**ap**
tertiary education 20**t**, 54, 56, 58, 116, 118, 120, 121
  difference in 21
  employment rates 31
  general 26
  mobility 33
  private rates of return 27, 28, 28**t**, 118–119
  type-A 18
  type-B 28
Third International Math and Science Study (TIMSS) 47, 47**n**, 48, 51
To, T. 159, 160**n**
Topel, R. 115, 257
Topo, A. 299**ap**
trade policies 159
trade unions 160, 170, 179**ap**, 233, 239–243, 244–245, 245**t**, 285
  labour supply, control 174
  and training 171, 172**t**, 172, 173–175, 233–234, 248, 251–252
  wages 173
training characteristics:
  individuals 205–206, 207**t**–208**t**, 221**apt(b)**–224**apt(a)**, 224**apt(b)**–225**apt**, 226**apt**, 228**apt**–230**apt**
training incidence 232, 248, 262, 287, 288
  and age 251
  and schooling 154**f**
  see also workplace training
training participation 47**f**, 190, 193**f**, 194, 194**f**, 195**f(a)**, 195**f(b)**, 196, 201, 202**f(a)**, 205**f**, 209, 219**t(b)**, 242, 248, 255, 261, 262, 266, 267, 273–274, 289

training participation (*Cont.*)
  by finance 218t
  by hours 202f(b)
  older workers 211
training policies 293ap–310ap
Trajtenberg, M. 69n
Trannoy, A. 119n
tuition fees 119, 278
Turner, S. 66
turnover *see* labour, turnover

UK 22, 147, 194, 196, 196f, 199, 204,
    212, 213, 214–215, 232, 235
  comprehensive schools 177
  higher education 61
  literacy 48
  mobility 33, 34, 77, 85, 88
  over-qualification 98, 99
  R&D 243
  schooling 238, 245
  skills 45–46
    mismatch 93, 96
  trade unions 233, 240
  wages 199–200, 234
    inequality 52; returns 261–262,
    264, 265
under-provision, of
    training 273–278, 282
unemployment 9, 13, 25, 34, 74, 91, 98,
    101, 112, 155, 232, 246, 246t, 346
  ratios 30t, 31
  training 158, 248, 263, 267, 341
unions *see* trade unions
university reforms 120
UNESCO 15–17
unskilled labour 12
upper-secondary education 18, 28, 47,
    239, 280
  earnings 25
    private rate of return 27
US Census of Population 61, 68
USA 147–148, 153, 155–156, 170, 193,
    199, 232, 346

earnings 26
economy 61
education 18, 20, 54
  attainments 149; growth 56; wages
    returns to 25, 258; years of 22
employment rates 28–29
  female 31
expenditure 24, 25
foreign-born residents 60t(b), 61–62,
    68–70, 89
  quality of 66–68
human capital 39, 115
immigration 34, 59–63, 65
jobs:
  for life 114–115; separations 277
literacy 37, 38
mobility 71–72, 74
  high-skilled workers 88–89
productivity 268
schooling 238
  by cohort 39, 39f; student/teacher
    ratios 49, 49t; tertiary 22, 23,
    56, 118; upper-secondary 21
skills 36, 38, 40, 47, 51, 55
unemployment 31
wages 67, 72, 88, 234
  inequality 52, 53; losses 115

van den Brink, M. 92, 208
Van Reenen, J. 173n, 268
Veeken, N. 306ap
Verdugo, N. 104
Verdugo, R. 104
Veum, J. 233, 258, 277
Vignoles, A. 245n
Violante, L. 248
vocational skills 16–17
vocational education 26, 116, 177, 238
vocational qualification 285
vocational training 189, 190, 197,
    330–331, 332, 338
voluntary quits 276–277
Vroman, S. 92

wages 13, 14, 90, 92, 120, 152, 156,
        159, 164, 248, 253, 267, 337
    competition, effects on 176
    compression 165–167, 173,
        179ap–181ap, 249, 269, 298, 339
    foreign-born residents 68
    growth 56, 253, 257, 261, 268, 330,
        335–336
    inequality 36, 40–41, 52–54
    losses 116
    over-qualification 102, 102t, 103
    penalties 103–104 , 110
    and productivity 253, 254
    profiles 254
    rates of return 258, 259t–260t, 261,
        268, 270, 271
        to education 25–28, 262; to
            training 258, 265–267, 270
    selection 210
    and skills 53
        mismatch 101–103t, 104
    trade unions 173, 240
    training 146, 160, 161, 162, 163f,
        167, 178, 199–200, 267;
    see also earnings; minimum wages
Walden, G. 300ap
Walker, I. 265
Walsh, P. 66

Wang, P. 168n, 169
Wang, Y. 163n
Wascher, W. 234, 235
Wasmer, E. 14, 111, 112, 344
Weiss, Y. 13
Westergaard Nielsen, N. 265
Westerlund, O. 74, 79, 86
Western Europe:
    EU-14 18
        skills, mismatch 109
Whalley, J. 303apn
Wilkinson, D. 233, 234, 270n
Wolfers, J. 112, 232
Wooden, M. 208, 233
Wooldridge, J. 206n
women see females
workplace training 198f(b)
    basic theory 157–159
    distribution 193–196;
    see also training characteristics;
        training incidence; training
        participation; training policies

Ziderman, A. 163n, 303apn
Zilibotti, F. 58
Zoega, G. 160n, 163n, 165, 169n, 171,
        173, 173n, 179ap, 180ap, 234
Zwick, T. 263, 268

Printed in the United Kingdom by
Lightning Source UK Ltd., Milton Keynes
139145UK00007B/140/P